Russian Traditional Culture

Russian Traditional Culture

Religion, Gender, and Customary Law

EDITED BY
Marjorie Mandelstam Balzer

M.E. Sharpe
Armonk, New York
London, England

Library of Congress Cataloging-in-Publication Data

Russian traditional culture : religion, gender, and customary law /
edited with an introduction by Marjorie Mandelstam Balzer.
p.   cm.
Includes bibliographical references and index.
ISBN 1-56324-039-4 (c) —ISBN 1-56324-040-8 (p)
1. Russian S.F.S.R.—Social life and customs.
2. Ethnology—Russian S.F.S.R.
3. Folklore—Russian S.F.S.R.
4. Russians—Intellectual life.
5. Russians—Folklore.
I. Balzer, Marjorie Mandelstam.
DK510.32.R87   1992
947—dc20
92-4775
CIP

Printed in the United States of America

The paper used in this publication meets the minimum requirements of
American National Standard for Information Sciences—
Permanence of Paper for Printed Library Materials,
ANSI Z39.48–1984.

BB   10   9   8   7   6   5   4   3   2   1

Contents

Customary Law, Daily Life, Medicine, and Morality

Contributors

Marjorie Mandelstam Balzer teaches at Georgetown University, and is editor of the M. E. Sharpe journal *Anthropology and Archeology of Eurasia* (formerly *Soviet Anthropology and Archeology*), in which these translations first appeared. She is author of numerous articles on Siberian peoples and on nationalities issues, editor of *Shamanism: Soviet Studies of Traditional Religion in Siberia and Central Asia* (Armonk, NY: M. E. Sharpe, 1990), and author of the monograph *The Tenacity of Ethnicity* (forthcoming). Her anthropological fieldwork has included research on Russians of Siberia and Central Russia, in 1975–76, 1983, 1985–86, and 1991.

Igor' Iakovlevich Froianov is a professor and doctor of historical sciences in the history department of St. Petersburg (Leningrad) State University. He is author of numerous books and articles, including *Kievskaia Rus'. Ocherki sotsial'no-politicheskoi istorii.* (Leningrad, 1980).

Andrei Iur'evich Dvornichenko is a professor and doctor of historical sciences in the history department of St. Petersburg (Leningrad) State University. His works include (with I. Ia. Froianov) *Goroda-gosudarstva drevnei Rusi* (Leningrad, 1988).

Iurii Vladimirovich Krivosheev is a candidate of historical sciences and an assistant professor in the history department of St. Petersburg (Leningrad) State University. His research is on early Slavic religion and Kievan Rus'.

V. G. Vlasov is a senior researcher in the Academy of Sciences Institute of Archeology in Moscow. He has written both archeological and ethnographic works on early Slavic folk culture and conceptions of calendrical time.

Tat'iana Aleksandrovna Bernshtam is a doctor of historical sciences and head of the Sector of Ethnography of the Eastern Slavs in the Academy of Sciences Institute of Ethnology and Anthropology, St. Petersburg. She is author of numerous articles, reviews, and books on Russian material and symbolic culture, including *Pomory (Formirovanie gruppy i sistema khoziaistva)* (Leningrad, 1978).

N. N. Veletskaia is a senior researcher at the Institute of History, Philology, and Philosophy of the Siberian Section, Academy of Sciences, in Novosibirsk. She is the author of numerous works on Slavic folklore, including *Iazycheskaia simvolika slavianskikh arkhaicheskikh ritualov* (Moscow, 1978).

F. F. Bolonev is a senior researcher at the Institute of History, Philology, and Philosophy of the Siberian Section, Academy of Sciences. He has done extensive research on the folklore of the Semeiski sect of the Baikal region.

N. G. Velizhanina is an art historian at the Academy of Sciences in Novosibirsk, and a scholarly consultant to the Novosibirsk Picture Gallery (*Kartinaia Galereia*). She has written several works on the sources and development of icons in Siberia.

Natal'ia L'evovna Pushkareva is a candidate of historical sciences and a researcher in the Russian section of the Academy of Sciences Institute of Ethnology and Anthropology in Moscow. She is author of several important works, including *Zhenshchiny drevnei Rusi* (Moscow, 1989).

Tat'iana A. Listova is a candidate of historical sciences and a researcher in the Russian section of the Academy of Sciences Institute of Ethnology and Anthropology in Moscow. She is author of a growing number of published works, and coeditor (with M. M. Gromyko) of a volume featured here, *Russkie: semeinyi i obshchestvennyi byt* (Moscow, 1989).

Iulia Kuz'mina is a reporter for the journal *Nauka i religiia*.

Nina Adamovna Minenko is a doctor of historical sciences and senior researcher at the Institute of History, Philology, and Philosophy of the Siberian Section, Academy of Sciences, in Novosibirsk. She is editor of several collections and author of many monographs on Siberian social history, including *Russkaia krest'ianskaia sem'ia v zapadnoi Sibiri (XVIII– pervoi poloviny XIV v.)* (Novosibirsk, 1979).

Marina Mikhailovna Gromyko is a doctor of historical sciences, senior researcher, and head of the Russian section of the Academy of Sciences Institute of Ethnology and Anthropology in Moscow. She is author of many books and articles on Russian traditional culture, including *Traditsionnye normy povedeniia i formy obshchenia russkikh krest'ian XIXv* (Moscow, 1986).

Irina V. Vlasova is a doctor of historical sciences and a senior researcher in the Russian section of the Academy of Sciences Institute of Ethnology and Anthropology in Moscow. She is author of numerous articles and books, including *Traditsii krest'ianskogo zemlepol'zovaniia v Pomor'e i Zapadnoi Sibiri v XVII–XVIII vv.* (Moscow, 1984).

Ben Eklof is professor of history at Indiana University, with specialization in Russian social history. He received the Ph.D. from Princeton University; he has had postdoctoral grants from the Princeton Davis Fund, the International Research and Exchanges Board, and numerous other sources. He is author of many articles and the well-received book *Russian Peasant Schools: Officialdom, Village Culture, and Popular Pedagogy, 1861–1914* (Berkeley: University of California Press, 1986). He is also coeditor (with Stephen P. Frank) of *The World of the Russian Peasant: Post-Emancipation Culture and Society* (Boston: Unwin Hyman, 1990). His sharing of a working bibliography on Russian peasant culture is greatly appreciated.

Leslie English is assistant editor in the Russian and East European studies program at M. E. Sharpe, Inc.

Introduction

Marjorie Mandelstam Balzer

Political and historical context

The surge of national and historical consciousness jolting peoples of the post-Soviet, deconstructivist world has been nowhere stronger than among the Russians themselves. This consciousness is not necessarily chauvinist or even outer-directed, but rather, for many, is an inner searching for lost cultural values and traditions. While Russians' popular awareness of their history may have been stimulated by comparable movements among national groups on their peripheries, the process has more complex dynamics. Since the Khrushchev period, Russian historians of the Middle Ages, of pre-Christian beliefs, and of peasant life have had a considerable following, as have scholars of Russian folk art, ritual, and music. Small folk culture museums opened and were supported by private funds in the Brezhnev era, joining a few large outdoor state-organized complexes such as Kizhi. With the very first glimmers of *glasnost'*, writing on Russian folk culture became a growth industry.

Several main themes permeate recent historical scholarship on Russian traditions. The first is military glory, including the heroism of Russian empire builders before and after the Russian Revolution. Some who stress this "single stream" of Russian military might are indeed in a chauvinist camp, justifying historical expansion of Russians into the Baltic, Ukraine, Caucasus, Central Asia, and Siberia. Others are simply interested in the lives of specific generals and tsars.[1]

A second theme involves the search for political legacies, whether democratic or authoritarian. The popular historian Dmitri Likhachev, one of the founders of the Culture Fund supported by Raisa Gorbacheva, has sought roots of folk democracy in traditions of Kievan Rus' as well as the peasant *mir* (commune).[2] Others point to the rules of authoritarian leaders from Peter the Great and Ivan the Terrible to Stalin to stress (both critically and approvingly) Russian reliance on urban-based central planning and traditions of reform from above.[3]

Themes centering on village life are similarly controversial, since idealization of village tradition continues to vie with progress-oriented views that recall the muddy squalor of prerevolutionary peasant existence. Pleas to save the dying Russian village have rallied those who wish to recapture "peasant" values they fear they have lost.[4] Such values, inculcated through traditional socialization, include more than the clichés of Russian collectivism, patriarchalism, submission to fate, and long-suffering stoicism. They also encompass soul-satisfying concepts of spirituality, hospitality, charity, fighting for one's honor, and atonement for permissible binges through confession. After the August 1991 coup, Boris Yeltsin touched a deep resonating chord among villagers and urbanites alike when he asked forgiveness from the families of three young men killed during the coup, "for not being able to save your sons." He was not merely grandstanding, but also rejuvenating an ancient Russian value of seeking repentance that came easily for him, given his roots.[5]

Religion and ritual

However traditional values are currently defined, they are based on Russian Orthodox roots, variously interpreted through the centuries by Russians with strong pre-Christian beliefs. Religion too has become a central issue in Russian nationalist thought, for the introduction of Christianity and the long subsequent process of Christianization are seen as key elements in forming the Russian people into a nation. Historians of Russia are by no means in agreement on when Russian national consciousness developed or how long "pagan" influences, often with strong local flavoring, were significant.[6]

In 1988, to the surprise of many Russians used to Soviet policies of atheism and persecution of believers, the government supported elaborate and widespread celebrations of the Millennium of Christianity—commemoration of the baptism in 988 when Vladimir of Kiev declared his people Christian. While some Ukrainians explained that the main actors in this historical drama were not Russians but Ukrainians (or at least proto-Ukrainians), others (Ukrainians, Belorussians, and Russians) stressed common Slavic roots.[7] Despite some ethnic discord, the celebration was an official affirmation of the historical and living significance of Orthodoxy, signaling a revival of worship, the return of hundreds of previously seized churches to believers, and renewed respect for Christian charity and morality. Some cynics claimed this was merely a governmental grasp at a Christian work ethic that had evaporated among workers of the socialist workers' state. But tangible results were impressive. The energies of believers were harnessed for massive church and monastery restorations, some completed for the official Millennium. In several places where decrepit churches (used as dumps, factories, offices, book repositories, museums, and concert halls) were not returned, congregations organized protest demonstrations and even hunger strikes. On a more symbolic level, church bells rang in Red Square for the first time in decades, and a joyous yet tearful service was held in the Church of the Annunciation in the Kremlin. Numerous scholarly conferences were organized to commemorate the Millennium. Their published papers, including some translated in this volume, gave a boost to the legitimacy of research on religion, using both Marxist and non-Marxist perspectives.[8]

The lead chapter here, by three St. Petersburg scholars, tackles the issue of "Christianization" during the time of Vladimir by arguing that Vladimir and his followers saw Orthodoxy through a pre-Christian, "pagan" prism. Since conversion is rarely as definitive or abrupt as the word implies, the narrative of I. Ia. Froianov, A. Iu. Dvornichenko, and Iu. V. Krivosheev is plausible, albeit highly conjectural. The chapter provides glimpses into early Slavic rituals, rationales, and reforms, gleaned from early Christian sources that are themselves a mix of history and mythology. We see the pagan god Perun literally dethroned, replaced with a miracle-making God perceived to be nearly as utilitarian as Perun.[9]

The second chapter expands traditional ideas about Christianization and "dual faith" (*dvoeverie*) by focusing on the peasantry. The author, V. G. Vlasov, argues that different social groups received and perceived Christianity in different ways, in various periods. The peasantry itself was not monolithic, and was not thoroughly Christian for many centuries, despite an Orthodox self-identity. Vlasov identifies consolidation of Christianity with the first decades of the sixteenth century and the widespread adoption of the church (Julian) calendar. Yet he maintains that popular "folk" Orthodoxy remained quite different from official Orthodoxy.

The next chapter develops the idea of folk Orthodoxy still further. T. A. Bernshtam rails against earlier academic conceptions of *dvoeverie* that describe it as a superficial, "formal" coexistence of two faiths—Christianity and "paganism." Instead, she argues for the evolution of a "multifaith" (*mnogoverie*) Russian culture, in which pagan–Christian syncretism was both more profound and more varied than previously admitted. To illustrate the significance of her thesis, Bernshtam delves into the complex history of sectarianism, notably by reanalyzing the Old Believers' passionate fight against the official Orthodoxy they saw as profane.[10]

Two chapters on specific aspects of folk religion follow. N. N. Veletskaia tackles the problem of deciphering pre-Christian beliefs. Her analysis is more in the style of James Frazer than Karl Marx as she focuses on Old Believer rituals that appear to be from sources deep in "pagan" antiquity. She traces the important and highly controversial tradition of ritually "dispatching" old people into the afterlife. Given that many peoples, both in the North and in Indo-European tradition, had similar rituals but endowed them with remarkably nuanced meanings, Veletskaia's theories on "genetic roots" and her assumptions about "degeneration" of traditions may seem to Western readers to be speculative and value-laden. But her descriptions are worth reading because she identifies variations on the poignant theme of how Slavic and other peoples tried to ritually ensure an afterlife for elders whose productive time in this world was perceived to be over, usually by themselves as well as others. At its core, the theme of death with dignity is very much with us in current debates about "extraordinary measures" for the dying, and about aiding voluntary death with suicide machines.[11]

F. F. Bolonev studies the cultural persistence of ritual poetry—specifically, the incantation or "charm." His material comes not only from archives but from Siberian field data. Some of the charms are strikingly powerful as artistic creations. This has indeed enhanced the perception of their users that they are powerful spiritual tools to affect sickness, love relations, jealousies, and other aspects of the human condition. Through the charms, much can be learned, or, more accurately, hypothesized, about pre-Christian beliefs.[12]

The section culminates with historian N. G. Velizhanina's careful description of a range of icon styles introduced from Russia into Siberia, as well as the evolution of more specifically Siberian traditions. By detailing particular icon patrons, painters, and subjects, she provides a solid feel for the early, rather large scale of icon production in Siberia, and for a few personal stories behind that production.[13]

Gender and family life

The evolution of folk attitudes toward Christianity is reflected in changing approaches to family life. Through changes in familial values and views of women one can see the eventual establishment of Orthodox norms. N. L. Pushkareva suggests the critical time period for study of these processes is the tenth to fifteenth centuries. Her work is meticulous, acknowledging gaps in sources yet utilizing every crumb she can find to reconstruct gender relations of urban and rural populations. Pushkareva concludes that Christianity did not uniformly improve the lot of women. On the contrary, traditions represented in marriage ritual and folklore reveal a stronger, more competitive position for Slavic women of the tenth than the sixteenth century. Yet customary gender relations and legal norms gave both men and women advantages and disadvantages through the Middle Ages.

A symbolically powerful example of gender bias is the famous (Russian or Slavic?) proverb "a chicken is not a bird, a woman is not a person."[14] Pushkareva cites a less well known and more subtle one: "In turbid water you cannot see the bottom, and in a bride you will not understand the truth." Scholars too will see only murkily until biases rampant in the study of Slavic gender relations are confronted. Pushkareva has begun to do this. Hers is too complex a narrative to squeeze into the muddy Marxist generalization that patriarchy follows matriarchy.

The often secret folk practices of Russian midwives provide another glimpse into concepts of gender and the persistence of cultural traditions nurtured by women. Ethnographer T. A. Listova's essay contains a sympathetic view of the midwife, seen through the eyes of elderly grandmothers whose children were delivered by midwives, through interviews with former midwives, and through ethnographic sources. Far from the old crones of some stereotypes, Listova's midwives are moral, upstanding community members with successful families of their own. If they so much as ate meat on Mondays (in one community), or performed an abortion, they lost their profession forever. Their payments came mostly in ritual form, and were rarely questioned or deviated from in close-knit, gossip-prone communities. Listova delves into a realm of folk belief that some Western medical and symbolic anthropologists have categorized as "pollution" concepts, including beliefs about menstruation and the impurity of childbirth.[15] Yet her analysis is filled with examples of the ambiguity of notions concerning the spiritual power of women, of midwives and of fertile mothers. Russians are seen to have three mothers—their birth mother, their godmother, and the more ancient *Mat' syra zemlia* ("moist mother earth" or "mother damp earth"). Concepts of menstruation come directly from ambiguous feelings regarding the power of fertility: monthly periods are described as "cleansing," yet menstrual and childbirth blood is seen as "impure." Christianity and folk beliefs are shown to be deeply intertwined, so that mothers and midwives did not always know where their folk Christianity left off and the Orthodoxy of the local priest began.

The chapters discussed thus far were written by scholars inspired by *glasnost'* to fill in perceived "blank spots" of history and ethnography. The chapter by Iu. Kuz'mina goes a step further, for it is a fascinating account on a topic far from the mainstream of Soviet or post-Soviet life: a still-functioning Russian Orthodox convent. At the start, it appears to be one of the first discussions of monastery life to be presented in a neutral, even sympathetic, light in the Soviet period. But by the end the author reveals her own love of the noncloistered world. Indeed, this is a tale of two women as well as two worlds. Kuz'mina cleverly features the thoughts of one kind-hearted monastery novice as she prepares to become a nun, while also disclosing her own, journalist's reactions. The result is not antireligious propaganda, but rather a sincere effort to understand something Kuz'mina feels belongs in history. Each woman, representing contrasting worlds, is self-righteous and self-justifying. Yet the reader is able to see not only a continuity of religious tradition, but also the psychology behind the reason that a young woman might want to join a convent in current times.

Customary law, daily life, medicine, and morality

Crucial in the lives of "traditional" Russian peasants were concepts of morality, honor, personal and social health, and proper ways to have fun. This is not to deny there were improper ways rampant in Russian villages.

But to be improper, one still had to know what was considered proper, socially approved, communal and individual behavior. Peasants living in close-knit communities in Russia and Siberia, before and after the revolution, were fully aware of societal norms. Public opinion played a strong constraining role, even for folks in far-flung tough frontier villages of Siberia. Nonetheless, social norms were not embedded in some static genetic or "character" code. Definitions of appropriate behavior changed with place and over time. The interplay between village life and urban centers influenced the moral tone in villages and the morale of villagers. Tensions over what was "proper" or "normal" might wrack a village or a family, and could land them in rural courts.

The section on customary law and village life features themes that have been developed in legal and medical anthropology, taking advantage of remarkably detailed data in the recent "revisionist" work of three social historians, N. A. Minenko, M. M. Gromyko, and I. V. Vlasova. To understand revisionist historical anthropology, one must know what is being debunked. The Russian women writers featured here have been active in changing common (Russian and Western) perceptions of agriculturalists in Siberia and Russia. Stereotypes of drunken, illiterate, and lazy peasants disintegrate under their careful reconstruction (not deconstruction) of village life and morality.[16]

Three Russian words used in this discussion require clarification: *mir*, usually glossed as the peasant commune; *muzhik*, an informal word for a peasant; and *krest'ianin*, the more dominant term for peasant, which has roots in the word "cross," i.e., Christian. *Krest'ianin* is the word most used by soil tillers themselves, for example as used by the Peasant Association in new-found mobilization. *Muzhik* has connotations of the crude fellow with muddy boots who puts his feet on the table. This is the word for "peasant" used in Chekhov's nineteenth-century stories of debauchery and squalor.[17] Yet some Russians, in self-irony or reverse snobbery, still proudly proclaim themselves and their close friends *muzhiki*—just folks.

Mir is a word of extraordinary multivocal versatility, rooted in the prerevolutionary village commune and its council, with additional meanings of "world" and "peace." It is "no accident," as the Russians often say, that *Mir* was chosen as the name for the Soviet space station. Today, in echoes of the past, some Russian villages are named "Mirnyi." Folk proverbs revealing past significance of the *mir* include: "God alone directs the *mir*"; "The neck and shoulders of the *mir* are broad: throw everything upon the *mir*, it will carry all"; "Trees are felled in the forest, and splinters fly in the *mir*"; "No one in the world can separate from the *mir*."[18] Numerous regional and general histories provide perspective on the village commune, ruled by a council of usually male household heads. These "elders" served as the basis for a rough-and-ready folk democracy, in ideal form based on consensus or two-thirds majority, but often dominated by several strong personalities. Some villages had only one *mir*, while larger ones had two or even three. Before the Great Reforms of the 1860s, the *mir* decided issues as diverse as allocation of land, military draft selection, and charity for widows. Its significance lingered into the Soviet period and is touted today as a possible exemplar of partial local autonomy. The accounts provided here bring the reader into the world of the not always peaceful, sometimes celebratory, peasant *mir*.

The strength and continuity of customary law regarding land use is depicted in the chapter by I. V. Vlasova. She explains that most prerevolutionary northern peasants had rights to dispose of at least some of their land as they saw fit, and that many, when in need of more land, got permission from the local commune to expand into unused forest. This may not seem earthshaking, but it is significant because it stresses local history and the interrelation between ecology and political power. Vlasova discusses the crucial dynamic between the state and the peasant, a topic of considerable comparative interest in legal anthropology.[19] A basic historical distinction is between "state peasants" and peasants on private estates. Vlasova views the state peasants as relatively better off, because they had more *de facto* control of their usually more considerable lands. Some behaved as though state ownership of land was a mere technicality to be remedied by good peasant sweat. It is this spirit that is precisely what members of the expanding Peasant Association are searching for today, in an atmosphere not yet conducive to farming or homesteading.[20] Vlasova's approach toward the rich peasants, called *kulaki* well before Stalin made them the victims of his collectivization campaign, is somewhat surprising. While many in Russia today are looking back at this "class" of wealthy peasants with sorrow and nostalgia, wishing the wisdom of their success could have been shared with future generations, Vlasova seems to take a more orthodox and scornful view.

Methodological issues

As post-Soviet anthropologists and social historians emerge from the intellectual cocoon of automatic Marxist analytical structures, some struggle to find new ways of digging for and deciphering data. A heightened sensitivity to regional differences is one manifestation of emerging theory tied to local conditions without being lost in overwhelming detail or thwarted by grand evolutionary schemes. Seasoned historians such as N. A. Minenko were attuned to a balance between theory and specificity well before the Gorbachev period, but many were not. The most striking regional contrast evident in this volume is that between Siberian and Central Russian traditions. North, Central, and South Russian differences are also salient.[21]

Russians whose families have lived in Siberia for many generations, or who have committed themselves voluntarily to staying in Siberia, often call themselves Sibiriaki. They have created and inherited a culture based extensively on old Slavic folk traditions that were preserved with pride in

Siberia, sometimes long after the same traditions had been forgotten in European Russia. Russian culture was not, however, some static idolized or idealized thing. Sibiriaki adapted to their varied Siberian circumstances, and syncretized aspects of native Siberian cultural traditions. Siberian-centered scholarship and fieldwork has much to offer for an understanding of the interplay between themes of Russian roots and Siberian culture, colonial legacy and frontier independence, urban polish and backwoods life, Christianity and "paganism," regionalism and federalism.[22]

A second main methodological issue concerns historical reconstruction. Authors featured here vary in their degree of adventurousness, some presenting highly speculative narratives as historical fact, especially when dealing with the Kievan or pre-Christian periods. Western readers can interpret these as texts revealing current political debates. But some of the historians offer exciting, direct tastes of their sources. These include court records of local household and land disputes, petitions and wills, personal observations by literate peasants, doctors and officials, and even peasant letters.

Recent anthropology fieldwork in Russian villages has been spotty and uneven.[23] Yet new worthwhile projects are getting off the ground. Two examples are reflected in the protocols of T. A. Listova and I. V. Vlasova, printed here in the appendices. These protocols reveal their authors' methodologies and worldviews, enabling us to glimpse priorities seldom made explicit in Russian anthropology. These "programs," from which further questions, field research, and results are emerging, show a balance between not wanting to ask loaded questions and not wanting to appear ignorant. They are wish-lists for information on cultural practices and culture change, designed to gain community respect for their authors' detailed prior knowledge, yet also to ferret out regional differences. Less structured field studies through multiyear residence in villages are a new goal.

The idea of filling in "blank spots," laudable though its intentions are, implies that history and ethnography are like detailed geographical maps to be filled in with uninterpreted nuggets of information. But even maps require selectivity, history and ethnography far more so. This volume provides a sampling of recent Russian scholarship that expands the horizons of both disciplines. But more anthropological work in the fields and homes of the fast-changing Russian village is critically needed for multidimensional understanding of past and present data.

Notes

I am grateful to scholars Valentina Baktina, Olga Balalaeva, Harley Balzer, William Brumfield, David Goldfrank, Jovan Howe, Edward L. Keenan, Nancy Shields Kollmann, Eve Levin, Margarita Mazo, Demitri B. Shimkin, Richard Stites, Valery A. Tishkov, Gelian M. Prokhorev, David Ransel, and Christine Worobec for advice on diverse aspects of this volume. Editorial observations or analysis not specifically credited stem from my own fieldwork in Russia and Siberia in 1975–76, 1983, 1985–86, and 1991.

1. Historian Dmitri Balashov and philosopher Eduard F. Volodin are associated with nationalist views that stress Russian heroism. O. Trubachev created a stir in 1987 (*Pravda*, 28 March) by condoning Russian repression of the Polish 1830 uprising (and Pushkin's poem about it). The *Voenno-istoricheskii zhurnal* in 1989–91 published articles on imperial heroes. The serial publication of General A. I. Denikin's memoirs *Ocherki russkoi smuty* in *Voprosy istorii* (1990, nos. 3–12) is a related but not quite comparable issue. Few of those best known for views that are clearly empire-justifying, anti-Western, and anti-Semitic, such as Dmitri Vasil'ev, Viacheslav Gorbachev, and Vladimir Begun, are academic historians. One of the first proponents of "single streamism" was publicist Viktor Chalmaev, whose 1968 *Molodaia gvardia* tracts are reprinted in John Dunlop, *The Faces of Contemporary Russian Nationalism* (Princeton: Princeton University Press, 1983), pp. 312–22. See also John Dunlop, "Soviet Cultural Politics," *Problems of Communism*, November–December 1987, pp. 34–56; and his "A Conversation with Dmitrii Vasil'ev, the Leader of Pamyat," *Radio Liberty Report on the USSR*, 15 December 1989, pp. 12–16; also Roman Szporluk, "Dilemmas of Russian Nationalism," *Problems of Communism*, July–August 1989, pp. 15–35; R. W. Davies, *Soviet History in the Gorbachev Revolution* (Bloomington: Indiana University Press, 1989); Mark Galeotti, "The Soviet Army's New Interest in Imperial Traditions," *Radio Liberty Report on the USSR*, 28 December 1990, pp. 8–10. The controversial orientalist Lev N. Gumilev, sympathetic to some Russian nationalist positions, stresses not militarism but peaceful Russian relations with Asians in *Drevniaia Rus' i velikaia step'* (Moscow: Mysl', 1989).

2. D. S. Likhachev outlined the rather idealistic argument in "The National Nature of Russian History" (The Second W. Averill Harriman Lecture, Columbia University, pamphlet, 13 November 1990). See also his "Rossiia," *Literaturnaia gazeta*, 12 October 1988, no. 41, pp. 5–6; *Chelovek v literature drevnei Rusi* (Moscow, 1970 [original 1958]); *Poetika drevnerusskoi literatury* (Moscow, 1979); *Literatura—realnost'—literatura* (Leningrad, 1981); "Preliminary Results of a Thousand-year Experiment," in *The Soviet Multinational State*, ed. Martha B. Olcott (Armonk, NY: M. E. Sharpe, 1990); and V. D. Likhacheva and D. S. Likhachev, *Khudozhestvennoe nasledie drevnei Rusi i sovremennost'* (Leningrad, 1971). The Culture Fund has actively supported church renovations and other projects associated with the rebirth of Russian traditional culture.

3. See B. G. Mogil'nitskii "Alternativnost' v istorii Sovetskogo obshchestva," *Voprosy istorii*, 1989, no. 11, pp. 3–16; Alexander S. Tsipko, "Istoki stalinizma," *Nauka i zhizn'*, 1988, no. 11 (English translation: "The Sources of Stalinism," *Soviet Law and Government*, vol. 29, nos. 1 and 2 [Summer and Fall 1990]); N. I. Pavlenko, "U istokov Rossiiskoi Biurokratii," *Voprosy istorii*, 1989, no. 12, pp. 3–17; N. F. Demidova, *Sluzhilaia biurokratiia v Rossii XVII v. i ee rol' v formirovanii absoliutisma* (Moscow, 1988); E. V. Anisimov, "Petr I: Rozhdenie imperii," *Voprosy istorii*, 1989, no. 7, pp. 3–20 (English translation: *Soviet Studies in History*, vol. 30, no. 2 [Fall 1991], pp. 6–29). Popular fascination with the monarchy has stimulated and been spawned by press articles on the death of Nicholas II.

4. The nationalist group Pamiat' (Memory) even sponsors its own farm. The Brezhnev-era campaign to abolish "villages without a future" (*neperspektivnyi*) is widely resented, and debates over Stalinist collectivization and new land ownership laws are sharp. See especially Pavel Voshchanov, "Kulaki," *Komsomol'skaia pravda*, 8 September 1989, p. 2, and the ensuing debate in *Komsomol'skaia pravda*, 2 December 1989, pp. 2–3 (English translation: "History and Ideology," *Joint Publications Research Service*, 11 January 1990, pp. 67–71). See also V. P. Danilov, *Rural Russia under the New Regime* (Bloomington: Indiana University Press, 1988); Viktor Il'in, "My Village of Rechnoe," *Soviet Anthropology and Archeology*, vol. 24, no. 3 (Winter 1985–86), pp. 3–46. For background, see Stephen P. Dunn and Ethel Dunn, *The Peasants of Central Russia* (Prospect Heights, IL: Waveland Press, 1988 [original 1967]); Sula Benet (American ed.), I. P. Kushner (Russian ed.), *The Village of Viriatino* (New York: Doubleday, 1970 [original Moscow, 1958]); Moshe Lewin, *Russian Peasants and Soviet Power* (Evanston: Northwestern University Press, 1968); Teodor Shanin, ed., *Peasants and Peasant Societies* (Harmondsworth: Penguin, 1971); R. E. F. Smith, ed., "The Russian Peasant 1920 and 1984," *The Journal of Peasant Studies*, vol. 4, no. 1, pp. 1–120; Wayne S. Vucinich, ed., *The Peasant in Nineteenth-century Russia* (Stanford: Stanford University Press, 1968); Sir John Maynard, *The Russian Peasant and Other Studies* (New York: Collier, 1942); Lawrence Krader, "Recent Studies of the Russian Peasant," *American Anthropologist*, 1956, vol. 58, pp. 716–20.

5. Yeltsin's speech was during the funerals on August 24, 1991. Stress here is on changeable, consciously socialized values rather than on "national character." Russians themselves discuss both values and "character," sometimes in highly generalized terms. See D. S. Likhachev,

"Rossiia," *Literaturnaia gazeta*, 12 October 1988, no. 41, pp. 5–6; M. M. Gromyko, *Traditsionnye normy povedeniia i formy obshcheniia russkikh krest'ian XIX v.* (Moscow: Nauka, 1986). Journalist Hedrick Smith (*The New Russians* [New York: Random House, 1990]) is in a long American tradition of risky attempts to probe (and overgeneralize) Russian character. Cf. Margaret Mead, *Soviet Attitudes toward Authority: An Interdisciplinary Approach to Problems of Soviet Character* (New York: Schocken, 1951); Margaret Mead and Rhoda Metraux, eds., *The Study of Culture at a Distance* (Chicago: University of Chicago Press, 1953); Geoffrey Gorer and John Rickman, *The Peoples of Great Russia: A Psychological Study* (New York: Norton, 1962 [original Cresset, 1949]). Clyde Kluckhohn, the psychological anthropologist who headed the 1950s Harvard Refugee Interview Project, declined to write a monograph on Russian character. A powerful approach to Russian traditional values remains through literature, including the nationalist, often xenophobic "village" writers Valentin Rasputin, Iuri Bondarev, Vasilii Belov, and Viktor Astaf'ev. Cf. "The Russian Complex: The Eidelman–Astafiev Correspondence," *Detente*, Winter 1987, pp. 5–7. See also the moving story by Alexander Solzhenitsyn, "Matriona's Home," in *Half-way to the Moon*, eds. Patricia Blake and Max Hayward (New York: Anchor, 1965), pp. 13–53.

6. The usual Soviet Marxist view was that the people (*narod*) formed first, and then the state. This remains valid for many historians, but not all. Compare B. I. Krasnobaev, *Russkaia kul'tura vtoroi poloviny XVII–nachala XIX v.* (Moscow: Moscow State University Press, 1983), pp. 41–62; D. S. Likhachev "Rossiia," *Literaturnaia gazeta*, 12 October 1988, no. 41, pp. 5–6; V. S. Rumiantseva, "Tendentsii razvitiia obshchestvennogo soznanii i prosveshcheniia v Rossii XVII veka," *Voprosy istorii*, no. 2, pp. 26–40; I. Ia. Froianov and A. Iu. Dvornichenko, *Goroda-gosudarstva drevnei Rusi* (Leningrad: Leningrad State University Press, 1988); Iu. V. Krivosheev, "Sotsial'naia bor'ba i problema genezisa feodal'nykh otnoshenii v severo-vostochnoi Rusi XI–nachala XII veka," *Voprosy istorii*, 1988, no. 9, pp. 49–63; E. A. Mel'nikova and V. Ia. Petrukhin, "Nazvanie 'Rus'' v etnokul'turnoi istorii drevnerusskogo gosudarstva (IX–X vv.), *Voprosy istorii*, 1989, no. 8, pp. 24–38; I. V. Dubov, "Spornye voprosy etnicheskoi istorii severo-vostochnoi Rusi IX–XIII vekov," *Voprosy istorii*, 1990, no. 5, pp. 15–27; V. P. Filippov, "Iz istorii izucheniia Russkogo natsional'nogo samosoznaniia," *Sovetskaia etnografiia*, 1991, no. 1, pp. 25–33. For Western views placing the gradual formation of Russian ethnicity well beyond the Kievan or Mongol periods, see Edward L. Keenan, "Royal Russian Behavior, Style, and Self-Image," in *Ethnic Russia in the USSR: The Dilemma of Dominance*, ed. Edward Allworth (New York: Pergamon, 1980), pp. 3–16; idem, "Moscovite Political Folkways," *The Russian Review*, 1986, vol. 45, pp. 115–81; Henrik Birnbaum and Michael S. Flier, eds., *Medieval Russian Culture* (Berkeley: University of California Press, 1984). Cf. Gail Lenhoff, *The Martyred Princes Boris and Gleb: A Socio-cultural Study of the Cult and the Texts* (Columbus, OH: Slavica, 1989). Edward Keenan gave early warnings of Russian national chauvinism in historical analysis, both before and during the Gorbachev period.

7. A few Ukrainians have also decided that the true roots of their culture lie with the pre-Christian cult of Iarilo. For discussion of Orthodoxy, see "Kruglyi Stol. Rol' pravoslavnoi tserkvi v istorii Rossii," *Voprosy istorii*, 1990, no. 3, pp. 84–106. With the Millennium, the journal *Voprosy istorii* instituted a section "Ocherki Istorii Russkoi Pravoslavnoi Tserkvi" including writings of Orthodox clergy; see, e.g., 1989, no. 8, pp. 54–75. See also A. B. Golovko, "Khristianizatsiia vostochnoslavianskogo obshchestva i vneshniaia politika drevnei rusi v IX–pervoi treti XIII veka," *Voprosy istorii*, 1988, no. 9, pp. 59–71. Cf. James H. Billington, "Russia's Quest for Identity" and "Looking into the Past," *Washington Post*, 21 January 1990, p. B7; 22 January, p. A11. In March 1989 a new pan-Slavic cultural organization was formed, *Fond slavianskoi pis'mennosti i slavianskikh kul'tur*, whose leaders are mainly Russian nationalists. See John Dunlop, "Two Noteworthy Russian Nationalist Initiatives," *Radio Liberty Report on the USSR*, 26 May 1989, pp. 1–4. In July 1991 a well-attended religious procession carried the remains of St. Sarafim of Sarov through Central Russia. See A. Vasinsky and A. Yershov, "Pilgrimage to a Miracle," *Izvestiia*, 31 July 1991, p. 6 (and *Current Digest of the Soviet Press*, vol. 43, no. 31, pp. 29–30; vol. 43, no. 29, pp. 27).

8. A Russian–American volume commemorating the Millennium is William C. Brumfield and Milos Velimirovic, eds., *Christianity and the Arts in Russia* (New York: Cambridge University Press, 1991). For a summary of religion and change under Gorbachev, see Sabrina P. Ramet, ed., *Religious Policy in the Soviet Union* (Cambridge: Cambridge University Press, 1992). See also the 1990 USSR "Law on Freedom of Conscience" (*Current Digest of the Soviet Press*, vol. 42, no. 40, pp. 6–8, 31), being adapted for Russia in 1992.

9. The word "pagan" is itself problematic, since some see it as pejorative. It is recently used neutrally in the West and Russia for a wide range of pre-Christian beliefs and practices. "Christianization" is also seen by some as not respectful enough of religious conversion. However, the word is used here to indicate the gradual nature of the adoption of Christianity by a highly diverse Slavic population. An example of speculative history on Slavic pre-Christian beliefs is B. A. Rybakov, *Iazychestvo drevnei Rusi* (Moscow: Nauka, 1987). Cf. N. K. Chadwick, *The Beginnings of Russian History: An Enquiry into Sources* (Cambridge: Cambridge University Press, 1946 [reprint 1966]); and idem, *Russian Heroic Poetry* (New York: Russell and Russell, 1964). Two basic sources on Russian folk religion are V. I. Dal', *Tolkovyi slovar'*, 4 vols. (Moscow: Russkii iazyk, 1981 [original 1863–1866]); and M. Zabylin, *Russkii narod* (Moscow: Kniga Printshop, 1990 [original 1880]).

10. For discussion of *dvoeverie* see George P. Fedotov, *The Russian Religious Mind: Kievan Christianity* (New York: Harper & Row, 1960), pp. 7–8, 395; Nikolai Andreyev, "Pagan and Christian Elements in Old Russia," *Slavic Review*, 1962, no. 21, pp. 16–23; Russell Zguta, "Witchcraft and Medicine in Pre-Petrine Russia," *Russian Review*, 1978, vol. 37, no. 4, pp. 338–448. Cf. Pierre Pascal, *The Religion of the Russian People*, Rowan Williams, trans. (Oxford: Mobray, 1976), pp. 8–10; James Billington, *The Icon and the Axe* (New York: Vintage, 1970), p. 18. See also S. A. Tokarev, *Religioznye verovaniia vostochno-slavianskikh narodov* (Moscow: Nauka, 1957), p. 21; Gelian M. Prokhorov, "Proshloe i vechnost' v kul'ture kievskoi Rusi," in *Chelovek i istoriia v srednevekovoi filosofskoi mysli russkogo, ukrainskogo i belorusskogo narodov* (Kiev: Naukova dumka, 1987). On sectarianism, see N. A. Kazakova and Ia. S. Lur'e, *Antifeodal'nye ereticheskie dvizheniia na Rusi XIV–nachala XVI veka* (Moscow: Nauka, 1955); A. I. Klibanov, *Reformatsionnye dvizheniia v Rossii v XIV–pervoi polovine XVI vv* (Moscow: Nauka, 1960); idem, "Fifty Years of Scientific Study of Religious Sectarianism," *Soviet Sociology*, vol. 8, no. 3–4 (Winter–Spring 1970), pp. 239–78; and idem, *History of Religious Sectarianism in Russia (1860s–1917)*, trans. Ethel Dunn, ed. Stephen Dunn (Oxford: Pergamon, 1982), pp. ix–xv and 1–66. Cf. George P. Fedotov, *The Russian Religious Mind: The Middle Ages*, ed. John Meyendorff (Cambridge: Harvard University Press, 1966).

11. Tensions over American approaches to euthanasia were also reflected in debates in the 1970s about Eskimo (Inuit) cultural studies in our schools. On Siberian religion, see A. I. Klibanov, *History of Religious Sectarianism in Russia*; L. P. Kuzmina, "Ethno-cultural Aspects of Research in the Oral Tradition of the Russian Population of Siberia," *Review of Ethnology*, 1982, vol. 8, pp. 126–31; Russian revolutionary exile Vladimir Zenzinov, *The Road to Oblivion* (New York: National Travel Club, 1931). See also V. A. Aleksandrov, ed., *Na putiakh iz zemli Permskoi v Sibir: ocherki etnografii severnoural'skogo krest'ianstva XVII–XX vv.* (Moscow: Nauka, 1989); V. V. Bunak and I. M. Zolotareva, eds., *Russkie starozhily Sibiri* (Moscow: Nauka, 1973); V. A. Lipinskaia, *Russkoe naselenie Altaiskogo kraia* (Moscow: Nauka, 1987); G. S. Maslova and L. M. Saburova, eds., *Etnografiia Russkogo naseleniia Sibiri i srednei Azii* (Moscow: Nauka, 1969); Serge Zenkovskii, *Russkoe staroobriadchestvo* (Munich, 1970); V. I. Zorkin, *Vklad politicheskikh ssil'nykh v izuchenie fol'klora Sibiri* (Novosibirsk: Nauka, 1985).

12. Few Western studies cover Slavic incantations (relatively elaborate poetry with a purpose) and charms (relatively simple spoken formulas for protection) in any systematic way. See Linda J. Ivanits, *Russian Folk Belief* (Armonk, NY: M. E. Sharpe, 1989); Felix J. Oinas and S. Soudakoff, eds., *The Study of Russian Folklore* (The Hague: Mouton, 1975). Two important collections are L. N. Maikov, "Velikorusskie zaklinaniia," *Zapiski imperatorskogo Russkogo geograficheskogo obshchestva po otdeleniiu etnografii*, 1869, vol. 2, pp. 417–580; N. N. Vinogradov, "Zagovory, oberegi, spasitel'nye molitvy i proch.," *Zhivaia starina*, 1908, vol. 17, no. 1, pp. 1–24, no. 2, pp. 25–40; no. 3, pp. 41–64; and no. 4, pp. 65–94. Incantations were collected by folklorists, and also written down and passed on by and for the people who used them, so that by the nineteenth century they were both an oral and a written art. Some were accompanied by rituals, including one for cursing a former lover that involved placing a frog in *kvass* (mildly alcoholic beer) or wine.

13. A major historical source on icons in Siberia is A. I. Sulotskii, *Istoricheskie svedeniia ob ikonopisanii v Sibiri* (Omsk, 1863). See also A. N. Kopylov, *Ocherki kul'turnoi zhizni Sibiri XVII–nachala XIX v.* (Novosibirsk: Nauka, 1974). For a few, varied sources (among many) on Siberian church history, see Avvakum, *The Life of Archpriest Avvakum by Himself*, trans. J. Harrison and H. Mirrlees (London: Hogarth Press, 1924); I. V. Barsukov, *O zhizni i podvigakh Innokentiia* (St. Petersburg: Tip. Katankogo, 1893); N. M. Iadrintsev, *Sibir' kak koloniia* (St. Petersburg, 1882); K. V. Kharlampovich, *Archimandrit Makarii* (St. Petersburg, 1905); G. F.

Miller (Müller), *Istorii Sibiri*, 2 vols. (Moscow: Nauka, 1941 [original 1763]); Pierre Pascal, *Avvakum et les débuts du Raskol: La crise réligieuse au XVIIe siècle en Russie* (Paris: Gallimard, 1938); G. M. Soldatov, *Mitropolit Filofei, v skhime Feodor, Prosvetitel' Sibiri* (Minneapolis: Soldatow, 1972).

14. The use of proverbs to illustrate folk belief is nonetheless problematic, since proverbs can be found to express contradictory positions within the same culture or region and the age of proverbs is hard to determine. See V. I. Dal', *Poslovitsy russkogo naroda* (Moscow: Nauka, 1957 [original 1878]); Demitri B. Shimkin and Pedro Sanjuan, "Culture and World View: A Method of Analysis Applied to Rural Russia," *American Anthropologist*, 1953, vol. 55, pp. 239–348; and Felix J. Oinas and S. Soudakoff, eds., *The Study of Russian Folklore* (The Hague: Mouton, 1975). On gender role complexity, see Barbara Evans Clements, Barbara Alpern Engel, and Christine D. Worobec, eds., *Russia's Women: Accommodation, Resistance, Transformation* (Berkeley: University of California Press, 1991); Nancy Shields Kollmann, *Kinship and Politics: The Making of the Muscovite Political System, 1345–1547* (Stanford: Stanford University Press, 1977); Eve Levin, *Sex and Society in the World of the Orthodox Slavs 900–1700* (Ithaca: Cornell University Press, 1989); Serge A. Zenkovsky, *Medieval Russia's Epics, Chronicles and Tales* (New York: Dutton, 1974 [2nd ed]), especially "Igor's Death and Olga's Revenge" and the apocrypha "The Descent of the Virgin into Hell"; and Wendy D. O'Flaherty, *Women, Androgynes, and Other Mythical Beasts* (Chicago: University of Chicago Press, 1980). In folklore, concepts of *rusalki* (drowned maidens) and *Baba Yaga* (witch-sorceress) exemplify negative female images. See Linda J. Ivanits, *Russian Folk Belief* (Armonk, NY: M. E. Sharpe, 1989); Aleksandr N. Afanasyev, *Russian Secret Tales: Bawdy Folktales of Old Russia* (New York: Brussel and Brussel, 1966 [original 1872]). Cf. Joanna Hubbs, *Mother Russia: The Feminine Myth in Russian Culture* (Bloomington: Indiana University Press, 1988), pp. 42–51.

15. See, for example, Mary Douglas, *Purity and Danger: An Analysis of Concepts of Pollution and Taboo* (London: Routledge and Kegan Paul, 1966); Marjorie Mandelstam Balzer, "Rituals of Gender Identity: Markers of Siberian Khanty Ethnicity, Status and Belief," *American Anthropologist*, 1981, vol. 83, no. 4, pp. 850–68; and Thomas Buckley and Alma Gottlieb, eds., *Blood Magic: The Anthropology of Menstruation* (Berkeley: University of California Press, 1988). Cf. Micaela de Leonardo, *Gender at the Crossroads of Knowledge: Feminist Anthropology in the Postmodern Era* (Berkeley: University of California Press, 1991).

16. Historiography of the Russian peasantry reflects oscillations between images of a romanticized, idealized peasant and a drunken brute. Relevant documentary films include *The Peasant Women of Riazan* and *Early on Sunday*; for feature films, see *Vasily and Vasilisa, Sibiriad*, and *Kalina Krasnaia*. For comparative concepts in legal anthropology about process, change, social tensions, and norms, see Sally Falk Moore, *Law as Process: An Anthropological Approach* (London: Routledge and Kegan Paul, 1978). For perspective on the social ramifications of medicine and medical beliefs, see Arthur Kleinman, *Patients and Healers in the Context of Culture: An Exploration of the Borderland between Anthropology, Medicine, and Psychiatry* (Berkeley: University of California Press, 1980); Lola Romanucci-Ross, Daniel R. Moerman, and Laurence Tancredi, eds., *The Anthropology of Medicine: From Culture to Method* (Westport: Bergin and Garvey, 1991 [revised]).

17. *Fermer* (farmer) is used by those trying to escape traditional connotations linking soil tillers with an exploited class. Cf. Anton P. Chekhov, "Muzhiki," in *Muzhiki i drugie rasskazy* (Moscow: Akademiia, 1932, [original 1897]); or *Peasants and Other Stories*, trans. Edmund Wilson (New York: Doubleday, 1956, pp. 249–88). See also Sula Benet, ed. and trans., *The Village of Viriatino* (New York: Doubleday, 1970, [original 1958]); Dunn and Dunn, *The Peasants of Central Russia*; Olga Crisp and Linda Edmondson, eds., *Civil Rights in Imperial Russia* (Oxford: Oxford University Press, 1989); Ben Eklof and Stephen P. Frank, eds., *The World of the Russian Peasant: Post-Emancipation Culture and Society* (Boston: Unwin Hyman, 1990); Esther Kingston-Mann and Timothy Mixter, eds., *Peasant Economy, Culture and Politics of European Russia 1800–1921* (Princeton: Princeton University Press, 1991); Sir John Maynard, *The Russian Peasant and Other Studies* (New York: Collier, 1962 [original 1942]); Vucinich, *The Peasant in Nineteenth-century Russia*. For theories about peasantry see A. Chayanov, *The Theory of Peasant Economy*, eds. and trans. D. Thorner, B. Kerblay, R. E. F. Smith (Homewood, IL: 1966); Michael Kearney and Carole Nagengast, *Reconceptualizing the Peasantry* (Boulder: Westview, forthcoming); Sydel Silverman, "The Peasant Concept in Anthropology," *Journal of Peasant Studies* vol. 7, 1979, pp. 49–69; Teodor Shanin, *The Awkward Class: The Political Sociology of the Peasantry in a Developing Society: Russia, 1910–1925* (New York, 1972); Eric R. Wolf, *Peasants* (Englewood Cliffs,

NJ: Prentice-Hall, 1966); idem, *Europe and the People without History* (Berkeley: University of California Press, 1982).

18. August von Haxthausen, *Studies on the Interior of Russia*, ed. S. Frederick Starr, trans. Eleanore L. M. Schmidt (Chicago: University of Chicago Press, 1972, [original 1847–52]), p. 277. Relevant histories include Jerome Blum, *Lord and Peasant in Russia from the Ninth to the Nineteenth Century* (Princeton: Princeton University Press, 1971 [original 1961]); Steven L. Hoch, *Serfdom and Social Control in Russia (Petrovskoe, a Village in Tambov)* (Chicago: University of Chicago Press, 1986); Geroid Tanquary Robinson, *Rural Russia under the Old Regime* (Berkeley: University of California Press, 1969 [original 1932]). A few basic sources include: V. A. Aleksandrov, *Sel'skaia obshchina v Rossii (XVII–nachalo XIX v.)* (Moscow, 1976); S. V. Bakhrushin, *Nauchnye trudy*, 3 vols. (Moscow, 1952–54); B. Chicherin, *Opyty po istorii russkago prava* (Moscow, 1858); A. Efimenko, *Issledovaniia narodnoi zhizni* (Moscow, 1884); K. Golovin, *Selskaia obshina v literature i deistvitelnosti* (St. Petersburg, 1887); the document collection *Krest'ianskaia reforma v Rossii 1861 goda: sbornik zakonodatel'nykh aktov* (Moscow, 1954); the journal *Krest'ianskaia Rossiia* (1920s); P. L. Liashchenko, *Ocherki agrarnoi evoliutsii Rossii*, 2 vols. (St. Petersburg, Leningrad, 1913–1926); V. I. Semevskii, *Krest'ianskii vopros v Rossii v XVIII i pervoi polovine XIX veka*, 2 vols. (St. Petersburg, 1888); A. Skrebitskii, *Krest'ianskoe delo v tsarstvovanie imperatora Aleksandra II*, vol. 4 (St. Petersburg, 1862–68); P. A. Zaionchkovskii, *Otmena krepostnogo prava v Rossii* (Moscow, 1968).

19. Cf., for example, Eric R. Wolf, *Europe and the People without History* (Berkeley: University of California Press, 1982); and Sally Falk Moore, *Law as Process: An Anthropological Approach* (London: Routledge and Kegan Paul, 1978).

20. The political mobilization of rural residents is complex and evolving. An Independent Peasants' Union was founded in 1989, but one of its leaders, V. A. Starodubtsev, was discredited for participation in the August 19, 1991 coup. A Peasants' Association (Russian acronym AK-KOR) developed in 1990, and a new Peasant Party, claiming membership of 20,000 families, represents some, but not all of the membership of the earlier groups. See A. Protsenko, "A Peasant's Exchange for Private Farmers," *Izvestiia*, 12 August 1991, p. 1 (translated in *Current Digest of the Soviet Press*, vol. 43, no. 32, 1991, pp. 20–21); *Current Digest of the Soviet Press*, vol. 43, no. 5, pp. 26–27; and vol. 40, no. 34, pp. 37–38. Privatization of land has been slow, with long-term leasing arrangements often made through the very collectives that the more enterprising families were trying to leave. On the dismal conditions, see (for just one example) David Remnick, "Soviet Farm Legacy: Dead Souls in a Dying Countryside," *Washington Post*, 21 May 1990, p. A1.

21. For an anthropological approach to local history as defined through "power regions," see Claudio Lomnitz-Adler, "Concepts for the Study of Regional Culture," *American Ethnologist* 1991, vol. 18, no. 2, pp. 195–214. For Russian case studies, see Stephen L. Hoch, *Serfdom and Social Control in Russia (Petrovskoe, a Village in Tambov)* (Chicago: University of Chicago Press, 1986); and Shimkin and Sanjuan, "Culture and World View."

22. Sibiriaki are treated as a self-conscious ethnic group in M. M. Balzer, "Sibiriaki," *Encyclopedia of World Cultures: The USSR*, ed. Paul Freidrich (Yale: Human Relations Area Files, forthcoming). See also Terence Armstrong, *Russian Settlement in the North* (Cambridge: Cambridge University Press, 1965); Basil Dmytryshyn, E. A. P. Crownhart-Vaughan, Thomas Vaughan, eds., *Russia's Conquest of Siberia, 1558–1700: A Documentary Record* (Portland: Oregon Historical Society North Pacific Studies Series, 1985); James R. Gibson, *Feeding the Russian Fur Trade: Provisionment of the Okhotsk Seaboard and the Kamchatka Peninsula 1639–1856* (Madison: University of Wisconsin Press, 1969); George Kennan, *Siberia and the Exile System* (New York: Praeger, 1970 [original 1891]); George V. Lantzeff and Richard A. Pierce, eds., *Eastward to Empire: Exploration and Conquest on the Russian Open Frontier* (Montreal: McGill-Queens University Press, 1973); John Massey Stewart and Alan Wood, eds., *Siberia: Two Historical Perspectives* (London: School of Slavonic and East European Studies, 1984); and the journals *Sibirica* (edited by Alan Wood) and *Siberica* (edited by Thomas Vaughan and Elizabeth A. P. Crownhart-Vaughan). Cf. A. P. Okladnikov, ed., *Istoriia Sibiri*, 5 vols. (Leningrad: Nauka, 1968); L. M. Russakova and N. A. Minenko, eds., *Kul'turno-bytovye protsessy u Russkikh Sibiri (XVIII–nachalo XX v.)* (Novosibirsk: Nauka, 1985). The most sensational case of peasant isolation in Siberia was that of the Old Believer Lykhov family, discovered by geologists: see *Current Digest of the Soviet Press*, 1982, vol. 34, no. 40, pp. 1, 3, 5; no. 41, pp. 13–16; no. 42, pp. 14–16; 1983, vol. 35, no. 37, pp. 12–13; 1984, vol. 36, no. 34, pp. 21–22. On Siberian regionalism, see N. M. Iadrintsev, *Sibir kak koloniia* (St. Petersburg, 1882); M. G.

Seniunina, *Potanin i Iadrintsev: ideologi sibirskogo oblastnichestva* (Tomsk: Tomsk University Press, 1974); Henry K. Norton, *The Far Eastern Republic of Siberia* (New York: Hyperion Press, 1982); John Stephan, "Far Eastern Conspiracies? Russian Separatism on the Pacific," *Australian Slavonic and East European Studies*, 1990, vol. 4, no. 1/2, pp. 135–52; "Iamal—vybor puti," *Krasnyi Sever*, 10 December 1988, pp. 1–14; and "Kolyma vzyvaet o poshchade," *Soiuz*, August 1991, p. 4.

23. Valery A. Tishkov, director of the Institute of Ethnology and Anthropology (formerly Ethnography), argues that there is a widespread need for trained field anthropologists. See, e.g., "Vystupleniia," *Vestnik akademii nauk SSSR*, 1990, no. 7, pp. 109–12. A lack of field-oriented anthropologists to study Russian villages is especially bemoaned by scholars of Russian culture. See, e.g., A. Sh.'s report "Etnograficheskoe izuchenie russkogo naroda," *Voprosy istorii*, 1990, no. 4, pp. 189–90, on a paper by M. M. Gromyko. A few ethnographers, linguists, musicologists, and folklorists have, however, remained active, for example E. Alekseev, V. Baktina, O. Budina, S. Dmitreva, G. Durasov, V. Gatsak, S. Guseva, I. Kremleva, V. Lipinskaia, and M. Schmeleva. A Russian–American project on Old Believers and Molokhans, sponsored by the Smithsonian Institution, involves the ethnomusicologist Margarita Mazo, with Irina Pozdeeva and Serafima Nikitina. Historian Richard Morris worked in the 1980s with Old Believers in the Novosibirsk region on a collaborative project with Russian colleagues. Ethnographer Jovan Howe, of the University of Tampere, Finland, has begun a field exchange with the St. Petersburg Institute of Ethnology and Anthropology, through Tat'iana Bernshtam.

Russian Traditional Culture

Religion and Ritual

The Introduction of Christianity in Russia and the Pagan Traditions

I. Ia. Froianov, A. Iu. Dvornichenko, and Iu. V. Krivosheev

The importance of pagan traditions in the process of Christianization of Russia remains largely unstudied in historical science.[a] Nor is the question as such even brought up, since it is customary to believe that Christianity, having replaced paganism, could not become established with the help of pagan means and methods, which it had repudiated. Orthodox theologians draw a sharp line between Eastern Slavic paganism and Christianity. However, a careful analysis of the sources clearly points to pagan elements in the process of institution of Christianity in the old Russian society.

What is noteworthy is the fact that the "conversion of Russia" took place no more than eight years after the so-called pagan reform of Prince Vladimir (980). Such a short time between the implementation of this reform and the acceptance of Christianity cannot be explained either by a shift in worldview of Vladimir and the nobles of Kiev or by external reasons, for such explanations are inconsistent with the findings of scholars, who have refuted any deep influence of Christianity in the formation of the ideology, culture, and social psychology of archaic societies.[1] As for Kievan Russia, we may say with confidence that the introduction of Christianity in 988, lacking any sufficiently solid social and political soil, did not bring about a radical change in the consciousness of the society during the entire course of ancient Russian history.[2]

Stories of the adoption of the Christian faith by Russia appeared in the pages of chronicles at least half a century later; moreover, they were written down by a church scribe who interpreted them largely through the prism of a Christian way of thinking. Yet even undergoing such "censorship," they preserve information that makes it possible for us to portray the "conversion of Russia" in a way somewhat different than it appeared to the Chris-

Russian text © 1988 by "Nauka" Publishers and "Sovetskaia etnografiia." "Vvedenie khristianstva na Rusi i iazycheskie traditsii," *Sovetskaia etnografiia*, 1988, no. 6, pp. 25–34. A publication of the Institute of Ethnography, USSR Academy of Sciences.

tian chronicler, and as it is still viewed by most scholars occupied with this subject today.

The introduction of Christianity in Kiev was preceded by a number of pagan reforms, all of which were directed at preserving the grand league of tribes [*plemen'*], subject to the authority of the princes of Kiev, that had come into being in the expanses of Eastern Europe.[3] What is important here is not the social tendency of these reforms but their pagan nature. In particular, an attempt was made to convert Kiev into the religious center of Eastern Slavdom. For this purpose, a pagan temple with a sculpture of Perun, originally located within the precincts of the old citadel of Kiev, was moved to a new spot,[4] accessible to all Polian arriving at the capital. The sources make it possible to ascertain the approximate time when this occurred.

Upon conclusion of the treaty of 907 with the Greeks, Oleg and "his men" swore "by their arms, and by Perun, their god, and by Volos, the cattle god."[5] As the investigations of specialists have revealed, the cult of Perun was primarily distributed in the southern regions of the Eastern Slavic territories, while that of Volos (Veles) was in the northern.[6] The presence of two deities (Perun and Volos) in the oath is perfectly natural, since both southern and northern tribes of the Eastern Slavs took part in Oleg's campaign against Constantinople.[7] The makeup of those participating in the 944 campaign against Constantinople led by Oleg's successor, Igor', was almost unchanged.[8] But the oath marking the new agreement mentions only Perun and not Volos. Moreover, the chronicle states clearly that the heathen of Kiev (headed by Igor') during the "ratification" of the treaty swore before the temple of Perun alone: "The next day, Igor' summoned his messengers and went to the hill where Perun stood, and put down his arms and shields and gold, and Igor' took an oath, as did his people, who are the heathen of Rus'. . . ."[9] Is this happenstance? It does not appear to be so. The desire of the Kievan rulers to assert Perun's priority over other gods of the Eastern Slavs can be glimpsed here.

Consequently, in the reign of Igor' but before the conclusion of his treaty with Byzantium, the god Perun of the Polian was proclaimed the supreme deity of the Slavic collectivity. This was needed for ideological fortification and establishment of the dominating position of Kiev over the Eastern Slavic tribes. But in the middle of the tenth century, the relations of Kiev with the subordinate tribes worsened drastically. The death of Igor' in the Drevlian forest inaugurated active resistence of the tribes "oppressed" by Kiev. The Kievan leaders were forced to make peace with the "warring tribes."[10] At the same time, the rulers of Kiev also retreated on the religious question. And thus, in the treaty of 971 between Sviatoslav and the Byzantine emperor Cimiskhius, we again find Rus' swearing by Perun and Veles.[11] Therefore, Kiev's attempt to confer on Perun the status of god of all the Eastern Slavs suffered a defeat.

But a new religious reform was undertaken soon thereafter. In 980, Vladimir "placed the idols on a hill outside the palace courtyard: wooden Perun, with silver head and golden beard, and Kh″rs, Dazh′bog, and Stribog, and Simar′gl, and Mokosh′. And they made an offering to them, calling them gods."[12] This was yet another attempt to aggrandize Perun, but more cautious and flexible.

The "placement of the idols" was an ideological action, by means of which the Kievan community hoped to retain power over the conquered tribes and halt the beginning collapse of the grand tribal confederacy headed by Kiev. Therefore, Perun was placed in the midst of the other tribes' gods, symbolizing their unity. The capital of the Polian was again declared the religious center of Eastern Slavdom.

Yet the pagan reform of Vladimir, although more supple, nevertheless failed like the preceding ones. The cardinal mistake was to attempt to assert the primacy of Perun over the other gods. As a result, his cult once again had to be forced on the tribes of the confederacy. In certain instances, Perun entirely supplanted the local idols. This happened in Novgorod, where Dobrynia, dispatched from Kiev, "placed the idol Perun at the river Volkhovo, and the Novgorodian people made offerings to him as god."[13]

The failure of this reform made necessary further transformations. And thus, the apotheosis of Vladimir's reforming activity was the adoption of Christianity. The very chronological proximity and logical connection with the preceding pagan reforms permits one to ask the question: was not the "introduction" of Christianity perceived by the inhabitants of the Dnepr region at that time in a pagan mode?

A "pagan" perception of Christianity already had some precedents. Interesting in this connection is an episode with the Varangian Christians. A chronicler, recounting Kievan human sacrifices, explained that lots cast by the Kievans fell to the son of a certain Varangian. "For this Varangian [merchant] had come from Greece and held the Christian faith," says the chronicler. How much of the Christian dogma was assimilated by the Varangian we learn from his following philippic against the Russian gods. "They are not gods, but wood, today they are here, but tomorrow they will rot; they do not eat, nor drink, nor speak, for they are made by hand in wood."[14] Thus, in the Varangian's mind, gods were supposed to eat, drink, speak, and commune directly with believers. Such an anthropomorphism of the gods is characteristic of pagan religion. According to pagan conceptions, the deity, like any other living being, requires a domicile, food, clothing, and so forth.[15]

The procedure for "choosing faiths" is permeated with pagan motifs. On what basis does Vladimir reject this or that faith? What are his criteria for the choice? At first, Vladimir heard the apostles of Islam. "But he did not like the cutting of the members [circumcision], and as for not eating pork and not drinking at all he said: 'Drinking is a joy to the Russians, we cannot do without it.' " A facetious attitude to this pronouncement of the prince often prevents one from seeing the reality of that time behind the words of Vladimir. For what is being discussed, in veiled terms, are the pagan feasts, which were an important social institution in the life of Kievan Russia, a form of communion for the princely ruler with his retinue and the people.[16] Scholars also point out the ceremonial, ritual magic origin of the feast and the ceremonial common meal.[17] Eating together with the people made it possible to bridge that gulf between the princely power and the common folk that was just beginning to emerge in society. For kinship by food and drink, along with kinship by blood, is known among various peoples.[18] Of course Vladimir did not want to give up the feasts. And at the same time, what is striking is the prince's persistence in searching for new gods.[b] And new gods were sought not only by Vladimir, but also by the "common folk," the inhabitants of the towns and villages.[19] When Vladimir explained the results of his conversations with the representatives of various faiths, "the boyars and elders said: 'O Prince, no one will condemn you, but instead give praise, as your followers. But if you want to try the issue aright, you have your men here; send them to try each kind of worship, to see how they worship god.' And this speech was pleasing to the prince and to all the people."[20] This chronicle not only testifies to the general nature of the "pagan quests," but also informs us that Dnepr region residents wanted to learn about religions professed by neighboring peoples. This was the "worship," i.e., the ritual aspect of religion. Ritual and ceremonies play a special role in paganism. "Therefore, the [pagan] cult included, in addition to operations ensuring the physical well-being and comfort of the deity, also solemn processions, theatricalized actions, and various spectacles."[21] All these presentations warmed pagan emotions to the point of ecstasy. Of course, the more vivid and beautiful the religion, the more true the "worship," and the greater the imprint made on the religious consciousness of the pagans. This motif is also evident in the famous "faith choosing." Joyfulness and beauty were chief attractions in the religious ceremony of the pagan Slavs. The religion of the Bolgars (the Moslem Bolgars of the Volga) was not pleasing because "there is no joy among them, but sorrow and great stench [*smrad*]." They rejected the Western European variant of Christianity because "we saw in the churches many worship services, but nowhere did we see beauty." The Greek religion was a different story. When the Russian envoys arrived in Constantinople, "the patriarch ordered that the priest [*krilos*] be summoned, and he performed the customary ceremony, and sprayed incense, and there was singing and rejoicing. And he [the patriarch] went with them to the church, and placed them in a spacious seat, showing them the beauty of the church, the singing and the high liturgy, and the presence of the deacons. . . ."[22] Here, as we see, are all the elements of rich ceremonial ritual, so favored by the pagans. Hence their impression of the Byzantine liturgy was: "And we came to Greece, and they brought us to where they worship their god, and we did not know if we were on earth or in heaven: for there is no such beauty on earth, and we are not able to describe it; all that we know is that god dwells with man there, and their worship is better than that of all the other countries. For we cannot forget this beauty, as though if a man were to eat something sweet, he does not have bitterness afterwards, and so we also do not have it, being here."[23]

Thus, already in the chronicle explanation of "faith choosing" there are vivid pagan motifs, indicating that the prince, bodyguards, and "commoners" in Kiev perceived everything connected with the new faith through the prism of pagan survivals and traditions.[24] The same may be discerned in subsequent events.

Noteworthy in this connection is the following chronicle account. After the successful campaign against Korsun' and the baptism of Vladimir and his bodyguard there, the prince of Kiev, departing from this place, "took the queen, and Nastas, and the priests of Korsun', with the relics of Saint Kliment and his pupil, Fif, took the church vessels and icons for his own liturgy. . . . He also took two copper *kapishche*, and four copper horses, which now stand behind the Blessed Virgin, and who the ignorant think are living creatures of marble."[25] As we see, in addition to other things there are "two copper *kapishche*" here. What were these *kapishche*?

In Russian etymological dictionaries, the term refers first and foremost to a heathen temple.[26] In the present case, however, this meaning is ruled out: certainly Vladimir did not take a temple, and a heathen one at that, from Korsun'. The other basic meaning of this term is a picture, a statue.[27] A copper picture could hardly be intended. More likely is the version that identifies *kapishche* with statue. Yet one of the few to investigate this matter, L. A. Dintses, has rejected such an explanation. He supposed that the "local architectural term—*kapishche*—was transferred in the present case 'by analogy' to the 'bronze *kivorii*'[28] or altar that was carried away, beneath which the mystery of the Eucharist was performed (yet the altars were by no means pagan, not even pagan antiquities)."[29] As proof, he presents a number of arguments.

First, Dintses points to the miniature in the Radziwill chronicle depicting the baptism of Prince Vladimir. In the picture, Vladimir is sitting inside a large font, on top of which a *kivorii* is erected. His bodyguard are also baptized in the very same font. Second, he writes, "for anthropomorphic statues the chronicler uses two invariable terms, *kumir* and *idol*." And third, in the opinion of Dintses, "it is not clear why the chronicler, who has often expressed opprobrium on the subject of idols, would not do so again in relating how Vladimir, full of conviction to extirpate heathenism in his own land, carried away statues of pagan goddesses [?], the 'Hellenic' nature of which was well known to zealots of the ancient Orthodox faith."[30] Yet these judgments can be questioned.

As for the miniature, it is known that the Radziwill illustrated chronicles were created at the beginning of the thirteenth century, i.e., more than two centuries after the baptism.[31] Therefore, it can hardly be claimed that they reflect certain details of this event. More likely, the picture in them was closer to the reality of the thirteenth century. As for the meaning of the term, I. I. Sreznevskii writing on Vladimir has already interpreted *kapishche* as statue (picture) and only as such,[32] even though (as we have seen) this word also had other meanings. Furthermore, he presents a number of examples from written sources, where *kapishche* refers to a statue[33] or picture. Hence, the designation of statues was not confined to *kumir* and *idol* but also included *kapishche* as a related term.

The third thesis of Dintses comes down to the dichotomy "what is heathen to the heathens, and what is Christian to the Christians." And this applies both to the chroniclers and to Prince Vladimir. We find this a somewhat simplified approach to the events of the tenth century and several of the following centuries, when the pagan worldview was still considerable in society, including its upper classes.[34] We should consider here the question of which statues were carried away to Kiev and for what purpose.

In his own day, N. M. Karamzin expressed the belief that these may have been "elegant productions of ancient art," which "stood in Nestor's time in the town square of old Kiev, near the famous Church of Andrew and the Tithe."[35] This thought was later elaborated by the expert in old Russian art, D. V. Ainalov. He presumed that Vladimir wanted to beautify the town square of Kiev after the model and likeness of the Byzantine and other cities, "imitating in this respect decorations in squares of the capital cities of that world. . . . Korsun' during this time was also a wealthy Byzantine city, decorated with various statues of the emperors and illustrious citizens, set up at various periods. It was from among these statues that Vladimir took the 'two copper *kapishche*,' by which must be understood, evidently, 'two copper human statues.' " "Thus," he concludes, "ancient Rus', which derived its familiarity with ancient statues from its relations with Constantinople and Korsun', could now become closely acquainted with them through the intermediacy of the statues carried away by Vladimir."[36]

Despite the elegance of this thought, we believe that the acquisition by Vladimir and his carrying away of both horses[37] and statues[38] conceals a deeper meaning than a passion for beautification or even a desire to accustom the Kievans to classical art. In our opinion, this is all interconnected with pagan traditions. D. V. Ainalov also associated the "undoubtedly pagan" *kapishche* with paganism. He considers that they could only have been taken by Vladimir "for the needs of a pagan cult." Therefore, they appear in the capital on the Dnepr "already at the time when Vladimir was a pagan." There is no reason to "push them back to the period before Vladimir, nor to assume that Vladimir brought them here when he was already a Christian."[39]

Indeed, based on the above considerations, there is no reason to grant that the *kapishche* were brought here by Vladimir the Christian. But neither is there data to push back this event to the times of Vladimir the pagan.

We think that Vladimir, having already been baptized at Korsun', may very well have performed this action. Moreover, this would appear to be a natural process. The fact of the carrying away of the horses and *kapishche*-statues, in our view, is inseparably connected with the preceding events, which go back to pagan times. For as we have seen, one of the critical moments in the pagan reforms preceding the introduction of Christianity was the "bringing" of gods. The first to become settled in Kiev was, perhaps, Veles—as the outcome of the unification of Novgorod and the Dnepr territories of Russia. In any case, it is known that Prince Oleg and "his men" swore "by their arms, and by Perun, their god, and by Volos, the god of cattle."[c] The "resettlement" of Veles began the "gathering of the different tribal deities under the aegis of Perun. Such pantheon replenishment occurred among many peoples, generally as the result of conquest. On occasion, major deities of the conquered tribes could be purchased. A third channel was marriage of foreigners by leaders."[40] In ancient Greece, when a city-state was conquered, a defeated god's statue would be transported to the temple of the victorious god. In ancient Rome, "new gods were accepted into the community of the Roman gods much as immigrants who received Roman citizenship were accepted into the Roman civil society, provided that they conform to the laws and practices binding on the citizens."[41]

Let us assume that, in ancient Russia, reform expressed as an adoption of a new faith—Christianity—can be arranged in this series. In pagan eyes, the fact of bringing to Kiev (in 988) new trophies from conquered Korsun'—horses (and we know that there was a zoomorphic being, the winged dog Simargl, in the pagan pantheon of Vladimir) and certain statues or idols—continued, as it were, the transfer of deities, embodying the new victories of the Kievan community. From the standpoint of the Christians, this action was hardly meaningful or significant. But for the former pagans, it symbolized a kind of continuity of traditions, hallowed over the centuries, and, thus, a more painless adoption of the new faith, which (at least from external features) was a continuation of the former pagan faith. The Korsun' figures [*kumir*], like their predecessors, the pagan gods, were installed in one of the central places of the city, which clearly shows that they were made accessible to all. And only after the Church of the Blessed Virgin was built did they find themselves placed behind it.

Incidentally, the fact of building churches on the site of pagan cult objects, which can be discerned in many regions, also reveals (in our opinion) a

certain permanence to religious ideas. It has become common in the literature to hold that the demolition of heathen temples and altars and the
building of churches on these sites signified a battle of the church against
paganism.[42] We see here not so much a gulf as a linkage, a continuity between Christianity and paganism.[43] Such a perception also made itself felt
afterwards, when the church building (like formerly the pagan edifice) was
seen by the old Russian townsman as the symbol of the entire community
and the property of all.

Thus, the introduction of Christianity in Russia outwardly continued a
chain of tenth-century religious reforms.[44] But whereas in paganism new
gods are added to the old and the pantheon generally increases, with the
adoption of Christianity in 988 the pantheon diminished; the former gods
were cast down. E. V. Anichkov reduces this act exclusively to a Christian
"revenge" according to "Biblical traditions."[45] Yet it is he who has pointed
out how even the Christian scribes viewed the moribund pagan gods. He
presumes that the "stories of Perun as a living creature were inevitable."
"For otherwise, the scribe of those days, and especially the Russian scribe,
could not have understood the tremendous event of adopting the new, the
true faith. Beliefs are more easily acquired than lost from consciousness."
The first step in this direction was the destruction of the pagan gods' statues.
"The overthrown idol," writes Anichkov, "by that very action ceases to be a
god, and belief in it perishes at the same time as it is desecrated."[46] It must
be stipulated at once that the destruction of Perun in no way signified a total
break with the pagan tradition. In archaic societies, the gods did not have
the status of inviolability. Only in societies with a developed class differen-
tiation, an antagonistic government, and a monotheistic religion do they become *persona grata*. But the people of "archaic society on occasion might
not even stop at throwing the idols from their pedestals," writes V. B. Iordanskii,[47] and he gives corresponding examples from the history of African
societies. What is of interest to us in the present case is how the Eastern
Slavs' gods were destroyed.[d] While the other gods were smashed and burned,
the procedure in the case of Perun was singular. In Kiev, "he [Vladimir]
commanded that Perun be tied to a horse's tail and dragged from the mount,
by way of Borichev to Ruchai, and twelve men set upon him with a staff.
Treating him not as wood, but as a demon to be desecrated, having seduced
humans, deserving human revenge. . . . But as he was dragged along the
Ruchai to the Dnepr, the unbelieving people wept for him, as they had not
yet taken the holy baptism. And when he was dragged to the Dnepr, they
threw him in. And Volodimer said: 'If he touches land anywhere, throw him
away from the shore; until he passes the rapids, only then grab him.' And
they did what was commanded. And as he passed the rapids, the wind blew
against the *ren'*, and since then Perun was called Ren', as he is still to this
day."[48] Perun was subjected to a similar execution in Novgorod: "And the

archbishop Akim of Korsun' came to Novgorod, and destroyed the altars, and cut up Perun, and ordered that he be dragged to the Volkhovo, and be tied with ropes, and they dragged him through the mud, beating him with staves; and no one refused the command."[49]

Recently, a view was expressed according to which Perun's overthrow was simply "a description, not understood by the chronicler, of the annual procession of the god, the pagan festival of the 'dying and reborn god.' " "For the most part," writes L. S. Klein, "the procession and burial of the god took place by drowning or floating him in the river, with the participants of the festival being divided into two groups, those who beat him and those who wept for him." In explaining the case of Perun, he argued by deduction from the rituals that took place during the later pagan ceremonies (Maslenitsa, Kupala, etc.). "What is noteworthy in this connection is the repetition of the chronicle's call, *Vydybai bozhe!* [Farewell, God], in the song during the burial of Kostroma."[50] These observations are interesting. However, the ritual of the overthrow of Perun may also be connected with other pagan traditions. The dragging, the beating with a staff, and especially the "water procedures" are all pagan actions. Everything here was done to humiliate Perun and condemn him. The god, cast down, is tied to the tail of a horse (this is in itself a humiliation) and dragged "by way of Borichev to Ruchai." The ritual of dragging, judging from diverse data, was highly humiliating in Eastern Slavs' conception. It is no accident that, during the familiar events of 1146–47 in Kiev, Prince Igor', already killed, was dragged "through the women's marketplace to the Blessed Virgin."[51] There were twelve men placed alongside Perun, beating him with a "staff." These men are more likely a kind of pagan jury, which also appears in the Old Russian Law. Let us remember the "trial before twelve men."[52] Archaic consciousness was characterized by "sacred numbers," whether it be the number of witnesses or a civil court [*obshchinyi sud'*]. But how was the unfortunate Perun tormented? Usually, *zhezlie* is translated as "rods." But a different reading is also possible. Perun may have been beaten with his own staff, i.e., his club, about which more will be said below. The throwing into the water must be interpreted as a kind of tribute to the pagan deified water element. And water also appeared as a "judge." Let us recall that as late as the nineteenth century, those suspected of sorcery (usually women) would be thrown into the river.[e] If they floated, they were incriminated and subjected to punishment; if they sank, they were presumed innocent and vindicated.[53] Basically, Perun was subjected to a similar trial. There was an attempt to discredit him before the pagan population of Kiev and Novgorod. And he did not withstand the test— the fact that he did not sink is a testimony of his guilt and, consequently, of the necessity for a new god. According to the chronicles, these purposes were achieved. The Novgorod chronicle contains a valuable corroboration of this. Relevant is the episode of the man Podblianin from the outskirts of Novgorod. "And Podblianin went in the morning to the river, wishing to carry his pots to town; and Perun had floated to shore, and he pushed him off with a pole: saying 'You, Old Perun, have eaten and drunk enough, and now float on'; and he floated away."[54] Besides the attitude toward Perun in this account, the conception of him is also of interest. It is pure paganism; the pagans believed that their gods ate and drank (recall the Varangians, mentioned above). It is interesting that the chronicler portrays a somewhat different stratum of the archaic consciousness. Recounting the events in Novgorod, he ascribes the words spoken at the instant of execution not to Perun, but to a demon: "and at that time, a demon had come into Perun, and he cried: 'Oh, oh me! I have fallen into these unkind hands." Also curious is another detail, that of Perun's club: "He floated through a large bridge, and threw his club onto the bridge, and now beating foolish ones with it the demon had great fun."[55] This reflects very interesting information, connecting Perun's club with a whole complex of pagan conceptions. In any case, we see that this club possessed supernatural power.

After Perun was dealt with, the baptism procedure ensued. We shall not speculate on the thoughts of the Kievans as they stood in the water of the Dnepr, but it would not be stretching the issue to suppose that this, too, was not a painful experience, but quite within the main current of pagan ceremonies. It is known that water played a major role in Slavic paganism. Bathing was also used as a means of summoning rain, and a water cult was widespread.[56]

The facts given above allow us to infer that the Christian religion was accepted in Russia in a kind of pagan wrapping, and the actions of Vladimir and of the entire Kievan community were imbued with paganism. The introduction of Christianity was only a link in the chain of development of religious reforms in Russia of the tenth century and was viewed as a standard replacement of the deity in the spirit of the prevailing pagan beliefs.

Editor's notes

a. For a version of the Primary Chronicle depiction of "Vladimir Christianizes Russia," see Serge A. Zenkovsky, ed., *Medieval Russia's Epics, Chronicles and Tales* (New York: Dutton, 1974), pp. 65–71. Paganism and its relation to Christianity has been widely and variously discussed, e.g., Nikolai Andreyev, "Pagan and Christian Elements in Old Russia," *Slavic Review*, 1962, no. 21, pp. 16–23; George P. Fedotov, *The Russian Religious Mind: Kievan Christianity* (New York: Harper & Row, 1960), pp. 344–412; Linda J. Ivanits, *Russian Folk Belief* (Armonk, N.Y.: M. E. Sharpe, 1989); Pierre Pascal, *The Religion of the Russian People*, trans. Rowan Williams (Oxford: Mobray, 1976), pp. 8–10; Russell Zguta, "The Pagan Priests of Old Russia: Some New Insights," *Slavic Review*, 1974, vol. 33, no. 2, pp. 259–66. See also E. V. Anichkov, *Iazychestvo i drevniaia Rus'* (St. Petersburg, 1914); S. A. Tokarev, *Religioznye verovaniia vostochno-slavianskikh narodov* (Moscow: Nauka, 1957), p. 21; B. A. Rybakov, *Iazychestvo drevnei Rusi* (Moscow: Nauka, 1987).

b. This story is so stereotyped as to strongly resemble others, such as that of the Khazars, concerning a contest of faiths. The authors of the article insist that such contests reflect "reality" (e.g., note 24), although they can just as easily be seen as a blend of relatively accurate history with borrowed mythology or texts. Vladimir's rejection of any religion prohibiting drinking seems highly plausible, although it is missing from Zenkovsky's version of the Primary Chronicle (note a). On the culture of Russian Saints' Days drinking in later periods, see Stephen P. Dunn and Ethel Dunn, *The Peasants of Central Russia* (New York: Holt, Rinehart & Winston, 1967), p. 29; and the Anton Chekhov story "Muzhiki" (e.g., in *Muzhiki i drugie rasskazy* [Moscow: Academiia, 1932, original 1897]; or *Peasants and Other Stories*, trans. Edmund Wilson [New York: Doubleday, 1956], pp. 249–88).

c. On Veles (also spelled Volos), the god of cattle (or beasts) and wealth, see Fedotov, *The Russian Religious Mind*, pp. 10–11, 357–58; G. Alexinsky, "Slavonic Mythology," *Larousse Encyclopedia of Mythology* (New York: Prometheus, 1960), pp. 304–5, 310. Alexinsky claims folk beliefs in Volos far outlasted beliefs in Perun.

d. It is not necessary to look to Africa for examples of idols being harmed or discarded when they are believed to have displeased. This was done by Finno-Ugric peoples, who then rescued their sacred wooden idols for further worship. See, for example, John Bernard Muller, "The Manners and Customs of the Ostiaks," in Frederick C. Weber, ed., *The Present State of Russia*, vol. 2 (London: Taylor, Innys and Osborn, 1722), p. 76.

e. The word used here for sorcery is *koldovstvo*, in contrast to *vedma* (witch) and *znakhar* (folk curer). See Russell Zguta, "Witchcraft and Medicine in Pre-Petrine Russia," *Russian Review*, 1978, vol. 37, no. 4, pp. 338–448; Valerie A. Kivelson, "Through the Prism of Witchcraft: Gender and Social Change in Seventeenth-century Muscovy" in Barbara Evans Clements, Barbara Alpern Engel, and Christine D. Worobec, eds. *Russia's Women: Accommodation, Resistance, Transformation* (Berkeley: University of California Press, 1991), pp. 74–94; N. I. Novombergskii, *Koldovstvo v moskovskoi Rusi XVII veka* (St. Petersburg: Suvorin, 1906); N. A. Nikitin, "K voprosu o russikh koldunakh," *Sbornik Muzeia antropologii i etnografii*, 1928, vol. 7, pp. 228–92.

Notes

1. M. I. Steblin-Kamenskii, *Mir sagi. Stanovlenie literatury* (Leningrad, 1984), p. 93; W. B. Wilinbachow, "Spoleczno-psychologiczny aspekt chrystianizacji Rusi. Kijowskiej," *Kultura i spoleczenstwo* (Warsaw, 1974), V.XVIII. N2. S.14.

2. I. Ia. Froianov, "Ob istoricheskom znachenii 'kreshcheniia Rusi,' " *Genezis i razvitie feodalizma v Rossii* (Leningrad, 1987), p. 57; idem, "Nachalo khristianstva na Rusi," *Khristianstvo: Antichnost'. Vizantiia. Drevniaia Rus'* (Leningrad, 1988), pp. 253–54.

3. Froianov, "Ob istoricheskom znachenii 'kreshcheniia Rusi,' " p. 48.

4. P. P. Tolochko, *Drevnii Kiev* (Kiev, 1983), pp. 29–30, 39–41. Tolochko assumes that this took place "already toward the end of the reign of Igor'" (pp. 39–40).

5. *Povest' vremennykh let* (hereafter *PVL*), pt. 1 (Moscow-Leningrad, 1950), p. 25.

6. V. V. Ivanov and V. N. Toporov, *Issledovaniia v oblasti slavianskikh drevnostei* (Moscow, 1974), pp. 55, 62; B. A. Uspenskii, *Filologicheskie razyskaniia v oblasti slavianskikh drevnostei* (Moscow, 1982), pp. 32–33.

7. *PVL*, pt. 1, p. 23.

8. Ibid., p. 33.

9. Ibid., p. 39; see also Tolochko, *Drevnii Kiev*, p. 39.

10. For more details see Froianov, "Ob istoricheskom znachenii 'kreshcheniia Rusi,' " p. 49; idem, "Nachalo khristianstva na Rusi," p. 288.

11. *PVL*, pt. 1, p. 52.

12. Ibid., p. 56.

13. *Novgorodskaia pervaia letopis' starshego i mladshego izvodov* (Moscow-Leningrad, 1950), p. 128.

14. *PVL*, p. 58.

15. I. A. Kryvelev, *Istoriia religii*, vol. 1 (Moscow, 1975), pp. 91–92.

16. I. Ia. Froianov, *Kievskaia Rus'. Ocherki sotsial'no-politicheskoi istorii* (Leningrad, 1980), pp. 141–42.

17. E. V. Anichkov, *Iazychestvo i Drevniaia Rus'* (St. Petersburg, 1914), p. 178; V. E. Vetlovskaia, "Letopisnoe osmyslenie pirov i darenii v svete fol'klornykh i etnograficheskikh dannykh," *Genezis i razvitie feodalizma v Rossii* (Leningrad, 1987).

18. Ibid.

19. Froianov, *Kievskaia Rus'*, p. 129.

20. *PVL*, p. 74.

21. Kryvelev, *Istoriia religii*, vol. 1, p. 99.

22. *PVL*, p. 75.

23. Ibid.

24. The "faith choosing" itself is interesting in this respect. The historical parallels at our disposal testify that this process was rather common in traditional societies. It is known that the Bulgars, Khazars, Scandinavians, and other peoples found themselves in similar situations (*Vvedenie khristianstva na Rusi* [Moscow, 1987], pp. 15–17). This is not a popular folklore plot, but a historical reality. Under conditions of unequal economic and political development, surrounded by different ethnic communities, at a time when their own gods had been compromised, the ruling circles or the society as a whole might turn to the ideological baggage of neighboring peoples in the hope of finding something suitable for themselves.

25. *PVL*, p. 80.

26. A. G. Preobrazhenskii, *Etimologicheskii slovar' russkogo iazyka*, vol. 1 (Moscow, 1959), p. 294; M. Fasmer, vol. 2 (Moscow, 1986), p. 185; *Etimologicheskii slovar' russkogo iazyka*, vol. 2, issue 8 (Moscow, 1982), p. 55. *Kapishche* has been interpreted more broadly—as the scene of pagan ceremonies—by I. I. Sreznevskii, "Materialy dlia slovaria drevnerusskogo iazyka," vol. 1 (Moscow, 1958), col. 1192–93. See also N. M. Gal'kovskii, *Bor'ba khristianstva s ostatkami iazychestva v drevnei Rusi*, vol. 1 (Khar'kov, 1916), p. 9; Anichkov, *Iazychestvo i Drevniaia Rus'*, p. 323.

27. Sreznevskii, "Materialy dlia slovaria drevnerusskogo iazyka," vol. 1, col. 1193; Preobrazhenskii, *Etimologicheskii slovar' russkogo iazyka*, vol. 1, p. 294; Fasmer, *Etimologicheskii slovar' russkogo iazyka*, vol. 2, p. 185. Also see A. Afanas'ev, *Poeticheskie vozzreniia slavian na prirodu*, vol. 2 (Moscow, 1868); D. I. Ilovaiskii, *Istoriia Rossii*, vol. 1 (Moscow, 1876), p. 299; A. S. Famintsyn, *Bozhestva drevnikh slavian* (St. Petersburg, 1884), p. 38; E. E. Golubinskii, *Istoriia russkoi tserkvi* (Moscow, 1901), vol. 1, first complete volume, p. 231, note 2; L. Lezhe, *Slavianskaia mifologiia* (Voronezh, 1908), p. 34.

28. *Kivorii*: 1—the arc in which the consecrated bread is kept, the coffer for donations; 2—the canopy beneath which donations are blessed on the communion table (see *Slovar' tserkovnoslavianskogo i russkogo iazyka*, vol. 2 [St. Petersburg, 1867], col. 355).

29. L. A. Dintses, "Dokhristianskie khramy Rusi v svete pamiatnikov narodnogo iskusstva," *Sovetskaia etnografiia*, 1947, no. 2, p. 69.

30. Ibid. The second and third arguments of the author are a repetition and development of the views previously expressed by D. V. Ainalov ("Letopis' o nachal'noi pore russkogo iskusstva," *Otchet o sostoianii i deiatel'nosti Sankt-Peterburgskogo universiteta za 1903 god* (St. Petersburg, 1904), pp. 19–20). In his work, Ainalov does not come to a definite conclusion: the *kapishche* were "two altars or two statues" (p. 21). Afterwards, however, he preferred the statues.

31. "Drevnerusskie letopisi i khroniki," *Trudy Otdela drevne-russkoi literatury*, vol. 39 (Leningrad, 1985), pp. 141, 143.

32. Sreznevskii, "Materialy dlia slovaria drevnerusskogo iazyka," vol. 1, col. 1193.

33. This is how the word is interpreted in the Nikon Chronicle, where the "two *kapishche*" are replaced by "two tree stumps." *Poln. sobr. russkikh letopisei*, vol. 9, p. 57.

34. B. A. Rybakov, *Iazychestvo drevnei Rusi* (Moscow, 1987); I. Ia. Froianov, *Ob istoricheskom znachenii "kreshcheniia Rusi,"* pp. 55–57.

35. N. M. Karamzin, *Istoriia gosudarstva rossiiskogo*, vol. 1 (St. Petersburg, 1892), p. 146.

36. Ainalov, "Letopis' o nachal'noi pore russkogo iskusstva," p. 21; idem, "Iskusstvo Kievskoi Rusi," *Russkaia istoriia*, ed. M. V. Dovnar-Zapol'skii, vol. 1 [no place, no date], pp. 496–97. Also see Ilovaiskii, *Istoriia Rossii*, p. 73; K. V. Sherotskii, *Kiev*, 1917, p. 98.

37. L. A. Dintses entirely ignores the fact that, along with the *kapishche*, there were also four "horses" (evidently, the "quadriga of classical horses"—Ainalov, "Letopis'," p. 21). We believe that the horses and the *kapishche*-statues are to be considered in a single context of meaning, and not separated from each other. Certain copies of the manuscript have "4 icons" [*ikone*], instead of "4 horses" [*kone*]. This version has been analyzed in detail and rejected by D. V. Ainalov (ibid., pp. 19–20).

38. It is hard to say what these statues portrayed. Classical or pagan gods (and not only goddesses, as Dintses writes)? Or perhaps they were sculptures of specific great people. I. S. Sven-

tsitskaia mentions the existence, in the Roman empire at the start of our era, of cults of the divine emperors, the deified Demos, Council, and Roman Senate. Statues and reliefs for worship were erected for all of these (I. S. Sventsitskaia, *Ot obshchiny k tserkvi* (Moscow, 1985), pp. 38–40). Anyway, this is not so important for us. More important is the fact that statues were brought to Kiev from Korsun', conquered by Vladimir.

39. Ainalov, "Letopis'," pp. 21–22.

40. V. B. Iordanskii, *Khaos i garmoniia* (Moscow, 1982), p. 131; N. N. Kharuzin, *Etnografiia*, pt. 4, "Verovaniia," (St. Petersburg, 1905), pp. 171, 172, etc. ("Given the intimate relationship between the spirit of the deity and his external surroundings, the custom of carrying away the idols of conquered tribes to the victors' residences naturally arises," wrote Kharuzin.)

41. *Kul'tura drevnego Rima*, vol. 1 (Moscow, 1985), p. 149.

42. B. A. Rybakov, "Iazycheskoe mirovozzrenie russkogo srednevekov'ia," *Voprosy istorii*, 1974, no. 1, p. 20.

43. Scholars also see a preservation of pagan ideas in the internal division of the space of the Christian church (G. K. Vagner, *Kanon i stil' v drevnerusskom iskusstve* (Moscow, 1987), pp. 98–99).

44. The "Korsun' expedition" itself, in addition to the mentioned pagan motifs, also reveals others. Vladimir demonstrates the model of pagan behavior. His pagan "demanding" attitude toward Christianity appears despite the prism of Christian texts. He is always making conditions. The baptism itself is the result of the fulfillment of these conditions, and not of "enlightenment." One such condition is the taking of the city, another is his marriage to the Byzantine princess. Even his "disease of the eyes" and recovery from it are a kind of condition and at the same time a touchstone to test the power of the new deity. The "miracle" also affected his bodyguard: "The *druzhina* having seen this, many of them were baptized" (*PVL*, vol. 1, p. 77).

45. Anichkov, *Iazychestvo i Drevniaia Rus'*, pp. 106–7.

46. Ibid., pp. 109–10.

47. Iordanskii, *Khaos i garmoniia*, pp. 177–78.

48. *PVL*, p. 80.

49. *Novgorodskaia pervaia letopis'* (hereafter *NPL*), pp. 159–60.

50. L. S. Klein, "Pokhorony boga i sviatochnye igry s umrunom," *Konferentsiia "Baltoslavianskie etnokul'turnye i arkheologicheskie drevnosti. Pogrebal'nyi obriad," Tez. dokl.* (Moscow, 1985). Already in 1937, A. Krappe had pointed out that the legend of Perun's fall and his dip in the Dnepr was based on a description of a ritual of bathing idols in the Dnepr, performed each year in Kiev in order to summon rain, a ritual that is common to many peoples. The chronicler took this ritual for the overthrowing of Perun (A. A. Krappe, "La culte du paganisme à Kiev," *Revue des études slaves*, 1937, vol. 17, no. 3, p. 217).

51. *Poln. sobr. russkikh letopisei*, vol. 1, col. 318.

52. *Pravda russkaia*, vol. 1 (Moscow-Leningrad, 1940), pp. 71, 398.

53. A. N. Afanas'ev, *Drevo zhizni. Izbrannye stat'i* (Moscow, 1983), p. 395.

54. *NPL*, p. 160.

55. *Pskovskie letopisi*, issue 1 (Moscow-Leningrad, 1941), p. 9.

56. J. Fraser, *The Golden Bough*; Rybakov, *Iazychestvo drevnei Rusi*, p. 681.

The Christianization of the Russian Peasants

V. G. Vlasov

The acceptance of Christianity by Russian peasantry evidently took place later than the official baptism of Rus'. The idea of E. V. Anichkov is well known: "Christianization of the countryside was the work, not of the eleventh and twelfth, but of the fifteenth and sixteenth or even the seventeenth century."[1]

There are various and convincing proofs that the process of Christianization of Rus' was extremely extended in time.[2] At the same time, it is inaccurate to generalize about the spread of Christianity among the "population as a whole"; more productive is the view that this process took place in different ways and at different times among the various social groups of Russian society—the ruling class, the lower orders in the towns, and the peasantry. Such an approach lets us presume that both the forms and the reasons for adopting the new faith by each social group were different.

It would be appropriate here to define exactly what is understood by Christianization with respect to each social group. However, detailed examination of specific religious, ethical, and economic views of the first two groups would far exceed the limits of this article. In general terms, Christianization may be considered to be the partaking by each group of Christian spiritual values (its mythology, dogma, rituals, symbolism, etc.), to the extent they are acknowledged, more or less sincerely, by the majority of representatives of a particular group. In other words, it is the situation in which the majority of a group's representatives one day acquire a new definition of self: "we are Christians," reflected in the documents and in the monuments of material and spiritual culture of the particular period.

It is necessary to dwell in greater detail on the concept of peasant Christianization, since this is the least determined event, given complete absence of direct testimony in the written sources. Which complex of ideas, which phenomenon in the realm of Christian realities was the major, decisive fac-

Russian text © 1988 by "Nauka" Publishers and "Sovetskaia etnografiia." "Khristianizatsiia russkikh krest'ian," *Sovetskaia etnografiia*, 1988, no. 3, pp. 3–15. A publication of the Institute of Ethnography, USSR Academy of Sciences.

tor in claiming the Russian peasants for Christianity? Clearly, it was not the rite of mass conversion, which after Prince Vladimir and Monk Kuksha of Kiev was not repeated in the following centuries. Nor was it the mastery of the proper level of Christian teachings, which was not even accomplished as the twentieth century approached. Closest of all to the essence of the peasant's understanding of Christianity is the belief in its rituals, of which we must emphasize one aspect—the economic basis. In moving from the town to the countryside, Christianity had to respond "to the economic needs, to the great problems of fertility, of proper distribution of rainfall, of the flowering of useful plants, of the pasturing of livestock."[3] The response to these problems involved not just a replacement of pagan charms with Christian prayers: most of the ritual events in the agrarian cycle were calendar events, and thus in replacing the former with Christianized rituals the problem of switching to the Christian calendar system was presented.

The rhythm of life of the tiller of land is the rhythm of nature, which is understood by him through the seasons of the calendar. The calendar is the linchpin of the peasant's entire existence, and his main problems are calendar ones: when to plow, when to sow, when to invoke the harvest, when to thank the earth, when to celebrate the rebirth of the sun. . . . On the other hand, the calendar is the framework on which the annual ritual cycle of any religious system is hung. The ritual existence in each system flows continually: each day of the year, if not a holiday (i.e., a nexus of ritualistic actions), is such-and-such day after or before the next holiday. Thus, it is clear that one may make occasional use of the calendar of a different religious system even without being an adherent of that system; but once having become such, it is absolutely imperative to switch to the new calendar. Hence, the mark of the appearance of a Christian self-awareness among the people was not the act of baptism, nor the quantity of Christian truths assimilated, but the fact that Christmas–Easter–Whitsunday became the calendar milestones of existence, in place of Koliada–Iarilo–Kupala.

Analysis of the menology, or popular Christianized agrarian and ritual calendar, reinforced with data from popular astronomy and medieval history, leads to the conclusion that the church (Julian) calendar was adopted by the Russian people in the sixteenth and seventeenth century. Such an analysis even makes it possible to narrow the time of occurrence of the "calendar reform"—around sixty years—within these two centuries.[4] The transition to the Julian calendar is a reliable indication that the Russian peasantry had adopted the Christian annual ritual cycle at this time, which in turn means that they had joined the church and Christianity. This step completed the process of tentative familiarization with Christianity, a process that lasted little more than half a century.[a] With the adoption of Christianization, the elements of the pagan beliefs and rituals of greatest importance to the peasant were not rejected: in part they continued to exist independently, and in part they were joined to the Christian rituals. Thus, in the popular mind, Christianity was not viewed as a religion, vying for a spiritual monopoly, but was accepted in accordance with the pagan, not the Christian tradition, in which "the new does not displace the old, but is layered on top of it, is added to the old."[5]

The reasons for the change in faith of the Russian peasants were undoubtedly complex and multifarious. In general, they may be understood as a response to the radical change in the social situation in Russia in connection with state centralization. All classes and social groups of the community were drawn into the process of centralization. For the topic of the present paper, it is important that certain of the government policies, beginning in the fifteenth century, were applied directly to the peasantry and required their incorporation into the Christian ritual system. One example is the reorganization of the bodies of local government, bringing into the administrative activity the "best people" among the feudal peasantry, each of whom was supposed to undergo the procedure of "kissing the cross." It is indicative that a number of legislative documents of this kind included time periods that were based on the church calendar. Among these documents were the temporary or permanent binding of the peasants to the land (with the deadline for possible "repudiation" on Autumn Iurii's Day, 26 November, Old Style); and a prescription that local authorities should bring monetary levies [obrok] to Moscow "on Shrovetide"[6] or on Sreten's Day.[7]

In Russian history, there were also events not as significant, yet touching all of the peasants more directly and sharply. We are speaking of the precipitous rise of the towns, starting in the second half of the fifteenth century, the population of which was replenished by an inflow from the villages and countryside.[8] The towns brought together sizable groups of peasants in the status of seasonal workers, brought as part of the feudal service—the "townwork."[b] Thus, the "First Novgorod Chronicle" under 1430 states: "The peasants were driven to Novgorod to build the town, and four provisioned the fifth,"[9] that is, one out of every five men went to build, and the other four supplied him with food. Many new problems were created in this way, which it is important to examine "from the inside."

On this foundation, a secondary system of relationships (economic, marital, etc.) was constructed.

In order to establish a close temporal framework for the Christianization of the peasantry, we shall briefly discuss certain events in Russian history and cultural phenomena in which this process found a reflection.

One may approach this problem by the "method of contradiction"—establishing the epoch during which Russian tillers were surely not Christian. Weighty "negative" testimony is afforded by archeology, revealing that mound [kurgan] burials with objects, antithetical to Christian norms, were a universal phenomenon in Russia up to the fifteenth century; in certain areas, they are attested in the thirties of the sixteenth century.[10]

The "Pskov Chronicle" reports, under the year 1544, an unusual conflict: the village and "suburban" priests petitioned to be removed from town councils,[11] and the separation took place. In this way, the clergy outside the towns gave notice that they were conscious of their independence and, furthermore, they began to receive considerable revenues, which they did not want to share with the town clergy. All of this may also be explained by the fact that a new and important flock had appeared among them—the farmers. This conclusion is consistent with the data of N. M. Nikol'skii, who observed that, up to and including the fifteenth century, no rural churches existed for the general use of the populace; churches existed only at the courts of boyars and princes.[12]

In the documents from the thirties to the fifties of the sixteenth century there are reports that the rural inhabitants of Russia were incorrectly celebrating the church holidays and behaving unseemly in church. Thus, in 1538–41, in the cloister of Ilarion Iloezerskii, the people of the district took to burying their dead, christening infants, performing weddings, and in the warm refectory "ate meat and brought in strong drink and consumed it there."[13] "Stoglav" tells of a remembrance of the dead, performed on Whitsaturday, and of "many a day" in pure pagan tradition.[14] Since the rural inhabitants were celebrating very Christian holidays, they naturally considered themselves to be Christians. The ceremonies were not orthodox: they combined major Christian dates with the rituals of the closest pagan dates, creating new ritual complexes.[c]

In the modern study of religions, the idea has become fixed that the church calendar during the Christianization of the European peoples was constructed by the method of attuning it to the local pagan traditions: the church "designated the Christian holidays on approximately the same days where previously pagan holidays fell."[15] However, this judgment, while true in principle, does not allow for the factor of time: in a process stretching over centuries, the relationships between Christian and pagan cultures could not remain unchanged, and in fact did not. We know that the status of the church in Russian society changed radically from the eleventh to the sixteenth century; during this time, the social strata with which the church worked also changed. Thus, in establishing the day of commemoration of Boris and Gleb (May 2) in the twelfth century, the church evidently "covered over" a certain pagan festival,[16] although not necessarily an agricultural one. It may have been connected with the ancestor cult, for example.[17] The Russian church was also weak during the period when Christianity was adopted in the town outskirts (second half of the thirteenth century). The church holidays formed during this time (Il'ia's day, the festival of the Thunderer, July 20; the day of Flora and Laura, or the "horse-breeder's day," August 18) absorbed the popular traditions and were conditioned by the popular calendar. Evidently, on the soil of the town suburbs, the selfless Roman physicians Cosma and Damian (November 1) were turned into the patrons of the blacksmith trade—"the holy blacksmiths." But starting in the middle of the fifteenth century, the confessional situation in the country began to change: the church began its ascent, and already by the end of this century was endeavoring (on a church of Rome model) to play the leading role in Russian society. (A striking example was the inveighing of the grand prince Ivan III to carry out the execution of "heretics.") By the start of the sixteenth century, it had become clear that the church had no real chance of surpassing the grand prince, and it took its place alongside him, as his closest advisor—this was the high point.

Under these conditions, the new wave of Christianization and the new clash of the two calendars would not necessarily result in a compromise. The peasants affiliated with the church found themselves compelled to switch entirely to its calendar, and this change was expressed not only as a replacement of the old calendar by the new one, involving an alternation of holiday events and days in commemoration of the saints, but also as a deformation of the ancient calendar tradition—a displacing of the rituals and omens or prognosticating events from their former fixed dates to the triumphant Christian ones (Shrovetide, Easter, Whitsunday). Individual attempts at local calendar creativity (such as the institution of the "horse festival" on June 26 or 27 under the name Nikola the Ordinary, the celebration of Saint Vlasia's day on Shrove Thursday or on the Saturday before Whitsun, and the day of Flora and Laura on the first Sunday after Peter's day)[18] were not accepted by the church and remained local customs. The most that the paganism of the peasants could accomplish in this area was an "embellishment" of church calendar rituals: thus, the worship of the birch on Whitsun, the holidays of *pervin* on Spas' days (August 1, 6, and 16), the harvest festival on the Assumption (August 15), and others penetrated into the church canon.

Yet the hierarchs, gathered at the Stoglav council, failed to appreciate properly the efforts thanks to which the Russian church was destined to assume an intense national tone; nor could they comprehend the first faltering steps of the latter-day Christians: "Fearlessness has come into the people, in God's churches . . . they stand fearlessly, in their bonnets, fresh from the plow . . . and [there is] talking, and murmuring, and every sort of contention, and gossiping, and shameful words."[19] Apparently, it was not so much that fearlessness had become rampant, as that "fear" [*strakh*] was not yet common to these people, who had only just entered the Church and did not yet know how to comport themselves in a Christian manner. Freedom in behavior was encouraged in large measure by the traditions of pagan holidays, to which silence and immobility were foreign.

The first half of the sixteenth century was a time during which the congregation of Russian saints was substantially increased, and those born among the peasants joined their number: Aleksandr Oshevenskii (died 1489), Aleksandr Svirskii (1533), Filipp Irapskii (1527 or 1537), Antonii Siiskii (1556), Nil Stolbenskii (1554), Nikifor Vazheozerskii (1550s or 1560s). As dissimilar as their biographies were, there is one common feature in their lives: children of peasant families, they become monks, then founders of monasteries, and then Russian saints. There were also other ways to join the elect and the devoted—in 1544, laborers Ioann and Loggin Iarengskii of the Solovetsk Monastery drowned in the White Sea and were added to the congregation of saints after 1624; in 1545, the young Artemii Verkol'skii, the son of a peasant, was struck by lightning and became a "saint" in 1639–40.[20] The phenomenon of canonization of members of the peasantry suggests that the Christianization of the Russian tillers had reached such a level that they required their own solicitors and intercessors before God.

In the estimation of the modern literature, the elevation of one or another Russian saint was motivated by religious propaganda or politics. Thus, for example, the massive miracles at the grave of Metropolitan Aleksei, mentioned by the chroniclers at the end of the second and beginning of the third decade of the sixteenth century, are explained by the worsening relations between Moscow and the appanage principalities.[21] But Metropolitan Aleksei, who died in 1378, had already been canonized in the middle of the fifteenth century; in the 1520s his authority was borrowed to resolve the current difficult political situation. Such an approach could hardly be used in the canonization of new saints, much less as a general rule, since the appearance of each particular "miracle" cannot be explained as the "decree of Moscow." It is possible to name dozens of persons active in church or public affairs who, for political considerations, should surely have held a place in the Christian pantheon, yet they are either totally absent therefrom (such as Vladimir Monomakh, Iurii Dolgorukii, Ivan Kalita, Dmitrii Donskoi), or were canonized much later (the Grand Prince Georgii Vsevolodovich, killed during Baty's invasion, Grand Prince Daniil Aleksandrovich of Moscow, the Moscow metropolitans of the fourteenth and fifteenth centuries Feognost, Kiprian, Fotii, and others). Meanwhile miracles—like a claim for sainthood—took place at the graves of quite different and ordinary people. Among these can be mentioned, for example, Princess Evfrosin'ia of Suzdal', who lived in the first half of the thirteenth century (canonized in 1572–81),[22] and Iakov Borovichskii, an unknown person whose coffin, along with his remains, was carried by an ice floe during the spring flood to Borovichi (1540s). He appeared in a dream to several inhabitants of the town and said that his name was Iakov (canonized in 1577).[23] In this same year (or, according to the contemporary church calendar, in 1522), the maiden Glikeriia was also canonized. The coffin with her remains was discovered "above ground" in Novgorod.[24] The miracles associated with these personages can only be explained by the sympathy of the lower strata of society for them. The fact that the circle of the venerated saints was growing indicates an increased contingent of the faithful, desirous of glorifying their local monastery or church and of making it one of the national Russian Christian shrines.

The legend "About the appearance of the Apostle Andrew the First Called in the Russian land" experienced a revival in the early sixteenth century. The situation was somewhat similar to that which accompanied the confirmation of the legend in Kiev in the second half of the eleventh century in unofficial circles: the first Russian metropolitan, Ilarion (middle of the eleventh century), did not know of this legend, and in his "Sermon on the law and grace" he named Prince Vladimir as the enlightener of the Russian lands, just as Peter and Paul, John, Thomas, and Mark announced Christianity among the other nations.[25] The same is said in the chronicle: "the apostles were not here in body";[26] the role of the apostles is similarly portrayed in the "Tale of Boris and Gleb"[d] (early twelfth century).[27] The "Tale of Bygone Years" (around 1113) names the apostle Paul as the first teacher of the Slavs,[28] and only after being revised by the Father Superior Sil'vestr of Vydubitsa monastery does the account of the apostle Andrew appear. The legend had a clearly anti-Novgorodian tendency, to which the Novgorodians responded in different ways. For example, the "First Chronicle of Sofia" asserts that, on the day of the conversion [of Russia], "the devil groaned the words: '. . . I am defeated by a know-nothing, and not by an Apostle, nor by a martyr' ";[29] according to another version of the response, the apostle not only spent time in the land of Novgorod, but also preached there and even left behind his staff.[30]

Kievan Rus' displayed no particular zeal in planting the cult of Andrew— evidently there was no special need for this. Basically, there was no "quest for apostles," but rather a collection of itinerant themes. Not surprisingly, the legend was soon forgotten, and by the late fifteenth and early sixteenth century it had come to be believed that "the faith of Christ was revealed to the Russian tongue, to one of the last apostles, who had never been in the land of Russia." Iosif Volotskii resolved the matter of why the apostle Andrew did not preach here: "He was forbidden by the Holy Spirit, but his destinies are endlessly many, and therefore they are not recounted."[31] It is impossible to ignore the polemical flavor of this statement (similar to the tone of the early chroniclers); the legend, it seems, had again gained currency among the faithful, and Iosif dismisses it as an unworthy fabrication. Nevertheless, in subsequent decades the idea of the apostle's blessing became a firm part of the "historical fund" of Russian Orthodoxy: the legend of Andrew the First Called is contained in the Makarov Minei; it was well known by Ivan the Terrible and used by him as an argument in his dealings with the Catholic world.[32]

The opinions of more recent scholars regarding this legend are well known: its truth was doubted by N. M. Karamzin, it was repudiated by prominent church historians—Platon, Filaret, E. Golubinskii[33]—which, however, in no way affected its status as a perfectly orthodox production. Yet the legend itself shows most accurately its place in the system of Christian values. By the significance of the event, it could have been just another chapter of the canonical "Acts of the Apostles," yet it has no element resembling this book. Approximately half the text of the legend is devoted to describing the apostle's itinerary, giving special attention to the future Kiev and Novgorod, while the other half presents an interesting depiction of a Russian-style bath.[34] In manner of exposition, the legend does not differ from the pronouncements of the maiden Glikeriia of Rostov, who as prophetess counseled people not to curse with foul language, or the precepts of the "false prophets" of "Stoglav," not to work on Wednesdays and Fridays. The fate of the legend was determined by the fact that its intrinsic popular spirit, contributed by the Kievan chronicler, was akin to the way of thinking of the tillers who had converted to Christianity: the legend took on a second life, receiving the approval of the people. The Russian church of the sixteenth century legitimized it for lack of a better course of action; this step is directly related to the adoption of the title "apostolic" for the church. In principle, every church is hereditarily apostolic, since the legendary founders of this institution were the apostles Peter and Paul; the assumption of the title apostolic by a local church was based on the special role of one particular apostle in its history. It should be pointed out that the term "apostolic" is almost never found in church documents from the eleventh to the fifteenth century. It was freely used by the patriarchs of Constantinople (e.g., the Patriarch Nil in the Pskov writ, ca. 1382);[35] but the Russian princes and metropolitans call their city church God's Holy Conciliar Church of Kiev.[36] And only at the council of Stoglav was the "Holy Conciliar and Apostolic Church" proclaimed "in full voice."[37] Milestones in the establishment of Russian church independence are the years 1448 (separation from the patriarchate of Constantinople) and 1589 (creation of an independent patriarchate).[e] With these should be grouped the ideological move by which the church became "proven" apostolic (first half of the sixteenth century). The latter is particularly interesting in connection with the changes in church building that occurred at this time.

From 1530 to 1532, the Church of the Ascension was built in the village of Kolomensk, outside of Moscow. This edifice inaugurated a new architectural trend—the creation of stone temples with a hipped roof. In the composition of the Kolomensk church, one clearly senses the influence of such architectural forms as were previously rendered only in wood, as is openly declared by the chronicler of the sixteenth century, who states that it was built "aloft in wooden work."[38] Wooden churches of this time and earlier, built on the outskirts of the towns and in the northern villages, had a hipped top: the oldest surviving temples are the Church of the Resurrection of Lazarus of the Muromsk Monastery on the shore of Lake Onega (1391, now part of the Kiev Conservatory Museum), the church of the village of Borodavo in Vologda territory (1486, now on the grounds of the Kirill Belozerskii Conservatory Museum), and that of the village of Iuksovichi of Leningrad Oblast (1493);[39] such was the Church of the Ascension in the outskirts of Vologda, built in 1493.[40] Religious construction with a hipped roof is typologically derived from the pagan temple.[41] This type of roof was widely used in the popular culture: it can be seen in the tall shelter made of branches for an idol shrine, constructed in a sacred grove during yuletide,[42] and also in the images of towerlike structures for cult purposes in folk embroidery.[43]

As we know, the traditional covering of the Christian temple was different—a dome, going back to Byzantine models. How highly the original form of the temple was praised is witnessed by the fact that, a little more than fifty years before the building of the Kolomensk Ascension, one of the principal tasks in the construction of the Cathedral of the Assumption (Uspenskii Sobor) of Moscow was to imitate as closely as possible the shape and proportions of the "classical" Cathedral of the Assumption in Vladimir. That which occurred in the 1530s—the transfer of the hipped shape from wood to stone, from the small suburban or village church to the massive temple, the main religious structure of the time—is nothing less than a complete revolution in church architecture. This revolution was a reflection of a certain major "revolution" in society, and the question of why suddenly a new model for the temple was needed and why indeed a popular model was selected may be answered by recognizing that a process of Christianization of the peasantry was taking place in Russia during this time and that this process had been noticed and properly understood by the Moscow government (twenty years before the Russian hierarchs slowly began to realize this with annoyance). The temple was "commissioned" by Grand Prince Vasilii III; his actions may be explained as a political calculation to win over the Christianized people and even become the head of "popular Christianity."

Thus, the Russian church, as a congregation of the faithful, having become apostolic, chose for its liturgical service a church building with a hipped roof. This is a single event, both sides of which have popular roots: the apostolicism from traditions outside the church, the hipped roof from pagan cult structures.

Also associated with this is the adoption into church practice of a number of distortions in the performance of ritual actions, which in little more than one hundred years would be among the most important reasons for the church schism: the two-fingered sign of the cross, the special (twice pronounced) hallelujah, and the walking in deasil (with the sun) direction during the wedding rite and in the procession of the cross around the church.

All these norms certainly took shape by the middle of the sixteenth century, as is indicated by the Old Believer formula "as commanded by the grand-fathers and the great-grandfathers," which was first pronounced in 1656: the generation of the great-grandfathers was active slightly more than a hundred years before this date. Certain of the above norms were confirmed by the Stoglav council of 1551. For the topic of the present work, the walking in the path of the sun is of special interest.

Christianity is characterized by a ritual movement against the path of the sun. This, evidently, was true in Russia from the time of the "conversion" till the end of the fifteenth century. The first critical attitude toward the rite is observed in 1479, during the consecration of the Cathedral of the Assumption in Moscow: it seemed to one of the entourage of Grand Prince Ivan III that the metropolitan was performing the procession of the cross "incorrectly." A dispute arose, which lasted for three years and ended with acknowledgment that the metropolitan was right[44]: the Christian norm was confirmed. Yet by the middle of the sixteenth century, the processions of the cross in the Russian church were already being performed "with the sun." When, by whom, and on what basis was this established?

A deasil ritual movement is characteristic of the circle dance [khovorod]—a pagan cult dance of the sun. The circle dance moves in the same direction as the sun, and thereby acts magically on it. This ritual tradition, which goes far back in time, may also be discerned in routine farming: folk wisdom advises the tiller "Plow with the sun, and the horse's head will not turn."[45] Deasil movement was implicit in every custom of the peasant's existence. For example, the livestock were counted out into the village flock and the hired shepherd served his terms in the houses following the path of the sun.[46] It is interesting that the opposite movement (withershins) was also employed in the popular magical rituals, but in diametrically opposite situations: when it was necessary to act, not in consonance with nature, but in order to change the existing state of affairs. For example, when certain ritual bans were violated during fishing, such as might affect the catch, the following ritual was performed: a hot kettle was turned upside down, and on its bottom, smeared with fat, the guilty party was placed bare-bottom and turned against the path of the sun; the person punished in this way was later called the "twirled one" and treated contemptuously by everyone.[47]

It is highly probable that the Russian people, having begun a vigorous adoption of Christian rites, performed those resembling the traditional circle dances in the customary mode. The reform of Patriarch Nikon in 1656 restored the correct Christian rite; the Old Believers, adhering to the deasil movement, were in this case actually defending "ancient piety," but a popular and pagan one, and not Christian.[48]

But how could the people impose on the church a clearly perverted action? Unfortunately, this significant episode in the history of Russian Orthodoxy has not been described by contemporaries. The time of its "legitimization" can only be determined by conjecture, on the basis of everything that we know today about events of this period. Most likely, it happened during a certain pompous and well-attended church holiday, when the norm that had spread spontaneously was approved for the entire Russian populace by the method of public display. Such solemn event may have been the consecration of the Temple of the Ascension in Kolomna province (1532). This temple, built as a manifesto of the folk architecture, would also have been consecrated in as public a way as possible, i.e., with the attendance of priests from the suburban and rural hipped-roof churches. The actions performed by them, including the procession of the cross around the church, not being repudiated, took on an obligatory form. The head of the Russian church during this time was Metropolitan Daniil.

At the same time as the "distortions" in the sphere of Christian culture, other changes occurred during this time. Certain of them went unnoticed by the church, and their consequences were not branded as errors. Among such innovations must be mentioned the custom, taking shape in the late fifteenth and the first half of the sixteenth century, of singing certain prayers that were formerly spoken,[49] as a result of which it became usual to think of the church service as one continuous song. This idea found a documentary reflection: the "Resurrection Chronicle," speaking of the church worship of this time, invariably calls it "singing."[50] Evidently, the mechanism of this innovation was similar to the previous one: singing, a crucial component of folk culture, could have entered the Christian liturgy from a popular source. Novelties of a different kind, which may be judged the result of mistakes in understanding the Christian concepts, were immediately rejected by the church, yet firmly entered the customs of the citizens. Of these, in particular, one must mention the appearance of the term *voskresenie* ("resurrection") to designate the day of rest (Sunday), which occurred in the sixteenth century.[51] The mere fact that the image of the Christian Easter was extended to all "weeks" of the year indicates that those who created this tradition were completely ignorant of the Christian mythology, and clearly reveals its origin in the lower classes.[f]

In the sixteenth century, Petr and Fevroniia of Murom became popular literary figures and afterwards Russian saints.[52] The plot of all stories concerning them is very simple: the sick prince Petr is healed by the peasant girl Fevroniia, after which the prince and the peasant are married.

There is no doubt that Fevroniia was a heathen prior to her meeting with Prince Petr: she prayed, not in church and not in her hut before an icon-case, but beneath a walnut bush,[53] i.e., in a "grove." She performed the healing of Prince Petr in purely pagan tradition: "She took a small vessel, and filled it with her brew and blew on it and said: 'Arrange a bath for your prince, and smear this on his body, . . . and he will be well.' "[54] Not a prayer to the Virgin, nor a "Lord bless," nor even a hanging of the cross over him; but instead sorcery, magic, witchcraft. Actually, it proved quite effective.[g]

The legend says nothing of the conversion of Fevroniia, as being an episode of little importance to the people, although it is clear that the heroine, having become the wife of a Christian and later a Christian saint, surely adopted Christianity. This metamorphosis, theoretically very important, is eclipsed here by the central event of the story—the wedding. The interest in this, of course, is no accident: it is appropriate and even essential in the context of the adoption by the peasantry of the complex of Christian realities, among which were the institution and the rite of the Christian matrimony.

Having become a Christian, Fevroniia kept her ability to perform miracles, although now they took on a more or less Christian coloring.[55] The paganism is simply and directly transfused into Christianity, the heathen magic becomes Christian miracle, and the sorceress or witch becomes a Christian saint—such is the popular philosophy of the time.

The Legend of Petr and Fevroniia of Murom is a reflection of the process of Christianization of the Russian peasantry, which took place on the level of family and matrimonial relationships, reflecting a peculiarly popular view of the relationship between heathenism and Christianity.

The commencement of the veneration for Merkurii of Smolensk evidently belongs to the sixteenth century.[56] As shown by V. N. Basilov, the legend of Merkurii and a number of other personages who lived and performed deeds for a certain time after their decapitation is based on the agricultural cult of the dying and reawakening Nature. The decapitation is not consistent with the familiar myths of dying and resurrected deities of Near East origin, forming an independent variant on this theme that was widely represented in the religious views and ritual practice and poetics of Central and Western Europe.[57] The Slavic material reveals a confinement of the decapitation ritual to the summer cycle,[58] where it forms part of the harvest rites. It appears that this deep-lying pagan stratum was fertile soil enabling symbols to be understood by the people, so that the "militaristic" in form and intensely local cult of Merkurii became, unnoticed by the church, common to all of Russia.

The process of formation of fable plots is a phenomenon for which it is hard to discern an origin (usually characterized as "deep in the past"), but its conclusion appears much more clearly. In the opinion of many scholars (N. P. Andreev, V. Ia. Propp, E. V. Pomerantseva, and others), this process in Russia evidently came to an end in the sixteenth century, since the period of conservation of the genre already occurs in the seventeenth.[59] Let us discuss the group of plots in which the protagonists are two smart brothers and a third one having an original way of thinking and usually called Ivan the Fool, and a portion of the story time is taken up with the quest for "another realm."[h] The situation itself, in which the youngest son in a peasant family is forced to make his own way far from the father's house, suggests a significant break with the traditional ideas and norms of common law, as well as a situation in which the main bulk of the land was already owned and under cultivation (such state of affairs obtained in the central regions of Russia in the middle of the sixteenth century).[60]

Students of folklore are quite right in pointing out the high moral virtues of Ivan the Fool.[61] Less convincing is the interpretation of the "other realm." The great chronological depth of this concept and its connection with the mythology and the rites of initiation has been noted; for the "other world" in this case was zoomorphic, particularly reptilian in nature, and one of the directions in the subsequent development of the theme of this realm was the slaying of dragons.[62] But the "other realm" was also reinterpreted in other ways. For example, its location beyond the sea, on a high mountain or underneath the earth served as the foundation for a fabulous geography: "Genetically descended from the 'other realm' is the forest where resides Morozko [Frost], and the underwater realm of the King of the Sea, and the realm of the Serpent Gorynych."[63] But all of this is mere external characterization. A number of observations suggest that later tradition did not lose the function of the "other realm" as a place of rebirth, although clearly not in an initiatory form. The "other" values proper to this world have no relationship to the sacral traditions, they are simply other, different from the customary secular Christian manners and ideas. The searchers are actuated by a disgust with *this* life, and the very fact of searching begins with a breach from it: the hero, for no apparent reason, "took it into his head to go on a journey" or desires "to go whither I myself know not." The philosophy of the searchers reveals two main groups of ideas: (1) rejection of common sense and life's teachings; (2) a negative attitude toward work: the hero is demonstratively committed to idleness (he lies in bed, catches flies), and unfailingly receives happiness and riches without effort. Very instructive is the fable in which an old mother wants to apprentice her son "to such a science that he can do no work (!), eat and drink well, and wear clean clothes."[64]

This mode of thought and behavior is not new in the history of European ethics: similar doctrines were advanced during the formation of the early Christian ideology: (1) "the wisdom of this world is foolishness before God," "we are fools for Christ's sake" (I Cor. 3.19, 4.10); (2) "do not be concerned . . . what to eat and drink . . . Behold the birds of the sky: they sow not, neither do they reap, nor gather in the harvest; and your heavenly father feeds them" (Matt. 6.25–26), "I sent you to harvest that for which you have toiled not: others have toiled, and you have come into their toil" (John 4.38).

After examining the above features of similarity, E. Trubetskoi was not able to determine how they were inspired: by the spontaneous development of the people's philosophy of life, or by the many centuries of influence of Christianity on the soul of the people and, through this, on the fable.[65]

Carried along by an objective course of social development, Christianity itself came to the philosophical precepts of the world that is represented by the town and the state and sanctified by the Christian church. The fable does not betray a full and adequate assimilation of these precepts.[i] The "other realm" is only sought, not yet found: it is *another* realm, not this one. The distinctive peasant ideas reflecting a degree of understanding of the "other realm" are created deep within the pagan worldview and are evaluated from this standpoint. This is pointed out by B. A. Rybakov: in this area, "much is still obedient to the pagan ritual; the hero of the fable only attains his goal if he unswervingly fulfills all the injunctions of this ritual, obeys the all-knowing warlock, and placates the evil spirits along the way."[66] At the same time, this "quest" is by no means static; it is not one of the routine itineraries of the fable, laid out in two dimensions. The "quest" travels into other dimensions, it is an ascent: the hero, having begun the journey, will no longer return to the starting point, or to what he was before crossing the threshold of his parent's house. Clearly, Trubetskoi was correct in assuming that the "quest for the 'other realm' in the fable is . . . a definite stage in the ladder raising the consciousness of the people from paganism to Christianity"[67] (let it be noted that he is speaking of the later form of "quest"). The creation of these stories may be definitely assigned to the second half of the fifteenth and beginning of the sixteenth centuries.

*   *   *

Thus, the Russian peasants were brought to the necessity of adopting Christianity in the late fifteenth and early sixteenth centuries, motivated by the emerging relationships of the feudal order in the centralized state. It is characteristic that the process of Christianization did not result in a study of Christian dogma or understanding of the inner meaning of Christian rites, but in a conversion to the ritual calendar system of the church and a fusion of this with the entire complex of age-old agrarian and meteorological observations. Since the adoption by the people of the church (Julian) calendar occurred in the sixteenth and seventeenth centuries, it may be inferred that the Russian tillers of soil had begun to adopt Christianity in the first decades of the sixteenth century. Certain events of Russian history and cultural monuments whose features are explained by the influence of the now-Christian people, closely grouped together in the first half of the sixteenth century, prove that the process of Christianization of the peasantry mainly occurred at this time. The most significant milestones are: the formation of a new architectural style—the construction of stone churches with hipped roof (the Temple of the Ascension in Kolomna province, 1532); the appearance in the towns of special assemblies (corporations), bringing together the priests of the villages and those of the municipal outskirts (1544); the canonization of the main core of Russian saints, including those of peasant origin (1547, 1549); the adoption in church practice of the deasil procession, which along with the two-fingered sign of the cross and the special hallelujah later resulted in the schism of the Russian church (1532, 1551).

This time frame and nature of the process should not be viewed as something exceptional, differing greatly from the corresponding events among the other peoples [narod]. On the basis of calendar information, it may be declared that the time of adoption of Christianity by the peasants of most of the Western European countries was the fifteenth century: the turning point in the winter cycle, which is remembered as the shortest day in the year, was Lucia's Day, December 13,[68] which had formerly been the day of the winter solstice. The solstice on this day (by the Julian calendar) occurred in the fifteenth century; thus, it was in this century that the Julian calendar was adopted and the final conversion to Christianity took place. This inference is supported by ethnographical material. For example, the pagan funerary banquet, or strava, was observed among the Czechs and the Poles right down to the fifteenth century.[69]

A number of other nations of Eastern Europe did not accept Christianity at once, and their missionary conversion occurred on several occasions at intervals of 100 or 200 years. Thus, for example, the Chud' were baptized by Ioann Ustiuzhskii in the twelfth or thirteenth century, and then by Kirill Chelmogorskii and Avraamii Chukhlomskoi in the second half of the sixteenth century; the Lapps [Saami] were brought into the bosom of the Christian church in the late fifteenth century by Lazar' Muromskii, and then also by Feodorit Kol'skii and Trifon Pechengskii in the middle of the sixteenth century.[70]

The Russians were not alone in recognizing the missionary role of the apostles. The very same apostle Andrew was made their patron saint by the Scots. Curiously, in this case as well there were several periods in his worship: the last, when the image of the cross on which the apostle Andrew was crucified was placed on the Scottish banner, falls in the fifteenth century.[71] In Sweden, Saint Sigfrid is worshipped as an apostle;[72] on the island of Sardinia, the emperor Constantine the Great is regarded as the thirteenth apostle.[73]

In the article, we have not been able to capture the full spectrum of both confessional and cultural aspects of the event in question—the voluntary and spontaneous adoption of Christianity by the Russian tillers of soil. The issue of the "popular orthodoxy," which N. K. Nikol'skii once raised in his own time,[74] is surely not answered definitively by the adoption of the Julian calendar, the building of hipped-roof churches, and the distortion of certain ritual operations of the church. The people displayed a vivid interest in the hagiology and in compositions of moralistic nature, seeing no difference between the apocrypha and the works of the fathers of the church. An echo of this was found in the idea of the monastery, which the people used extensively during the difficult years of the schism (the remarkable poetic fantasy of the invisible city of Kitezh was based on this). The popular orthodoxy was far from official Orthodoxy, as is shown both by the survival of *dvoeverie* (dual faith) and by the ongoing spiritual quests, either within the context of Christian doctrine (sectarianism) or outside of it (the legends of the White Water, the Opon'skie Islands, etc.).

Editor's notes

a. For additional sources on Russian peasant Christianity, see Donald W. Treadgold, "The Peasant and Religion," in Wayne S. Vucinich, ed., *The Peasant in Nineteenth-century Russia* (Stanford: Stanford University Press, 1968), pp. 72–107; Pierre Pascal, *The Religion of the Russian People*, trans. Rowan Williams (Oxford: Mobray, 1976); Eve Levin, *Sex and Society in the World of the Orthodox Slavs 900-1700* (Ithaca: Cornell University Press, 1989).

b. See Jerome Blum, *Lord and Peasant in Russia from the Ninth to the Nineteenth Century* (Princeton: Princeton University Press, 1961), on peasant obligations and rights. A tradition of more voluntary, temporary, often seasonal, work away from one's village, *otkhodnichestvo*, lasted into the twentieth century. See Stephen P. Dunn and Ethel Dunn, *The Peasants of Central Russia* (New York: Holt, Rinehart & Winston, 1967), pp. 18–20, 81–85.

c. For calendrical correlations of pagan diety festivals with Saints' Days, see George P. Fedotov, *The Russian Religious Mind: Kievan Christianity* (New York: Harper & Row, 1960), pp. 357–62.

d. For a Laurentian text translation on Apostle Prince Andrew, and on Boris and Gleb, see Samuel Hazard Cross and Olgerd P. Sherbowitz-Wetzor, *The Russian Primary Chronicle* (Cambridge: Medieval Academy of America, 1953), pp. 53–54, 126–29.

e. For contrasting perspectives on these milestones, see George P. Fedotov, *The Russian Religious Mind*, vol. 2: *The Middle Ages–the Thirteenth to the Fifteenth Centuries*, ed. John Meyendorff (Cambridge: Harvard University Press, 1966); George Florovsky, *Collected Works* (Belmont: Norland, 1976); V. G. Ovchinnikov, "Pravoslavnaia tserkov' v istorii nashei stranei," *Voprosy istorii*, 1988, no. 5, pp. 111–21.

f. Compare Michael S. Flier, "Sunday in Medieval Russian Culture: Nedelja versus Voskresenie," in *Medieval Russian Culture*, eds. Henrik Birnbaum and Michael Flier (Berkeley: University of California Press, 1984), pp. 105–49.

g. Folk curers, *znakhari*, were believed to deal with "clean [supernatural] strength," whereas witches or sorcerers dealt with "unclean strength." See Russell Zguta, "Witchcraft and Medicine in Pre-Petrine Russia," *Russian Review*, 1978, vol. 37, no. 4, pp. 338–448; G. I. Popov, *Russkaia bytovaia meditsina* (St. Petersburg: Suvorin, 1903); N. I. Novombergskii, *Koldovstvo v moskovskoi Rusi XVII veka* (St. Petersburg: Suvorin, 1906).

h. For Ivan the Fool stories, see A. Afanasyev, *Russian Fairy Tales* (New York: Pantheon, 1945); and Alex E. Alexander, *Russian Folklore: An Anthology in English Translation* (Belmont: Nordland, 1974). See also E. M. Meletinskii, "The Low Hero of the Fairy Tale," in *The Study of Russian Folklore*, eds. Felix J. Oinas and S. Soudakoff (The Hague: Mouton, 1975), pp. 236–54; Linda J. Ivanits, *Russian Folk Belief* (Armonk, NY: M. E. Sharpe, 1989); Roman Jakobson, "Slavic Folklore and Slavic Mythology," in *Standard Dictionary of Folklore and Mythology*, ed. Maria Leach, vol. 2 (New York: Funk and Wagnell, 1950), pp. 1019–28.

i. The issue of folklore revealing less than full assimilation of Christianity is also discussed in Oinas and Soudakoff, eds., *The Study of Russian Folklore*; Ivanits, *Russian Folk Belief*; and Joanna Hubbs, *Mother Russia: The Feminine Myth in Russian Culture* (Bloomington: Indiana University Press, 1988).

Notes

1. E. V. Anichkov, *Iazychestvo i drevniaia Rus'* (St. Petersburg, 1914), p. 306.
2. N. M. Nikol'skii, *Istoriia russkoi tserkvi* (Moscow, 1985), pp. 21–57.
3. Anichkov, *Iazychestvo i Drevniaia Rus'*, p. XXI.
4. V. G. Vlasov, "Russkii narodnyi kalendar'," *Sovetskaia etnografiia*, 1985, no. 4, pp. 22–33.
5. B. A. Rybakov, "Iazycheskoe mirovozzrenie russkogo srednevekov'ia," *Voprosy istorii*, 1974, no. 1, p. 4; idem, *Iazychestvo Drevnei Rusi* (Moscow, 1987), p. 754.
6. *Pamiatniki russkogo prava*. no. 4 (Moscow, 1956), pp. 186–88, 191, 197–98.
7. *Akty Arkheologicheskoi ekspeditsii*. vol. 1 (St. Petersburg, 1836), pp. 266–67.
8. L. V. Cherepnin, *Obrazovanie russkogo tsentralizovannogo gosudarstva v XIV–XV vv.* (Moscow, 1960), pp. 329–46; M. N. Tikhomirov, *Srednevekovaia Moskva v XIV–XV vv.* (Moscow, 1957), pp. 98–100.
9. *Novogorodskaia pervaia letopis' starshego i mladshego izvodov* (Moscow-Leningrad, 1950), p. 416.
10. *Dopolneniia k Aktam istoricheskim*, vol. 1 (St. Petersburg, 1846), no. 28.
11. *Pskovskie letopisi*, issue 1, (Moscow-Leningrad, 1941), p. 111.
12. Nikol'skii, *Istoriia russkoi tserkvi*, p. 52.
13. I. U. Budovnits, *Monastyri na Rusi i bor'ba s nimi krest'ian v XIV–XVI vv.* (Moscow, 1966), p. 296.
14. "Stoglav," *Rossiiskoe zakonodatel'stvo X–XX vv.*, vol. 2, (Moscow, 1985), pp. 309, 310.
15. N. M. Nikol'skii, *Istoriia russkoi tserkvi*, p. 25; G. A. Nosova, *Iazychestvo i pravoslavii* (Moscow, 1975), p. 14.
16. B. A. Rybakov, "Iazycheskoe mirovozzrenie russkogo srednevekov'ia," p. 21; idem, *Iazychestvo Drevnei Rusi*, pp. 186–87, 670–74.
17. Vlasov, "Russkii narodnyi kalendar'," p. 35.
18. B. A. Uspenskii, *Filologicheskie razyskaniia v oblasti slavianskikh drevnostei (Relikty iazychestva v vostochnoslavianskom kul'te Nikolaia Mirlikiiskogo)* (Moscow, 1982), p. 47.
19. "Stoglav," p. 273.
20. E. Golubinskii, *Istoriia kanonizatsii sviatykh v russkoi tserkvi* (Moscow, 1903), pp. 100, 125, 128, 150, 155, 196; L. A. Dmitriev, *Zhitiinye povesti russkogo Severa kak pamiatniki literatury XIII–XVII vv.* (Leningrad, 1973), pp. 213–61.
21. A. M. Sakharov, "Religiia i tserkov'," *Ocherki russkoi kul'tury XVI v.*, pt. 2 (Moscow, 1977), p. 82.
22. Golubinskii, *Istoriia kanonizatsii sviatykh v russkoi tserkvi*, p. 89.
23. Ibid., pp. 87, 114.
24. Ibid., pp. 114–15.
25. M. E. Fedorova and T. A. Sumnikova, *Khrestomatiia po drevnerusskoi literature* (Moscow, 1969), p. 31.
26. *Polnoe sobranie russkikh letopisei* (hereafter *PSRL*), vol. 1, (St. Petersburg, 1846), p. 35.
27. *Zhitiia Borisa i Gleba* (Petersburg, 1916), p. 3.
28. *Povest' vremennykh let* (Moscow-Leningrad, 1950), pt. 1, p. 23.
29. *PSRL*, vol. 5 (St. Petersburg, 1851), p. 119.
30. *PSRL*, vol. 21, 1st half, (St. Petersburg, 1908), p. 7.
31. E. Golubinskii, *Istoriia russkoi tserkvi*, vol. 1, 1st half, (Moscow, 1901), p. 28.
32. *Istoricheskie sochineniia o Rossii XVI v.* (Moscow, 1983), p. 79.
33. Golubinskii, *Istoriia russkoi tserkvi*, vol. 1, 1st half, p. 30.
34. *Povest' vremennykh let, Izbornik* (Moscow, 1969), p. 31.
35. *Russkaia istoricheskaia biblioteka* (hereafter, *RIB*), vol. 6 (St. Petersburg, 1908), p. 191.
36. *Drevnerusskie kniazheskie ustavy XI–XV vv.* (Moscow, 1976), p. 169; *RIB*, pp. 8, 432, 599, 700, 717, 893.
37. "Stoglav," pp. 263–64.
38. *Istoricheskie zapiski*, 1942, vol. 13, pp. 88, 268.
39. *Istoriia russkoi arkhitektury* (Moscow, 1951), p. 64.
40. M. N. Tikhomirov, "Moskva i kul'turnoe razvitie russkogo naroda XIV–XVII vv.," *Voprosy istorii*, 1947, no. 9, p. 14.
41. L. A. Dintses, "Dokhristianskie khramy Rusi v svete pamiatnikov narodnogo iskusstva,"

Sovetskaia etnografiia, 1947, no. 2, p. 77.

42. I. M. Snegirev, *Russkie prostonarodnye prazdniki i suevernye obriady*, vol. 3 (Moscow, 1838), pp. 106–7.

43. G. S. Maslova, *Ornament russkoi narodnoi vyshivki kak istoriko-etnograficheskii istochnik* (Moscow, 1978), pp. 108, 141.

44. *PSRL*, vol. 6 (St. Petersburg, 1853), pp. 221, 233–34.

45. *Poslovitsy russkogo naroda. Sbornik V. Dalia* (Moscow, 1957), p. 906.

46. E. N. Kletnova, "Zapiska o metakh i znakakh sobstvennosti Viazemskogo uezda," *Etnograficheskoe obozrenie* (Moscow, 1916), no. 1–2, pp. 40–41.

47. D. K. Zelenin, "Tabu slov u narodov Vostochnoi Evropy i Severnoi Azii," *Sb. muzeia antropologii i etnografii*, vol. 8 (Leningrad, 1929), p. 118.

48. D. O. Sviatskii, "Ocherki istorii astronomii v Drevnei Rusi," pt. 1, *Istoriko-astronomicheskie issledovaniia* (Moscow, 1961), issue 7, p. 78.

49. Golubinskii, *Istoriia russkoi tserkvi*, vol. 1, 2nd half (Moscow, 1904), pp. 360–61.

50. *PSRL*, vol. 8 (St. Petersburg, 1859), pp. 202, 229, 235, 248, 256, 263, 265, 267, 284, etc.

51. S. I. Seleshnikov, *Istoriia kalendaria i khronologiia* (Moscow, 1970), p. 170; A. P. Pronshtein and V. Ia. Kiiashko, *Khronologiia* (Moscow, 1981), p. 86.

52. A. K. Leont'ev, "Nravy i obychai," *Ocherki russkoi kul'tury XVI v.*, pt. 2 (Moscow, 1977), p. 46.

53. M. O. Skripil', "Povest' o Petre i Fevronii Muromskikh i ee otnoshenie k russkoi skazke," *Tr. Otdela drevnerusskoi literatury*, vol. 7 (Moscow-Leningrad, 1949), p. 156.

54. Ibid., Texts, p. 233.

55. Ibid., Texts, pp. 237, 241.

56. Golubinskii, *Istoriia kanonizatsii sviatykh v russkoi tserkvi*, p. 141.

57. V. N. Basilov, "Sledy kul'ta umiraiushchego i voskresaiushchego bozhestva v khristianskoi i musul'manskoi agiologii," *Fol'klor i istoricheskaia etnografiia* (Moscow, 1983), pp. 118–48.

58. Fraser, *The Golden Bough*.

59. N. M. Vedernikova, *Russkaia narodnaia skazka* (Moscow, 1975), p. 26.

60. L. I. Ivina, *Vnutrennee osvoenie zemel' Rossii v XVI v.* (Leningrad, 1985), pp. 27–28, 233.

61. Iu. I. Iudin, "Russkaia narodnaia bytovaia skazka" (author's abstract of doctor of philology dissertation), (Leningrad, 1979), p. 24.

62. V. Ia. Propp, *Istoricheskie korni volshebnoi skazki* (Leningrad, 1946), pp. 51, 88, 213–23.

63. Vedernikova, *Russkaia narodnaia skazka*, p. 38.

64. *Narodnye russkie skazki A. N. Afanas'eva, V 3-kh tomakh*, vol. 2 (Moscow, 1957), p. 291.

65. E. Trubetskoi, *Inoe tsarstvo i ego iskateli v russkoi narodnoi skazke* (Moscow, 1922), p. 41.

66. B. A. Rybakov, "Prosveshchenie," *Ocherki russkoi kul'tury XIII–XV vv.*, pt. 2 (Moscow, 1970), p. 161.

67. Trubetskoi, *Inoe tsarstvo i ego iskateli v russkoi narodnoi skazke*, p. 45.

68. O. A. Gantskaia, N. N. Gratsianskaia, and S. A. Tokarev, "Zapadnye slaviane," *Kalendarnye obychai i obriady v stranakh zarubezhnoi Evropy. Zimnie prazdniki* (Moscow, 1973), p. 206.

69. L. Niderle, *Slavianskie drevnosti* (Moscow, 1956), p. 53.

70. I. U. Budovnits, *Monastyri na Rusi*, pp. 71, 117, 127, 151, 262–63, 266; E. Golubinskii, *Istoriia kanonizatsii sviatykh v russkoi tserkvi*, p. 142.

71. I. N. Grozdova, "Narody Britanskikh ostrovov," *Kalendarnye obychai i obriady v stranakh zarubezhnoi Evropy. Zimnie prazdniki*.

72. N. V. Shlygina, "Finny," *Kalendarnye obychai i obriady v stranakh zarubezhnoi Evropy. Vesennie prazdniki* (Moscow, 1977), p. 123.

73. N. A. Krasnovskaia, *Proiskhozhdenie i etnicheskaia istoriia sardintsev* (Moscow, 1986), p. 141.

74. N. K. Nikol'skii, "O drevnerusskom khristianstve," *Russkaia mysl'*, 1913, bk. 6, pp. 3–22.

Russian Folk Culture and Folk Religion

T. A. Bernshtam

A number of sciences in our time deal with Russian folk culture. All of them have their own research topic and their own perspective on both the given topic and culture as a whole. The volume of continually arriving new information is so huge that not only can we not assimilate it for personal and scholarly enrichment, but we cannot even keep track of the disappearance of the lacunae in the cultural heritage. It may be said that this heritage is growing "before our very eyes," and each discipline claims to be that "droplet of water" in which the entire world is reflected, i.e., to represent its domain of knowledge as the one that reflects most fully the folk spiritual values: the study of literature, folklore, art—from the icon paintings to practical folk arts, architecture, music. The outstanding successes in the study of the above fields of culture are familiar to every contemporary person interested in the history of their country, since a majority of the cultural testaments can be seen, read, or heard. Their anonymity and quantity are a testimony to their mass origin, born from the vigor of the people, while the masterpieces among them have become symbols of Russian culture, in which the artistic genius of the Russian people is particularly evident.

Yet the term "folk culture" is not subsumed by the totality of knowledge regarding exalted cultural symbols, no matter how vast. Historians of folk culture have treated this term in different ways—as the culture of the lower strata of society, as that of the "illiterate" lower strata and "unlettered" upper strata, or as something created by the elite and "bestowed" on the lower orders. These and other definitions have cognitive and investigative value only when viewed in proper historical context. In Russia (as, incidentally, in

Russian text © 1989 by "Nauka" Publishers and "Sovetskaia etnografiia." "Russkaia narodnaia kul'tura i narodnaia religiia," *Sovetskaia etnografiia*, 1989, no. 1, pp. 91–100. A publication of the Institute of Ethnography, USSR Academy of Sciences.

The article is based on a paper given by the author at the Twenty-first Scientific-Technical Conference "Ancient Russian Culture and Contemporary Musical Art (Commemorating the Millennial Anniversary of the Adoption of Christianity in Russia)," held on April 13, 1988, in Leningrad. The conference was organized by the Leningrad State Institute of Theater, Music, and Cinematography and the Leningrad State Conservatory.

a number of countries of Western Europe), the center of gravity of the socioeconomic life was the village, right up to the turn of the nineteenth century, even allowing for the full range of influence of the town culture, beginning in the Middle Ages.

Traditional peasant culture was formed, we know, on the basis of religious awareness, which was not only the spiritual "core," but also the spiritual fulfillment [*napolnenie*] of life, conditioning feelings for the world (the way of looking at and perceiving the world), ways of assimilating the sensual and the suprasensual, the emotional plane, and the moral code. Religious awareness did not divide life's experience or culture into profane (secular) and sacred aspects, so that we are justified in following A. Ia. Gurevich and equating the terms "folk culture" and "folk religion" (religiosity).[1]

In the nineteenth century, folk religion of the Russians was given two designations in scholarly and church circles, defining its essence as a synthesis of the Christian dogma and "pagan" beliefs—dual faith [*dvoeverie*] and customary orthodoxy [*bytovoi pravoslavie*] The term *dvoeverie* is still used to this day in scholarly works and is understood by certain scholars as a straightforward and rather formal, superficial blending of "dual faiths" in folk religion. In many general and particular investigations of Eastern Slavic religious beliefs, including the Russian, ethnographers' main interest is focused on "pagan survivals," their interpretation and the reconstruction of archaic forms, usually directly traceable to a proto-Slavic mythological source.[a] Such an approach is often determined by the conception that "paganism" comprises the greater and essential component of a folk system of beliefs, poorly and transparently covered over by Christianity, which has only to be "stripped away" to reveal pre-Christian archaism in almost "pure" form. In the best of cases, we subscribe to the conclusion of A. N. Veselovskii as to the constancy of myth-creating, thanks to the uniformity of the mental process which recreates similar forms at different historical times.[2] Interest in paganism and Eastern Slavic mythology is understandable, since there is still a notable backwardness in this field, as shown by the encyclopedia *Myths of the Peoples of the World* [Mify narodov mira]. At the same time, great harm is done to scholarship, especially Russian ethnography, by our biased attitude toward Christian culture, our lack of education in the history of Christianity, and by restrictions on making use of its enormous heritage of books and writings—from the first historians, the Old and the New Testament, to the theological literature. Without this, it is not possible to examine the phenomenon of Russian folk culture/religion as an integrated unity and equal blending of constituent worldviews—"paganism"[3] and Christianity.

I present the following discussion as an attempt at a *new* approach to the ethnographic study of folk culture/religion in view of the formation and development of both official Russian orthodoxy and the Christianity of the people.[4] I shall begin with historical generalizations as to the relationship between two processes of mass Christianization: *from the top*, the "teaching Church," and *from the bottom*, the "church of the flock." The two paths were inseparable from the beginning, although their relationship and the evolution of each were not the same during different periods.

1

Christianization took place in the course of Eastern Slavic ethnic history, a characteristic feature of which among the Russians was continual *migration*. During the period of the Ancient Russian State and after its demise, the European territory of the future Great Russian massif expanded. After the formation of the Russian state, there was active colonization of the north and east of Europe, including the lands along the Volga and the Urals, while in the late seventeenth century it passed beyond the Urals, into Siberia and the Far East. A vast number of indigenous peoples of Europe and Asia were drawn into this process and underwent Christianization. This fact alone was responsible for the many centuries' duration of Christianization and the continuing need to solve the highly *practical* problems that confronted the church until the very beginning of the twentieth century: temple [*khram*] building, parish organization, increasing priestly ranks, missionary activity, etc. All of this demanded proper spiritual preparedness, starting with the elementary education of priests and ministers, which the church was not in a position to provide.

The symbolic act of the "christening of Rus'" gave notice of the advent in the Christian world of fledgling nations who thus far had not realized the essence of the new religion, or what it meant to them. The ancient Russian church was also in a state of "birth" and had to cultivate and introduce the received religion in the difficult circumstances of the division of the Christian church into the Orthodox and the Catholic. Vladimir was presented with the Symbol of the Faith and the collection of dogmata and established truth as adopted by the Council of Nicaea/Constantinople, under the title of the "Orthodox rite."[5] The first dogma of Orthodoxy was the trinity of the deity, which was traced back to the New Testament tradition of the Epiphany and Christ's blessing of the apostles for universal proselytization (Matt. 28.16–20, Mark 16.15–18). The Orthodox church, unlike the Catholic, continued to hold unchanged the ancient dogma, which asserted that divine truth, so far as the essence of the teaching of the faith is concerned, is given in revelation and formulated by the *church* alone, whose authority is incontestable to the Christian. Thus, from the perspective of the upper strata, Christianization was to involve an adoption by the people of the Symbol of the Faith and the dogma as expounded by the church, which in turn would alter consciousness, moral behavior, and lifestyles. In order to introduce the Orthodox canon, the Russian church followed the ancient Christian technique: church worship, oral preaching and personal example (the ascetics, missionaries, monks), and the spread of Christian literature—the canonical code and the theology.

Let us consider how the situation developed in these three areas, especially during the first five centuries of Christianization, which laid the foundation for the specific nature of Russian Orthodoxy as a whole and its folk variants. Unfortunately, my sources are not sufficiently complete, and therefore I consider the following remarks to be tentative.

1. It is known that the period of feudal fragmentation corresponded to cult fragmentation. The centers of religious life were the courts of the princes and boyars, so that Christianization at first encompassed the population of the towns and large commercial settlements, where temples and monasteries were concentrated.

The Orthodox metropole received from Byzantium a minimum set of canons and material ritual "accoutrements"—books for public worship, including psalters (the Evangelium and Apostle-aprakos, the Minen, the Triode, the Breviary, etc.),[6] icons, vessels, and the like. The practice of ritual proper was not constant, but developed along with the church—certain rites would vanish and others appear. This was permissible since ritual was identified with neither the faith nor the dogma.[7]

The local churches were supposed to construct their worship on the model of the metropole, but it was here that the first impossibility of similarity appeared, giving rise to *disparities* between central and local Orthodox cults, since the individual churches arose at different times and were not identical in position, ability to acquire the necessary implements of worship, or stature of priests. In the best position, of course, were the town churches of the Russian princedoms (Kiev, Novgorod, Pskov, Vladimir, Suzdal'), where the metropolitan, the bishops, and the grand princes were initiators and participants in the development of church affairs.[8] From the late eleventh to the early twelfth century, the Russian church began to create its own pantheon of saints and relics, to commemorate events, to institute holidays, and to compose prayers, canons, and services for them. Thus, in the second version of the Prologue (copies from the twelfth to fourteenth centuries are known), in the section on holidays, proper "Russian" ones are now listed: the translation of the relics of Boris and Gleb, the memory of Feodosii Pecherskii, the Lives of Ol'ga, Vladimir, the Varangian Martyrs, Bishop Leontii Rostovskii, the coming of the apostle Andrew to Russia, the translation of the relics of Nikolai Mirlikiiskii.[9] The local churches, along with accepting these innovations (but occasionally not even knowing of them), created their own pantheons, consisting of saints, miraculous icons, and patrons; among the latter, a large place is held by the feudal lords (and their families). Closed worlds were formed of "our" faith, at war with the "foreign" faith of one's neighbors, by capture of icons, destruction and desecration of shrines, denial of the veracity of miracles, and so on. This was the epoch during which, in the words of the author of the Life of Prokopii Ustiuzhskii, "each land and town blesses and praises and boasts of its own wonder-workers."[10] In this epoch, the provincial versions of the Christian culture of the upper and lower strata, the common calendars, rites, and customs of church and secular life were formed. Local fragmentation was also increased by a lack of uniformity in the divine service (personnel, regulations, implements, and actions) and—even more so—by the unrefined nature of *personal religious rites*[b] for the populace, part of church "customary law" (even up to the twentieth century).[11] Customary law encompassed life-cycle rituals (baptism, matrimony, obsequies), domestic holiday celebrations, participation in village holidays and processions around fields and crossroads, and succor in natural disasters.[12] Many church customs in smaller towns sprang from popular forms and were organically incorporated into the people's ritual life. Only at the centers did the church try to define a canonical ritual performance "by Christian law." This did not have broad resonance at the time and remained within the confines of the metropole or the theology: for example, the questions of Kirik Novgorodets and the replies of the archbishop Novgorodskii Nifont as to the church law and rituals (twelfth century), the sermon of Petr, the metropolitan "of all Rus'," regarding the performance of the rites of baptism, marriage, etc. (fourteenth century).[13] We may add that comprehension of spoken or sung texts was the exception, and not just in peripheral areas: "uncomprehension" and learning "by ear" were universal (and continued to be observed in rural localities even in the nineteenth century).

2. While official Orthodoxy nonetheless endeavored to follow the canon, many representatives of the oral preaching—local priests, theologians, missionaries—made use of all Christian sources known to them in their sermons, a huge number of which at the time were comprised of *apocrypha*.[c] Given that oral preaching had great importance for the Christianization of the illiterate (upper and lower strata), and that the problem of Christian apocrypha is intimately connected with the "interface" between *oral* and *written* traditions, I shall hereafter consider them together.

From the beginning the Apocrypha were prime spiritual nourishment for peoples undergoing Christianization, although at different times and in differing milieux the term "apocryphos" was invested with different meaning, and different books were taken to be apocryphal. The apostles made use of Old Testament traditions and books not included in the Biblical canon, since they were written after the latter was formed; the apocalyptic book of Enoch was reflected in the Revelation of the Prophet John; the fathers and consecrators of the church called "holy" not only Biblical apocrypha with prefigurings of Christ (such as that of Melchizedek), but also ancient treatises foretelling the coming of the Messiah ("Sybilline Books") or containing his image ("Orpheus"). Apocrypha appeared very early among the Slavs, and their flourishing coincided with the rise of the Bogomil movement in the thirteenth century, which had great influence on Southern Slavic Christianization and penetrated into Russia. (The creation of a number of apocrypha is also ascribed to the Bogomils.)

In the twelfth to fifteenth centuries, a considerable number of copies of translated apocrypha and writings containing individual apocryphal stories were in circulation in the Russian world. The church could hardly find its bearings in this flood, much less control its spread. Not even the higher clergy and theologians were always able to distinguish canon from apocrypha, and combined them in their sermons, commentaries, prayers, and preachments. As the most striking examples, we mention the Epistle of Vasilii Kalika (archbishop of Novgorod) to Feodor, Lord of Tver', on the "earthly paradise" (cf. the apocryphos "On Macarius of Rome" with the same story)[14] and the establishment in the fifteenth century of a divine service honoring the Prophet Elijah on July 20 (on the basis of the apocrypha "Il'ia's Tale" depicting his ascent into the sky in a fiery chariot). Apocrypha stories were included in the *Palea, Chet'i-Minei, Khronograf,* and *Zhitiia,* which led to the appearance of stories of Russian origin[d] (the "Tale of Lazarus's Resurrection," the "Sermon of the Heavenly Forces," twelfth to thirteenth centuries).[15] Apocrypha were widely depicted in icon painting and miniatures—for example, the Life of the Virgin Mother in Snetogorsk monastery frescoes (thirteenth century), the "Tale of the Unicorn," in the Kiev Psalter of 1397, "Kitovras and Solomon," "Scenes from the Life of David," the "Descent into Hell," on the royal gates of Sofia Cathedral in Novgorod (mid-fourteenth century), and many others.

The deep penetration of the apocrypha into the written and pictorial culture of the Middle Ages is a testimony to their early and extensive oral distribution, as well as their power to leave a lasting impression. Thus, along with the "words of the false teachers," with the voices of the "zealots for the true faith" and the illustrious canonists such as Kirill of Turov, there were the sermons of Abraham of Smolensk, who used apocrypha in his prayers to summon rain during drought, and Moses, who spoke out against paganism "without quotations" from Holy Scripture.[16] Furthermore, the apocrypha (even for the church and the theologians) supplemented the basic lack of canonical literature, since the full corpus of New Testament books was translated into Church Slavonic much later, while the "liturgical types" of the Evangelium and the Apostle-aprakos (i.e., excerpts in the sequence of the calendar service) could only be acquired and transcribed by the large churches and monasteries (as we have already mentioned). Only a few Evangelium-aprakos are known from the eleventh and twelfth centuries: for Russia as a whole (Savva's Book, the Ostromir Evangelium) and for the provinces (Arkhangel'sk, Mstislav, Iur'evsk, Galich, Dobrilo). Later on, events from the Old and New Testament were included as separate cycles in the Chronograph and Chronicles, where they existed alongside historical events (such as the "History of the Hebrew War" of Josephus Flavius), apocrypha, the Conversations of the Fathers of the Church, the Hexameron, and so forth.[17] During this period, literature was accessible only to a narrow circle of educated people, its influence being felt only much later, with the development of printing, literacy, the advent of "popular pictures," and so on.

The distinctiveness of folk religion first appeared "in full measure" during church and state centralization in the fifteenth and sixteenth centuries. During this period, a gradually emerging gap between the "cultures" of the upper and the lower orders widened, and a dialogue or conflict began between them. The centralized church initiated a campaign to eradicate the "false" faith of the masses, whom it called "half-pagan." Church councils produced an increasing flood of sermons and pronouncements. None of this filtered down fully to the masses. Real Christianization remained the duty of the *local* (village or parish) church, which in terms of church building and officiant literacy and authority among the parishioners occupied an extremely low position throughout the vast majority of the Russian territory right up to the turn of the twentieth century.[e] Being part of the rural collectivity (the *obshchina* or parish), the village clergy willingly (or unwillingly) continued to take part in the creation of folk religion.

In the second half of the seventeenth century, Orthodox Christianization encountered serious obstacles in connection with the schism of the church and the conversion to the "Old Belief" (in its broad meaning) of a large number of the Russian and other ethnic populations. The Old Believers (of all persuasions) constituted a significant contingent of the settlers in the European and Asiatic regions, finding sympathy among local inhabitants. From this time onward (even until the twentieth century), the Orthodox missionary activity, especially in the North and in Siberia, had the goal of converting to the official church not only the "pagan peoples," but also the "Old Believer heretics," who possessed great zeal in the oral preaching of their ideas and an extremely well-developed written culture, combined with literacy, initiative, and internal consolidation.[18] The constantly arising Russian sects also grouped themselves around the Old Belief (especially the priestless sect).[19f]

Let us now turn to the Christianization "from the bottom."

2

Scholars now admit that no elaborate pagan religion with an "institution" of priests [*zhretsy*] took shape among the Eastern Slavic tribes. One reason for this was the fragmentation of the tribal communities, constantly moving through Eastern Europe. The vast bulk of the Eastern Slavs were christianized (after the fall of the Ancient Russian State) within the Russian princedoms, as we have already mentioned above. In the thirteenth to fifteenth centuries, the princedoms were gradually broken up into appanages. The princes needed men to colonize their domains and guaranteed newcomers the "freedom of resettlement" (otherwise none would have responded). The settlement of the appanages made progress, helped by the devastation of the central princedoms during the Mongol conquest, the extensive form of natural resources utilization, the "seminomadic" cultivation of the forest zone, and other factors.

Having founded his church, Vladimir issued no legislation as to its possessions, rights, legal, or other functions; the "Statutes" [Ustavy] ascribed to him and Iaroslav belong, in the opinion of scholars (including church scholars),[20] to the fourteenth century. As new bishoprics were founded, the local princes endowed them with lands and granted them charters; among the early privileges of the church was the right to invite settlers to their lands, and the exemption of the clergy and their workers from taxes and service. The khans of the Golden Horde confirmed all rights of the church with written decrees [iarlyki]. All of this undoubtedly attracted colonists to the church and monastery lands. During the thirteenth to the sixteenth centuries, the church and monastery possessions increased with amazing speed, which gave rise to opposition not only from the state, but also within the church.

In mentioning these familiar historical facts, I wish to point out the following. In the eleventh to fourteenth century, the *town* and *village* population of the princely *centers* (and their appanages), the church and the monastery holdings, became Christianized, i.e., were more or less brought into Christianity. This same population, in the fifteenth to seventeenth centuries, developed and settled the lands of the growing Russian state. The settlers brought with them Christianity in the local variants that had formed during the time of cult fragmentation, and the subsequent Christianization in the old and new places depended on specific ethnocultural and social factors, in the general context of statewide processes.

Two processes, *official* and *spontaneous*, continually interacted in the popular Christianization. But while prior to the formation of the Russian state this interaction brought together the "unlettered" upper and lower classes, after this time a separation occurred. And the spontaneous element prevailed among the settlers, who in the fifteenth to seventeenth centuries organized religious life in the new towns with their own hands and according to their own "Christian understanding": building chapels or temples, choosing those to lead services and administer personal rites, and celebrating their church holidays selectively. The parish clergy who subsequently came here on occasion had to deal with this independently organized church and religious order. People came to the church from hundreds of *versts* away to be baptized and, at the same time, anointed with the last rite (there are many accounts of this by the clerics of the towns, even in the early twentieth century).[21] Thus, cult fragmentation, the low stature of the local church, the varying nature of the Christian "documents" and their commentaries, the different times and extent of Christianization of the lower classes gave rise to extremely diverse Christian ideas, which were not just incorporated into the archaic system of belief, but actively *influenced* it, forming local and regional peculiarities of the folk religion.

The multiplicity of folk religion forms is not the only consequence of Christianization during the first five centuries. In the words of B. D. Grekov, there was a *"Russification* [my emphasis— T.B.] of the Christian faith and church," which began very early and moved in two directions: the struggle for their own national church organization among the upper classes and the struggle for their own folk beliefs among the masses; "both tendencies ultimately led to a single result."[22] On the national level, this was expressed, by the turn of the seventeenth century, in the formation of a Russian *self-consciousness*, in an identification of the terms *Russian* and *Orthodox*—not only in their Russian-speaking milieu but also in that of other Christianized peoples (for example, in Karelia).

This spiritual outcome warrants identification of the preceding period as the *first stage* of Russian Christianization (with due regard to its internal structure), distinguished by the prevalence of *apocryphal phenomena* in the Christian faith assimilated by the upper and the lower classes, at least until the turn of the sixteenth century. Apocrypha (as we briefly demonstrated) also lay at the foundation of the Orthodox faith itself, as revealed by the well-known lamentable history of the correction of the liturgical books in the sixteenth and seventeenth centuries, when the elders of Afonsk burned the Moscow books "with heresies" and canonical books were brought in by order of Nikon for a new translation. The important role of the apocrypha in the foundation of Orthodoxy is not peculiar to Russian Christianization alone: this norm was repeated at the initial stage of any mass Christianization at all times and among all peoples (for example, witness the struggle with the "heresies" in the Acts of the Apostles and the Epistles of Paul). Christianity as an ideology brought about a revolution in the pagan world: it rejected state and tribal boundaries, proclaimed the equality of people, and spoke of the worth of the human being; "liberation of the person was understood as a moral perfecting, the establishment of a personal connection with God and personal responsibility for sins."[23] As shown by the history of Christianity and the church, these ideals always conflicted with socio-economic processes, with state and national self-determination. The problems of socialization, as well as the determination of its position under the formation of the states and nations, became of paramount importance to the church, and it allowed the "flock" a chance to determine for themselves a hierarchy of spiritual values in Christian teaching. The objective role of Christianization in the course of the ethnic history of the Russian people was to enable *spiritual* formation as a communal entity (*sobornaia lichnost'* in the words of F. M. Dostoevsky), i.e., it should have led, ideally, to a new level of collective (social) consciousness. Yet despite its conviction in the effective force of the Christian teaching, the early church had no realistic way of influencing the archaic collective consciousness. And in this situation, spontaneous help was supplied by "apocryphal Christianity," in which (thanks to its half-pagan, half-Christian nature) there were from the outset chances of appealing not only to the individual, but also to the collective consciousness. In other words, the apocrypha performed the role of a *transitional* link in the process of Christianization, if we may express ourselves thus, in the changing of the *stereotype* of the collective worldview. And from this standpoint, it is hard to overvalue the importance of the apocrypha during the initial stage of Russian Christianization and in the formation of the folk culture (or that of any other people, incidentally).

From the turn of the eighteenth century it is customary to date a new stage of Christianization, clandestinely maturing in the preceding centuries, yet only publicly announcing itself after the schism in the church. With the subsequent spread of the Old Belief among a broad spectrum of people, the Christian denomination split, so to speak, into "two beliefs." There was a paradoxical contradiction between what the terms and subjective content of "old and new belief" meant to the ideologues of the oppositions and what their objective meaning was on the level of folk Christianization and changes in the cultural order. The "New Belief," to the population who had remained loyal to Orthodoxy, was basically restricted to mere changes in the "liturgy," for which (however) the church blamed the adherents of the Old Belief. But to the latter, the conflict in liturgy was only an external cause, giving expression to deep spiritual aspirations, testifying, incidentally, to the growth in *Christian* collective consciousness: an active interest in the canonical and liturgical literature, an independent thinking about early Christian ideas and symbolism, an aspiration for moral improvement and literacy for all community members, so as to achieve total understanding of the nature of Christ and his teaching. The very term "spirituality" took on special meaning among the Old Believers, as revealed by the recognition of their own faith as "spiritual," in contrast to the "worldly," "bureaucratic," and "townspeople" faith of the Orthodox Christians.[24] Not being homogeneous, the Old Belief in large measure helped the development of dissident thought [*inakomyslie*] in Russian Christianity, captivating in the eighteenth and nineteenth century considerable numbers of the formerly Orthodox population, primarily along the Volga, in the central and southern provinces. Eyewitness accounts speak of the dominant popularity of the priestless sect and the "Dukhobors,"[25] which satisfied people's demand for "spiritual nourishment," which a church long since removed from the people could not provide.[g]

Summarizing the foregoing, it may be said that a *second stage* of Christianization *shattered* the idea of the church and the upper classes with respect to Orthodox unity and revealed its fluidity and evolution into a "multifaith" [*mnogoverie*], including the development of a higher level of Orthodoxy itself. These changes greatly influenced the folk culture and the previously developed forms of pagan-Christian syncretism. Obviously, in view of this picture, it is no longer advisable to employ the learned terms "dual faith" and "customary Orthodoxy"; rather, investigations of folk religion within the entire Russian bloc will have to be conducted by studying the Old Believer and sectarian groups, attested in Russia since the seventeenth century.[26]

The second stage, strictly speaking, also brought out the role played by the apocrypha in the folk Christianization of the preceding centuries, as well as its further evolution and its relationship with the canonical codex, which became accessible to the broad masses after the development of printing, literacy, and creation of "books for the people," as well as the broad dispersal of the manuscript tradition. The "purification" of the Orthodox teachings, accompanied by complete and accurate translation of the canonical books (including the liturgical ones) and development of theological literature and printing, was inseparably connected with the declaration of ongoing lists of apocryphal content and compilations of indexes of "banned or renounced" literature. These indexes were continually updated, and the Ecclesiastical Regulations of the eighteenth century already contained more than 100 titles of various manuscripts from different periods. The dismal reputation for the apocrypha in the eyes of official Orthodoxy was created mainly by so-called "superstitious books," of which a multitude eventually appeared in Russia, with a very heterogenous composition: from compilations of ancient cosmogonic/astrological ideas and magical lore to works of the lowest "mass consumption." The superstitious books were both translations and Russian productions; the latter variety also reflected the stages of Christianization, since magic, animism, and the like, appear in them, blended with apocryphal stories and motifs (the various *lunniki, koliadniki*, etc.).[h] The close interaction of such literature with the apocryphal and popular archaic ideas led to those popular beliefs existing in the manuscript traditions— eventually being placed on the lists of "false teachings": the collections of charms, prayers, folk medicine (herbals), mythological fables (such as those about shape changers), and so forth.

The Christian self-awareness of the Old Believers was also nourished by the traditional canon and, to an even greater extent, the apocrypha, which underwent a cleansing in this setting, similar to that of the Orthodox teaching in the church: thus, it is curious that both the church and the Old Belief were unanimously intolerant (although from different perspectives) with respect to magic and sorcery, holding (in particular) that charms [*zagovory*] were a major sin.[27] The dominant personal religious-ethical aspect in the Christian worldview of the Old Believers increased the importance of the ideas of retribution and redemption, the fleeting nature of existence and responsibility for sin, which were reflected in the different kinds of eschatological writings, graphic culture, and religious verse.

Religious verse is a remarkable and little-studied phenomenon of Russian Christian culture. Its origins are lost far back in the centuries, yet it is evident that religious verse was born as a cross between oral and written traditions of paganism and Christianity (as were the apocryphal legends, mystery plays, etc.). In the course of its evolution, the forms, kinds, and themes of religious verse changed, making it a sort of "mirror" of the continuing Christianization of the folk culture/religion—from the verse of epic (*byliny*, apocrypha) and ritualistic (charms and prayers, "yuletide" wishes, moon calendars) genre to the hymns (such as the "Evangelical Song").[28] The significance of Russian religious verse is clearly attested by the "Poem of the Book of the Dove" [Stikh o Golubinoi(Glubinnoi) Knige], a work that V. N. Toporov has called "an encyclopedic compendium of the mythopoetic cosmology from the time of the creation until the beginning of the fall of Holy Russia."[29] Its composers believed in the existence of this "Book," that it was preserved in "Old Jerusalem," and identified it with the Psalter or attributed its authorship to Jesus Christ, one of the prophets or apostles.[30] The recently proposed interpretation (by A. A. Arkhipov) of the title "Golubinaia Book" as a translation of the word "Pentateuch"[31] basically addresses the tendency toward creation of a Russian "Holy Scripture" in the oral tradition—a testimony to the particular outcome and independence of popular Christianization.[i] The social category of the transmitters of religious verse— wandering minstrels, beggars, "itinerant cripples"—and the content of the verse itself in the "older texts" (such as the "One and Forty Minstrels") reveal the existence of yet another aspect of the Christianization of the people (already mentioned at the outset)—its dissemination in the course of continual movement, whether it be pilgrimage to the holy places, colonization, or the later "wandering Rus'."

Editor's notes

a. An example is V. Ia. Propp, "The Historical Bases of Some Russian Religious Festivals," in *Introduction to Soviet Ethnography*, eds. Stephen P. Dunn and Ethel Dunn (Berkeley: Highgate Road Social Science Research Station, 1974), pp. 367–410. Propp's structuralism is different from that of Claude Lévi-Strauss (e.g., *The Raw and the Cooked: Introduction to a Science of Mythology* [New York: Harper & Row, 1975]) in that he searches for European archaic roots rather than universals.

b. The italicized term is *chastnyi treb*, a rite required for personal special occasions—what in the anthropological literature is called life crisis (or life passage) ritual.

c. For apocrypha see Serge A. Zenkovsky, ed., *Medieval Russia's Epics, Chronicles and Tales* (New York: Dutton, 1974), pp. 153–66.

d. These are Old Testament, Martyrologue, Chronicle, and Saints' Lives sources. See George P. Fedotov, *The Russian Religious Mind: Kievan Christianity* (New York: Harper & Row, 1960), pp. 42, 389.

e. On the life and history of the rural clergy, see Gregory L. Freeze, *The Parish Clergy in the Nineteenth Century: Crisis, Reform, and Counter-Reform* (Princeton: Princeton University Press, 1983), *The Russian Levites: Parish Clergy in the Eighteenth Century* (Cambridge: Harvard University Press, 1977); and Jack Edward Kollmann, "The *Stoglav* Council and Parish Priests," *Russian History*, 1980, vol. 7, nos. 1–2, pp. 65–91. For an atheism-oriented collection of anti-priest folklore, see V. P. Vilchinsky, ed., *Russkoe narodno-poeticheskoe tvorchestvo protiv tserkvi i religii* (Moscow-Leningrad: Nauka, 1961).

f. See also Serge A. Zenkovsky, *Russkoe staroobriadchestvo: Dukhovnye dvizheniia semnadtsatogo veka* (Munich: Wilhelm Fink, 1970); N. A. Kazakova and Ia. S. Lur'e, *Antifeodal'nye ereticheskie dvizheniia na Rusi XIV–nachala XVI veka* (Moscow: Nauka, 1955); A. I. Klibanov, *Reformatsionnye dvizheniia v Rossii v XIV–pervoi polovine XVI vv.* (Moscow: Nauka, 1960); idem, "Fifty Years of Scientific Study of Religious Sectarianism," *Soviet Sociology*, 1970, vol. 8, nos. 3–4, pp. 239–78; idem, *History of Religious Sectarianism in Russia (1860s–1917)*, trans. Ethel Dunn, ed. Stephen Dunn (Oxford: Pergamon, 1982); Robert O. Crummey, *The Old Believers and the World of Antichrist* (Madison: University of Wisconsin, 1970).

g. *Dukhobor*, literally meaning fighter for the spirit, refers to one of the sects that was Protestant in orientation. Many Dukhobortsy fled to communities in Siberia, or moved to Canada.

h. *Lunniki* were guides to the phases of the moon, sometimes used by folk curers as guides for when to gather medicinal herbs. *Koliadniki* were caroling books associated with the New Year and Christmas holidays, when singers customarily went door-to-door singing for money, food, and good cheer.

i. The *Pentateuch* refers to the first five books of the Old Testament. It was used, in forms such as the *Golubinaia Book*, as a guide for traveling, often impoverished, minstrels of religious and secular verse. See V. I. Dal', *Tol'kovyi slovar' zhivogo velikorusskogo iazyka* (Moscow: Russkii iazyk, 1978 [original 1863–66]).

Notes

1. A. Ia. Gurevich, "Ved'ma v derevne i pred sudom (narodnaia i uchenaia traditsii v ponimanii magii)," *Iazyki kul'tury i problemy perevodimosti* (Moscow, 1987), pp. 25–26.

2. A. N. Veselovskii, "Zametki i somneniia o sravnitel'nom izuchenii srednevekovogo eposa," *Sobranie sochineniia* (Moscow-Leningrad, 1938), vol. 16, pp. 10–12.

3. By "paganism" I mean the stratum of ideas of non-Christian origin or archaic forms of syncretism.

4. Special aspects in the Christianization of the Ukrainian and Belorussian people require an independent investigation.

5. In the Eastern church, the contemporary meaning was "teaching, exposition of the faith"; the word "symbol" came later, from the West.

6. These books are known from the eleventh to thirteenth centuries (*Slovar' knizhnikov i knizhnosti Drevnei Rusi*, vol. 1, eleventh century to first half of thirteenth century [Leningrad, 1987], p. 98; hereafter *Slovar'*).

7. See (Reverend) S. Markov, *O prave tserkvi izmeniat' tserkovnye postanovleniia, obriady i obychai, sushchestva very ne kasaiushchiesia* (Moscow, 1901).

8. In the eleventh to fourteenth centuries, services and sermons were written and liturgical books transcribed by the metropolitans Kiprian, Ioann, Maksim, the bishops Ioann and Leontii of Rostov, Vasilii of Novgorod, Serapion of Vladimir, the grand princes Andrei Bogoliubskii, Vladimir Vasil'kovich Volynskii (*Slovar'*, pp. 37, 95, 98, 159, 164, 206, 211, 254, 387–90).

9. *Slovar'*, pp. 377–78.

10. N. M. Nikol'skii, *Istoriia russkoi tserkvi*, 3rd ed. (Moscow, 1983), p. 53.

11. *Entsiklopedicheskii slovar'*, eds. F. A. Brokgauz and I. A. Efron, vol. 24-a, pp. 914–15

(customary law of the church).

12. Thus, e.g., the medieval custom of singing praise in all houses and on all holidays (not just on Christmas) was retained in many places after its abolition by Peter I.

13. *Slovar'*, pp. 215–16, 281, 328.

14. Apocrypha of the fourteenth century in the "forbidden books" (*Slovar'*, pp. 42, 95).

15. Ibid., pp. 428–31.

16. Ibid., p. 257.

17. There were also complete translations of the books of the Bible: Genesis, Leviticus, Numbers, Deuteronomy, Judges, Ruth, Kings 1–4 in the Archival (fifteenth century) and Vilenski (sixteenth) Chronograph; both copies can be traced back to the thirteenth century (*Slovar'*, pp. 475–77).

18. "The individual communities of Dissenters are in constant communication with each other: for this, they have their own post service, language, numbers, even 'police force'. . . . The sectarian communities organize councils and congresses" (A. S. Prugavin, *Raskol i sektantstvo v russkoi narodnoi zhizni* [Moscow, 1905], p. 54).

19. Ibid., pp. 79–80.

20. See, e.g., N. Suvorov, *Kurs tserkovnogo prava*, vol. 1 (Iaroslavl', 1889).

21. In place of the newborn it was possible to "baptize" an object that symbolized the child, such as the father's headgear (regarding one such case see M. G., "Dorozhnye zametki," *Olonetsk. gub. vedom.*, 1868, no. 23–24).

22. B. D. Grekov, *Kievskaia Rus'* (Moscow, 1953), p. 392.

23. S. I. Kovalev, *Proiskhozhdenie khristianstva: osnovnye voprosy* (Moscow-Leningrad, 1964), p. 47.

24. One member of the priestless sect told I. S. Aksakov, who was studying the "schism" in Iaroslavl' province: "Your Orthodox faith is a bureaucrat's faith, a townsman's faith, not based on living, sincere conviction, but serving as one of the arms of the government to maintain order" (see Prugavin, p. 18).

25. Ibid., pp. 64–65.

26. (Archpriest) T. I. Butkevich, *Obzor russkikh sekt i ikh tolkov* (Khar'kov, 1910), pp. 18–21; for example, the Khlysty in Vladimir province.

27. S. E. Nikitina, "Zhanr zagovora v narodnom predstavlenii," *Etnolingvistika teksta: semiotika malykh form fol'klora*, 1, *Tez. v predvaritel'nye materialy k simpoziumu* (Moscow, 1988), pp. 25–26.

28. P. Bezsonov, *Kaliki perekhozhie*, I, 1–3 (Moscow, 1861).

29. V. N. Toporov, " 'Golubinaia Kniga' i 'K ploti': sostav mira i ego raspad," *Etnolingvistika teksta*, pp. 169–74.

30. Bezsonov, no. 76–92.

31. A. A. Arkhipov, "K istolkovaniiu nazvaniia 'Golubinaia kniga,' " *Etnolingvistika teksta*, pp. 174–77.

Forms of Transformation
of Pagan Symbolism
in the Old Believer Tradition

N. N. Veletskaia

Since our subject is the genetic derivation of surviving forms of pagan rituals and the transformation of early symbolism preserved in the Old Believer tradition, it is appropriate to single out from the complicated, prolonged, and dramatic history of the Old Belief those aspects that influenced the restoration and preservation of rudimentary forms of pagan ideas and cults.

The Sermon of Nil Sorskii and his followers had considerable impact on the Old Believers' doctrine and the lifestyle of the adherents of the old piety. On the far bank of the Volga, not far from the Kirill Belozersk Monastery, in the hermitage created by Nil Sorskii, the *zavolzhskie startsy*, or elders, stubbornly preached the old Christian commandments in the first half of the fourteenth century, attacking the dogmatic tendencies of the national state church advocates. The essence of their teaching came down to the following: " . . . there is much written, but not all is God's work: that which is, are God's commandments, most teachings of the Fathers, but only some human customs." In the thinking of the Old Belief ideologues, the written word must be treated critically (only the Evangel and the Apostle were exempt from criticism).

The *zavolzhskie startsy* were consistent advocates of separation of church and state, each to be independent of the other. "The prince has no reason to consult with monks," or with "those who have died" to the world, yet neither should the church have to obey the world: the shepherds should not "be frightened of power," they should calmly stand for the truth, since "holiness is greater than tsardom," and the secular ruler is not the judge in religious matters. Faith is the personal affair of each person's conscience, and therefore a secular power has no right to persecute religious convictions. To

Russian text © 1987 by "Nauka" Publishers. "Formy transformatsii iazycheskoi simvoliki v staroobriadcheskoi traditsii," in *Traditsionnye obriady i iskusstvo russkogo i korennykh narodov Sibiri*, edited by by L. M. Rusakova and N. A. Minenko (Novosibirsk: Nauka, 1987), pp. 78–99. A publication of the Institute of History, Philology, and Philosophy, Siberian Division, USSR Academy of Sciences.

judge the righteous and the guilty is not the duty of the church, which should act through conviction and prayer. Neither the splendor of the church nor expensive icons and adornments constitute a blessing, but "spiritual acts." True followers of Christ must work with their own hands, monasteries should not own property, and monks should be "poor and humble" [*nestiazhateli*].

The ideas of the *nestiazhateli*, which in large measure declared the inviolability of the old Russian pillars of the church, and which had religious and secular authority in the sixteenth century, were condemned as schismatic in the seventeenth century. Of course, the religious and ethical doctrine of the *nestiazhateli* also underwent various transformations in the Old Belief. First and foremost, this involved the very concept of poverty; the monasteries [*skity*] of the Old Believers, as we learn from the eloquent descriptions of P. Mel'nikov-Pecherskii,[1] for example, became owners of great wealth, and the way of life in most of them quickly left the ascetic ideal far behind. But the basic doctrines of *nestiazhatel'stva* (firm following of one's convictions and moral principles founded on the ancient Christian teaching; the idea that perfection of the soul was more important than the value of life; great interest in old manuscripts and the desire to understand their inner meaning and not simply accept the written word without thought; to live by one's own efforts, not becoming wealthy at another's expense) played an important role in the formation of the Old Believers' worldview.

One of the extreme forms of expression of the firm following of religious principles and disregard of secular authority was self-immolation. "Death by fire" reached an acme in the second half of the 1680s, as a result of the ukase of Empress Sofia in 1684 (which in fact presented the adherents of the "old piety" with a choice between self-immolation and burning at the stake). Many thousands were burned along with the preachers of "death by one's own hand" in the conflagration of houses, barns, and specially built frameworks, until the early 1690s, when persecution of the Old Belief ceased to be the dominant internal policy, thanks to a change of rulers.[a]

To be sure, the claim that there was only one possible outcome in the struggle against the official church—"into the fire or into the water"—could not go unchallenged even among Old Believers. A clear expression of this was the "Repudiation of the Newly Invented Path of Death by Suicide," written by the elder Evfrosin in 1691.[2] From this and the writings of his contemporaries[3] it becomes evident that old prejudices had been reborn in new forms in the Old Believer movement. To the ancient beliefs (surviving until the seventeenth century) of the cleansing force of fire, against which not even the most stringent and enduring penance [*epitimiia*] could prevail, were joined the Christian beliefs about the end of the world, when a river of fire would flow and nothing would escape its flames. It is not entirely clear how the Old Belief came to the dogmatic conclusion that the true disciples of the "old piety," in sacrificing themselves to fire, would be redeemed from the flames of hell. The genetic roots of this phenomenon go back to the old Indo-European belief in an eternal round of metamorphoses, in which future transformations are dependent on earthly existence, especially its most recent period. But the main factor, apparently, which governed reincarnation in higher forms, was firmness in adherence to established principles of existence and uplifting the soul and intellect at the moment of passing from life. It is this that caused ancient Hindus to enter the flames of the funeral pyre, and these same beliefs sustained the ancient tradition of escaping to "another world" during the Middle Ages.[4] Among Old Believers, the tradition of self-immolation also flared up at later times, but no longer in such mass forms.[b] Self-immolation was primarily a local or even isolated phenomenon, generally being connected with an Old Believer reaction against renewed persecutions. At the same time, there was a marked and growing tendency toward proliferation of "runaways," "wanderer-pilgrims," and "hermits."

The Old Believer self-immolations are rather well known, but other forms of "escaping to the other world" are poorly and quite fragmentarily represented in the sources. This topic deserves not only historical but also ethnographic study. As a matter of fact, we have almost no ethnographic studies of the Russian Schism. This situation was pointed out by V. Bogdanov[5] in the early twentieth century, and since then little has changed.

The "glorious death" [literally "Red Death"] in its genetic roots is a particularly archaic phenonemon, of which death by fire is one form. This term is also used to designate other forms of self-willed death—smothering with a red pillow, entombing, or starvation. A forty-day fast in the forest could also end in death by starvation. Information about the "glorious death" is so sparse and random that no detailed examination of the phenomenon is possible, and it can be comprehended only in general outline.

First of all, let us note that Old Believers valued a voluntary death over a natural one. The explanation for this as an emulation of martyrdom[6] is somewhat limited. This may well be how Old Believers themselves saw the matter, but its roots should be sought in the ritual of "going to the other world." However meager the data on the "glorious death," comparison of it with the ritual of dispatching someone to the "other world" among the Slavs and other peoples of Europe leads to the conclusion that the "glorious death" is a rudimentary form of a protoslavonic ritual of sending someone to the world beyond. It is of note that the "glorious death" is a remnant of an early stage of certain other ritual forms known among the Slavs, such as "putting someone on the bast" ("on the sled"), or the Southern Slavonic forms of going into the deep forest, being hit on the head, being placed in a barrel covered with felt, etc.[7] All such residual forms resembled the enactment of an age-old barbaric custom, where the victim displayed not voluntary motivation but compulsory obedience. The "glorious death" is closer to the ancient Indo-European form of ascending the funeral pyre.

The basic elements of the "glorious death" resemble the custom of voluntary death among the smaller nationalities of the North. This applies, first of all, to the very understanding of it. Those undertaking this step were revered as ancestor-protectors of the family, such a death being considered above a natural death, and the burial of those dying a voluntary death followed a more archaic custom, with observance of an elaborate ritual.[8]

An important element in the "glorious death" is that the individual making the decision to go to the "other world" should not lay hands upon himself. "What is required on his part is the firmness to take the last step, but the forces of nature or the hand of another person should do the rest."[9] Here again are analogies with the ritual of the smaller nationalities of the North (where those willingly parting with earthly existence were pierced with a spear or arrow, stabbed with a knife, strangled with a belt, or buried alive) and the residual forms of the ritual of dispatching someone to the "other world" among Slavs, especially burying old men alive or abandoning them in the deep forest.[10]

The "glorious death" exemplifies degeneration of the ritual of dispatching to the "other world," which also characterizes the other surviving forms known among the Slavs. However, certain elements place the "glorious death" in the distant pagan past. This concerns not just self-immolation, where analogies with the ancient Indo-European form of the ritual for cosmic travel to gods and deified ancestors remain valid despite layers of stratification. Such elements are also discerned in the smothering with a red pillow—the performance of the main event by the son, another relative, or the "strangler," and the use of the color red in the ritual. A degeneration of the pagan ritual is clearly seen in the fact that a daughter also could perform the rite.[c]

Information about "stranglers" that may be obtained from twentieth-century materials is so meager that it is hard to form a clear impression of these individuals. All that may be gleaned is that stranglers differed greatly in their way of life from Old Believer "elders," "priests," and "preceptors," who adhered to strict ritual and moral norms. The existence of a special officiant takes the genetic roots of the "strangler" back to pagan magicians [*volkhvy*], who performed ritual acts. Rudimentary forms of the dispatching ritual in traditional calendrical ceremonies indicate a paramount role for the magician in the pagan dispatching ritual, an indirect confirmation of which is found in medieval written sources.[11]

The color of the cushion used for suffocation is a vital and revealing element. The symbolism of the color red, associated with fire and the deified Cosmos, indicates the direction of the action itself—that of dispatching someone to cosmic ancestors. A link to such deified Cosmos ritual symbolism is indicated by analogy with the red color of the caftans worn by the "elders" of the Bukhtarminsk Old Believers when performing mass on major holidays.[12] Since records of "glorious death" by suffocation with a red cushion refer to a later time, it may be that this form of "going to the other world" is a comparatively later one, an "easier" substitute for self-immolation. This assumption is probable in view of evidence that the burning of a wife alive on a husband's funeral pyre was replaced, in pre-Christian times, by first strangling the wife.[13]

In view of the foregoing remarks on the symbolism and function of the red cushion, it is hard to agree with the statement of D. K. Zelenin: "The red cushion was most likely a simple sound association with the 'Red Death.' "[14] The symbolic essence of ritual actions plays a crucial role in folk tradition: the red color of the cushion indicates the direction of the action. It seems likely that the very designation of Red Death is more ancient than its attribute—the red cushion—and echoes or perhaps preserves its ancient title. Based on the connotation of the Russian word for "red" [*krasnyi*] (meaning wonderful, superb, excellent),[15] it may be surmised that the term "Red Death" involves the idea of the willing relinquishing of life as a better and higher form of crossing over to the "other world," where higher forms of the new life have been made ready for the soul as a consequence of this act. It may be that echoes of this ritual are preserved in such sayings as "Even death is good [*krasna*] in this world"; "Life is merry, death splendid [*krasno*]";[16] just as the ritual of dispatching to the "other world" may be reflected in such proverbs as "He placed his father on the bast [*lub*], and expects the same for himself"; "We do not live for joy, and there is none to dispirit us"; "Thou art living in a different age, it is time to 'bast' [*lobanit'*] thee," and others.[17]

In fact, the preservation of the Old Russian stratum among the Old Believers makes one consider the meaning of *kras'nyi—kras"—kres"* in Old Russian. *Kras'nyi*, along with its primary meaning of "excellent," was also analogous to *kresnyi*, just as *kras"* [beauty] was used in place of *kres"*, while *kres"* also had the meaning of the "turning of the sun."[18] Since the performance of the ritual of dispatching to the "other world" in the pagan ceremonial was associated with a definite change in solar inclination, turning "into summer" or "into winter,"[19] it may be surmised that the term "Red Death" connotes forms more ancient than those occurring under this title among Old Believers. In all likelihood, most residual forms of "going to the other world" among the Old Believers reflected back to the pagan ritual of dispatching someone to deified ancestors as an element of a [calendrical] ritual complex.

The ritual of sending someone to the "other world" also found a reflection in the archaic forms of burial practiced by the Old Believers, especially burials in forests. Along with small graveyards in forests on the other side of the Volga, there were also isolated graves, located beneath a huge pine tree or next to an isolated forest spring [*kliuchik*]. Such graves with Old Believer tombmarkers, in the form of massive tall crosses or chapels [*chasovenki*], were also found in the woods around the Holy Lake (Svetloiar), famed in the legend of the sunken city Kitezh, and in the dense forests of the former Kostromsk Province and those of the Russian North, as well as other places of Old Believer settlement. This form is a transformation of the previous custom of abandoning old people in the forest beneath a tree.

Another surviving form of the pagan ritual of sending someone to the "other world" is the bog burial. Thus, certain groups of flagellants [*khlysty*] practiced burial in a swamp without digging a grave, shrouding the deceased in new homespun cloth [*novina*].[20] In this connection, the findings of Danish archeologists, who discovered the remains of people who had been buried alive in bogs, are of great interest.[21]

And finally, the schismatics of the Kalagur sect threw corpses into a lake.[22] Such burial goes back to the pagan custom of dispatching human mediators to the deified Cosmos in rituals of mediation with the forces of nature.[23] The throwing of corpses into a bog, a lake, or other bodies of water, as well as the sinking of a boat in the sea by the Lusatian Serbs, is a residual form of this ritual; such kinds of burial are related by certain elements to the ritual of dispatching mediators to the deified ancestors and are the result of transformation of the ritual.[24]

The archaic lexicon reveals that the word for death among Bukhtarminsk Old Believers—*navalit'sia*[25]—is apparently derived from *navalki*, that which is heaped or piled up by someone.[26] It evokes an association with the red cushion used in the Red Death; the significance of the expression is its reflection of what is involved in the event. It is similar to the word for death in the former Smolensk Province (*zalivnai*, "a pouring or spreading upon"), which preserves echoes of the ritual of sending someone to the "other world" (correlate this with bog burials occurring in Belorussia),[27] as well as the archaic *oprudit'*, to deprive of life [*prud* = pond].

In connection with the latter example, we should mention the Old Believer ritual performances at Lake Svetloiar. Enough relevant literature discusses the legend of the "Kitezh chronicler," Old Believer pilgrimages to this lake and their prayers, that this deserves special investigation. Yet the nature of the lake cult remains an open question. Without entering the debate, the most significant elements of this Old Believer cult can be described.

The clear lake is surrounded by tall hills (sometimes called mountains), and the shore is low only in one spot. The people think it is bottomless (recent efforts by scuba divers to reach the bottom in the deepest places have not succeeded). Its water does not putrefy even when kept for the longest time in ordinary conditions. It is considered sacred and curative, and pilgrims take it away with them. The shoreline ("mountains") is pitted with "holes" dug by hermits who have withdrawn from the world, and are rimmed with "chapels," or tombmarkers of the Old Believers interred here. On the summit of the tallest hill stood an Old Believer chapel where services were held. On the summit of another hill are three very old and large pines, growing close together as though springing from the same root and believed to be sacred. They were festooned with icons and pieces of cloth by pilgrims, who would perform a ritual procession around them with prayerful singing. The bark of one of them, believed to be curative, was scraped off near the root and taken away by one individual. The clear lake was considered the main shrine of the Volga Old Believers, and a pilgrimage to it was formerly undertaken on foot and with a vow.[d]

For us, Svetloiar is interesting because major ritual activities occurred on June 24 (Old Style). The Old Believer rituals were interwoven here with the calendrical [Ivan] Kupalo ceremonies. Pilgrims from the most diverse Old Belief persuasions congregated on the "mountains." At night, the Kupalo bonfires were lit. The main event was a ritual procession around the lake with candles and ritual singing at dawn, before the rising of the sun,[28] concluding with each pilgrim launching his candle on a board in the water. On the eve of Ivan Kupalo, the "mountains" seemed aflame with the bonfires and the entire lake shone with the fires of the candles floating on it. The Kupalo ceremony seems to have a genetic link with the ritual of sending someone to the "other world"[29] and the symbolism of sending a mediator to the forefathers in a *pomana* (one of the later varieties of transformation of the ritual of sending to the "other world"—sending a candle downstream in a ritual vessel).[30] Thus it may be conjectured that the ritual activities on June 24 were based on the ritual of sending mediators to the deified ancestors.[31]

The intertwining of pagan and Christian cult performances on Ivan's Day is in large measure understandable since the ancestor cult lay at the basis of both the activities associated with the Kitezh legend (concerning the invisible city and monastery of the Old Believer tradition), and the ritual of sending to the "other world." Of course, the pagan cult underwent transformation and was reinterpreted in the process of the origin and elaboration of the Christian tradition, but even so the events around the sacred Lake Svetoiar were imbued by the common folk with reverence for the ancestors concealed in the lake. Both the candles burning on the water and the offerings placed by the pilgrims in the chapels on the lake shore are essentially for remembrance of the dead. Perceived by those who performed them as an integral part of "the old piety of the Orthodox priesthood," these actions are quite important to understand a range of referential and symbolic rudiments in the proto-Slavic ritual.[e]

In studying archaic cultural phenomena whose roots go back to paganism, diversity must be acknowledged since restoration of pagan lifeways and rituals, and searches for true sources of the "olden piety of the Orthodox priesthood," took different forms among the Old Believers. While the return to old ways among educated city dwellers was primarily seen as a heightened interest in ancient manuscripts, monks living in hermitages went to extremes of self-torture in their efforts to instate the old monasticism. And manifestations of paganism in the ritual cycle occurred mainly among the peasantry. Here, it seems, there was not so much a restoration as a conservation of the old principles.

This conservation is explained not just by the desire to preserve as much as possible the old lifeways; a considerable part was also played by the isolation of the rural Old Believer groups and monasteries from the outside world. This was so not just for groups that settled far from the lines of communication on the fringes of the Russian North, Siberia, and the Far East; even in the heart of Russia the Old Believers dwelt in regions that were sometimes literally cut off from the surrounding population of Slavs and other peoples by impenetrable forests, swampy marshland, and steep cliffs. Over a lengthy period of time, their settlements closed in on themselves, virtually walled off from the outside world. It is not surprising that Old Believers of the Vetluga or Pereiaslavl'-Zales'e settlements preserved archaic features not found (or not attested, which unfortunately is often accepted as a proof of absence of a particular element of culture or lifeway) among the groups that lived near the state borders, surrounded by foreign-speaking populations.

The Old Believers living across the Volga were particularly conservative. Scientific expeditions to this region have encountered phenomena found neither in the Russian North, nor among the Cossacks of the Urals, nor among the "Austrians" of the Altai. These same Old Believers, when the talk turned to rudiments of deep antiquity, would sometimes observe: "That is not here (or "no longer here"). Perhaps at Vetluga (or "only at Vetluga")." But in the 1950s the Vetluga settlements of Old Believers were linked up by arteries of communication to a much greater and better degree than those across the Volga, and the decay of the former lifeways, the vanishing of traditional cultural forms in the late fifties and early sixties became much more pronounced. At the same time, the group of Old Believers hidden in the Ussuri forests and totally unconnected with the outer world continued to live its "Late Middle Ages" existence, just as it had done from the time when it fled the motherland,[32] most likely searching for the promised "White Waters."

E. E. Blomkvist, one of the most authoritative representatives of the Russian ethnology school, which won worldwide recognition in the early twentieth century,[f] defines as follows the general importance of research among the Bukhtarminsk Old Believers: "Materials on the peripheral population, torn away from the main Russian core, are of great ethnological interest, chiefly because of the desire of the peripheral population to preserve the oldest forms and given the very recent imposition of modern city culture, so that the most recent stratum is easily separated from the primary, earlier forms in analysis of these materials."[33] This dictum is fully applicable to the materials of other isolated groups of Old Believers.

K. Zavoiko, who spent time at the Vetluga settlements before the revolution, wrote: "Once in the Kostroma woods, I immediately felt as though . . . I were in another world, . . . a foreign one, as though I were far away, at the very end of the earth. . . . The life of the people is simple and stark. . . . You need only look closely at the existence of these forest dwellers to see that their life has halted many centuries ago and can no longer advance; . . . it is stuck in the fifteenth or sixteenth century, perhaps earlier."[34]

The thick woods along the reaches of the Vetluga River became one of the first refuges for Old Believer adherents, hiding from the persecution of the authorities. Information from an early-twentieth-century source is wholly consistent with a depiction from an ancient Old Believer manuscript, "The Edifying Narrative of the Life and Times of Our Most Excellent Father Cornelius, Who Lived on the Vyga River near Lake Onega," which describes the founding of the Vygoretsk monastery by the first champions and teachers of the Old Belief, who came from the Vetluga monastery. This manuscript is very important for a study of Old Believer history, especially the Vygoretsk monasteries, one of the " . . . chief places among the other schismatic communities in Russia. Hence came and still come those collections of manuscripts which, since the waning of the L'vov (Lemberg) typography, have served as the enticement of printed books. . . . In the Vygoretsk community are the root and fountainhead of all those strange sects that [became] not uncommon in a great many places in Russia: the flesh-mortifiers [*morel'shchiki*], the self-burners [*samosozhigateli*], the flagellants [*khlysty*], the castrati [*skoptsy*], the child-killers [*detoubiitsy*], and other fanatics.[g] From these Vygoretsk monastery complexes, in the shortest time, the schism spread and engulfed the whole of the Russian North, beginning at the state border with Sweden and ending at the distant boundaries between Siberia and China and the non-Christian tribes of Siberia,"[35] so wrote S. Maksimov in the late nineteenth century. The "Narrative," no less valuable to ethnological research, begins with a description of the Vetluga monastery: "In the distant dark forest of Vetluga lives the monk Kapiton, and under his tutelage another thirty novices. . . . This place is desolate."[36]

The way of life in the first Old Believer hermitages is of great interest to the study of the formation and early history of monasticism: the renunciation of the comforts of existence was, in all likelihood, manifested here in forms more ancient and primitive than those of Byzantine and, perhaps, Eastern monasticism. A comparison of the existence of the early Old

Believer hermitages with the way of life of the Byzantine and Ancient Eastern monasticism would probably yield positive results for investigation of the genesis and the primitive forms of the very institution of monasticism, but such an investigation is a matter for specialists on the history of the culture of Byzantium and the ancient East. We shall confine ourselves to the conjecture that the institute of monasticism itself may have arisen in the early stages of the transformation of the ritual of retreating, in old age, to an ancestral (original) homeland. A monasticism similar to the archaic Tibetan type probably existed in addition to symbolic and referential variations of the dispatching ritual, separate from degenerated forms leading to the killing of old people.[37]

The basis for such a presumption is furnished by certain aspects of the Old Believer way of life, beginning with the transition (in old age) to a different "rank," when life was confined to the strict observances of spirituality: public prayers and reading of sacred manuscripts and old printed books; when devout performance of the chores of the field and hearth and total renunciation of ordinary entertainments—singing songs, dancing on holidays, even telling stories[38]—became the norm. Very informative in this respect is *stolpnichestvo*, borrowed from Byzantium, but taking on extreme forms in Russia, evidently testifying to a degeneration of the original phenomenon. The *stolpnik*, going to the highest point of a mountain or hill,[39] having only a railing for hand support, would stay there until the end of his days (sometimes several years), with only his clothing for shelter, covered with ice in the harsh winter frost, soaked to the skin in downpours, entirely exposed to the burning rays of the sun in July.[h]

In comparing this form of retreat from the world with going to a mountain at the end of one's life and dying on the summit, it is clear that no major difference exists. Voluntary leaving of home as a form of dispatching ritual came into being via rules established for all community members; the later, residual forms of the ritual involved leading (or carrying) away an old person when he reached a customary age or decrepitude. With a small amount of provisions (a loaf of bread, a bowl of porridge), he was left to himself (on the mountain or in the forest, sitting under a tree, on a sled in a snow drift in the field, etc.).

The *stolpniki* did not even permit themselves the luxury of sitting; the main difference in their status from that of the old people destined to die in residual forms of the dispatching ritual was that the *stolpniki* were given food and drink, whatever they required in the minimum quantity needed to sustain life. It is quite likely that a comparison of Byzantine pillar-sainthood with the ritual or retreat to the "other world" will reveal genetic links, but such an investigation is a matter for specialists on Byzantium and ancient Eastern civilizations, as is the comparison of forms of monasticism (in particular Tibetan) with the way of life of monks in Old Believer monasteries.

The harsh norms of existence in the Vetluga monastery founded by the monk Kapiton offer a basis of comparison of monastic retreat with the ritual of going to the "other world": although the first Old Believer monasteries differed among themselves in way of life, as dictated by the physical setting, religious zeal, general level of culture and education of the preceptors or monastery founders, and so forth, on the whole the strict norms of shared living, fasting, and providing the essentials of life by one's own hands were common and obligatory.

In comparing the way of life in the original Old Believer monasteries with the ritual of going to the "other world," we should not look for direct links here, or a conscious adherence to ritual operations of pagan origin. Apparently efforts were made to follow diligently the old Russian ritual norms in the way of life. And while Kievan Rus' preserved only echoes of the tradition (an eloquent testimony of which is the vivid phrase of Vladimir Monomakh, "sitting on the sled"), among the ordinary folk on the outskirts of what had been Kievan Rus' residual forms of the dispatching ritual endured until the nineteenth century. It is also known that cudgels—an attribute in the performance of this ritual—were preserved in Scandinavian churches until the Late Middle Ages.[40] Certain echoes of ancient beliefs as to the necessity of leaving earthly existence in a state of maximum clarity of mind and spirit, of the necessity of observance of strict rules of life in order to attain this state, may have had an impact (indirect, of course, refracted through the Christian dogma) on the formation of Old Believer monastery ideology, and might appear in certain of the more extreme Old Believer sects.

It is instructive that mentors of Old Believer monasteries—the founders of this emerging Old Believer institution—set even greater restrictions on themselves, no matter how stringent the norms already were. Kapiton, the founder of the monastery in the impenetrable thickets of the Vetluga woods, "ate every two days a little stale bread and raw vegetables at sundown. He slept little, spending all his time either in singing the psaltery or in working. . . . He did not sleep on his ribs, but always sitting or standing. . . ."[41] The power of the Christian teachings appeared here in the reading of the psaltery and in the refusal to sleep "on the ribs" (in connection with the legend of the creation of man from a rib). But all of the rest—the strictly limited food, consisting of dry bread and raw plants, the acquisition of the means of existence by one's own labor, the prayerful psalms, and especially the directing of one's entire being to the deified Cosmos—was essentially identical with the atmosphere and the circumstances in which victims of the pagan ritual of sending to the "other world" were left.

The first monasteries in the Russian North, as close as possible to the natural environment, evoke associations with another form of going to the "other world"—ending one's life in caves, grottoes, etc. "The cell . . . is natural, formed on three sides by granite walls; on the fourth, the monks have cut a door and window; the ceiling and roof were made of wood, and inside a stove was placed. . . ."[42]

Of great interest for study of those elements of the ritual of sending to the "other world" relevant to burial is the ending of the letter of a certain Ioann, a member of the Mezen' monastery, written by himself "near . . . death's door": "If the Lord God hath mercy on my sorrowful sinful soul . . . , pray for my wretched self, and for my wretched body, unworthy and foul, a string set up on legs, throw it from the monastery or wherever it might suit, in an unpleasant place, in a swamp or a ditch, to be food for the dogs, and the beasts, and the birds."[43] This method of burial evokes associations with dispatching a person to the "other world," on the one hand, and with the ancient burial rite, on the other.[44]

The clearest correspondence between the burial rite and the ritual of going to the "other world" in its ancient Indo-European forms (ascending the funeral pyre) is seen in the self-immolations of Old Believers. The ancient Indo-European tenet of the necessity of leaving existence on earth in a state of maximum elevation of the spirit is manifested here by the desire to leave one's earthly existence while fully preserving faith, conviction, and lifelong principles. Accordingly, self-immolation was solemnly enacted. This is shown by the description of self-immolation at one of the Mezen' monasteries, besieged by government troops in the first half of the eighteenth century. It should be mentioned that the besieged had been threatened with demolition of the monastery but not execution or forcible conversion to "Nikonism"; furthermore, the besiegers guaranteed preservation of life to all inmates of the monastery and tried in every way to prevent self-immolation. "And they . . . (the Old Believers—N.V.) gathered in a temple [*khramin*], prepared for this purpose, locked themselves in readiness . . . , where the brethren performed the church service, and smashed the ladders, and put shields on the doors and windows, and began . . . to prepare tar and birch bark for the burning, . . . and those unneeded books and icons they took away first, and those to secret cells that were specially arranged in the woods they sent two men good, where they might be concealed, who knew of these." During the siege the members of the monastery sang holy psalms, and as soon as the ladders were brought up to attempt to take them alive and prevent their dying in the flames, "the temple was lit and burned, and the noise of the flames was like thunder, and in an instant the fiery flame engulfed the entire temple. . . ."[45]

In the folklore tradition we find confirmation of the link between the Old Believer self-immolations and the ancient Indo-European belief of ascending the funeral pyre as a way of rising with the fire and smoke into the cosmic world of the gods and sacred ancestors. The legend attested from the coastline of the White Sea, telling how in the eyes of a child a self-immolator rose in the fiery flame with a column of smoke into the sky and was carried away by a cloud,[46] brings to mind the ancient Eastern mythological motifs of culture heroes, who upon completion of their mission on earth were taken away into the sky in a fiery flame, enveloped in a cloud of smoke, and thus went away to continue their life on the other planets. From Slavic beliefs we are reminded of the motif of the ascent of the soul into the sky with a column of smoke.

Of course, Old Believers could hardly have known about ancient Eastern mythological motifs. Yet it is these motifs that were the soil giving rise to the ancient Indo-European ideas as to the ways of leaving earthly existence, and these latter should be examined for the sources of the forms of leaving life, primarily by self-immolation, that were adopted by the Old Believers. That the folklore motif involving self-immolation has gone through a lengthy process of reinterpretation is shown especially by the fact that it is placed in the mouth of a child: the appearance of a child as an "attribute" of an important ritual performance or the associated folkloric motif bears evidence of a degeneration of the motif itself.[47]

Thus, the Old Believer tradition reveals residual forms of the proto-Slavic ritual of going to "another world," refracted through the desire to find ways of following the old Orthodox faith.

*   *   *

Like all phenomena in the history of culture, the Old Believer movement and philosophy with its concomitant ritual operations, lifestyles, and various persuasions underwent a process of formation, growth, and decay, resulting in degeneration of rituals and transformation of former norms into formal routine. One of the most eloquent testimonies of this process was the formation and degeneration of the "pilgrim" trend. We have already mentioned one of the forms of "going from the world" that was popular in the seventeenth century—going into the deep forest to starve to death. Even more popular at that time and during the occasional revivals of official persecution was retreat to hermitages. We should not forget that these hermits in the beginning lived a primitive life, deliberately restricted to the minimum needed to sustain life. They settled in deep forests, on the shores of a river or lake, in holes with no windows or doors, having only a trapdoor in the top and an opening for the smoke to escape and the minimum necessary ventilation, fitted out with a small thin pipe or even an old pot; frequently, one could only sit or lie down in these domiciles, so low and small were they; fire was produced by the primitive method of friction; and so forth. By the end of the eighteenth century, a "pilgrim" trend had formed, basically continuing the traditions of the hermits of the late seventeenth and early eighteenth centuries, yet most likely without their asceticism.

"Wandering pilgrims," seeing themselves as "the last of the old piety" and founded on the commandment of "the Lord God Himself" to the apostles to flee Babylon, and also relying (after the hermits) on the teaching of Kirill of Jerusalem as to only two possible paths for the truly righteous—either uncompromising war with Satan or flight from him—advanced the postulate for the true successors of "those who were once Christians": "To have no city, nor village, nor home." That is, the idea of perpetual "nomadism" was the underlying foundation of the "wandering pilgrims."[48]

But already by the start of the nineteenth century a split had taken place in this movement, mainly on the basis of the renouncement of strict asceticism. A separate group had formed, that of the "pilgrim welcomers" (who also called themselves the "lovers of Christ"). Living in ordinary houses and not basically differing in manner of life from ordinary profane people, they saw their service to the old faith in sheltering "pilgrims" ("Christ's people"). For this purpose, they built special rooms in their houses, hiding places, exits concealed from the uninitiated, and camouflaged doors. The former eternal wandering was limited for them to the idea of needing to pass before death into the ranks of the true pilgrims. The process of transformation of the pilgrim movement was not limited to this; the "wandering pilgrims," one of whose prime postulates was (in keeping with the ancient Christian ideal) to renounce the right of property, gradually admitted this right, especially when the principles of religious tolerance were established. This began with receiving certain articles from the "pilgrim-welcomers" to keep, and then led to the customary use of others' goods. But the most important transformation, extremely vital for an understanding of the processes of degeneration of cultural phenomena over the course of the tradition's history, took place with the "lovers of Christ." Their moving into the ranks of the pilgrims before death ended with their being carried, expiring, to the nearby woods, and then simply to their own garden, or even only into the yard.

This form of parting with life by the "lovers of Christ," which appeared through lengthy transformation of pagan ritual and its merging with Christian teaching, and which also endured historical vicissitudes altering its original meaning, illustrates what became the ultimate synthetic end of degenerated pagan and Christian cultural phenomena in the later folk tradition.

The proto-Slavic ritual, which was directed to the deified Cosmos, ultimately became a residual phenomenon, the very essence of which was contrary to the philosophical idea on which it had been formed.

*　　*　　*

Examination of the rudiments of paganism in the rituals brings to mind the dictum, clearly enunciated as far back as P. Miliukov: "The Russian Old

Belief, being the conservator of antiquity, has always kept exclusively to the common masses, the peasants and the merchant class."[49] The ritual tradition of Old Believer peasant settlements, as well as that of the common folk of the urban population who remained within the "old faith," can basically be characterized, in terms of its special features, as one that preserves in a more integrated form the archaic elements of ancient Slavic rituals.

We know that the traditional folk ceremonial tied to the Christian calendar is basically a synthesis of pagan and Christian ideas and cults, the pagan philosophy often dictating the nature and outlook of the ritual operations and their attributes. Christianity itself took up many elements of the pagan philosophy and rituals, adapting itself to the customary pagan ritual cycle. The Byzantine *brumalia*, for example, clearly reveal specific forms of adaptation by the Byzantine Christian church, in the initial period of its history, of customary pagan rituals to Christian holidays in the calendrical ceremonial cycle.[50]

The Christian church set Christ's birth celebration to fall on December 25th so as to overcome (largely through absorption) the cult of Mithra—the most popular deity of the sun, the light of day, and truth; the mediator between people and the deified Cosmos; the patron of peaceful, benevolent, well-regulated relations in society, of harmony and general welfare in the family—the celebration of his birthday being connected with the winter solstice.

The calendrical ceremonial complex is concentrated at the most significant moments of the solar year: the winter and summer solstice, the vernal and autumnal equinox, and the declinations of the sun, which usher in seasonal change. The central event is the ritual complex of the New Year. Just as the turning of the sun, one of the most important sources of life, toward "summer" indicated the imminent blossoming of everything vital on earth, so too the New Year ceremonial was intended to invoke blessings in the coming year. The New Year ritual actions were conceived as being of exceptional influence on the prosperity of the entire year. From them were drawn the threads connecting to the seasonal rituals.

Of special importance in understanding the nature of the reinterpretations and transformations in the folk tradition of Christian beliefs is the motif of "unclean strength" in the Christmas and New Year activities. It is commonly known that this was supposed to run rampant during Yuletide; of the various forms of activity spawned by this belief, we will concentrate on the most archaic patterns. The Yuletide mummery of long-established Russian inhabitants of Eastern Siberia as "demons"[51] harkens back to a "devil" masquerade in the Vetluga hamlets: plant fiber was tied to the head, "so that he would be tasseled, shaggy, with face blackened (without horns)."[52]

Shagginess, tassels, yet no horns—the symbolic mark of the devil in Christianity—evoke associations with traditional dramatic depictions of

Kostroma-Kostrubon'ka in rituals of mediation with the forces of nature and other such personages of anthropomorphic aspect in the spring and summer rituals.[53] The darkened face is tantamount to a death mask and signifies belonging to the "other" world. As we know, all of religious history, beginning with ancient Sumer, has been characterized by an ongoing process of reinterpretation of former deities and deified ancestors as demons. In Christmas and New Year mummery we perhaps encounter the images of the pagan ancestor-protectors, inhabitants of the deified Cosmos, transformed into demons, devils, witches, and spirits over the course of the history of the Christian era. We find an echo of the transformation of pagan supernatural beings into female spirits [*kikimory*] in medieval documents.[i] Thus, the "Prikaznyi stol" no. 95, p. 225, states that, in the early seventeenth century, "in Galitskii district the peasant Mitroshka the Lame . . . had dealings with the 'impure' supernatural and the evil spirit is called *kikimora* in their waking dreams."[54] Various forms of "burning a demon," "burying a witch," and similar customs among European peoples reveal rudiments of the ritual of sending mediators to the deified forefathers.[55]

Depiction of *ved'ma-kikimora* images in the Christmas tradition amounts to the following. "The mummers were dressed as old women with every kind of rag and scrap, a rag-covered pot on the head, to resemble as much as possible *kikimory*, or witches."[56] For an understanding of the genetic roots of such a masquerade, the form of its existence in the Vetluga hamlets is of special importance. "In former times the old women at Christmas came to visit disguised as assorted spirits [*shishimory*]: they dressed in tattered clothes (*shobolki*) and, with a long pointed stick, sat on the hearth planks with their feet dangling from the timber beam, and spun in this position. They placed yarn (*kopyl*) between their legs; they tied tow fiber onto the yarn and twisted the thick strand about their long staff. The girls would laugh at the spirit, grabbing her legs, and she would beat them with the stick."[57] Three elements in this form of mummery are of particular interest. The old women dressed in rags evoke associations with the procession moving through the village toward the Shrovetide hill, with mummers dressed as beggars seated on sleds, with an old woman on the front sled, and also with a crowd of old women and beggars in the spring and summer rituals of mediation with the forces of nature, i.e., rudimentary forms of the ritual of sending to the "other world" during other calendrical seasons.[58]

The old women on the hearth planks, disguised in this fashion, evoke associations with old men dispatched to the "other world" by being left on the stove in an unheated shack.[59] The long sticks with pointed tip resemble cudgels—implements for ritual dispatch of old men to the forefathers, preserved in Scandinavian churches as recently as the Late Middle Ages. Alternatively, they correlate with swords—the main attribute of ritual dispatching to the "other world" among the Goths, the peoples of the North, and so on, as well as with staffs and wooden implements that are attributes of funerary games. The symbolic meaning of the pot on the head is significant. In various forms of mummery (and in more archaic ritual performances), the pot represents a head, and breaking or smashing it by blows simulates killing (the "bull," festivities after a wedding, etc.). An intact pot on the head of the "spirit" is a very telling feature. And the spinning itself, the winding of thick strands of yarn about the long staff, is associated with the earliest Indo-European conceptions concerning spinning the thread of life, its breaking signifying the end of earthly existence for whomever the thread is broken.

In view of the above, this form of mummery represents one of the symbolic forms of the archaic ritual of sending mediators to the forefathers, in which the ritual is actually transformed into a farce. The symbolic meaning of the transformation of ancestral cult forms in this kind of mummery is extremely vivid: the thick strand on the long staff signifies a long and secure life, while the blows with the staff rain down on the maidens for their mockery; these elements, plus the leg-grabbing (signifying, ostensibly, futile efforts to throw the old woman out of the house) indicate a complete transformation and rethinking of pagan custom through dislocations of the actions of the former ritual targets: the older generation, formerly dispatched to deified ancestors for the sake of the young generation, who have not yet lived their allotted time on earth, by their resolute actions nip in the bud the efforts of the young to perform the physical action. Such dislocations, transforming the object of a pagan ritual to the subject, or officiant, constitute a typological phenomenon in the history of folk traditions; they have taken on their most vivid embodiment in the carnival, essentially a synthesis of various transformed pagan rituals for sending to the "other world."

All of this acquired especially vivid expression in the European carnival election of a "king," who appeared in comical costume and was the object of comical obedience for the duration of the carnival and taunting toward its close; upon completion of the carnival ceremonies, however, he went his own way unscathed, after watching the burning of the straw man, which replaced the earlier pagan object of culmination of the ritual performance. The primary elements of the European carnival, like elements of the Eastern Slavic Christmas and New Year mummery, including burning a "demon" ("witch") or "execution of a criminal," plus the episodic "grandfather-burning" (*palenie dida*), "burial" (*pohreben*), throwing a boy into the sea and his safe return to shore, under comparative historical analysis are seen as rudiments of the pagan ritual of sending to the "other world." Yet taken in their entirety, they must be regarded as a transformed, distorted form of the pagan ritual, mocking its barbarity and declaring a victory in being delivered from the barbaric custom.[j]

The connectivity of worlds, the outwardly unseen but permanent links between the deified ancestors and their earthly descendants, ancestral protection over their earthly kinsmen—these ideas form one of the cornerstones of the ancient Indo-European worldview, and were also incorporated in medieval pagan philosophy. Those who "departed for the other world" were seen as becoming one with the company of sacred ancestors, similar to those in whose presence the Vedic first ancestor Yama "drank with the gods";[60] only priests were allowed to consort with them. When the pagan beliefs were corrupted, the former deified images were turned into demonic ones, into an "unclean spirit," while the priests and soothsayers were transformed into sorcerers. The *kikimora* from the late medieval document is seen as a vague "evil spirit," while in the olden mummery it is the image of a frightening crone. The idea that demonic beings run rampant during Christmas is evidently a transformation of the ancient pagan belief that celestial ancestors return to their descendants in their earthly abode on the New Year and other major calendrical periods associated with change in solar inclination or lunar phases, and reside there for the duration of the ritual season (which has been retained to some extent in the Belorussian *dziady*).[k]

The symbolic meaning of the transformation of ancestral cult forms during their history is vividly seen in archaic mummery forms, exhibiting its various stages. Illustrative are dramatized performances based on zoomorphic images. Disguise as an animal and the conception of animals as substitutes for humans in certain residual forms of ritual performance are revealed in a special literature, reflecting a multitude of manifestations and interpretations. Even so, the interpretations offered do not account for all of the archaic forms of mummery, so that we must again interpret their genetic roots and symbolic meaning.[61] The Yuletide leading of a goat in procession by mummers among the Lake Baikal Semeiski,[62] apart from indicating that such a ritual performance in antiquity was common to all Eastern Slavs (in itself rather important), is of special interest for an understanding of the transformational lines of archaic rituals during the history of the tradition. Comparison of this with the form of masquerading as a goat in the Carpathian Mountains of the Bucovina, where the goat mummer is the central personage of a dramatized festival, demonstrates the genetic antiquity of this zoomorphic personage in archaic ritual performances.[l]

The very shape of the "goat" image bears archaic features: a man (or boy) is totally covered with straw, with a cone-shaped straw headpiece pointing upward and a goat mask on his face. The central action—the circle dance, in whose center is the goat, who is rewarded with blows at the close—evokes associations with the circle dance of Balkan Gypsies that concludes with a ritual dispatching to the "other world": a lethal blow is given to the doomed person in the center.[63] And the carnival personage of the "goat," in turn, evokes associations with the ritual Christmas pastry of zoomorphic shape, known on the Tersk coast of the White Sea, in Olonetsk province, and in certain other places of the Russian North as "roebucks" [*kozuly*], "idols" [*istykany*], and "images" [*bolvany*].[64] While "idols" and "images" may be equated with anthropomorphic symbols replacing humans in archaic rituals, we must search in deepest antiquity for the roots of the holiday pastry apellation "roebucks." Pausanias wrote that the adolescents brought in sacrifice to Dionysus were replaced with goats, adorned with wreaths and ribbons and with gilded horns,[65] clearly revealing the direction of the action (gold being a cosmic symbol).

Since the roots of the cult of Dionysus go back to the world of the Sumerians and Babylonians, the ancient Babylonian seals are of special interest as a material expression of the nature of the performance. One of these shows the sacrificing of goats. They are being brought to an altar and handed over in a prayerful attitude to the mediator between the sacrificers and the deity. At the other side of the altar, these goats are shown frolicking and fawning before the deity.[66] The scene on the Babylonian seal evokes associations with the dispatching of a dog to the "other world" among the Northern peoples, the dispatching of a herald to a deified ancestor among the Goths, and the ancient Slavic belief that a killed animal can take messages to ancestors and deities.[67]

The influence of the Sumero-Babylonian culture on the ancient Greek, the ancient Roman, and (through them) on the formation of the medieval European culture is discerned in many manifestations;[68] in traditional beliefs and rituals, it is felt more or less throughout the entire history of the tradition. In the present instance, it is especially important to point out that the goat was the first substitute for humans in the ancient Babylonian sacrifices.[69] As for the "roebucks" or "images," it is known from later sources of information that they were made by elderly men at home, from rye dough or clay, placed on a table and in the window, not only at Christmas and New Year's, but also during the observance of other calendrical rituals (the first driving of livestock to pasture on Egor's Day, Seventh Thursday, etc.), containing elements of the ritual of dispatching to the "other world." The setting of the "roebucks" or "images" in the window and on a table is essentially analogous to the placing of a mask in the window at Christmas and a statuette of dry fruit on the Christmas/New Year table, the anthropomorphic puppet-cross in the icon corner and at the gate, and also the clay figure called German beside a river—symbols of people in transformed forms of the ritual of sending to the "other world."[70]

The carnival "goat" is the counterpart of the "goat" personage of funeral games, the goat that is thrown from a bell tower at the end of carnival, and finally the "rock of the old men" in Abkhazia, from which old men were thrown into the sea, and similar ritual actions of the Ligae and Tabarenes.[71] There is also a parallel with the throwing of a goat from the cliff of Azazel in ancient Babylon, while the man who was replaced by the goat went into the desert forever. From this, perhaps, tenuous links can be traced to the Old Believers withdrawing into hermitages, through similar forms of Byzantine monasticism and the earlier Eastern form.

Hence, rudimentary forms of archaic ritual action show how manifold and complex are the ways and means for transforming pagan phenomena, and how differently pagan symbolism is interpreted in folk tradition. Identification of the roots and functional nature of archaic phenomena, reaching proto-Slavic antiquity, and determination of semantic transformational laws make it possible to discern a sequence of transformational forms in both a horizontal direction (analogies among different peoples) and a vertical direction (relating to laws of development in calendrical and funeral ceremonials). The Old Belief stands before us as the custodian of the earliest traditions, having gone through several stages of semantic transformation but nevertheless preserving certain conceptual meanings.

Editor's notes

a. In addition to other sources cited in the introduction on Old Believer history, see Robert O. Crummey, *The Old Believers and the World of Antichrist* (Madison: University of Wisconsin Press, 1970).

b. Self-immolation has not stopped in the twentieth century, evidenced by the young Gulf War protester who burned himself in a town square in Massachusetts in 1991, the Southeast Asian Buddhist immolations during the Vietnam war, and the Islamic women who have burned themselves as a last resort in Central Asia. Most of these cases involve the concept of fire as a purifying way to reach an afterlife. See Stephen P. Dunn, ed., "Through the Flames: Central Asian Women Protest," *The Station Relay: Facts and Views on Daily Life in the Soviet Union*, Sept. 1988–May 1989, vol. 4, nos. 1–5, pp. 53–66.

c. The word "pagan" (*iazycheskii*) in this article refers to the pre-Christian past without being as condemnatory as our word "heathen." The degree of scientific specificity (complete with archeological metaphor) that is claimed here in arguing for "degeneration" is probably not warranted by existing data. Yet the author's confident tone is part of the expected Soviet culture of ethnographic analysis. People were not trained to be circumspect, to present such theories as speculation.

d. This is clearly the author's description from her own fieldtrip (scientific pilgrimage) to Lake Svetloiar, still believed sacred, purifying, and curative by some.

e. The author is making a useful semiotic distinction here between referential and symbolic, which could be more developed. Cf. Charles Pierce's explanation of icon, index, and symbol: *Collected Works: Elements of Logic*, eds. Charles Hartshorne and Paul Weis (Cambridge: Belknap, 1960), vol. 2.; A. S. Myl'nikov, *Etnograficheskoe izuchenie znakovykh sredstv kul'tury* (Leningrad: Nauka, 1989).

f. In addition to E. E. Blomkvist, prominent Russian ethnologists included N. I. Nadezhdin, V. Dal', G. I. Popov, N. Kharuzin, and D. K. Zelenin. The early history of Russian ethnography is covered in A. N. Pypin, *Istoriia russkoi etnografii* (St. Petersburg, 1890–92, 4 vols.).

g. These names, capitalized in prerevolutionary sources, were used first by outsiders rather than by the groups themselves. The sects were often "without priests" and sometimes had ecstatic group religious experiences. Missing from the list are the *skakuny*, or jumpers, an offshoot of the *khlysty*; the *sokratil'shchiki*, [life] shorteners; the *tiukal'shchiki*, hackers; and others. The *detoubiitsy* were also called *detogubiitsy*, meaning child-spoilers (ruined with improper religion?) rather than child-killers. For more on the sects, see Crummey, *The Old Believers and the World of Antichrist*; A. Leroy-Beaulieu, *The Empire of the Tsars and the Russians*, trans. Z. A. Rogosin (London, 1905, vol. 3); A. Shchapov, *Russkii raskol staroobriadchestva* (Kazan', 1859); Serge Zenkovskii, *Russkoe staroobriadchestvo* (Munich, 1970).

h. *Stolpnichestvo* means going to the heights for God. The root is *stolp* or *stolb*, meaning column or tower, but *stolp* is also used metaphorically as a pillar of strength, especially religious. It applied particularly to the most revered hermits, some of whom became saints, e.g., St. Simeon.

i. See G. Alexinsky, "Slavonic Mythology," *Larousse Encyclopedia of Mythology* (New York: Prometheus, 1960), pp. 299–300 on the *kikimora* spirit (sometimes depicted as the wife of the *domovoi*).

j. For other interpretations of carnival, see Mikhail M. Bakhtin, *Rabelais and His World*, trans. Helen Iswolsky (Cambridge: MIT Press, 1965); Natalie Zemon Davis, *Society and Culture in Early Modern France* (Stanford: Stanford University Press, 1975), pp. 97–123, 180–84; Priscilla Rachun Linn, "Chamula Carnival: The 'Soul' of Celebration," *Celebration: Studies in Festivity and Ritual*, ed. Victor Turner (Washington: Smithsonian Institute Press, 1982). Analyses of two non-Christian masquerades are also relevant: Abdellah Hammoudi, *La Victime et ses masques: essai sur le sacrifice et la mascarade au Maghreb* (Paris: Editions du Seuil, 1988); and Iurii Iu. Karpov, "The Communal Winter Festival among the Tsezy," *Soviet Anthropology & Archeology*, vol. 22, no. 2 (Fall 1983), pp. 37–48.

k. On the *dziady*, or feasts with incantations honoring the "grandfathers" (ancestors), see George P. Fedotov, *The Russian Religious Mind: Kievan Christianity* (New York: Harper & Row, 1960), pp. 17, 355.

l. For a powerful rendition of this masquerade see the film by the late Sergei Parajanov, "Shadows of Forgotten Ancestors." A translation by Steven P. Hill of Parajanov's "confessions" about the making of this film appears in *Film Comment*, 1968, vol. 5, no. 1, pp. 38–49.

Notes

1. His well-known works "In the Woods" and "In the Mountains," which are brilliant in artistic form, provide excellent material for a study of the life of the Old Believers beyond the Volga, as I had occasion to learn during expeditionary research and examination of the sources; at the present day, this statement no longer causes any doubt among experts.

2. *Pamiatniki drevnei pis'mennosti* (St. Petersburg, 1895), vol. 108.

3. See, e.g., D. I. Sapozhnikov, *Samosozhzhenie v russkom raskole* (Moscow, 1891), and others.

4. N. N. Veletskaia, *Iazycheskaia simvolika slavianskikh arkhaicheskikh ritualov* (Moscow, 1978), pp. 60–78, 100.

5. V. Bogdanov, " 'Dushila' u russkikh raskol'nikov," *EO*, 1904, no. 2, p. 160.

6. D. K. Zelenin, " 'Krasnaia smert' " u russkikh staroobriadtsev," *EO*, 1904, no. 3, p. 68.

7. Veletskaia, *Iazycheskaia simvolika*, ch. 2.

8. D. K. Zelenin, *Obychai 'dobrovol'noi smerti' u primitivnykh narodov* [no place given] (1935) (special offprint).

9. Zelenin, "Krasnaia smert'," p. 68.

10. Veletskaia, *Iazycheskaia simvolika*, ch. 2.

11. Ibid., ch. 2, sect. 2; ch. 3, sect. 1.

12. N. N. Grinkova, "Odezhda bukhtarminskikh staroobriadtsev," *Bukhtarminskie staroobriadtsy* (Leningrad, 1930), p. 376.

13. A. Ia. Garkavi, *Skazaniia musul'manskikh pisatelei o slavianakh i russkikh* (St. Petersburg, 1870), etc.

14. Zelenin, "Krasnaia smert'," p. 68.

15. V. I. Dal', *Tolkovyi slovar' zhivogo velikorusskogo iazyka* (Moscow, 1955), vol. 2, p. 187.

16. Ibid., p. 188.

17. Veletskaia, *Iazycheskaia simvolika*, pp. 158–59.

18. I. I. Sreznevskii, *Materialy dlia slovaria drevnerusskogo iazyka* (St. Petersburg, 1893), vol. 1, pp. 1318, 1355.

19. Veletskaia, *Iazycheskaia simvolika*, ch. 3.

20. V. Smirnov, *Narodnye pokhorony i prichitaniia v Kostromskom krae* (Kostroma, 1920), p. 19.

21. Gracious communication from V. N. Basilov.

22. N. Linder, "Raskol'nich'ia sekta 'kalagury,'" *Novoe vremia*, 1891, no. 5243.

23. N. N. Veletskaia, "Rudimenty indoevropeiskikh i drevnebalkanskikh ritualov v slaviano-

balkanskoi obriadnosti mediatsii sil prirody," *Materialy od VI Megunaroden simpozium za balkanskiot folklor. Makedonski folklor* (Skopje, 1979), pp. 88–94.

24. Veletskaia, *Iazycheskaia simvolika*, ch. 3, sect. 3; ibid., "O rudimentakh iazycheskikh ritual'nykh deistv v slaviano-balkanskoi pogrebal'noi obriadnosti," *Materialy od VII Megunaroden simpozium za balkanskiot folklor. Makedonski folklor*, 1982, pp. 202–5.

25. N. P. Grinkova, "Materialy dlia slovaria," *Bukhtarminskie staroobriadtsy* (Leningrad, 1930), p. 457.

26. Dal', *Tolkovyi slovar'*, vol. 2, p. 383.

27. I take this opportunity to thank L. V. Alekseev for courteous information.

28. Crawling around the lake on the knees by a vow is apparently a relatively later phenomenon, developing from the soil of certain Old Believer persuasions which involved self-mortification.

29. N. N. Veletskaia, "Iz istorii kupal'skikh ritualov u slavian," *Materialy od V Megunaroden simpozium za balkanskiot folklor. Makedonski folklor*, 1977, pp. 73–79.

30. Veletskaia, *Iazycheskaia simvolika*, pp. 155–57; cf. the ritual remembrance of the dead among the Japanese—floating a lighted candle or lantern on a lake. (I am grateful to N. A. Iofan for information on the medieval ritual observances.)

31. Cf. the pagan idea of the link between flowing and bottomless waters with the Cosmos.

32. Cursory information was courteously provided me by L. V. Markova, who obtained it from a philologist who found himself among this group of Old Believers of the Ussuri in entirely unforeseen circumstances.

33. E. E. Blomkvist and N. P. Grinkova, "Zakliuchenie," *Bukhtarminskie staroobriadtsy*.

34. K. Zavoiko, "V Kostromskikh lesakh po Vetluge-reke: Etnograficheskie materialy, zapisannye v Kostromskoi gubernii v 1914–1916 gg.," *Etnograficheskii sbornik* (Kostroma, 1917), issue 8, pp. 3–4.

35. S. V. Maksimov, *Sobranie sochineniia*.

36. Ibid. Stories from the history of the Old Believers (from the manuscripts of the sect).

37. See Veletskaia, *Iazycheskaia simvolika*.

38. A feature especially characteristic of the rural Old Believer way of life of certain persuasions, particularly the Pomeranians, evidently involving a replacement of the traditional entering of a monastery in old age with passage to a special rank within the same environment.

39. On the meaning of mountains in the ritual of going to the "other world" see Veletskaia, *Iazycheskaia simvolika*.

40. Ibid., ch. 2, sect. 2.

41. Maksimov, *Sobranie sochineniia*.

42. Ibid.

43. S. V. Maksimov, "Rasskazy is istorii staroobriadchestva," p. 332.

44. Veletskaia, *Iazycheskaia simvolika*, ch. 2, sect. 2; ch. 3, sect. 2.

45. Maksimov, "Rasskazy is istorii staroobriadchestva," p. 331.

46. S. V. Maksimov, "Samosozhigateli na Mezeni," *Sobranie sochineniia*, vol. 17.

47. Veletskaia, *Iazycheskaia simvolika*, pp. 171–73; idem, "Iazycheskaia simvolika antropomorfnoi ritual'noi skul'ptury," *Kul'tura i iskusstvo srednevekovogo goroda* (Moscow, 1984), pp. 81–84.

48. P. Miliukov, *Ocherki po istorii russkoi kul'tury* (St. Petersburg, 1902), vol. 2, pp. 91–92.

49. Ibid., p. 142.

50. L. A. El'nitskii, "Vizantiiskii prazdnik brumalii i rimskie saturnalii," *Antichnost' i Vizantiia* (Moscow, 1975), pp. 345–46.

51. *ETGM*, 1901, issue 12, p. 118.

52. Zavoiko, "V Kostromskikh lesakh," p. 25.

53. Veletskaia, "Rudimenty indoevropeiskikh i drevnebalkanskikh ritualov."

54. Cited in L. V. Cherepnin, "Iz istorii drevnerusskogo koldovstva XII v.," *Etnografiia*, 1929, no. 2, p. 100.

55. Veletskaia, *Iazycheskaia simvolika*, ch. 3, sect. 1.

56. Zavoiko, "V Kostromskikh lesakh," p. 25.

57. Ibid., p. 38.

58. Veletskaia, *Iazycheskaia simvolika*, ch. 3, sect. 1.

59. P. Litvinova, "Kak sazhali v starinu liudei starykh na lubok," *Kievskaia starina*, 1885, June, pp. 354–56.

60. *Rigveda* (Moscow, 1972), p. 253. "Under the tree with beautiful leaves/Where Yama drinks with the gods/Thither our father, the head of the clan/Heads toward the ancestors."

61. N. N. Veletskaia, "Iazycheskaia simvolika arkhaicheskikh antropomorfnykh i zoomorfnykh obrazov slavianskikh karnaval'nykh deistv," *Materialy od VI Megunaroden simpozium za balkanskiot folklor. Makedonski folklor* (in press).

62. F. F. Bolonev, *Narodnyi kalendar' semeiskikh Zabaikal'ia* (Novosibirsk, 1978), p. 48.

63. Veletskaia, *Iazycheskaia simvolika*, ch. 3.

64. D. K. Zelenin, *Opisanie rukopisei uchenogo arkhiva Imperatorskogo Russkogo geograficheskogo obshchestva* (Petersburg, 1915), issue 2, p. 924.

65. See N. N. Evreinov, *Azazel i Dionis* (Leningrad, 1924), p. 39.

66. Ibid.

67. K. Sosenko, *Kulturno-istorychna postat' staroukrains'kykh sviat Rizdva i Shchedrogo Vechera* (L'viv, 1928).

68. G. Vinkler, *Vavilonskaia kul'tura v ee otnoshenii k kul'turnomu razvitiiu chelovechestva* (Moscow, 1913); S. N. Kramer, *Istoriia nachinaetsia v Shumere* (Moscow, 1965), etc.

69. Evreinov, *Azazel i Dionis*.

70. Veletskaia, *Iazycheskaia simvolika*, ch. 3, sect. 1; ibid., "Rudimenty indoevropeiskikh i drevnebalkanskikh ritualov."

71. V. V. Latyshev, *Izvestiia drevnikh pisatelei grecheskikh i latinskikh o Skifii i Kavkaze* (St. Petersburg, 1890), vol. 1, pp. 454, 657, etc.

Archaic Elements in the Charms
of the Russian Population of Siberia

F. F. BOLONEV

In the past two decades many works have been published on ritual folklore. This is no accident; this complicated and diversified stratum of oral folk creativity furnishes valuable material to scholarship. It is important for study of a people's worldview, having scientific and practical significance. Survivals of religion and magic in folk consciousness can be contested only when the sources and forms of existence of such beliefs, their role and functions, are known. Ritual folklore is also important in the reconstruction of the history of folklore in general, as it helps us discern laws of development in oral and poetic productions of folk creativity.[a]

The least studied aspect of ritual folklore are charms [zagovory]—an old sacral element of folk religious culture. Present-day investigators are finding in the Russian (Eastern Slavic) forms and texts of charms "visible features of the Indo-European and Old Slavic conjuring skill."[1] In the literature, particular attention has been given to charms that are curative, amatory, and social; their structure, motives, and poetics have been examined as a way of learning about their sources.[2] But the system of images in the conjuratory texts, their classification, formation, and archaic features, have scarcely been studied.

The charm is a vanishing genre. It is losing its sacral and secret nature in our time, becoming, in the words of N. I. Tolstoi, "demystified." This scholar rightly confronts Slavic folklorists with the task of orderly collection, classification, and publication of these charms. "We cannot wait calmly," he writes, "until the tradition of the charm, like that of the epic, has disappeared."[3]

The sacredness of the ritual forms and the high artistic values of the charms (the "gold of genuine poesy," in the words of Aleksandr Blok) attracted the attention of and were highly appreciated by many prominent So-

Russian text © 1987 by "Nauka" Publishers. "O nekotorykh arkhaicheskikh elementakh v zagovorakh russkogo naseleniia Sibiri," in *Traditsionnye obriady i iskusstvo russkogo i korennykh narodov Sibiri*, edited by L. M. Rusakova and N. A. Minenko (Novosibirsk: Nauka, 1987), pp. 66–78. A publication of the Institute of History, Philology, and Philosophy, Siberian Division, USSR Academy of Sciences.

viet scholars and by those involved in the field of culture. A. N. Afanas'ev, F. I. Buslaev, A. A. Potebnia, D. K. Zelenin, N. F. Poznanskii, E. Eleonskaia, A. M. Astakhova, Iu. M. Sokolov, P. G. Bogatyrev, V. P. Petrov, A. A. Blok, A. M. Gorky, and others have written about them.

"The charms are important and interesting to ethnographers as material reflecting ancient human beliefs and ideas,"[4] wrote Astakhova, who did much to closely define the applied-artistic value of this folklore. The poetic and pictorial system of the charms reveals quite clearly archaic elements of ancient Slavic social consciousness, as well as superimposed layers involving the changing epochs, religious beliefs, and natural-climatic setting experienced by the Slavic communities and peoples. Charms performed a practical and utilitarian function; they were used to safeguard planted crops and livestock; they played an important part in folk medicine and in romantic and domestic relations. The use of charms involves irrational attempts to influence the surrounding world.

Incidentally, the use of charms in medicine may have had a positive result, as the psychotherapeutic value of suggestion is well known. In the present article we shall pay attention to some archaic elements of conjuratory formulas, images, and concepts often encountered in Siberian Russian charms.

The number of charms recorded in Siberia[5] is much greater than the number of those in the collections of L. N. Maikov, N. N. Vinogradov, and A. Vetukhov, who identified texts of charms that existed in the European part of Russia.[6] Many unpublished charm texts of the Siberian Russian population are kept in government archives, museums, manuscript departments of libraries and institutions in Moscow, Leningrad, and the cities of Siberia, and in the archives of collectors of Siberian folklore. The Institute of Russian Literature (Pushkinskii Dom) has in its archives the data of collectors of Siberian Russian folklore, including many charms collected by S. Guliaev, over 300 charm texts in the materials of M. V. Krasnozhenova, and others in the notes of A. M. Astakhova, who recorded them in 1934 from the old families who had settled in the Lake Baikal region.

At present, this form of folklore has been sharply curtailed, although in field expeditions in 1969–82 we recorded more than 100 charms and conjuratory formulas. These were predominantly charms against sickness or pertaining to household and community relations. Many texts have been gathered by students of folklore at the Institute of Social Sciences, the Buriat branch of the Siberian Division of the USSR Academy of Sciences. More than 180 charms were noted by students of the Krasnoiarsk Pedagogical Institute in the Krasnoiarsk territory. Over the past twenty years, M. N. Mel'nikov and students of the Novosibirsk Pedagogical Institute have collected several hundred texts of conjuratory formulas in Western Siberia alone.

Thus, the statements of certain scholars regarding the vanishing of charms from the daily existence of our people require correction.[7]

The systematic gathering of Siberian spells [*zaklinanie*] and incantations [*nagovory*] began in the first half of the nineteenth century, although records dealing with sorcery [*koldovstvo*] and "witches" [*ved'my*] who used conjuratory formulas and amatory incantations are found much earlier in Siberian archives, since the seventeenth century. Charms recorded in Siberia attracted the attention of a number of scholars, physicians, and psychologists. At present, individual groups of Siberian charms of an economic or curative nature have been partially examined. The philosophical and social aspects of the charms have been considered in greater detail.[8]

One scholar of Siberian ethnography wrote: "Despite references to saints, mention of the city of Jerusalem, or allusion to biblical wisdom, an ancient pre-Christian chaos is alive in [the charms]."[9] Indeed, the charms attested among the Russian old-livers of Siberia contain archaic ideas and images that belong to the epoch of early clan life and ancient Slavic paganism. Numerous charms were transformed over time, especially since Christianity in Russia took on many Orthodox features in Byzantine-Slavic form while retaining old images and ideas. This will be evident on examination of charm texts and the ritual actions associated with them.

The archaic nature of many charm texts recorded in Siberia appears through the lexicon, oral formulas, use of metaphor, metonymy, symbolism, vivid similes, and other imagery. Certain charms are perhaps the equal in artistic qualities to creations of Old Russian classical literature. Here, for example, are two charms.

Wedding Procession Charm
against Sorcerers and Shape-Changers

I arise, God's slave (say name), pray, go, making the sign of the cross, wash myself with cold spring water, rub myself with a fine towel, don my garments, girdled by the rosy dawn, protected by the bright moon, prodded by the many stars, and glowing with the glorious sun. I enclose myself (say name) and my party with ass foals surrounded by an iron stockade, with ground laid with steel, with sky covered by damask steel, so that none may penetrate it, from the east to the west, from the north to the summer (south), no male or female heretic, no male or female sorcerer, worthy or unworthy, whoever takes bread in this wide world. My head is a container, my tongue a lock.[10]

During the Wedding

I arose, God's slave (say name), prayed to God, washed with spring water, prayed to Michael the Archangel, and bowed in every direction. I went, God's slave (say name), out through the doors, out through the gates—into the clean field, to Father Ocean; I came closer, I bowed lower. Oh it is thee, Father Ocean, the blue sea, how you cling around all the land and all of the underworld: so too am I, God's slave (say name), [like] the young prince with the young princess, clasped by strong spells; with these words, no one—not an evil person, nor evil foes, nor an old witch, nor a bare-headed maid—can think evil thoughts; it is as though there is around me, God's slave (say name), and the young prince an iron screen from the ground to the sky, a copper roof, a cast-iron floor. The yellow fog of night flows over you, Father Ocean, the blue sea: so let the iron screen be around me, and let no evil person, no evil foe, neither the old witch nor the bare-headed maid see through the dark fog and the iron wall, under the copper roof or above the iron floor. Above this dark fog fly bright falcons through the air; so let good horses run to the gold crown and from the gold crown, and along all the [heavenly] path-roads. . . . [11]

Ritual poetry, like the above example, often employs the mighty image of an *iron* screen extending from the ground to the sky, with gates of damask steel, closed by golden keys, with a copper roof, with iron or steel floor. Thus, in the Siberian congratulatory song known as the "vineyard," the master's yard is open and there stands "for seventy versts, for seven mile-stones, an all-iron stockade around this yard." N. F. Poznanskii, a student of charms, has written on this matter: "The epithets 'copper,' 'iron,' 'damask,' and 'gold' are nothing less than an expression of sympathetic magic in words. All of them are used to emphasize the desired quality."[13] In the present instance, the security, solidity, and strength of the master's yard are demonstrated.

It is of some interest to inquire into how and when these epithets entered ritual poetry. There is no doubt that they arose in the age of metal, the discovery and smelting of which gave people such implements and means of defense as had never before existed on earth. The strength of copper and iron, the remarkable qualities of silver and gold not to tarnish or spoil, and in certain instances to cure, were noticed first by the olden smiths, sorcerers and healers, and priests. Noting these properties of metals, the ancient poets introduced their names into the lexicon of ritual speeches as though they had magical significance. Yet images of the *iron screen*, the *steel floor*, the *copper sky* did not yet definitively supplant the earlier images of the ritual tradition that had arisen during the Stone Age (the *stone screen*, the *stone sky*, *stone weapons*, etc.), which continued to survive in the oldest charms and religious rituals. We know that stone implements "played a leading role in the ancient religious ceremonies of the Romans. Such implements, devoutly kept in temples, were used to kill sacrificial victims. The most solemn of oaths were taken on the stone axe, kept in the Temple of Jupiter. . . ."[14]

Among the Semeiski of the Lake Baikal region we recorded one of the earliest charms, evidently going back to the dawn of agriculture and used to "safeguard" the grain: "Fire in front, water behind, a stone screen all around." These three elements (fire, water, and stone) were to ancient people a reliable means of protection against enemies and wild animals. They enhanced confidence in safety and thus were employed in the charm to safeguard grain.

Stone tools became part of the rituals of various peoples and have survived into modern-day ethnography, thanks to their preservation in ceremonial ritual.

According to our observations, stone was also used frequently in the ritual practice of the Russian Siberian population. Certain wounds were rubbed with stone, a person bitten by a mad dog would be drawn through an opening in stone, stones were placed with cabbages when they were planted so that the heads would be just as firm, etc. According to a belief we have recorded, stone cleanses by taking sickness into itself and neutralizes evil spirits. Even today the Semeiski say that "water in a stream is cleaned by forty stones." The image of the stone in archaic charms reminds us of the importance given to it by our distant ancestors.

With the birth of metallurgy, stone was displaced by iron. The daily life and folklore of many peoples preserve notions about the strength of iron: iron is feared by evil spirits and is used "against magic." Fortunetellers drew a circle about themselves with iron implements to be protected from demons. When digging up the roots of "wonder-working" herbs, the "wise people" also made a circle around themselves with an iron knife, to protect themselves against evil spirits guarding the plants.[b]

According to a belief attested among the Russian population of Lake Baikal, the best remedy against sorcery was a needle that had not yet been used for sewing. If this were kept on one's person, no magic need be feared. If a female sorcerer comes to the house, stick the needle in the door, and she cannot leave.

E. Taylor once observed: "The Eastern jinni (spirits inhabiting trees, stones, etc., according to pre-Muslim Arab beliefs) are so deathly afraid of iron that the mere word is used as a charm against them. Just so, in European beliefs, iron chases away wizards [*volshebniki*] and elves [*el'fy*] and destroys their power. These creatures, it seems, are the product of the old Stone Age, and the new metal is hateful and harmful to them." Iron implements and articles made from iron were considered to hold at bay unclean forces [*nechistaia sila*], witches, and house spirits [*domovye*].[c] For this reason, horseshoes were nailed to the entrance of a domicile to protect its inhabitants.[15]

Interesting facts of this kind are also mentioned by J. Frazer. Many prohibitions are connected with the use of iron. According to many peoples, "nothing of iron may touch the body of the ruler." Roman and Sabine priests were supposed to be shaved and their hair cut exclusively with bronze (never iron) razors and scissors. It was also forbidden to bring iron objects into the Greek sanctuaries. Shamans [folk healers] among the Hottentots, when making sacrifices or butchering meat, did not use iron knives but sharp pieces of quartz. Jews did not use iron tools in the building of the temple at Jerusalem or the construction of the altar. Evaluating these facts, Frazer writes: "The superstitious ban on the use of iron may go back to an extremely ancient period in the history of society, when iron was still a novelty and therefore regarded by many with suspicion and disapproval. All new things are capable of exciting fear and horror in the savage."[16]

Discussing similar facts, Frazer explains that this antipathy to iron was also extrapolated to the spirits, who were attributed a fear for the handmade material. The very origin of this metal enabled the presence of a magical component in the mind of early humans—hence the special attitude toward smiths. It was believed that "the antagonism of the spirits to iron is so great that they will not even permit themselves to approach objects or persons protected by this repulsive metal, [and therefore] iron can be used as a magical means of frightening away ghosts or other dangerous spirits."[17] That is why sharp piercing tools of iron (steel) came to be used as an amulet among the superstitious population. A needle, knife, or pin would be stuck into the door of the home so that a sorceress could not enter. A knife or scissors were also used in rituals to "drive off" sickness from the body of a person or animal. It is certain that piercing objects and tools also played an apotropeic [warding off evil] role. According to popular notions, the clanging of iron and the jingling of bells frightened evil spirits. This, it would appear, is the reason for the widespread use of iron, damask, and forged steel objects in the Russian charms of Siberia.

Iron was also used in purificatory rites, frequently combined with water, fire, garlic, and other substances that were taken to be amulets.

With the development of metallurgy, metal displaced stone tools and for a long time determined the development of the entire culture.

The Iron Age in Europe begins at the start of the first millennium B.C., while in the territory of the USSR it begins in the first century B.C.[d] The transition to metal tool fabrication was one of the powerful factors in raising productive capacities. Having mastered bronze and learned to smelt and work iron, people acquired tools of unprecedented strength, reliability, and durability. "In general, the advent of the age of metals produced a deep, almost revolutionary change in the history of early society."[18] Those specializing in the smelting and working of metals enjoyed particular respect. The smith was considered almost a sacred personage. In Rus', the smith was often an herb doctor and regarded as a sorcerer who could determine one's fate and "forge happiness."[19] He was feared and his craft was thought to depend on help from unclean supernatural strength. He held a special place in the community: his "bread" did not depend on the weather, the harvest, the whims of nature. Among many peoples of Africa and America the work of the smiths and smelters was surrounded with special secrecy and a nexus of bans and taboos, and protected by special purifying rituals. This work was the privilege of individual clans.[20] Since people did not understand how metal could be obtained from stone, they therefore thought that magic was essential for this process.

In the middle of the first millenium B.C., remarkable changes occurred in the ideology of various peoples over a vast area from China to Greece. Writers who study this period relate these ideological innovations in large measure to the spread of iron.[21] The technological innovation raised the economy to a new level, which could not help but bring changes in ideology and the social sphere. The mastery of the production technology of iron implements gave a new impulse to the human mind and strengthened faith in the human possibilities of remaking the world and nature in accordance with the needs of society. The image of iron as a symbol of reliability and firmness entered ritual and epic poetry (*"iron screen," "iron man,"* etc.). Thus, the Siberian charm "Against an Evil Charm" says: "There stands an iron man, leaning on an iron staff. Just as the mouth of the man will not open and his tongue not be lifted, so let the mouth of my enemy not open and his tongue not be lifted, from now until eternity."[22] The "iron hosts" of the famous "Lay of Igor's Campaign" have a source in common with these images.

We find the apotheosis of iron in a charm that was discussed at one time by E. Eleonskaia: "There is . . . the ocean-sea, on this ocean-sea there is another iron sea . . . , on this iron sea there is an iron pillar . . . , on this iron pillar stands an iron man, resting on his iron staff from east to west. . . ." This man demonstrates his power in protecting "his children—all iron and damask steel and blue forged steel and all ordinary iron . . . and he strengthens humanity with special clothing: [let him] place on me and my children a shirt of stone."[23] The charm is permeated with the epithet "iron," yet it contains the deeply archaic image of the *stone shirt.*[e]

N. F. Poznanskii believed that such objects as the key, the lock, and the iron stockade originally functioned as shepherds' amulets to protect the herd against roaming wild animals, evil people, thieves, and foes. Later on, the charms probably assumed broader functions; this is clear from the texts that we have already presented. In the Siberian cattle-drivers' charm published by D. A. Klements, this original function of a shepherd's amulet is brought out: "Holy Mother of God, place around my herd an iron stockade from the ground to the sky and close it with a golden lock. . . . I do not want the keys, the keys I shall throw in the water, and the keys will be eaten by a pike, and since no one can catch or hold this pike, so too will no one be able to do anything to my herd, neither ruin nor doom."[24]

The epithet "iron" was applied not just to images or objects through which one endeavored to protect people, flocks, or herds, but also during magic to work harm. Thus, to blight a turnip harvest, an evil person would conjure: "Copper turnip, iron ground, let mouse tails sprout."[25] In this instance, the "iron" fastness of the ground was to do the farmer ill. Such are the diverse meanings of the epithet "iron."

In the late nineteenth century, at the village of Kezhemskoe, Pinchug district, Eniseisk region (now the Krasnoiarsk territory), the ethnographer and folklorist V. S. Aref'ev recorded a charm against "curses" and the "evil eye," that says: "In the east there stands a white birch, beneath the white birch a white stone, beneath the white stone the heavenly pike; the heavenly pike has copper lips, iron teeth, pewter eyes. Remove, Heavenly Pike, from God's slave (the cursed person or animal is mentioned, depending on who is being conjured) the curse and the bad looks, and the hoarseness, and the lameness, and the fear, and the alarm."[26] What is remarkable in this charm are three images of ancient origin: the white birch, the white stone, and the heavenly pike. This fabulous pike, endowed with copper lips, iron teeth, and pewter eyes (the first three metals mastered by humanity!), is somehow able to deliver the sick one from three illnesses.

The use of the number 3 in the charm is no accident. In a number of traditions the number 3 opens the number series and is held to be perfect. It became a sacred, holy number. It is associated with ideas about the three worlds, the three whales, the holy trinity, and so on.[f] The recurring epithet "white," applied to the birch and the stone, also plays a certain semantic role. The color white in the mythopoetic system is the color of life and death; it is connected with death and rebirth and symbolizes purity, innocence, chastity, wealth, happiness, and well-being. The image of the holy tree—the healing birch, the amulet tree—is well known in Slavic ethnography. Notions concerning the birch have been well studied.[27] The image of the white stone, or stone-altar, belongs to the most ancient mythopoetic images. The white stone is the primordial stone, arising from the sea at the beginning of creation. This is well expressed in a Ukrainian song:

> And what we had in the beginning of the world,
> Oh! we had no shortage of blue water,
> Blue water, and a white stone,
> And the Lord covered the wet earth,
> And on it grew a cedar tree. . . . [28]

The "Poem of the Book of the Dove"[g] reveals other qualities of this primordial stone:

The white stone Latyr' is the father of all stones.
And why is it the father of all stones?
From under the stone, from under white Latyr'
There flowed the rivers, the fast rivers
Throughout the earth, throughout the universe,
To save the entire world,
To drench the entire world:
And that is why the stone is the father of all stones.[29]

The endowment of the stone with healing properties in popular belief probably had an influence: it came to be used in the folk medicine. According to the beliefs of the Eastern Slavs, "under that stone lies mighty power, endless power."

The image of fire is encountered in the conjuratory texts of the Russian population of Siberia. Fire is summoned for help in protecting the health of people or animals, kindling amorous passion, cleansing pollution, and so on. Thus, for example, folk doctors [*znakharki*] cured rashes, running face sores, and herpes blisters by conjuring: "Fire, fire, take your fire from God's slave (say name). I have been beyond the sea and have put out the fire."[30]

In amatory charms, fire was invoked to kindle a live spark in the heart of the loved one, as for example in this invocation:

My Tsar Fire, Tsarina Spark, Smokey Smoke! Fly, smoke, find, smoke, God's slave (say name) in the open field beneath the white birch, in the byways, in the alleys, in a happy chamber after honeyed victuals find him. His circle strike, twist, remove his white shirt, go into the white body, the lung, the liver, the hot blood, the entire frame, take him apart at the bone, at the joint, put in his heart a sad yearning, a painful pang, an inconsolable weeping, an unshakeable love. Let his heart rush and rage, let his blood be troubled for me, God's slave (say name). Let myself, God's slave (say name) be more beloved of God's slave (say name) than the white light, more beautiful than the beautiful sun, more dear than his father and mother and all his friends. In his food let him not eat for me, in his drink let him not drink for me, in his merrymaking let him not carouse. Let my words be strong and clinging. Amen.[31]

The cult of fire goes back to deep antiquity.

The meaning of fire in human life is commonly known. F. Engels noted: "The acquisition of fire by friction first gave people mastery of a definite force of nature and thus conclusively segregated them from the animal kingdom."[32] "Fire gave humanity the ability to live in all latitudes of the globe."[33] It also played a large part in rituals. Early humans worshipped fire as a living element, like the earth, water, sun, and so on. Fire could be good, it could heat, protect against wild animals, make food more tasty and digestible. It could be stern and ferocious, like a ravenous beast, destroying homes, forests, steppes, animals, inspiring people with fear and horror.

"Human helplessness before nature in the early stages of culture also produced in this case a superstitious feeling of significance, expressed by an ambivalent attitude toward fire: respect and at the same time fear."[34]

Fire was also worshipped in particular by Russian peasants in Siberia. Fire and the associated bonfire, hearth fire, stove, smoke, torches, embers, and ashes were endowed by the Sibiriaki with special sanctity and purity. Fire is one of the prime agencies in Siberian peasant purificatory and apotropeic rites. Important events in the life of the family and the community (weddings and funerals) could not be observed without these rites. During human and animal epidemics, special "living fire" was obtained by rubbing one tree against another, and this would be taken through the entire village, fumigating and driving out the foulness. In certain places fire was known as Tsar Fire. Thus, the Siberian charm recorded by V. Andrianov in the Kurgan region of Tobol'sk province says: "Oh Father, Tsar Fire, you are tsar of all tsars, you are fire of all fires. . . ."[35] In this context, "Tsar Fire" is used as a poetic determinant. The epithets "Tsar Fire" and "Tsarina Spark" are the product of a later order. The combination of the elemental force of nature with the force of the earthly sovereign, possessing great possibilities in the use of authority, seemed to humans in those distant times a substantial and inspired quality, which found its expression in the conjuratory epithet.

While "the term *living fire* . . . enhances the notion of purity, inviolability, the *newness* of the ritual flame,"[36] the concept of Tsar Fire enhanced the notion of its mightiness. It could protect humanity, ignite passionate love, heal sickness, and so on. "Living fire, used during epizoic diseases as an apotropeic and purificatory agent, has a function similar to that of *healing and living water* in Russian fables."[37] All of this shows the very old sources of such ideas.

The role of water in the Russian charms is multifarious. The image of water is especially frequent in invocation formulas designed to protect health.

Archaic notions generally appear in charm texts and actions when people are appealing for help to the elements (earth, water, fire, wind) and to cosmic objects (the sun, stars, new moon). There is no belief in gods or demons in the conjuratory formulas of this type: "Early humans, believing in the sympathetic power of word and deed, tries to elicit the desired effect by them. . . ."[38]

On the basis of animist ideas, early humans imagined sickness to be a living creature, a kind of foreign substance, harmful, entering into the body, and therefore capable of being driven out by such agencies as would "neutralize" it. For this purpose, along with pronouncing the proper words, noise would be made, striking with an axe, cutting with a cleaver, puncturing with a knife or arrow, cutting with shears, sucking out, washing, gnawing, and smoking it out, like an animal from its den.

None of the images or pictorial agencies in the charms are accidental. They were well understood and subservient to a main idea: in curative charms to drive out illness; in household charms to protect the home; in amatory charms to inspire love in the beloved or to cool and repel amorous feeling. In other words, "the images and personages of the charm are created in full correspondence with the functional purpose of the charm. . . ."[39] With the introduction of Christianity into Russia, the whole congress of Christian saints was adopted into the texts of conjurations alongside ancient personages and images, replacing and supplanting pre-Christian deities and personages in folk beliefs. The archangel Michael was seen as the protector against evil forces, Egorii the patron of horses, Vlasii replaced Volos (Veles), the cattle god of the ancient Slavs, Medost and Lavr were honored as horse gods in Siberia. Images of the Mother of God, Jesus Christ, Nicholas, and others were widely used.[b]

The origin of the charms is a complicated question. Some investigators assign the sources of the invocations to the Stone Age. It is surmised that people became aware of a "connective link" at this time, such as is often encountered in charm formulas of the type: "Join, grow together, body with body, bone with bone, sinew with sinew. . . ."[40] Evidently, Stone Age people already knew how to add and subtract serially based on the removal or addition of an object,[41] exemplified in the following charm text: "Ten worms were spawned in the red spotted cattle: from the ten nine, from the nine eight, from the eight seven, from the seven six, from the six five, from the five four, from the four three, from the three two, from the two one, from the one none."[42] The evolution of poetic images and symbols apparently followed the development of technology and culture, only rarely outstripping reality (stone walls—iron barrier, stone altar—iron pillar, stone sky—iron sky, but carpet—airplane etc.). Such are some of the data on archaic elements of charm texts preserved by the Russian old-liver population of Siberia.

Editor's notes

a. The author's Marxist approach is revealed here, since the two main legitimizing reasons for study of religious folk beliefs are to combat them and to reconstruct their history through identification of survivals. Nonetheless, Bolonev's interpretation is not entirely standard, for charms are seen as esthetic (worthy of symbolic interpretation), and they are acknowledged to be more persistent and meaningful than many Soviet researchers have understood.

b. This use of iron for spiritual protection is widespread among indigenous Siberian groups as well. See, for example, the Mansi ethnographer E. I. Rombandeeva, "Some Observances and Customs of the Mansi (Voguls) in Connection with Childbirth," in *Popular Beliefs and Folklore Tradition in Siberia*, ed. V. Dioszegi (The Hague: Mouton, 1968), p. 77.

c. Slavic peasants divided (and sometimes still divide) the supernatural into two kinds of power: "pure" or "clean strength" and "evil" or "unclean strength." The Christian God and all the saints fall into the "clean strength" category, while the Devil and many spirits of nature are "unclean." But one of the most ambiguous categories is the capricious house protector spirit, or *domovoi*. See Linda Ivanits, *Russian Folk Belief* (Armonk, NY: M. E. Sharpe, 1989); G. Alexinsky, "Slavonic Mythology," *Larousse Encyclopedia of Mythology* (New York: Prometheus, 1960), p. 298.

d. When the Iron Age came to Russia and the Caucasus depends on which region is discussed and what is considered a critical mass of iron. A gradient can be seen: the earliest iron discoveries come from southern areas near the Iranian border dating to the last centuries of the second millenium B.C. Further north, the timing is closer to that mentioned here. I am grateful to Phil Kohl for explanation of these issues. Cf. A. L. Mongait, *Archeology in the USSR*, trans. M. W. Thomson (Baltimore: Penguin, 1961, original 1955), pp. 152–78; Iu. V. Boltrik, "Sukhoputnye kommunikatsii skifii (po materialam novostroechenykh issledovanii ot Priazov'ia do Dnepra), *Sovetskaia arkheologiia*, 1990, no. 4, pp. 30–44.

e. A similar charm to cure hernia, collected by L. N. Maikov, "Velikorusskie zaklinaniia," *Zapiski imperatorskogo russskogo geograficheskogo obshchestva po otdeleniiu etnografii*, 1869, vol. 2, pp. 471–72, is strikingly shamanic. The "iron-man" of this ancient myth-like chant sits in a green oak, being served poison from the sickness of the living by a beautiful red messenger maiden who travels from the Blue Sea to various rivers where the sickness is to be found. She captures the sickness in a silken ribbon, delivering it to the green oak in a clear field.

f. The sacred trinity concept thus predates the Christian Father, Son, and Holy Ghost. The three worlds are heaven, earth, and the underworld; the three whales refers to a myth of three whales holding up the universe. (Nonetheless, in some versions there are four whales.) I am thankful to Linda Ivanits for clarification.

g. For discussion of this source, see T. A. Bernshtam, "Russian Folk Culture and Religion," in this volume, pages 34–48..

h. This fits with discussions of *dvoeverie*. See George Fedotov, *The Russian Religious Mind* (New York: Harper & Row, 1960), pp. 10–11, 357–58; Alexinsky, "Slavonic Mythology," pp. 304–5, 310.

Notes

1. N. I. Tolstoi, "Iz nabliudenii nad polesskimi zagovorami," *Slavianskii i balkanskii fol'klor: dukhovnaia kul'tura Poles'ia na obshcheslavianskom fone* (Moscow, 1986), p. 135.

2. V. N. Toporov, "K rekonstruktsii indoevropeiskogo rituala i ritual'no-poeticheskikh formul (na materiale zagovorov)," *Trudy po znakovym sistemam* (Tartu, 1969), issue 4, pp. 9–43; I. A. Chernov, "O strukture russkikh liubovnykh zagovorov," *Trudy po znakovym sistemam* (Tartu, 1965); Z. I. Vlasova, "K izucheniiu poetiki ustnykh zagovorov," *Russkii fol'klor* (Moscow, 1972), vol. 13.

3. Tolstoi, "Iz nabliudenii nad polesskimi zagovorami," p. 137.

4. A. M. Astakhova, *Khudozhestvennyi obraz i mirovozzrencheskii element v zagovorakh* (Moscow, 1964), p. 1.

5. See S. I. Guliaev, "Etnograficheskie ocherki Iuzhnoi Sibiri," *Biblioteka dlia chteniia*, 1848, vol. 90, division 3; M. F. Krivoshapkin, *Eniseiskii okrug i ego zhizn'* (St. Petersburg, 1865), vol. 1; D. A. Klements, "Nagovory i primety u krest'ian Minusinskogo okruga," *Izv. Vostochno-Sibirskoe otdelenie Russkogo geograficheskogo obshchestva* [hereafter *VSORGO*], 1902, vol. 19; A. A. Makarenko, "Materialy po narodnoi meditsine Uzhurskoi volosti Achinskogo okruga Eniseiskoi gub. S prilozheniem sbornika narodno-meditsinskikh sredstv toi zhe volosti," *Zhivaia starina* (St. Petersburg, 1898), issue 1–4; V. S. Aref'ev, "Obraztsy narodnoi slovesnosti: primety, gadan'ia, koldovstvo, nagovory i sueveriia," *Izv. VSORGO*, 1901, vol. 32, no. 1–2; M. V. Krasnozhenova, "Materialy po narodnoi meditsine Eniseiskoi gubernii," *Izv. VSORGO* (Irkutsk, 1908), vol. 39, pp. 10–23; (1911), vol. 42, pp. 65–86; P. M. Tolmachev, "Zagovory i pover'ia v Zabaikal'e," *Sib. arkhiv.* (Irkutsk, 1911), no. 2, 3; "Sibirskie zagovory," ed. Ia. O. Biriukov, *Altaiskii sbornik*, 1911, vol. 11; M. K. Azadovskii, "Zagovory amurskikh kazakov," *Zhivaia starina*, 1914, issue 3–4, pp. 5–15; G. S. Vinogradov, "Samovrachevanie i skotolechenie u russkogo starozhil'cheskogo naseleniia Sibiri," *Zhivaia starina* (St. Petersburg, 1915), issue 4; idem, "Pover'ia i obriady krest'ian-sibiriakov: materialy po etnografii Nizhneudinskogo uezda," *Sib. arkhiv.* (Irkutsk, 1915), no. 3–5.

6. L. N. Maikov, "Velikorusskie zaklinaniia," *Zapiski RGO po otdeleniiu etnografii* (St. Petersburg, 1869), vol. 2; N. N. Vinogradov, "Zagovory, oberegi, spasitel'nye molitvy i pr.," *Zhivaia starina* (St. Petersburg, 1907), issue 1–2; (1908) issue 1–4; (1909) issue 4; A. Vetukhov, "Zagovory, zaklinaniia, oberegi i drugie vidy narodnogo vrachevaniia, osnovannye na vere v silu slova," *Russkii filologich. vestn.*, 1907, issue 1–2.

7. *Russkoe narodnoe poeticheskoe tvorchestvo*, ed. P. G. Bogatyrev (Moscow, 1954), p. 219; *Russkoe ustnoe narodnoe tvorchestvo*, eds. N. I. Kravtsov and S. G. Lazutin (Moscow, 1983), p. 61.

8. M. M. Gromyko, *Trudovye traditsii russkikh krest'ian Sibiri XVIII–pervoi poloviny XIX v.* (Novosibirsk, 1975), pp. 130–50; idem, "Dokhristianskie verovaniia v bytu sibirskikh krest'ian XVIII–XIX vv.," *Iz istorii sem'i i byta sibirskogo krest'ianstva XVII–nachala XX v.* (Novosibirsk, 1975), pp. 86–102; N. N. Pokrovskii, "Materialy po istorii magicheskikh verovanii sibiriakov XVII–XVIII vv.," ibid., pp. 110–30; L. V. Ostrovskaia, "Mirovozzrencheskie aspekty narodnoi meditsiny russkogo krest'ianskogo naseleniia Sibiri vtoroi poloviny XIX v.," ibid., pp. 131–42; F. F. Bolonev, "O nekotorykh sposobakh narodnogo vrachevaniia u semeiskikh Zabaikal'ia," *Etnograficheskie aspekty izucheniia narodnoi meditsiny: Tezisy vsesoiuznoi konferentsii* (Leningrad, 1975); N. A. Minenko, "K istorii russkoi narodnoi meditsiny v Sibiri XVIII–pervoi poloviny XIX v.," *Traditsii i innovatsii v bytu i kul'ture narodov Sibiri* (Novosibirsk, 1983), pp. 88–103.

9. Klements, "Nagovory i primety," pp. 32–33.

10. Guliaev, "Etnograficheskie ocherki," p. 42.

11. Tolmachev, "Zagovory i pover'ia v Zabaikal'e," pp. 140–41.

12. *Kalendarno-obriadovaia poeziia sibiriakov* (Novosibirsk, 1981), p. 31.

13. N. F. Poznanskii, "Zagovory: Opyt issledovaniia proiskhozhdeniia i razvitiia zagovornykh formul," *Zap. ist.-fil. f-ta Petrogradskogo un-ta* (Petrograd, 1917), p. 171.

14. N. F. Vysotskii, *Narodnaia meditsina* (Moscow, 1911), p. 147.

15. E. Taylor, [*Primitive Culture*] (Moscow, 1939), p. 83.

16. J. Frazer, [*The Golden Bough*] (Moscow, 1983), pp. 216–17.

17. Ibid.

18. M. O. Kosven, *Ocherki istorii pervobytnoi kul'tury* (Moscow, 1957), p. 203.

19. Ibid., p. 205.

20. E. N. Chernykh, *Metall, chelovek, vremia* (Moscow, 1972), pp. 140–42, 184–86, 188–98.

21. A. I. Zaitsev, "K voprosu o proiskhozhdenii volshebnoi skazki," *Fol'klor i etnografiia. U etnograficheskikh istokov fol'klornykh siuzhetnykh obrazov* (Leningrad: Nauka, 1984), pp. 76–77.

22. *Altaiskii sbornik*, 1911, vol. 11, p. 6.

23. E. Eleonskaia, *K izucheniiu zagovora i koldovstva v Rossii* (Moscow, 1917), no. 1, pp. 43–44.

24. Klements, "Nagovory i predmety," p. 41.

25. Krivoshapkin, "Eniseiskii okrug i ego zhizn'," p. 44.

26. Aref'ev, "Obraztsy narodnoi slovesnosti," pp. 47–48.

27. D. K. Zelenin, *Totemy-derev'ia v skazaniiakh i obriadakh evropeiskikh narodov* (Moscow-Leningrad, 1937); V. Ia. Propp, *Russkie agrarnye prazdniki* (Moscow, 1965); B. A. Rybakov, *Iazychestvo drevnikh slavian* (Moscow, 1980); idem, "Drevnie elementy v russkom narodnom tvorchestve," *Sovetskaia etnografiia*, 1948, no. 1, p. 105; F. F. Bolonev, *Narodnyi kalendar' semeiskikh Zabaikal'ia (vtoraia polovina XIX–nachalo XX v.)* (Novosibirsk, 1978), pp. 134–52.

28. Quoted in N. I. Korobka, "'Kamen' na more' i kamen' alatyr'," *Zhivaia starina* (St. Petersburg, 1909), no. 4, p. 409.

29. Ibid., p. 423.

30. Recorded by the author in 1967 at Ulan-Ude from U. S. Nazarova, born 1906.

31. Recorded in Western Siberia. Kept at the M. N. Mel'nikov archive.

32. F. Engels, *Dialektika prirody* (Moscow, 1957), p. 108.

33. S. A. Semenov, "Dobyvanie ognia treniem," *Materialy po etnografii: Doklady za 1962 g.* (Leningrad, 1963), issue 3, p. 6.

34. S. A. Tokarev, *Religioznye verovaniia vostochno-slavianskikh narodov XIX–nachala XX v.* (Moscow-Leningrad, 1957), p. 65.

35. Maikov, "Belorusskie zaklinaniia," p. 514.

36. A. F. Zhuravlev, "Iz russkoi obriadovoi leksiki: 'zhivoi ogon'," *Obshcheslavianskii lingvisticheskii atlas. Materialy i issledovaniia* (Moscow, 1978), p. 228.

37. Ibid., p. 227.

38. E. V. Anichkov, *Vesenniaia obriadovaia pesnia na Zapade i u slavian* (St. Petersburg, 1903), pt. 1: "From the Ritual to the Song," p. 120.

39. V. P. Petrov, "Zagovory," *Iz istorii russkoi sovetskoi fol'kloristiki* (Leningrad, 1981), p. 102.

40. Maikov, "Velikorusskie zaklinaniia," p. 168.

41. V. N. Toporov, "K proizkhozhdeniiu nekotorykh poeticheskikh simvolov. Paleoliticheskaia epokha," *Rannie formy iskusstva* (Moscow, 1972), p. 82; idem, "K rekonstruktsii indoevropeiskogo rituala i ritual'no-poeticheskikh formul," pp. 9–13.

42. The charm was recorded by the author in 1976 in the Gremiachinskoe village, Pribaikal region, Buriat ASSR, from M. E. Trifonova, born 1895 (in the village of Kuitun, Tarbagatai region of Buriatiia).

On the History of Icon Painting in Western Siberia

N. G. VELIZHANINA

Publications on the icon painting of Siberia are few. There are primarily the materials of A. I. Sulotskii, who worked in the mid-nineteenth century in the churches of Tobol'sk and in the archives with documents that were later lost, who viewed icons whose location is now unknown.[1] Data on Siberian icons is found in articles by N. A. Abramov from the mid-nineteenth century and by P. N. Butsinskii from the end of that century.[2] Scattered references to Siberian icons and the masters who painted them are included in studies of ethnographers such as N. Kostrov and A. E. Novoselov. In connection with a study of Siberian culture, A. N. Kopylov discovered additional information on Siberian icon painting in archives.[3] A short article on the Siberian folk icon was published by N. Kazarinov.[4] T. A. Kriuchkova was interested in the history of icon painting in Eastern Siberia. The author of the present article sees her task as presenting, in general outline, the history of icon painting on the basis of the publications, documents, and productions in Western Siberia from the seventeenth to nineteenth centuries.[5]

In the first decades after Ermak's conquest, Siberia and its newly built churches, monasteries, and houses were provided with icons from European Russia. These icons were brought by the first Cossack pioneers, by the first representatives of the Siberian clergy, and also by settlers belonging to various social strata—from the highest administrators to runaway serfs. The tsar also donated icons to the first Siberian churches and monasteries.[6]

Icons for sale ("for barter," as was said then) also, in all likelihood, were brought to Siberia in the first half of the seventeenth century. According to Kopylov, in 1640 the peasants Semenov and Ivanov of the Prince of Pozharsk brought 360 icons to Tobol'sk. The facts of such journeys are corroborated by documents from the seventeenth to nineteenth centuries.[7] Virtually all primary icon-painting centers took part in the creation of the icon fund of Siberia: Moscow, Novgorod and Pomerania, Great Ustiug, the Vla-

Russian text © 1987 by "Nauka" Publishers. "K istorii ikonopisaniia v zapadnoi Sibiri," in *Traditsionnye obriady i iskusstvo russkogo i korennykh narodov Sibiri*, edited by L. M. Rusakova and N. A. Minenko (Novosibirsk: Nauka, 1987), pp. 125–41. A publication of the Institute of History, Philology, and Philosophy, Siberian Division, USSR Academy of Sciences.

dimir region, and (beginning with the eighteenth century) the south-west—Kiev and the Old Believer centers of southern Russia. The character of the emerging Siberian icon painting was dictated both by the influence of certain icon-painting schools and by the conditions of Siberia itself.

The beginning of Siberian icon painting is beyond doubt connected with the establishment of the Siberian eparchy with its center at Tobol'sk in 1621—both prerevolutionary and modern scholars who have dealt with this matter are agreed on this point.[8]

The first Tobol'sk and Siberian archbishop was Kiprian (Starorusenkov), the former archimandrite of the Novgorod Spasokhutynsk monastery and a skilled organizer. By the end of his tenure in 1625, there were twelve monasteries (generally including two or three temples) and thirty churches in Siberia. In setting out for his new appointment, Kiprian prepared himself for an ambitious construction program and brought along a considerable number of icons and church accoutrements.

We have discovered a copy by A. I. Sulotskii of an extremely interesting seventeenth-century writ, along with his interpretations. "You know" (writes the patriarch Filaret to the first Siberian archbishop, Kiprian) "how many treasures of beauty our devout son and great sovereign, Tsar Mikhail Fedorovich, and I have expended on behalf of God's church and human salvation, when he ordered that this bishopric be established in that faraway land (Siberia).[9]

However, given the extent of church building in Siberia, it was hard to supply all temples with imported icons, since an iconostasis in the Russian Orthodox Church usually included several dozen icons.[a] Therefore, Kiprian, setting out for Siberia with "his appointed staff" of twenty-five persons, according to P. Butsinskii "took along two icon painters among the other people."[10]

We know the names of several of the icon-painting masters who worked in Siberia in the 1620s. In a 1624 payment book, among tradepeople and service people of Tobol'sk, are registered the yards of the "Sofian archdeacon Matvei," the "tradesman Ivan Stepanov, iconist," and the "Cossack horseman, Fedotka the Iconist."[11] In the payment register of 1625–26, iconists Bogdan and Vtoroi appear in connection with the loss of a kettle of drying oil.[12]

One of the first Siberian iconists was the archdeacon of the Tobol'sk cathedral, Matvei Martynov, who in 1637 painted the icon of the Abalakskaia Mother of God [*Bogomater'*]. Subsequently, this was declared to be miraculous and became the most revered icon in Siberia. He came to Tobol'sk with Archbishop Kiprian and shortly thereafter painted two images of the Mother of God behind the altar and retouched the old icons.[13]

Thus, it is known that five icon painters were working in the 1620s in Tobol'sk, one in Tiumen', and one in Turinsk.

In the 1630s, the group of Siberian icon painters received reinforcements. According to the documents published by Kopylov, in 1636 Archbishop Nektarii, upon being appointed to Tobol'sk, brought from the "Nilor monastery the icon painter Monk Antonii," who held the position of icon painter of Tobol'sk Sofia House until 1645. On the request of this same Nektarii, Dmitrii Butusin of Sol' Vychegodskaia and Pervyi Tsyrkov from Great Ustiug were sent to Tobol'sk in 1638.[14]

N. A. Abramov mentions the icon painter Finis Cherkunov, who painted the large icon (3 x 2 arshins) "The Savior Pantocrator" [*Spas Vsederzhitel'*] for the Turinsk Krestovozdvizhenskii [Exaltation of the Cross] Monastery.[b] Abramov reports that, according to tradition, "this picture was painted in the first quarter of the seventeenth century."[15]

The first reliably dated Siberian icon belongs to 1624: it is the "Mother of God of the Sign" [*Bogomater' Znamenie*] in the Tiumen' Znamenskii Church [of the Sign], painted by Spiridon the Iconist, a native of Great Ustiug and patriarch of the Ikonnikov trading house, which became famous in Tiumen' in the seventeenth and eighteenth centuries. Having seen this icon, Sulotskii described it as octagonal, with nine angels around the Mother of God.[16] In this same Znamenskii Church we found an icon of equally unusual form, but of a later date, the mid-twentieth century. As the icon was in a glass-covered niche it could not be examined, so the question of whether a seventeenth-century painting lies beneath layers of renovation, or whether that icon was the legendary one, remains open.

The Tiumen' "Mother of God of the Sign" is important to the history of Siberian icon painting as one of the early testimonies of the ambition of the Tobol'sk bishop's house, and especially the Archbishop Kiprian, to make the Siberian church the successor of the Novgorod church, for this very icon is held to be the palladium of Novgorod, being venerated as miraculous, with its subject figuring as a heroine in the icon "The Battle of the Novgorodians with the Suzdalians."

The payment book of 1624 and the register books of 1625–26 list 368 icons at Tobol'sk cathedral and churches; on the basis of additional information, it may be assumed that no less than 200 of these were painted locally. This is also confirmed by the frequent shipments from Moscow of paints and other materials needed for icon painting. Thus, " . . . with the Protopope Ivan (Iosifov) the Tsar Mikhail sent to Kiprian various German paints for icon painting." On another occasion, Mikhail Fedorovich dispatched several church books thither, "and for icon work, 2,000 gold sheets, 500 silver sheets, several pounds of various paints, 5 pounds of chalk, glue, etc."[17]

Already in the 1640s the demand of Siberian churches for icons were being mainly satisfied locally. This conclusion is aided, in particular, by the reply of the military governor [*voevoda*] Pronskii to the Siberian Office regarding the fire in the Church of the Ascension on January 22, 1642, during which thirty-seven large icons were lost, not to mention the "icons painted for the church holidays." The governor was confident that pictures in place of those that were consumed "could be painted in Tobol'sk, except that paint, and gold, and Susal' silver must be sent from Moscow."[18]

A second document confirming this possibility is the order of Tsar Mikhail Fedorovich of February 10, 1644, from which it follows that as early as 1638, the Yakutsk governors Pushkin and Suponev were ordered to have icons for the Yakutsk church "painted right in Siberia, in Tobol'sk, by iconists sent to Tobol'sk to the archbishop from Great Ustiug and from Soli Vychegodskie."[19] Clearly, Siberian icon painters served not only the city and the island around Tobol'sk, but also worked for Eastern Siberia, although there were not yet many masters.

In this connection, the pulpit of Tobol'sk was faced with the task of teaching local residents, both those born in Siberia and those from elsewhere, to paint icons in Tobol'sk itself.

According to Sulotskii's data, in the mid-seventeenth century at the Tobol'sk archbishop's house two teachers of icon painting were salaried by the archbishop.[20] In 1669, in the outskirts of Eniseisk, and not "Tobol'sk the Capital," there were already five icon painters[21]—not counting the icon-painting masters among the clergy, who generally constituted a significant proportion of the painters. Sulotskii writes: "On the example of the bishop's house and the monastery of the Tobol'sk eparchy, some at least formerly had their own icon painters, either from among their patrimonial peasants and monastery servants, or from among their novices and monks."[22]

In the second half of the seventeenth century, we know of only one instance of icons being sent from Moscow to a Siberian church: in 1671, the icon "The Last Judgment" [Strashnyi sud'] on canvas was sent to the Troitskii [Trinity] Monastery of Kondinsk, with an inscription announcing its donation by "the great lord Fedor Alekseevich."[23] As we know, however, such offerings were not always motivated by an absence of icons at the monastery or church for which the gift was intended.[c]

In 1680, this same Fedor Alekseevich, while sending to the newly built stone cathedral of Tobol'sk two bells (103 and 40 poods), a silver cross, an evangelium, and "service vessels," sent no icons.[24] Paint, gold, and drying oil were now being transported to Siberia from Moscow. For example, in 1685 the scrivener Grigorii Iakovlev brought a pood of drying oil, as well as two thousand gold sheets, for the Sofia Cathedral. In February 1688, the Iamsk department has a "memorandum" of the passage of the Sofia priest Mikhail Vitiazev with church implements purchased in Moscow for the Tobol'sk Sofia Cathedral, including "paint for painting holy pictures."[25]

The extent of Siberian icon painting during this period was very large, as can be shown by easy computations. In 1625 there were about 50 temples in

Siberia and in 1702 there were 160; thus in seventy-seven years of the seventeenth century no fewer than 110 cathedrals and churches were built. The number of iconostases erected in them must be further increased by allowance for partitions, as well as the fact that some of the wooden churches that were built burned down. Each iconostasis had from one to several dozen icons. Furthermore, icons were required for many chapels—public and private, for the monastery cells and for houses.

The creation of Siberian iconography proper, i.e., the appearance of local variants of canonical themes, is dated to the middle and the second half of the seventeenth century. An active role was played here by the Sofia bishop's house, the superiors of which considered this work to be a means of strengthening the authority of the Tobol'sk Siberian pulpit.

One of the most vital measures of the bishopric in this direction was the establishment of the "Abalakskaia Mother of God" communion table in 1636 and the painting of an icon in her honor.[26] Sulotskii and Abramov mention the painting of the icon of the "Abalakskaia Mother of God" by Archdeacon Matvei Martynov.[27] A reproduction of an engraving from the mid-nineteenth century depicting this icon has been preserved and reproduced in many copies (Fig. 1, p. 90). In the foreground is the Mother of God of the Sign, on the left in the fields is depicted Nikolai the Miracle Worker [Chudovorets] in an attitude of worship to the Mother of God, on the right is Mary of Egypt. In the north, Nikola was especially popular.[d] Icons with saints in the fields were also extremely widespread in the Novgorod area (and at Great Ustiug). All of this shows that the clerical authorities of Tobol'sk were trying to make Siberia the successor to Novgorod.

In the second half of the seventeenth century, cults of the individual Siberian saints appeared, for Vasilii Mangazeiskii and Simeon Verkhoturskii. According to Sulotskii, L. Filippov painted the first icon of Vasilii Mangazeiskii, produced in 1687 after a vow of thanks "for salvation during the blizzard," "having inquired at Turukhansk into the external appearance of the martyr who was venerated there."[28] N. Kostrov dates the appearance of images of this saint to 1679.[29] It is possible that the first icons of Vasilii Mangazeiskii apared even somewhat earlier, since the first parts of his life (according to E. K. Romodanovskaia) were written in the 1650s.[30] V. K. Andrievich and N. Kostrov have pointed out the special reverence for this saint and the existence of icons with his likeness at Eniseisk, Turukhansk, and Krasnoiarsk.[31]

So far we have found no paintings of Vasilii Mangazeiskii. Perhaps this is due to the peculiarities of his cult: Vasilii was believed to have perished unjustly from the beatings of his master, the governor of Mangazei S. Pushkin, and he was revered as a righteous martyr. Of course, this was not very impressive to those who wielded power, ecclesiastical and secular, and rendered his canonization impossible. According to folk traditions, Vasilii

Figure 1. "Abalakskaia Mother of God." 1637. Tobol'sk. M. Martynov (early 1560s–after 1645). Reprinted from the book by A. I. Sulotskii, *Opisanie naibolee chtimykh ikon Tobol'skoi eparkhii* (St. Petersburg, 1864). Location unknown.

Mangazeiskii was the patron of hunters and trappers, which reflected the special nature of Siberian life.

Pictures of Simeon Verkhoturskii are met not uncommonly in Western Siberia—several life-size icons as well as model icons of various dimensions, including miniatures. Simeon is usually depicted in peasant dress, in a simultaneous composition, where alongside the main image is another identical figure in a different attitude, with a fishing pole cast in the river and a

Figure 2. "Simeon Verkhoturskii." Nineteenth century. Verkhotur'e. Novosibirsk Picture Gallery.

wooden bucket, against the backdrop of the buildings of the Verkhotursk monastery (Fig. 2). As Romodanovskaia declares, the first parts of the "Life of Simeon Verkhoturskii" were produced during the time of Archbishop Ignatii Rimskii-Korsakov, who himself participated in its creation—hence, in 1692–99.[32] According to Sulotskii, around 1695 the priest-monk Ioann painted icons of excellent quality for the newly built stone cathedral of Verkhotursk.[33] Since the cult of Simeon Verkhoturskii was being created during this same period, was his first icon not painted then and there? Analysis of the composition of the Simeon icons, which combine the distinguishing features of direct perspective in the rendering of the landscape, especially the monastery buildings, with the simultaneity of the Middle Ages, does not refute this hypothesis, so that the first and original icon may be assigned roughly to that period of transition in the history of Russian painting when the appearance of elements of two different pictorial systems (Old Russian and European) in the same production first became possible.

It would seem that the stylistic features of Siberian icon painting took shape under the influence of separatist tendencies of the secular and spiritual authorities of Siberia and the well-known special qualities of the culture of the local population. While it is not possible to characterize Siberian icon styles in their many varieties here, we shall point out the major ones among them.

The most characteristic Russian icon paintings of Siberia, according to D. A. Rovinskii, were "icons with faces and full figures, as though stepping forward in relief."[34] The Altai Museum of Graphic and Applied Art has an icon of the "Mother of Unexpected Joy" [*Bogomater' Nechaiannaia radost'*] with high (up to 7 mm) relief. In our opinion, the sources of its painting style may be considered to be the "Stroganov painting,"[35] while molded relief on wooden boards arose as a result of development of one of the variants of Byzantine icon painting, which had not become common in Russia up to this time.[36] Similar to the Stroganov style is a characteristic family-commissioned icon depicting three saints in the Novosibirsk Picture Gallery (Fig. 3).

The influence of icons with relief, revealed in particular by the existence of sculptured relief icons of various types, as well as the development of the stylistic direction characterized by prominent emphasizing of the musculature of the faces and bodies of the saints (Fig. 4), can be traced in Western Siberia up to and including the nineteenth century.

The second tendency of Siberian seventeenth-century icon painting is the typical orientation toward archaic traditions: laconic composition and form and "dark-face" coloring, as though the paint were covered with a layer of darkened drying oil. Examples of this are the "Mother of God of Kazan'" icons in the Tomsk Art Museum and Museum of Local History, evidently painted in the late seventeenth and early eighteenth centuries in Tobol'sk, and the "Mother of God of Smolensk" icon from the Tobol'sk Museum and Shrine of History and Architecture.

The third stylistic tendency of seventeenth-century Siberian icon painting

Figure 3. "Selected Saints: Antipa, Grigorii, Ekaterina." Late seventeenth century. Tobol'sk. Novosibirsk Picture Gallery.

was inaugurated, in our opinion, by the "Sofia—Divine Wisdom" icon in the Sofia Cathedral of Tobol'sk. Sulotskii describes it thus: "The wisdom of the divine word is depicted in the same way as at Novgorod and Moscow, i.e., in the form of an angel in royal raiment, seated on a seven-step platform, and

Figure 4. "Nikolai the Miracle-Worker." First half of the nineteenth century. Novosibirsk Picture Gallery.

so forth, but with the difference that Saint Sofia is placed in a tree, at the root of which are shown the Tsar Ivan Vasil'evich the Terrible and Metropolitan Dionisii of Moscow, during whose tenure Siberia was conquered by

Ermak, and on the branches of the tree are the first six Siberian bishops (the last Metropolitan Kornilii, who died in 1667)."[37] In our opinion, this composition was painted under the influence of an icon by Simon Ushakov, "Planting of the Tree of the Russian State," preserved in the State Tret'iakov Gallery, where the center of the composition is again a tree, at the root of which are shown Prince Ivan Kalita and Metropolitan Petr, who brought the pulpit from Vladimir to Moscow, and in the branches are medallions with portraits of all prominent political actors of Ancient Rus'.

It may be confirmed that the icon of Sofia Cathedral was painted in Tobol'sk on commission from the bishop's house, for nowhere else would they dare to compare the creation of the Tobol'sk eparchy with the founding of Muscovite Russia. Ushakov's composition is dated 1668. The Tobol'sk icon was evidently painted during the time of the seventh Siberian archbishop, Pavel I, who succeeded Kornilii. He spent twelve years in Siberia, from 1668 to 1681.[38] Having been the archimandrite of the Chudov monastery at the Kremlin in Moscow and at the same time a member of the patriarchal class in charge of the construction of churches and monasteries throughout Russia, he would certainly have seen the work of Ushakov and, once arrived in Siberia, with the impression fresh in his mind, would have ordered the masters to paint an icon of similar composition to glorify the Tobol'sk bishop's house. Whether he brought the icon painter with him or commissioned a local master for the icon is a question that is of paramount importance but thus far unanswered. In any case, with Pavel I the most modern Moscow courtly tastes of the time found an embodiment in Tobol'sk, especially the tastes of the Kremlin icon-painting studio led by Ushakov.

Evidently among the leaders of the spiritual and secular authority coming to live in Siberia, especially in Tobol'sk, were those who possessed rather "modern" artistic tastes: they brought with them icon painters whose understanding of the form and content of the art was equal to their time.

An extremely significant reorientation of the icon-painting tastes of the higher clergy of Siberia took place in the early eighteenth century with Filofei Leshchinskii's ascension to the Siberian pulpit (1702). From this time onwards graduates of the Kiev clerical academy became the archbishops of Siberia, and southern Russian and Ukrainian influences began to be felt in artistic productions. This is shown, in particular, by the replacement in 1710, on Leshchinskii's initiative, of the iconostasis of the Tobol'sk Sofia Cathedral, painted in 1686. Sulotskii writes: " . . . the iconostasis was taken down by the Metropolitan Filofei, whether because it did not suit the magnificence of the building or for another reason. This person explained to his sovereign, Petr I, the need to construct a new iconostasis, and after receiving 1,000 rubles from the treasury, he had an entirely new, sculpted one produced in 1710."[39] Sulotskii, rather indifferent to matters of stylistics, did not understand why the iconostasis was replaced. The reasons were these: Leshchinskii, a Ukrainian by birth, formerly the steward of the Kiev Pecherskaia Lavra, came to Siberia at a time when the "Ukrainian Baroque," so distant from the stark and mainly northern tastes of the seventeenth-century Siberian spiritual leaders, was in full flower in his homeland.

Sulotskii describes in detail one other local icon of the Tobol'sk Sofia Cathedral, "Sofia the Divine Wisdom," declaring that it is almost identical to the icon in the Kiev Sofia Cathedral. According to the data of Sulotskii and recently found documents, Filofei Leshchinskii "wrote to Kiev for some of its artists and artisans,"[40] and these worked in Tobol'sk and other Siberian towns such as Tiumen'.

From this time onwards Baroque forms were actively asserted—in architecture this trend was so pronounced that it received special designation as the "Siberian Baroque." There are several Siberian icons with elements of the Baroque style in Irkutsk—at the Museum of Art[41] and at local churches. Elements of the Baroque are perceptible in eighteenth-century Tobol'sk and Tomsk icons (Fig. 5). One such icon, preserved by the Tomsk Regional History Museum, is "The Fiery Ascent [Ognennoe voskhozhdenie] of the Prophet Il'ia" (1779), with opulent Baroque cartouches of oval medallions, with a conventional realistic landscape of the academic type, with garments twisting in the wind, and with a chariot of fiery colors.

The Demidov school at the Nizhnetagil'sk estate, oriented toward Western European principles of art, also became a source of new influences in Siberia in the early eighteenth century. A result of the Ukrainian and Demidov influences was the spread of Western European "Friazhskii" painting; in particular, oil on canvas work for the iconostasis became widespread from the mid-eighteenth century on.[42] A typical blending of canonical icon-painting traditions with the techniques of "Friazhskii" painting appeared in the eighteenth-century icon "The Annunciation" [Blagoveshchenie] from the Tobol'sk Pokrovskii Cathedral.[e]

Canonical icon painting also survived in Siberia during this period. Such is the import of a document from the archives of Tiumen', found by the present author: " . . . the main church of the cathedral, Troitskaia, [had] a magnificent iconostasis, contemporary with the building of the church itself (1710—N.V.), a Greek, very exquisite painting."[43]

The scale of Siberian icon painting was probably particularly vast in the first half of the eighteenth century: from 1702 to 1742, 288 churches were built here, and consequently no less than 300 iconostases (counting the partitions) were created, amounting to several thousand icons.

However, in the 1760s (in connection with the secularization of church land in 1764), the Tobol'sk bishop's house lost its free icon painters. "Some of the icon painters and sculptors returned to the places of their former habitation and forgot their skill there,"[44] others continued to pursue it, al-

Figure 5. "Mother of God of Kazan'." Tobol'sk Museum-Shrine of History and Architecture.

though on a lesser scale and gradually losing their high professional stature.[45] The Tobol'sk bishop's house endeavored to counter this by regulating icon painting—issuing certificates of work approval to painters and examining the icons. The Archbishop Varlaam himself was especially active in this.

By October 25, 1764, the Tobol'sk clerical consistory already had a "Department for Examination of Icon Painters": "The priest Andrei Mikhailov is commanded to examine the icon painters, to make sure that . . . they execute the holy icons correctly."[46] Since the teaching of icon painting was no longer being done at the Tobol'sk Sofia house, individual instruction by masters was instituted. A testimony to the organization of such teaching is the record of the Tobol'sk clerical consistory of July 1772, concerning a leave of absence for Ivan Pogrebtsov, sexton of the Pokrovskaia Church of Nizhnetagil'sk district, to study icon painting. In his request, the sexton writes: " . . . how I, a humble person, from childhood had a desire to learn the icon art, and when I was with the church, in my idle moments, I tried in every way to accomplish by desire by my own efforts, except that there are no skilled artists on this estate, and I am entirely uninstructed, and so I now have such a great desire. On this account, Your Grace, and Merciful Pastor, I humbly ask to be released from the duties of sexton for the space of a year."[47] Masters of icon painting are also mentioned here: the tradesman Abram Menshchikov (who is mentioned as having left Tobol'sk) and the tradesman Mikhail Cherepanov, from a famous family of icon painters. A term of study of three years was appointed for the sexton (previously, the icon-painting tutelage lasted for two years).

In the eighteenth century, Siberian craftsmen, including icon painters, began to form guilds. In particular, the documents of the Tobol'sk provincial magistrate of 1738 list nine icon painters of Tobol'sk and mention the guild leader, Aleksei Budrin; it is said of four of the masters that they are "from the trading class" [iz meshchan] and the other five "from the guild."[49]

By the start of the nineteenth century, signs of crisis in Siberian icon painting were evident. Even though icons were painted rather competently, and the special Siberian style was preserved, it was gradually eroding.

In order to maintain the level of icon-painting mastery, the leaders of the Tobol'sk eparchy resolved to teach icon painting to the local clergy, so that priests could themselves paint and revise the work of others. For this, in 1800, a class in drawing was started at the Tobol'sk religious seminary, where instruction was given by the teacher P. Misiurev and later by the steward of the Tobol'sk cathedral, M. Karpinskii. In 1818, the class was closed. Thirty-six years later, in May 1854, the Tobol'sk religious academy began to teach "drawing, sketching, and icon painting," while the seminary taught painting and icon painting. The instructors were Iakov Biserov and Mikhail Znamenskii, who had been specially sent for two years to the Petersburg seminary, where they studied with Professor Solntsev of the Academy of Arts.[50] In our opinion, this decisively strengthened the movement of the principles of Siberian church icon painting toward "Friazhskii" painting, i.e., the general European type. Yet the traditions of old Russian icon painting were preserved in part by domestic prayer icons.

In the nineteenth century in Siberia, as elsewhere in Russia, icon workshops were created in which masters acquired a particular specialization—the face, the background, the landscape, and so on. Icons were now produced collectively. However, there were relatively few such workshops in Siberia.

Throughout the existence of Siberian icon painting, the demand for its productions usually exceeded the supply, and therefore along with officially recognized icon painters there were always folk masters working. The peasant artists were frequently masters of both icon and decorative paint-

Figure 6. "The Almighty Savior." Suzun. I. V. Krest′ianikov (1858–1941). Novosibirsk Picture Gallery.

ing,[51] which defined the folk icon's esthetics. Folk icons were always produced here in greater numbers than in the European part of Russia; with the advent of the crisis in official icon painting their overall proportion increased. Productions of folk icon-painting masters in Siberia in the second half of the nineteenth and start of the twentieth centuries are a significant phenomenon. While there is a certain diversity given local features, these icons have in common a pictorial folklore structure and a "primitive" style (see Fig. 6 on page 99). Peasant icon-painting masters would often sell their works ("barter them to the people") at markets. A group of icon painters worked at Suzun, in the Altai Mountain Region, where from the middle of the nineteenth century onwards icons were sold at the Nikol'skii winter fairs (the largest in terms of goods in the south of Siberia).[52]

The work of icon painters employed by Old Believers also had specific features in Siberia, frequently with an orientation toward archaic tendencies in Russian icon painting.

Starting in the second half of the seventeenth century, icon-painting centers with distinguishing traits of iconography and stylistics gradually formed in Tiumen', Irkutsk, and certain other Siberian cities. Their discovery and study is one of the most vital tasks in the study of Siberian art today.

Editor's notes

a. The iconostasis is the major icon screen, usually floor to ceiling, separating the laity in the nave from the clergy in the sanctuary of a church. A door in the screen enables clergy to pass between the more and the less sacred part of the church, with service conducted in both areas. The icon screen often contains an ordering of icons, with lower-ranking saints, monks, and "soldier saints" at the bottom and more sacred images near the top. However, definitions of which Orthodox images belong in which places of honor vary locally. An important point made in this article is that the "high culture" associated with elaborate and diverse icons arrived in Siberia remarkably early. For more on the general history and meaning of Orthodox icons, see the works of the Russian authorities V. Lazarev and I. Grabar; plus L. Ouspensky, *Essai sur la théologie de l'icone dans l'Eglise orthodoxe* (Paris, 1960); T. Talbot Rice, *The Russian Icon* (London, 1947); N. J. Rothemund, *Ikonenkunst. Ein Handbuch* (Munich, 1954).

b. An arshin is .711 meters, or approximately 28 inches. Certain conventions are observed in translations of religious terminology, but the Russian original is preserved here as much as possible. Thus Turinsk has the Exaltation of the Cross (not the Cross Raising) Monastery. Especially noteworthy is that the terminology for Mary, Mother of God in Russian Orthodoxy does not stress her Virgin identification; rather, she is described as the "Bogomater'" (Mother of God) or the "Bogoroditsa" (Giver of birth to God). I am grateful to Father Dmitry Grigorieff and to Allison Hilton for clarification of church and icon translations.

c. The comment refers to diverse motivations for donations and for charity, particularly from Moscow tsars and nobility to Siberian churches and monasteries. Siberia, as a symbol of the penetration of Christianity into a frontier of heathenism, became a worthy object for reputation-enhancing religious gifts.

d. St. Nikolai (or Nikola) was probably the most revered of saints in Siberia: his life inspired admiration, exemplifying personal resources much needed in the north. His icons were in nearly every Russian (or Sibiriak) house, and in many native Siberian Christian homes as well, especially because of his miracle-working and healing abilities, and by extension, because of the perceived curative powers of his icons. St. Nikolai's wide renown reached the point that his image occasionally appeared on shamans' drums.

e. *Friazhkii* is an obsolete word meaning "foreign," with stress on connotations of Western European cultural difference. Given the strong influence of French culture on the Russian nobility and on art, *friazhkii* often meant French influence. The Tobolsk cathedral, like many Russian Orthodox churches, was named "Pokrovskii" denoting both "intercession" and "protection"—a concept more complex in Russian than its usual translation in English. The word *pokrov*, literally "cover" or "veil," refers to the veil of protection that Mary is believed to have extended over a crucial battle for Christendom.

Notes

1. A. I. Sulotskii, *Opisanie kratkoe vsekh ikon, sushchestvuiushchikh v Tobol'skoi eparkhii* (Moscow, 1852); idem, *Opisanie naibolee chtimykh ikon Tobol'skoi eparkhii* (St. Petersburg, 1864); idem, "Istoricheskie svedeniia ob ikonopisanii v Zapadnoi Sibiri," *Tobol'skie gubernskie vedomosti*, 1871, no. 17–18.

2. N. A. Abramov, "Starinnye ikony v Tobol'skoi eparkhii," *Izvestiia Imp. arkheol. o-va*, 1859, vol. 1; P. N. Butsinskii, "Otkrytie Tobol'skoi eparkhii i pervyi Tobol'skii episkop Kiprian," *Vera i razum*, 1890, no. 21; etc.

3. A. N. Kopylov, *Ocherki kul'turnoi zhizni Sibiri XVII–nachale XIX v.* (Novosibirsk, 1974).

4. N. Kazarinova, "Narodnye sibirskie ikony," *Tvorchestvo*, 1973, no. 8.

5. Certain aspects of the matter are discussed by the author in the articles: N. G. Velizhanina, "Narodnye ikony Novosibirskoi oblasti v Novosibirskoi kartinnoi galeree," *Muzei*, 1983, no. 4; idem, "U istokov sibirskoi ikonopisi," *Kul'turno-bytovye protsessy u russkikh Sibiri. XVIII–nachalo XX v.* (Novosibirsk, 1985); idem, "Novye dokumenty po reglamentatsii ikonopisaniia v Zapadnoi Sibiri vo vtoroi polovine XVIII–pervoi polovine XIX v.," *Istochniki po istorii russkogo obshchestvennogo soznaniia perioda feodalizma* (Novosibirsk, 1986).

6. Velizhanina, "U istokov," pp. 87–91.

7. Kopylov, *Ocherki*, p. 163; Velizhanina, "Novye dokumenty," pp. 144–47, 151.

8. N. A. Abramov, "Materialy dlia istorii khristianskogo prosveshcheniia Sibiri," *Zhurnal Ministerstva narodnogo prosveshchenie*, 1854, p. 16; Kopylov, *Ocherki*, p. 163.

9. Tobol'skii filial, Gosudarstvennyi arkhiv Tomskoi oblasti [TF GATO], f. 144, op. 1, d. 26.

10. Butsinskii, "Otkrytie Tobol'skoi eparkhii," p. 565.

11. *Tobol'sk: Materialy dlia istorii goroda XVII–XVIII stoletii* (Moscow, 1885), pp. 6–7.

12. Ibid., p. 24.

13. Butsinskii, "Otkrytie Tobol'skoi eparkhii," p. 575.

14. Kopylov, *Ocherki*, p. 164.

15. Abramov, "Starinnye ikony," p. 417.

16. Sulotskii, *Opisanie naibolee chtimykh ikon*, p. 139.

17. Butsinskii, "Otkrytie Tobol'skoi eparkhii," pp. 574–75.

18. Kopylov, *Ocherki*, p. 165.

19. *Dopolneniia k istoricheskim aktam arkheologicheskoi komisii* (St. Petersburg, 1887), vol. 2, p. 265.

20. Sulotskii, *Opisanie naibolee chtimykh ikon*, p. 8.

21. A. N. Kopylov, *Kul'tura russkogo naseleniia Sibiri v XVII–XVIII vv.* (Novosibirsk, 1968), p. 31.

22. A. I. Sulotskii, "Istoricheskie svedeniia ob ikonopisanii v Sibiri," *Tobol'skie gubernskie vedomosti*, 1871, no. 17, p. 98.

23. Abramov, "Starinnye ikony," pp. 355–56.

24. Sulotskii, *Opisanie kratkoe*, p. 32.

25. Tsentral'nyi gosudarstvennyi arkhiv drevnikh aktov SSSR, f. 214, op. 3, d. 1058, l. 394; d. 256, l. 1058. Documents found and graciously provided by N. N. Pokrovskii.

26. See E. K. Romodanovskaia, "Sibirskie povesti ob ikonakh," *Osvoenie Sibiri v epokhu feodalizma* (Novosibirsk, 1969), issue 3, pp. 82–96.

27. Sulotskii, *Opisanie naibolee chtimykh ikon*, p. 20ff.; Abramov, "Starinnye ikony," p. 356.

28. Sulotskii, *Opisanie naibolee chtimykh ikon*, p. 8.

29. Tobol'skii filial, Gosudarstvennyi arkhiv Tiumen'skoi oblasti [TF GATiuO], f. 144, op. 1, d. 10, l. 29.

30. Romodanovskaia, *Sibirskie povesti*, p. 84.

31. V. K. Andrievich, *Istoriia Sibiri* (St. Petersburg, 1889), pt. 1–2, p. 185.

32. Romodanovskaia, *Sibirskie povesti*, p. 84.

33. Sulotskii, *Opisanie naibolee chtimykh ikon*, p. 12.

34. D. A. Rovinskii, "Istoriia russkikh shkol ikonopisaniia do kontsa XVIII veka," *Zapiski Imp. arkheol. ob-va*, (St. Petersburg, 1856), vol. 8, pp. 27–28.

35. I. E. Grabaria, ed. *Istoriia russkogo iskusstva* (Moscow, 1955), vol. 3, p. 346.

36. N. P. Kondakov, *Ikonografiia bogomateri* (Petersburg, 1915), vol. 2, pp. 188, 217.

37. Sulotskii, *Opisanie kratkoe*, p. 23; V. I. Kochedamov, *Tobol'sk* (Tomsk, 1963), p. 25.

38. Sulotskii, *Opisanie naibolee chtimykh ikon*, pp. 34–35.
39. Ibid.
40. GATO, f. 85, op. 1, d. 192, l. 2.
41. See E. Pavliuchenkova, "Liki i litsa," *Sibir'*, 1981, no. 5, p. 128.
42. For example, to paint the iconostasis in the Naryma cathedral church in 1751, half a pood of hempseed oil was sent from Tobol'sk (TF GATiuO, f. 156, op. 1, d. 53, l. 10).
43. GATO, f. 85, op. 1, d. 192, l. 6.
44. Sulotskii, *Opisanie naibolee chtimykh ikon*, p. 149.
45. Velizhanina, "Novye dokumenty," p. 149.
46. TF GATiuO, f. 156, op. 1, 1764 g., b/N, l. 87.
47. Ibid., op. 1, 1772 g., d. 108, l. 1.
48. Ibid., op. 1, 1772 g., d. 108, l. 5.
49. Ibid., f. 341, op. 1, 1783 g., d. 40, l. 333.
50. Sulotskii, *Opisanie naibolee chtimykh ikon*, p. 19.
51. G. I. Il'ina-Okhrimenko, *Narodnoe iskusstvo semeiskikh Zabaikal'ia XIX–XX v.* (Ulan-Ude, 1972), p. 13.
52. Velizhanina, "Narodnye ikony," pp. 87–91; idem, *Narodnye ikony iuga Zapadnoi Sibiri: Katalog Novosibirskoi kartinnoi galerei* [no date].

Gender and Family Life

The Woman in the Ancient Russian Family (Tenth to Fifteenth Centuries)

N. L. PUSHKAREVA

The issue of the social status of women during the Middle Ages, especially that of Russian women, has been raised with increasing frequency at international scholarly forums of the recent decade.[1] This issue is also important for a general understanding of Russian history, governmental and cultural life, for in the words of the French utopianist C. Fourier, whom Marx was fond of quoting, "social progress can be precisely measured from the social status of the fair sex."[2] One of the most crucial aspects of the social status of woman in the tenth to fifteenth centuries is her family status and, as a reflection of this, the place of women in the system of ceremonies and ritual operations involved in the formation of a marriage, as well as the right to dissolve it.[a] In the evolutionary history of the Russian woman's social status, we may identify several major landmarks, the foremost of these (historically and chronologically) being the sixteenth century. At this time, a number of negative changes occurred in the material and family status of women of all classes. The occurrence of these changes was influenced by a multitude of factors: the many years of subjugation to the Golden Horde, the strengthening of a despotic political system (the family being a reflection and the basic unit of this system), the growing influence of an ascetic Christian doctrine, and the curtailment of personal, proprietary, and hereditary rights of women in privileged classes. Therefore, it seems appropriate to limit this study of the Russian woman's family status to the tenth to fifteenth centuries, as this characterizes a relatively high (for the Middle Ages) sociolegal and proprietary-legal status of the various classes of women.[3] Whereas the family status of the Russian woman during the later period of the sixteenth and seventeenth centuries is comparatively well described in the sources and somewhat reflected in the works of contemporary historians and ethnographers,[4] insufficient attention has been paid to the family status of women in the tenth to fifteenth centuries. The reason for such a situation lies in the

Russian text © 1988 by "Nauka" Publishers and "Sovetskaia etnografiia." "Zhenshchina v drevnerusskoi sem'e (X–XV vv.)," *Sovetskaia etnografiia*, 1988, no. 4, pp. 87–98. A publication of the Institute of Ethnography, USSR Academy of Sciences.

limited number of sources; the information characterizing the status of woman during the period of Ancient Rus' is meager and spotty, hindering comparative characterization (except in the material-legal sphere) of the status of representatives of the various classes and conditions, particularly their family status. The canonical collections of the church are the principal source for recreating a picture of the familial status of women. These consider a kind of average "wife," whose social position can be defined simply as the absence of a condition of servitude (slavery). But the chronicles, the archeological material, and the narratives of the tenth to fifteenth centuries make it possible to study the position of women in the family, especially women of the privileged class. However, although the sources do not permit an elucidation of the family status of women of different classes with the same completeness, a description of the earliest marriage ceremonies and certain domestic family customs enables a more complete characterization of a number of traditions that existed in the territory of Kievan Rus' (up to the middle of the twelfth century), and also in the northeastern and northwestern parts of Russia in the twelfth to fifteenth centuries. In this way, we can identify "mechanisms of social succession," which were an important means of stabilizing the relations that had become customary in this society and of reproducing them in the life of successive generations not only during the period under discussion, but also later, in the seventeenth to nineteenth centuries.

One of the earliest forms of contracting marriage that existed prior to the adoption of Christianity was "abduction"[5] "from the water," which was a traditional Indo-European form of marriage.[6] Festivals in honor of the god of marriage, Lad, during which the abductions took place, began in early spring and ended in summer (from Krasnaia Gorka till Ivan Kupalo Day).[7] In the earliest Russian chronicles the "taking" is described as nothing less than a symbol of mutual accord between the bride and groom and a manifestation of the free will of woman in the choice of a spouse: "And they carried off as wives those with whom they had agreed."[8] The ceremony, as well as the "games" in honor of Lad, were preserved among the "common folk" (dependent populations) a rather long time, right down until the sixteenth century.[9]

Along with abduction, there existed in early feudal Rus' the "bringing of the marriage" [brakprivedenie] with elements of bargaining: "the son-in-law did not come for his bride, but they brought [her] in the evening, and the next day that to be given for her was taken [to her family]."[10] During the proceedings, it was not the bride, but her parents or relatives who played a major role. The term privedenie is often used by the chronicler in describing the conjugal unions of princes, and also in cases where lack of [bridal] independence in matrimonial affairs is emphasized (the chronicles use the impersonal form—"that which is brought").[11]

After the conversion of Rus' and the monopolization by the church of the right to consecrate marriage, wedding rituals came into being that corresponded to norms of an emerging matrimonial law, which included numerous changes in both the family status and the rights of the various classes of women. This process unfolded in two ways: the ancient family and wedding customs, i.e., common law norms, were transformed into formal laws and legal custom; on the other hand, the decisions of church administrative bodies, relying in their activities on the Byzantine code of matrimonial law, were recognized as law, leading to the creation of new traditions. The influence of pre-Christian Russian rituals on tenth- to fifteenth-century betrothal and wedding ceremonies is witnessed by the earliest documents of the tenth and eleventh centuries,[12] which mention the preliminary wedding agreement, accompanied by a kind of *engagement* [*pomolvka*]. Thus, Prince Mal of Drevliansk sent matchmakers to the Grand Princess Ol'ga to bargain over her. According to ancient Russian custom, the engagement was accompanied by a meal at the bride's parents. Meat pies, gruel, and cheese were eaten. The cutting of cheese sealed the bargain, and if the groom rejected the bride after this procedure he would be punished, as he had offended her honor: "If the cheese has already been cut, one *griven* for the cheese, three *grivens* for the insult to her, and expenses for what she has lost."[13] Subsequently, the engagement became only a part of the *marriage agreement* [*brachnyi sgovor*], the main purpose of which among the small landholders and privileged class was to conclude a written contract, or *riad*. Not only did this reflect the accord between the parents of the bride and groom in contracting the marriage and stipulate the property conditions and time frame involved, but it also confirmed the acquiescence of the newlyweds themselves, particularly the bride. The articles of the "Charter of Prince Iaroslav Vladimirovich" imposed a special monetary fine on parents in favor of the metropolitan in such cases where "the maiden wishes to be married, and the mother and father do not let her." The semilegendary story of the Polotsk Princess Rogneda, who refused to marry the groom proposed by her father, is also preserved in the "Tale of Bygone Years."[14] It appears that the institution of the written marriage contract was definitively established for members of the ruling class no earlier than the thirteenth century. From this time, we have the remarkable Novgorod birchbark writ No. 377 ("From Mikita to Ul'ianitsa. Marry me. I love you, and you me, and let Ignato witness this"), as well as other documents.[15]

The concluding event in the marriage agreement in Rus' was the *handclasp* [rukhobit'e] *and betrothal* [obruchenie] *in church*. Several scholars believe that the term "betrothal" may have originated much earlier than the ceremony of the church betrothal (exchange of rings), since it designated the objective of the "contract," on which occasion they clasped hands ("were betrothed").[16] The handclasp when giving the bride in marriage and the

betrothal in the church were necessary for a girl's marriage, enforced by social morality—"he may not take another, but only have that one as wife."
Even if the betrothed were "tempted and defiled by another," church law
(taking its origin from folkways) commanded that the groom marry her.[17]
The ritual of the church betrothal has often been described in various
church collections: it culminated with the priest placing a gold ring on the
right hand of the future husband and an iron ring on the hand of the
betrothed.[18]

After the handclasp and the betrothal came a period that was later called
the *great week* [*velikaia nedelia*]. Its appointment was purely practical (for
wedding preparations, dowry collection, etc.), but it might last for two or
three months, or even much longer. In no ancient Russian document do we
find a time delimitation for this period, since the engagement, agreement,
and handclasp often took place before the bride and groom were of mar-
riageable age.

Women in Ancient Rus' were permitted to marry from the age of thirteen
or fourteen, although a church law prohibiting marriage of "maids younger
than twelve years" appeared only in the fifteenth century. Prior to this time,
the children of princes who had not even reached the minimum age of marriage were permitted to "enter into wedlock": Princess Verkhuslava Vse-
volodovna on her wedding day was "very young, eight years old," while the
son of Vasilii Vasil'evich Temnyi, the young Ivan, at the age of five, was
"bound to a beautiful girl" by the exertions of the prince of Tver', Boris
Aleksandrovich.[19]

Other traditional norms prohibiting marriage emerged in ancient Russian
society under the influence of the most diverse factors: socioeconomic, religious, common law. In particular, we know that the Orthodox Church
worked out rather clear canons, restricting the persons with whom a woman
could enter into marriage. Thus, women of any age were prohibited from
marrying blood relatives (six times removed), by marriage or by birth, potential or future (i.e., between persons intending to become related: it was not
possible to marry the groom of one's daughter, etc.).[20] The church also
endeavored to exercise a restraining influence on the processes of ethnic in-
tegration of the inhabitants of Ancient Rus' and the peoples of neighboring
countries by introducing a law that forbade "giving [girls] in marriage to another country," especially to infidels.[b] For a "highly unworthy and unseemly" union with an infidel, a Russian woman (she is termed *russka* in the
Charter of the Prince Iaroslav Vladimirovich) was punished by compulsory
admittance to a nunnery. Subsequently abandoning the effort to thwart objective processes, members of the orthodox clergy replaced forced entrance
into a nunnery with a monetary fine, even relaxing this ban with respect to
grand princesses, many of whom were married to foreign kings.[21]

Other norms forbidding marriage that were elaborated by the church involved social and class differences. Thus, socially mixed marriages were not allowed. A peasant girl or bondwoman in the best of cases was considered a "lesser" or second wife for members of the privileged class. In the worst case, the marriage of a dependent to a freeman made the latter a dependent (or indentured servant). Curiously, the reverse—i.e., that the marriage of an indentured servant to a freewoman would make the latter unfree—did not exist in the Russian codes. Nor was it applied in reality: for example, among the families of Novgorodians there were such in which the father was a bondman, while "his wife and daughters are free."[22] And he who endeavored to contract a lawful marriage with a woman of the lowest social status was supposed to be dissuaded by the "instructive" collections for edifying reading: for example, it is written in the "Pchela" ["The Bee"] (fourteenth and fifteenth centuries) that "A wife taken from the indentured servants is wicked and cruel. . . ."[23]

While tradition and common law did not regulate the number of marriages that a woman could enter into during her life, Christian mores allowed not more than two. Permission to contract a third marriage was given in the form of an exception, and this only in Novgorod and Pskov: "If one is young, and there are no children from the first marriage nor the second."[24] In the event of a fourth marriage, the church authorities demanded an immediate divorce: "the first marriage is law, the second forgiveness, the third a crime, the fourth an infamy, for it is a swinish way to live."[25]

Preservation of virginity up to the marriage was not traditionally a condition for conclusion of marriage. However, with the spread of Christian mores, it became the norm for future wives of members of the clergy. As for the main bulk of those contracting marriage, the law prescribed an *opitim'iu* (church penance, *epitimia*) for she who "entered marriage unclean."[26] Yet the ultimate goal for the clergy was not to restrict (by constantly introducing new bans), but rather to widen the range of people contracting marriage in the church. "Make them marry and live by church law . . . and when the girls are grown, give them in marriage, so that they do not do bad things . . ."[27]— such instructions are often found in the church collections. In view of pre-Christian ideas and traditions concerning parental responsibility for the fate of their children, the church introduced fines for parents who did not give their daughters in marriage at the opportune time ("they who have sat too long").[28]

The supplanting of pre-Christian marriage and wedding ceremonies by the church marriage and their contamination with new ceremonies was a slow process. Nevertheless, it was continual. This may be traced in the ancient Russian *wedding and marriage ceremonies* of the tenth to fifteenth centuries. True, the ancient Russian narrative and normative sources of the time contain only scattered accounts and reports of them. The first detailed descriptions of Russian weddings were compiled by foreign travelers in the late fifteenth century, and the majority of them even later, in the sixteenth and seventeenth centuries.

Since the domestic ceremonies generally remain unchanged over the centuries, in systematizing and generalizing the records of the earliest chronicles and documents concerning Russian weddings it is necessary to use certain descriptions of the fifteenth and sixteenth centuries as well.[c] Not without reason the author of the account of the marriage between Vasilii Ivanovich and Elena Glinskaia (sixteenth century) points out that everything was done "as of old, in the time of Grand Prince Semen Ivanovich," i.e., the fourteenth century.[29] A broad circle of friends and relatives of the bride and groom took part in the wedding ceremonies during the period in question. There were also women among them, such as matchmakers and friends.[30] It is hard to determine their place in the rituals from the early sources (tenth to fourteenth centuries). But since the bride, along with the groom, was the central figure in the wedding suite, we shall concentrate on her position and rights.

Shortly before the wedding, it was common to arrange a ritual *bath* [*bania*]. The preservation of the pre-Christian customs associated with "charmed water" in tenth- to fifteenth-century wedding rituals is explained by the desire of the bride to win the love and affection of her future spouse by means of magical rituals. After the bride's ritual ablution, the "charmed water" was carefully saved and given to the husband to drink after the wedding. Already in the twelfth century, Kirik of Chernoriz asked Bishop Nifont of Novgorod whether a weekly penance could be imposed on such brides; but the ritual actions associated with the "washing" and the bath continued to exist—they are also mentioned in later marriage records (fifteenth and sixteenth centuries).[31]

Without fail, the wedding was preceded by a maidens' party [*devichnik*]. At this gathering of girls, the wreath or *kokoshnik* (maiden headdress, leaving the upper part of the head exposed) was removed from the bride and her "head was combed," i.e., her tress (the symbol of maidenhood) was braided for the last time. All of this took place in a bride's "mansion" [*khoroma*], without the groom, pretending that the bride and groom did not know each other. The very word for bride [*nevesta*] is perhaps a synonym of the adjective "unknown" [*neizvestnaia*].[32] Among the "aphorisms" of the early Russian "Pchela," mentioned above, is the following: "In turbid water you cannot see the bottom, and in a bride you will not understand the truth."[33] Moreover, in Novgorod and its territories, the prewedding ceremonies were often performed without observance of the above rules, which gave reason for N. I. Kostomarov to mention these peculiarities of Novgorodian weddings.[34]

The central events on the wedding day were the rite of transfering the bride to the groom, the *okruchivanie* (hair winding), the church *venchanie* (wedding), the reception of the young bride in the *husband's house*, and the *podklet* (wedding bed). The rite of handing over the bride to the groom during this period began with preparations in the "middle chamber" (probably situated between the chambers of the bride and the groom) for reception of the young couple. The first to enter this chamber was the bride, before whom was carried a round loaf and money—signifying wishes for the future family's wealth and prosperity.[35] It is noteworthy that such wishes pertained specifically to the woman, who was seen as the future overseer of the household. The bride was "transfered" to the groom, who seated her alongside himself. Next came the hair winding: matchmakers or the "wife of the prefect"[36] braided the girl's formerly loose hair into two tresses (the symbol of wedlock), after which a *kika* or *povoinik* with bridal veil—the distinguishing headdress of married women in Rus' (differing from the maiden wreath in that all the hair was covered)—was placed on her head. It is noteworthy that as early as the twelfth century, a monetary fine was provided for deliberate removal of this headdress, for such a misdeed was punished as an affront to womanly honor.[37] The term *grebenshchina* was also long in existence—a term of abuse for women who replaced the headdress appropriate to their domestic status with a comb [*grebenka*].[38]

Before the trip to the altar, a large number of magical rituals were performed, customarily known as producing [*produtsiriushie*] rituals in the modern literature.[d] Thus, in particular, the bride and groom were bestrewn with hops ("for happiness"), fur coats were draped on the bride ("for a rich life"), straw mattresses with the seams unsewn ("for easy birth"), sheaves, etc. were thrown at her feet.[39] After this, the wedding cortege[40] headed for church. Here, the groom took up his place on the right hand of the priest, the bride on the left. Each received, in keeping with the "wedding rite" (contained in many old Russian prayer books), "a single burning candle." After exchanging rings, the newlyweds "clasped their right hands," the priest placed wreaths (*venets*, whence the word for "wedding," *venchanie*) on their heads, censed them, and prayed "very loud," turning toward the east. Next came the church blessing of the marriage, toward a "peaceable and long life," and a wish "to have many children and grandchildren, to fill the home with prosperity and beauty."[41]

After the church ceremonies came the traditional customs, the reception of the young woman into the husband's home and nuptial chamber. The custom of the wife removing the husband's shoes after the wedding, for example, is well known. It is mentioned as early as Nestor in the earliest Russian chronicle: the Princess Rogneda of Polotsk refuses to "unshoe the indentured servant's son."[42] This custom is not mentioned in descriptions of the weddings of fifteenth- and sixteenth-century grand princes or tsars. Yet it is mentioned in the accounts of foreigners visiting Russia in the sixteenth and seventeenth century as a game in which the husband and wife vie for primacy in the family and for their rights.[43] A similar meaning pertained in the sixteenth century to ceremonial goblet smashing, which is familiar from many descriptions of fifteenth-century weddings and was later described by foreign travelers.[44]

Under the influence of rigid patriarchal tendencies in marriage and the husband's growing domination, the smashing of the goblets entirely disappeared from the wedding rituals (with no descriptions of it in the seventeenth century).

The custom of receiving a young woman in the husband's home invariably included giving of gifts to the young family, and to the bride from the groom. Among the gifts were many symbolic ones, in particular, needles and a whip. While in more recent time such gifts were simply a confirmation of the authority of the man in the home, symbolically restricting the range of wifely duties to familial domestic work, in the tenth to fifteenth century these objects, given long-lived influence of pre-Christian rituals, might still be endowed with their old magical meaning, not involving a woman's humiliation and subservience (since the needles protected against the "evil eye," while blows with the whip were thought to bring about fertility).[45]

After the gifts and the wedding feast, at which savory pies [*pirogi*] and chicken were obligatory foods,[46] the young couple were led to the nuptial chamber. The "examination" of the bride, or determination of her "honorableness," sometimes described by foreigners of the leisure class, was never a folk custom, since it humiliated the dignity of woman. It came into being along with the spread of church matrimony and the associated requirement that the bride preserve her chastity until marriage.[47] With respect to the dependent population, it should be mentioned that the *jus primae noctis* [first night rights] was absent from Russia during this time.[e] This survival of group marriage had been replaced, in the opinion of V. N. Tatishchev, by monetary compensation as early as the time of Princess Ol'ga.[48]

From descriptions of old Russian wedding customs it is evident that both the domestic status of woman and the development of family and marital relations in the tenth to fifteenth centuries took place under the influence of not only common law and folkways, but also the increasingly prevalent Christianity. Consequently, subsequent relations within the family were also largely governed by norms of Christian morality. Marriage and the family, according to Orthodox doctrine, were not held to be "an impediment to the salvation of the soul," but they were beneath asceticism and celibacy: "For virginity is higher than marriage and much more seemly. . . . One should be a virgin, if possible."[49] The importance of "earthly things," including the procreative functions of woman in the family life, were belittled by theologians in comparison with transcendental values (love of God, self-abnegation): "Marriage of man is usually an *evil* [*zlo*] [my emphasis—N.P.]. . . ."[50]

The teaching of the relationship between "body and soul" played an important role in the church's definition of the purpose and place of woman in the family: "The nature of things does not allow the woman to be the superior," the clergy taught. "The man is the head of women, the prince the head of men, and God the head of princes."[51] The "kind," *dobraia* (read: ideal) wife should be "submissive," "quiet," "humble," and "uncomplaining."[52] "It is the greatest shame if one is owned by the wife," it is written in the Instructional Miscellany. "Such men are soft, shameless, thoughtless, unfree, servile, and vulgar."[53] But in actuality, the question of "familial authority" might be resolved in various ways. This is shown both by the chronicles of the princely families, where the wife "owned her husband,"[54] and the confessional miscellanies, containing a composite portrait of that "domestic recluse" who "barked" (i.e., cursed), "struggled" (i.e., quarreled), and even "spat in the face" of her own spouse.[55] Not uncommonly in their daily round the clergy encountered "husbands who owned towns, yet toiled for their wives."[56]

Ultimately, in the opinion of the authors of the church teachings, the microclimate in the family depended in fact on the woman. We find many appeals to the "husbands" in documents of the fourteenth and fifteenth century, such as "Do not deprive yourselves of your wife's counsel . . . "; "the wife should have her husband as the head on her shoulders, and the husband his wife as the soul in his body. . . ."[57] The chronicler, presenting examples of "harmony and solicitude" in old Russian families, mentions Ian and his wife Mar'ia (eleventh century),[58] Prince Mstislav Vladimirovich and his spouse Kristina (twelfth),[59] Prince Vladimir Vasil'kovich of Volynia and "his sweet princess Ol'ga" (thirteenth), Prince Mikhail Iaroslavich of Tver' and his wife Anna Dmitrievna (fourteenth), and many others.[60] And even though these are all members of princely families, endowed by the chronicler with an "inborn capital of virtues," it is nevertheless hard to deny that such descriptions express ideas of the people of those times with respect to the highly moral relations within families. At the same time, the specimen of a fourteenth-century love letter, written in Novgorod, confirms that many townsmen of that time were strangers to the ascetic ideal, imposed by the church: "As my heart and my body and my soul have been inflamed for thee and for thy body and for thy face, so too let thy heart and thy body and thy soul become inflamed for me and for my body and for my face. . . ."[61] Such "carnal love" was resolutely condemned by the clergy, and not just because it was contrary to the prescribed models of family relationships. For a long time the Russian church had to fight against pagan ways of "enchanting the spouse." For example, one of the "sorcerer's" ways of acquiring the love of a spouse was to prepare potions of "love root" (?),[f] woman's milk, sweat, and honey.[62] But while declaring all "delights of the body" sinful, the Orthodox Church encouraged large families, claiming that "it is a great evil if children are not born, a special curse."[63] Severe penalties existed in the thirteenth to fifteenth centuries for killing a child or attempting to abort or avoid pregnancy. The "Charter of Prince Iaroslav Vladimirovich" required those women who "being married, kill children" to be punished by being made nuns [literally, having their heads shaved].[64] Church ordinances protected the health of the future mother, forbidding her under threat of penance to do strenuous work in the fields,[g] to prostrate herself on the ground, etc.[65] There was also rigorous persecution of "idol-worshipping crones," who taught women how to avoid pregnancy by means of "herbs" and also "taking away the fruit"—performing abortions: "if alive, fifteen years; if a similitude [*obraz*] is there, seven years; if still an embryo, five years of fasting."[66] The fight against "witches" and "spell-binders" was also seen in the effort to stamp out remnants of pagan childbirth cults and related rituals. We may find echoes of such archaic ceremonies in prayers from the apocrypha: "if the woman is given pain from the child" and "if the woman starts to deliver the child too slowly"—these for the most part are descriptions of "child-bearing meals" of bread, cheese, honey, and gruel.[67] The "witches" in the old Russian village were not only midwives: they preserved and passed on the wisdom of folk healing. Already in the twelfth century, Kirik of Novgorod complained that "if a child should take ill" it will be brought to them, and not "to the priest for prayer."[68] The witches also attempted to cure barrenness. In keeping with the level of medical knowledge at the time, they recommended that the women eat "a child's umbilical cord" or the "afterbirth," which had long been attributed magical power.[69]

The birth of children in the old Russian family was traditionally looked upon as a "blessing," a "joy," an "honor to the home."[70] Their rearing was traditionally the wife's "dominion." It behoved the mother of the family to "reform a child's manners," to "watch over her children."[71] The church required that children be taught obedience, forbearance, respect for elders in the home ("A younger child should be silent before an elder child"),[72] and from the parents it demanded reasonable strictness ("do not become angry when punishing the child!"),[73] affection, and benevolence. The latter is observable in the affectionate nicknames parents gave to their favorite children; the Lavrent'ev chronicle cites the name "Izmaragd" (Emerald), which the parents called their daughter Efrosin'ia.[74] "Disobedience" of children to their mother was severely condemned: the church promised damnation in the afterlife to "evil-hearted sinners."[75] "Did you swear at your mother, or beat her, or shout at her?" or "Did you cause her grief?" Such queries were rife in the confessionals. Various punishments were prescribed for misbehavior—from obeisances and fasting to monetary fines.[76] Nevertheless, conflicts in the family were not a rarity. "Greetings from Fevroniia to Feliks, with a grievance. My stepson beat me and chased me from the yard . . . ," complains a certain woman to the court deputy of Novgorod. For his misdeed, the stepson evidently answered before a secular court (indemnity for bodily harm inflicted on a woman) and a church court, which imposed a penance "lifelong, and in future, until he comes into feeling. . . ."[77]

Becoming a widow, a woman received right of seniority in the family, even if there were adult sons; in the testaments that have come down to us, the princes demand: "honor and obey mother . . . in father's stead." The church teachings also demanded "not to reproach" the mother, even if she "grows meager in thought" in old age.[78]

Church law placed obligations of mutual care and keeping on the spouses themselves. "Grievous ailment, or blindness, or long illness," under no circumstances gave one the right to abandon a life's companion or to part. Meanwhile, many motives existed for divorce during this period. The chief of them (and the only one officially recognized) was adultery. But this was determined differently for each of the spouses. The husband was considered an adulterer if he not only had a mistress, but also children by her. Bigamy and concubinage are attested in the chronicles,[79] and they are also vividly portrayed in the birchbark writs: one of these contains a complaint from a lawful wife that the husband, after beating her, "dismissed" her and "took another."[80] The "lesser" or second wife was most often a woman of lower social standing, a servant.[81] The battle of the church against polygamy and concubinage was made difficult by the fact that the polygamists most often belonged to the ruling classes.

Church law was more strict with married women than with their husbands; they were considered to have committed adultery if they merely entered into a liaison with another man. The husband, learning of a wife's unfaithfulness, was supposed to divorce her, and a wife who was forgiven and not punished ("having been given her way") was especially punished. For a long time, women did not have the right to divorce an unfaithful spouse. Up to the middle of the fifteenth century, the priest merely imposed a monetary fine on the treacherous husband ("ransoming" him);[82] only in the middle of the fifteenth century did church law permit the woman to divorce on this ground.[83]

For a number of other motives that were equated with betrayal in church law, the husband alone had the right of divorce, specifically if the wife attempts to take his life; if the wife eats, drinks, and sleeps outside the home,[84] frequents [gambling] "games," directs "thieves" against the property of the husband, and several other grounds.[85] But a number of situations that were equated with betrayal in the twelfth century (such as talking to outsiders) were no longer considered grounds for divorce; instead, a fine was introduced.[86]

The right of "separation" (divorce) for material and physiological reasons (inability to perform conjugal relations, absence of children) was granted to each of the spouses.[87] The woman had the right to divorce in those cases when the husband concealed that he was a bondman, or if he sold himself into bondage without her knowledge (already in the late fifteenth century the norm prevailed: "a servant with a bondman, a bondman with a servant"), or if he accused his wife of "evil doing" without cause (including "if the husband slanders the chastity of his wife"), or if he used force to compel her to perform the conjugal duties ("she is not guilty in leaving him"), if he himself were impotent, and several other eventualities.[88]

In addition to "separation" with consent of the priest, up to the fifteenth century there existed the unauthorized divorce, or "dismissal." This was carried out on the initiative of either party. While the "Charter of Prince Iaroslav Vladimirovich" had already come out against "dismissals" on the part of the husband, coming to the defense of the "old" (or lawful) wives and demanding "punishment" for husbands' unfaithfulness,[89] in the thirteenth and fourteenth centuries the members of the clergy were fighting against analogous misdeeds committed by women ("if the wife leaves the husband and goes to another").[90] Bishop Feodosii of Novgorod ordered the priests of Ustiuzhna Zhelezopol'skaia not to marry such "leavers," who "reach unlawfully, restlessly, for other men. . . ."[91] The church documents reflecting the punishments for "dismissals" without the consent of the church authorities contain indications of clerical attention to the moral side of marital relations. If a husband wilfully left a wife, in addition to a fine on behalf of the church there was exacted from him compensation to the wife "for the insult." The size of this depended on the status and affluence of the broken family.[92] In the case of mutual agreement of the spouses to divorce, a monetary fine was also imposed on them.[93]

Dissension between the spouses, personal antagonism, and other motives of moral-psychological nature were least of all justifications for divorce, both in the eyes of the priest and before the bar of social opinion. In the thirteenth to fifteenth century, the tendency to restrict the grounds for divorce was strengthened. For example, Metropolitan Daniil in the late fifteenth century demanded that only one ground for divorce be legitimate: "It does not befit the husband to leave the wife, unless there is fault of lechery."[94] On the whole, the law remained more lenient to the man and stressed the responsibility of the woman for the strength of the marriage.

Thus, the material presented above from the narrative literature and canonical documents, reflecting marital and wedding traditions, customs, and rituals, provides a conception of a woman's rights in contracting and dissolving marriage and her place and role in the conjugal union. The traditional ritual for establishing familial bonds was transformed after several centuries into typical betrothal and wedding customs of the church marriage. In sanctioning this, the church acted as a kind of regulator in the handling of matrimonial affairs; accordingly, church laws also appeared, establishing certain punishments for forcible or untimely giving in marriage, for moral offense given by the groom withdrawing from the marriage, and for failure to observe other conditions in the conclusion of the conjugal union. At the same time, elements of the pre-Christian traditions, stressing the woman's important role in the family, remained in prewedding and wedding rituals. The preservation of such traditions in family life prevented the establishment of an ethic of submissiveness, or a moral concept of a woman's "social backwardness" and subservience to the will of the family head—the husband. The right to divorce, which women possessed despite the many reservations in the law code, testified to the relatively high domestic and social status of the woman in the tenth to the fifteenth centuries.

Editor's notes

a. See also Barbara Evans Clements, Barbara Alpern Engel, and Christine D. Worobec, eds., *Russia's Women: Accommodation, Resistance, Transformation* (Berkeley: University of California Press, 1991); Eve Levin, *Sex and Society in the World of the Orthodox Slavs, 900–1700* (Ithaca: Cornell University Press, 1989); Dorothy Atkinson, "Society and the Sexes in the Russian Past," in *Women in Russia*, eds. Dorothy Atkinson, Alexander Dallin, and Gail Warshofsky Lapidus (Stanford: Stanford University Press, 1977), pp. 3–38; Dan Kaiser, *The Growth of Law in Medieval Russia* (Princeton: Princeton University Press, 1980); William T. Shinn, "The Law of the Russian Peasant Household," *Slavic Review*, 1961, vol. 20, no. 4, pp. 604–12; Nancy Shields Kollmann, *Kinship and Politics: The Making of the Muscovite Political System, 1345-1547* (Stanford: Stanford University Press, 1987); idem, "The Seclusion of Elite Muscovite Women," *Russian History*, 1983, vol. 10, pt. 2, pp. 170–87. Cf. S. S. Shashkov, *Istoriia russkoi zhenshchiny* (St. Petersburg, 1879); S. N. Kaidash, *Sila slabykh. Zhenshchiny v Rossii (XI–XIX vv.)* (Moscow: Sovetskaia Rossiia, 1989).

b. Cf. Nancy Shields Kollmann, "Women's Honor in Early Modern Russia," in *Russia's Women*, eds. Clements, Engel, and Worobec, pp. 60–73; Ia. N. Shchapov, "Brak i sem'ia v drevnei Rusi," *Voprosy istorii*, 1970, no. 10, pp. 216–19. Church rules restraining interethnic marriage were not easily enforcible, and behavior also varied according to status.

c. A few additional sources on weddings include L. A. Pushkareva and N. M. Shmeleva, "The Contemporary Russian Peasant Wedding," in *Introduction to Soviet Ethnography*, eds. Stephen P. Dunn and Ethel Dunn, vol. 1 (Berkeley: Highgate Road Social Science Research Station, 1974), pp. 343–60; G. V. Zhirnova, "The Russian Wedding Ritual in the Late Nineteenth and Early Twentieth Centuries," *Soviet Anthropology & Archeology*, vol. 14, no. 3, pp. 18–38; M. Komarev, ed., *Opisanie trinadtsati starinnykh svadev* (Moscow, 1785).

d. "Producing" rituals, especially for healing and fertility, are explicitly functional according to native ideology. Explication of native functional concepts is often considered only a starting point for multiple anthropological approaches to ritual—i.e. social, semiotic, symbolic, and psychological interpretations. E.g., Victor Turner, ed., *Celebration: Studies in Festivity and Ritual* (Washington: Smithsonian Institution Press, 1982).

e. First night rights refers to a practice known (but very poorly documented) in various parts of feudal Europe of allowing a local lord to sleep with a peasant bride before her husband. The practice may well have become mythologized, being much less widespread than its reputation. Though Pushkareva sees it as a "survival of group marriage," there is no evidence for this. See Eve Levin, *Sex and Society in the World of the Orthodox Slavs 900-1700*, pp. 79–135, on marriage.

f. One "love root" may have been *ginseng*, obtained from the East. Local concoctions existed, both to attract and to repel partners.

g. Such rules were necessary because pregnant and nursing Russian mothers customarily continued strenuous labor in fields and peasant households, before and after the time period considered. See David L. Ransel, "Mothering, Medicine and Infant Mortality in Russia," Kennan Institute Occasional Paper, no. 236, 1990; idem, *Mothers of Misery: Child Abandonment in Russia* (Princeton: Princeton University Press, 1988).

Notes

1. "XV Congrès international des sciences historiques. Rapports," vol. 1 (Budapest, 1980), pp. 335–64; "Untersuchungen zur gesellschaftliche Stellung der Frau im Feudalismus," *Magdeburger Beiträge zur Stadtgeschichte*, no. 3 (Magdeburg, 1981).
2. K. Marx and F. Engels, *Sochineniia*, vol. 32, p. 486.
3. N. L. Pushkareva, "Pravovoe polozhenie zhenshchiny v Drevnei Rusi X–XV vv.," *Sovetskoe gosudarstvo i pravo*, 1985, no. 4, pp. 121–26; ibid., "Imushchestvennye prava zhenshchin v russkom gosudarstve X–XV vv.," *Istoricheskie zapiski*, vol. 114 (Moscow, 1986), pp. 180–225.
4. B. A. Romanov, *Liudi i nravy Drevnei Rusi (istoriko-bytovye ocherki. XI–XIII vv.)* (Moscow, 1948) (2nd ed., Leningrad, 1966); A. I. Kozachenko, "K istorii velikorusskogo svadebnogo obriada," *Sovetskaia etnografiia*, 1957, no. 1, pp. 61–70; M. G. Rabinovich, *Ocherki etnografii russkogo srednevekovogo goroda. Gorozhane, ikh obshchestvennyi i domashnii byt* (Moscow, 1978); *Russkii narodnyi svadebnyi obriad* (Leningrad, 1978); and others.
5. It must be admitted that abduction was not a regular form of marriage, even in the period of early feudalism in Rus'.
6. *Polnoe sobranie russkikh letopisei* (hereafter *PSRL*), vol. 2 (Gustynskaia letopis') (St. Petersburg, 1846), p. 257.
7. N. Khlebnikov, *Obshchestvo i gosudarstvo v domongol'skii period russkoi istorii* (St. Petersburg, 1872), p. 257.
8. *PSRL*, vol. 1 (Lavrent'evskaia letopis') (St. Petersburg, 1846), p. 6.
9. "Poslanie vladimirskogo episkopa k mestnomu kniaziu XIII v.," *Russkaia istoricheskaia biblioteka* (hereafter *RIB*), vol. 6 (*Pamiatniki drevnerusskogo kanonicheskogo prava XI–XV vv.*) (St. Petersburg, 1880), p. 137; "Poslanie mitropolita Fotiia v Novgorod 1410 g.," ibid., p. 272, etc.
10. *PSRL*, vol. 1, p. 6.
11. *PSRL*, vol. 1, pp. 12, 32, 118; vol. 2 (Ipat'evskaia letopis') (St. Petersburg, 1908), pp. 286, 290. See A. V. Artsikhovskii, *Novgorodskie gramoty na bereste* (hereafter *NGB*). *Iz raskopok 1951 g.* (Moscow, 1953), no. 9, p. 542.
12. This point has been clarified somewhat in the cited work of B. A. Romanov.
13. *Povest' vremennykh let* (hereafter *PVL*), ed. V. P. Adrianova-Peretts, vol. 1 (Moscow-Leningrad, 1950), p. 104 (this also contains the earliest mention of the wedding procession); *PSRL*, vol. 3 (*Novgorodskie i pskovskie letopisi*) (St. Petersburg, 1841), p. 52; "Ustav kniazia Iaroslava Vladimirovicha (XII v.)" (hereafter "Ustav Iaroslava"), *Pamiatniki russkogo prava* (hereafter *PRP*), vol. 1 (Moscow, 1952), article 33, p. 269.
14. "Ustav Iaroslava," article 20, 26, pp. 268–269; *PSRL*, vol. 1, p. 32.
15. *NGB. Iz raskopok 1958–1961* (Moscow, 1963), no. 377, pp. 76–77; "Riadnaia Teshaty i Iakima XIII v.," *PRP*, vol. 2 (Moscow, 1953), p. 278.
16. D. D. Khanykov, *Russkie byliny* (Moscow, 1860), p. 122.
17. *Materialy dlia istorii drevnerusskoi pokaiannoi distsipliny XII–XV vv.* (hereafter *MdRPD*) (Moscow, 1913), pp. 50, 146, etc.
18. "Chin obruchen'e devitse i muzhiu, tsarem i prochim (XIII v.)," M. Gorchakov, *O taine supruzhestva. Proiskhozhdenie, istoriko-iuridicheskoe znachenie i kanonicheskoe dostoinstvo 50 glavy pechatnoi Kormchei knigi* (St. Petersburg, 1880), supplement, texts, p. 6.
19. "Poslanie mitropolita Fotiia v Novgorod 1410 g.," *RIB*, vol. 6, p. 175; *PSRL*, vol. 2, p. 136; N. P. Likhachev, *Inoka Fomy slovo pokhval'noe o blagorodnom i velikom kniaze Borise Aleksandroviche* (St. Petersburg, 1908), pp. 37–38.
20. "Ustav Iaroslava," articles 20–26, pp. 268–269; "Rospisanie stepenei rodstva i svoistva, prepiatstvuiushchikh braku (XIV v.)," *RIB*, vol. 6, articles 1–4, pp. 143–44.
21. "Ustav Iaroslava," article 17, p. 268; "Kanonicheskie otvety mitropolita Ioanna II (XI v.)," *RIB*, vol. 6, article 13, p. 7; "Belozerskaia ustavnaia gramota 1488 g.," *PRP*, vol. 3 (Moscow, 1955), p. 173.
22. "Russkaia Pravda," *PRP*, vol. 1, article 10, p. 119; *Gramoty Velikogo Novgoroda i Pskova*, ed. S. N. Valek (Moscow-Leningrad, 1949), p. 168 (no. 110).
23. Rukopisnyi otdel Gosudarstvennoi Publichnoi biblioteki im. M. E. Saltykova-Shchedrina (hereafter *RO GPB*), f. p. 1, no. 44, l. 184.
24. "Poslanie mitropolita Fotiia v Novgorod 1410 g.," *RIB*, vol. 6, p. 273.

25. Ibid., pp. 273–74; "Poslanie mitropolita Fotiia vo Pskov o sobliudanii zakonopolozhenii tserkovnykh 1410 god," *RIB*, vol. 6, p. 281.

26. "Voprosy Kirika, Savvy i Il'i s otvetami Nifonta, episkopa novgorodskogo (XII v.)" (hereafter "Voproshanie Kirika"), *RIB*, vol. 6, article 81, p. 46; "Tri sviatitel'skie poucheniia dukhovenstvu i mirianam o raznykh predmetakh tserkovnoi distsipliny (XV v.)," ibid., p. 924, etc.

27. *MdRPD*, p. 92.

28. "Ustav Iaroslava," article 5, p. 267; the historical literature also contains other interpretations of the term "a maid who has sat too long" [*zasevshaia devka*], a sinful girl who was confined in a church house or monastery, a malefactress, etc. (see A. A. Zimin, "Istoriko-pravovoi obzor 'Ustava kniazia Iaroslava Vladimirovicha,' " *PRP*, vol. 1, p. 281). There was also a penance for owners of bondmen who did not give their indentured servants in marriage ("Tri sviatitel'skie poucheniia . . . ," pp. 918–19, 925).

29. I. Sakharov, *Skazaniia russkogo naroda o semeinoi zhizni svoikh predkov*, pt. 3, bk. 2 (St. Petersburg, 1837). *Dopolneniia. Russkie svadebnye zapisi* (hereafter *RSZ*), p. 20.

30. We find mention of women matchmakers only in late sixteenth-century sources, e.g., the notes of D. Fletcher (before this, only male matchmakers were mentioned; see *PSRL*, vol. 2, p. 136). In sixteenth-century law codes, the woman matchmaker is known as the "gossip" [*kuma*] or "marrying mother" (for more details, see Fletcher, *O gosudarstve Russkom* [St. Petersburg, 1906], p. 112; N. I. Ostroumov, *Svadebnye obychai v Drevnei Rusi* [Tula, 1905], p. 28). Data on the participation of the future mother of the groom in the wedding ritual also belongs to the sixteenth century; in particular, according to Fletcher, she made the "examination" of the bride and took part in the exchange of gifts during the bargaining (see *Domostroi po spisku Obshchestva istorii i drevnostei rossiiskikh* [hereafter *Domostroi*] [Moscow, 1882], pp. 170–72). Particulars on nuptial ceremonies and the involvement in them of the bride's matchmakers and girlfriends in the sixteenth century is described by Rabinovich (see M. G. Rabinovich, "Svadba v russkom gorode XVI v." *Russkii narodnyi svadebnyi obriad* [Leningrad, 1978], pp. 12–15).

31. "Voproshanie Kirika," p. 41; *Sbornik Russkogo istoricheskogo obshchestva* (hereafter *Sb. RIO*), vol. 35 (St. Petersburg, 1882), p. 187.

32. *RSZ*, p. 120.

33. "Pchela (XV v.)," RO GPB, f. p. I, no. 44, l. 184.

34. N. I. Kostomarov, describing a Novgorodian wedding of the fifteenth century, mentions the following ritual episode: before the trip, a [bride's] girl[friend] cried out, "'We did not come to look at the veil, but the bride!' The groom saw his intended . . . " (N. I. Kostomarov, *Istoricheskie monografy i issledovaniia*, vol. 1 [St. Petersburg, 1872], pp. 158–59).

35. *RSZ*, p. 26.

36. Ibid., p. 160.

37. Ibid., p. 34; "Dogovor Novgoroda s Gotskim beregom i nemetskimi gorodami 1189–1199 gg.," *PRP*, vol. 2, article 8, p. 126.

38. V. I. Dal', *Tolkovyi slovar' zhivogo velikorusskogo iazyka*, vol. 1 (Moscow, 1955), p. 393.

39. *Sb. RIO*, vol. 35, p. 186; *RSZ*, p. 34.

40. Women also took part in this: "girlfriends," "sponsoring mothers," "wives" of friends or masters of ceremonies, "boyar women." In the *Domostroi* and descriptions of foreigners who spent time in Russia in the sixteenth and seventeenth centuries, considerable space is devoted to them. In the early sources (up to and including the fifteenth century), they are not mentioned in the descriptions of wedding feasts, even though "wedding rites" apparently took shape at precisely this time. This is indirectly indicated by the presence of the wives of princes and boyars at princely wedding celebrations (see *PSRL*, vol. 2, pp. 134, 136, etc.).

41. "Trebniki (XV v.)," RO GPB, Sobr. Mikhailova, q. 9, l. 23–24-ob; Sobr. Gil'ferdinga, 21, l. 15 ob.-17; q. p. 1, no. 473, l. 243 etc.

42. *PVL*, vol. 1, p. 54.

43. "The young man places in one of his shoes money, gold and silver. . . . The young woman is supposed to remove whichever shoe she pleases. If she manages to take off the one that has the money, not only does she keep it, but in future she need not remove her husband's shoes . . . " ("Opisanie Rossii neizvestnogo anglichanina, sluzhivshego zimu 1557/1558 gg. pri tsarskom dvore" [hereafter "Neizvestnyi anglichanin"]), *Chteniia Obshchestva istorii i drevnostei Rossiiskikh pri Moskovskom Universitete* (hereafter *ChOIDR*), 1884, October, pp. 26–27.

44. *Domostroi*, p. 172; "Neizvestnyi anglichanin," p. 26.

45. N. I. Sumtsov, *O svadebnykh obriadakh, preimushchestvenno russkikh* (Khar'kov, 1881), p. 94.

46. F. I. Buslaev, "Istoricheskie ocherki russkoi narodnoi slovesnosti i iskusstva." Vol. 1, *Epicheskaia poeziia* (St. Petersburg, 1861), pp. 46–47.

47. "Opisanie svad'by Eleny Ivanovny, docheri velikogo kniazia Ivana III Vasil'evicha," *Sb. RIO*, vol. 35, p. 187.

48. V. N. Tatishchev, *Istoriia Rossiiskaia v 7-mi tomakh*, vol. 2 (Moscow-Leningrad, 1963), pp. 48–49.

49. "Kanonicheskie otvety mitropolita Ioanna (XI v.)," *RIB*, vol. 6, p. 70.

50. "Pchela (XIV v.)," Tsentral'nyi Gosudarstvennyi arkhiv drevnikh aktov (hereafter TsGADA), f. 180, no. 658/1170, l. 212.

51. "Prolog (XIV v.)," TsGADA, f. 381, no. 171, l. 195; "Pchela (XV v.)," RO GPB, f. p. 1, no. 44, l. 10-ob.

52. *Pamiatniki drevnerusskoi tserkovno-uchitel'noi literatury*, ed. A. I. Ponomarev, vol. 4, no. 60 (St. Petersburg, 1898), p. 120 (hereafter *Pamiatniki*).

53. "Pchela (XV v.)," RO GPB, f. p. I, no. 44, l. 10, 134, etc.

54. *PSRL*, vol. 2, pp. 265, 296.

55. "Ustav Iaroslava," article 39–40, pp. 269–270; "Sluzhebnik s trebnikom (XV v.)," Rukopisnyi otdel Biblioteki Akademii nauk SSSR v Leningrade (hereafter RO BAN (Leningrad); RO GPB, q. p. 1, no. 875, l. 133; "Trebnik (XV v.)," RO BAN, Leningrad, Fond Arkhangel'skoi missionerskoi biblioteki (hereafter Arkhan.), d-73, l. 44; "Sbornaia rukopis' (XV v.)," RO GPB, q. p. 1, no. 729, l. 174-ob.

56. "Otryvok iz pouchenia Efrema Sirina (XI v.)," RO BAN, Leningrad, 24, 4.20 (Fond Sreznevskogo 67), l. 3-ob.

57. "Trebnik (XV v.)," RO GPB, Sobranie novgorodskogo Sofiiskogo sobora (hereafter Sof.), 875, l. 134-ob.; *Pamiatniki*, pp. 118–120; "Izmaragd" (XV v.), RO BAN, Leningrad, 13.2.7, l. 81-ob.

58. "They lived according to the Lord's commandment and dwelled in mutual love . . . ," *PSRL*, vol. 1, p. 91.

59. "The princess Kristina very much loved me, and we lived in complete love, and although I did not stint with others' wives, she . . . did not curse. But today, the princess, as a young person, wants to make merry, has managed to learn indecent ways to do so—it is not easy for me to keep watch, it is enough that no one know of this . . . ," *PSRL*, vol. 2, pp. 76–79.

60. Tatishchev, *Istoriia Rossiiskaia*, vol. 2, p. 242; *PSRL*, vol. 2, p. 111; vol. 5 (St. Petersburg, 1851), pp. 210–13; vol. 7 (St. Petersburg, 1856), pp. 191–195; vol. 8 (St. Petersburg, 1859), pp. 197, etc.

61. V. L. Ianin, "Kompleks gramot no. 519–521 iz Novgoroda," *Obshchestvo i gosudarstvo feodal'noi Rossii* (Moscow, 1975), no. 521, pp. 36–37.

62. "Trebnik (XV v.)," RO BAN, Leningrad, Arkhan., d-71, l. 161-ob.; "Voproshanie Kirika," p. 60; "Sbornaia rukopis' 1482 g. Kirillo-Belozerskoi biblioteki," RO GPB, Q. p. 1, no. 6/1083, l. 97.

63. "Prolog (XV v.)," TsGADA, f. 381, no. 355, col. 256.

64. "Ustav Iaroslava," article 4, p. 266.

65. "Trebnik (XIV-XV vv.)," RO GPB, q. p. 1, no. 582, l. 254-ob.; see *MdRPD*, p. 59.

66. "Trebniki (XV v.)," RO GPB, q. p. 1, no. 1088, l. 360-ob.; q. p. 1, no. 473, l. 119; "Pouchenie dukhovnika ispovedaiushchimsia," *RIB*, vol. 6, article 28, p. 862.

67. *MdRPD*, p. 46.

68. "Voproshanie Kirika," article 16–18, p. 60.

69. "Trebnik (XV v.)," RO GPB, q. p. 2, no. 6/1083. l. 97–97-ob.; "Sbornaia rukopis' 1482 god," RO GPB, *Sof.* 875, l. 33.

70. "Pchela (XV v.)," RO GPB, f. p. 1, no. 44, l. 188-ob.; TsGADA, f. 181, no. 658/1170, l. 233.

71. "Pchela (XV v.)," l. 71-ob.

72. S. A. Shcheglova, *"Pchela" po rukopisiam kievskikh bibliotek* (St. Petersburg, 1910), Texts of the fifteenth to sixteenth century, article 7, p. 67.

73. *Pamiatniki*, vol. 4, no. 64, p. 125.

74. *PSRL*, vol. 2, p. 152.

75. *Pamiatniki*, vol. 4, no. 64, p. 126.

76. A respectful attitude of grown sons toward their mother is a distinguishing feature of old

Russian fables. See, e.g., *Pesni*, collected by P. N. Rybnikov, vol. 1 (St. Petersburg, 1861), p. 317; vol. 2, p. 21; *Pesni*, collected by P. V. Kireevskii, vol. 1 (St. Petersburg, 1860), pp. 14–15, 17, 21, etc.

77. *PSRL*, vol. 4, p. 107; "Dukhovnye i dogovornye gramoty velikikh i udel'nykh kniazei XIV–XVI vv." (Moscow-Leningrad, 1950), no. 12, 17, 20–22, 61, 71.

78. RO GPB, f. p. I, no. 44, l. 72-ob.; *Pamiatniki*, vol. 4, no. 64, p. 127.

79. *PSRL*, vol. 1, p. 29; vol. 2, pp. 563–564.

80. *NGB*, "Iz raskopok 1952 g., no. 9 (XI v.)" (Moscow, 1954), p. 41.

81. "Voproshanie Kirika," pp. 41–42; *MdRPD*, pp. 5, 68, etc.

82. "Knigi zakonnye, imi zhe goditsia vsiakoe delo ispravliati (XIII v.)" (hereafter "Knigi zakonnye"), *Sbornik otdeleniia russkogo iazyka i slovesnosti Akademii nauk*, vol. 38 (St. Petersburg, 1858), no. 3, razdel II (Zakon o kazniakh), article 16, 49, p. 73.

83. "Zapis' 'o razluchenii' (XV v.)," Ia. N. Shchapov, "Novyi pamiatnik russkogo prava XV v.," *Slaviane i Rus'* (Moscow, 1968), p. 207.

84. Despite the ban on talking, eating, drinking with "strange people," women evidently often behaved at odds with it. "[I am] drunk," complains a writer in one of the Prologues of the fourteenth century. "I would go to market, but there is no money. And the wife has gone visiting . . . (TsGADA, f. 381, no. 174, l. 31–34).

85. "Ustav Iaroslava," article 53 (3–6), p. 271.

86. "Knigi zakonnye," article 26, p. 58.

87. "Voproshanie Kirika," p. 48; "Ustav Iaroslava," p. 271.

88. "O razluchenii," p. 207; "Knigi zakonnye," p. 82; *MdRPD*, p. 9.

89. "Ustav Iaroslava," article 8, p. 267.

90. *MdRPD*, p. 92, *Akty istoricheskie, sobrannye i izdannye Arkheograficheskoi komissiei*, vol. 1 (St. Petersburg, 1841) (hereafter *AI*, vol. 1), no. 109 (1499g., "Pouchenie sviashchennosluzhiteliam").

91. *AI*, vol. 1, no. 298, p. 545.

92. "Ustav Iaroslava," article 3, p. 266.

93. Ibid., article 16, p. 268.

94. "Poslanie mitropolita Fotiia (XV v.)," *RIB*, vol. 6, p. 523.

Russian Rituals, Customs, and Beliefs Associated with the Midwife (1850–1930)

T. A. LISTOVA

Materials of the latter half of the nineteenth and the early twentieth century make it possible to reconstruct a vivid picture of social life in the Russian village, to study the interaction among community members in various areas of existence, and to identify the role of custom, tradition, and public opinion, which influence this interaction and determine a person's position in the community. The present article examines customs, rituals, and beliefs associated with a traditional personality in the prerevolutionary village—the midwife. In discussing her place in social, ritual, and practical life (that is, the actual assistance she rendered), we shall be concerned with issues such as what her duties were, how her activity was remunerated, what forms payment took, and what rituals were associated exclusively with midwives.

Our research is based on archival materials of the AGO, the GME (the V. N. Tenishev collection), the TsGIA, and the OLEAE,[1] ethnographical and regional historical publications, and field materials collected by the author in the Pskov, Smolensk, Perm', Voronezh, and Kursk oblasts.

No peasant family could do without the midwife. She not only handled the delivery but also (most importantly) knew how to perform necessary procedures (in the eyes of the community) for the infant and mother, accompanied by magical operations. The primary procedures were: cutting the umbilical cord (giving rise to local names for the midwife: *puporezka*, *puporeznitsa*, *pupoviaznitsa*), disposal of the afterbirth, bathing the infant, and washing the mother. All the midwife's actions with the newborn were subsumed by Russians under a single term, *babit'sia* (*babit'*, *babnichat'*, *obablivat'*, *babkat'*, *babchit'*).

The midwife was neither elected nor appointed, nor was she generally settled in one place. A woman who became a midwife voluntarily took on certain obligations that, while unwritten, were fully understood by her and

Russian text © 1989 by "Nauka" Publishers. "Russkie obriady, obychai i pover'ia, sviazannye s povival'noi babkoi (vtoraia polovina XIX–20-e gody XX v.)," in *Russkie: semeinyi i obshche-stvennyi byt* (Moscow: "Nauka" Publishers, 1989), pp. 142–71. A publication of the Order of Friendship among Peoples, N. N. Miklukho-Maklai Institute of Ethnography, USSR Academy of Sciences.

by the community where she practiced. She could not refuse to come to the aid of a woman in labor. Refusing to fulfill her obligations was impossible, not only because her neighbors would condemn her, but also because of superstitious beliefs: refusal was seen as an "unforgivable sin" that might entail immediate punishment—"turning to stone."[2] As a former midwife from Pskov oblast and a practicing midwife from Perm' oblast recalled, "no matter how reluctant you are to go to certain women as you will get neither a present nor gratitude, it is impossible to refuse; just shut your eyes and go."[3]

Usually the sources mention simply that each village had its own midwife, either one or several (evidently depending on the number of houses).[4] Sometimes the territory where a midwife practiced was defined more specifically by custom: "Each street has its own midwife and it is strictly forbidden for her to have patients in other streets."[5]

In places with a mixed religious composition (Orthodox and Old Believers), even granted the strict segregation of Old Believers from the "secular" that was maintained until recently, midwives were "nondenominational." Old Believers from Pskov oblast recall that they and the Orthodox in a neighboring village each had their own midwife, but in emergencies the midwife from the Old Believer's village would be invited to the Orthodox, and vice versa. We found the same situation in Perm' oblast, where both Orthodox and Old Believers of different faiths sometimes lived in the same village and used the services of the same midwife.[6] Perhaps this is because the special women who attended childbirth and took care of the newborn appeared before the adoption of Christianity, or at least before the schism in Orthodoxy. Furthermore, the actions they performed were not directly related to church ceremonies, and the possibility of a newborn's "defilement" was removed by later christening.

It is not clear whether a tradition of direct transmission of midwifery knowledge and experience existed in the nineteenth century. There are only a few reports that midwives "in very rare cases receive training from an older, more experienced woman, who supervises the pupil."[7] More often, descriptions draw a contrast between the obstetrician and the "self-taught midwife," who "acquired all her knowledge, to be sure, from experience alone, or better put, these women know nothing, yet their skill comes from native Russian common sense and ability."[8] Practical as well as ritual knowledge was acquired during many childbirths, when a mother became familiar with techniques used by midwives. Any village woman who took care of livestock acquired elementary knowledge about the birth process. Several informants have reported transmission of special spells (of which more will be said later).

The midwife was an obligatory and generally the sole attendant at childbirth. By unanimous eyewitness testimony, the peasantry appealed very seldom to obstetricians, who appeared in the village in the latter half of the nineteenth century.[9] This is explained by a number of reasons, chiefly the "polyfunctional role" of the midwife, who not only attended childbirth but also provided various services involving care of the mother and child. Trust in the midwife was nourished for centuries by belief in her knowledge of magical and practical techniques. It is often reported that peasants preferred the midwife because she could also charm away hernias.[10] To superstitious peasants, it was also significant that "obstetricians are for the most part girls, and what if they have the evil eye?"[11] Moreover, the use of obstetric instruments during childbirth "is considered a sin by most."[12] The obstetrician's services, as is occasionally mentioned, were used exclusively by the rich and prosperous, since "it was necessary to send a carriage a distance of eight to ten versts, prepare an expensive meal for her, and pay her a huge fee."[13] Social factors also played a large part. According to D. K. Zelenin, who studied Viatsk Province peasantry, an obstetrician was a "lady" or "gentleman" in the eyes of the peasant, i. e., a weak and helpless being whom the peasant woman could not permit to attend her. Added to this was the "necessary shame, on the part of the woman and her entire family, for the dirt and messiness, etc."[14]

Opinions as to the actual help offered by the midwife during childbirth are contradictory. A correspondent of the Russian Geographical Society writes that "hardly ten in a hundred women know what they are doing."[15] Such also is the opinion of a correspondent from Sebezhsk *uezd*, Vitebsk Province.[16] Skeptical opinions of the midwife's activity often were due to the correspondents' well-known prejudice toward all activities involving magic and superstition. Furthermore, many midwifery techniques did not conform to the rules of medicine and hygiene. However, materials of the nineteenth and early twentieth century as well as data collected by the author contain a positive assessment of midwifery. Many women aged seventy to eighty years old who gave birth attended by midwives report that the latter knew a number of techniques to facilitate childbirth and that their help was vital. The midwives made extensive use of medicinal herbs, primarily to stanch bleeding. During a difficult birth, the midwife called upon the husband and sometimes the household as well, to offer help and perform essential (in her view) magical actions. Everyone carried out her instructions unhesitatingly; her authority in the house was unquestioned during labor.

For village women with their large families, childbirth was a painful but customary occurrence. The postnatal period was viewed as much more dangerous for both child and mother. The midwife was often not called immediately at the start of labor (except for a first childbirth). Sometimes there was not time, but more often it was due to the superstition that the less people knew about the birth, the easier it would be. Even in such cases, the midwife had to perform all postpartum procedures. Interesting in this respect are baptismal songs of Smolensk Province, relating how, with or after the birth, the father of the newborn goes in search of the midwife and the godparents. The father addresses each in turn and asks them to perform their duties. He asks the midwife to come "and midwife [*pribabit'*] the child."[17] Local correspondence containing a description of childbearing customs frequently points out that, "once relieved of her burden, the mother arrives home with the child and lies down near the stove. Then they send for the midwife";[18] "women often give birth alone, and only then, fearing the evil eye, send for a midwife for one or two days."[19]

Immediately after the birth, the midwife made sure that the child was healthy, straightening its head and feet and checking for dislocations. Descriptions of midwives' therapeutic activity note their ability to cure hernias in children. Zelenin, who had high regard for midwives' skill, writes: "the midwife at any time will remedy birth pains or dislocation, and will cure a child's hernia in the blink of an eye with cinnabar or the like. Some village midwives have refined the skill of remedying birth pains or dislocation to an art. . . . The medicine of these homegrown midwives and herbalists, springing from the soil of village existence, is perfectly adapted to it. . . ."[20]

Practical assistance was necessarily accompanied by magical actions and spells. It is important to note that the knowledge and application of magic in no way made the midwife, in the eyes of her neighbors, a vehicle of the magical power possessed by fortunetellers [*vorozhei*] and sorcerers [*kolduny*]. To the contrary, it is often stressed that midwives are commonly "godfearing women."[21] One of the midwife's prime duties at childbirth is to protect the newborn and the mother from impure power [*nechistaia sila*]; for this, village midwives often employed appropriate Christian appurtenances— incense, holy water, and prayers.[a] Their spells usually include an appeal to various saints for help: Zosima and Sabbatia, Ann the Prophetess ("a prompt and willing helper"), Cosmos and Demian, and the Mother of God.[22] Sometimes the midwife acts in her spells as the mediator between the newborn and the surrounding saints: "On the Ocean sea, on the island of Buyan, at the river Jordan, stands Nikitii, Conqueror of evil spirits, and John the Baptist. They scoop water from the holy river, give it to the midwives and command: 'sprinkle this water, and give it to drink to the mother and child, the unchristened child, yet born of a christened woman.' "[23] Their main protectress and helper, according to materials from various Russian provinces, was "the old woman Solomonida" (Solomeia, Solomonia).[24] According to popular belief, Solomeia performed the same operations with the Christ child that the village midwife was supposed to perform. Illustrative in this connection is the story of a village midwife from Orlovsk Province. The midwife complains that the Flagellants are bothering her because she handles the filth of birth. In justification of her ancient profession she appeals to Christian legend: "As for helping women in labor, the Lord himself commanded this: the Mother of God gave birth by the Holy Spirit, and the old woman Solomonida was at her side and helped in her labor, and so on the icons she is in second place at the Mother of God's side, and we say a prayer to her: 'Remember, Lord, King David and the old woman Solomonida.' And so it is, the Lord God Himself has commanded us midwives to help women in labor, and only cattle loosen themselves, but a baptized person can in no way do this."[25] Thus, women giving birth begged in their prayers: "Holy Mother of God, forgive dear Solomonida, be not angry with her, poor sinner, help me during childbirth."[26] The midwives appealed to her for help: "Old Solomonida, lay your hands on God's slave (name)";[27] "Old Solomonida, who delivered Christ, help me."[28] Sometimes Solomonida is mentioned only as a person performing actions similar to those of the midwife or assisting the health of the mother and child: "Old Solomonida, who delivered Christ, who bathed Christ, who straightened his arms and legs, has prepared a bath for our child";[29] "the old woman Solomonida came from beyond the sea, she carried two baskets of health. She tripped, fell, landed on [her] bones, nothing to anybody, but let (name of mother) have the baskets' contents."[30]

Interesting spells exist in which the action to be performed by the midwife is simultaneously transferred to Solomonida: "It is not I, child, who delivered you, not I who washed you, but the old woman Solomonida";[31] "it is not I who washed you, not I who gave you a bath—dear old Solomoneia washed and bathed you."[32] "It is not I who bathed you, not I who straightened you—dear old Salamanida bathed and straightened you, she it was who told you: 'Grow, my child, every hour, every minute.' "[33]

Regrettably, many of the magical rituals and spells accompanying childbirth were not recorded by collectors. Sometimes this was hampered by a skeptical attitude toward village superstitions, but more often it was the difficulty of collecting the material. As reported by a correspondent from V. N. Tenishev's office, "it was not possible to obtain information on birth rituals because they constitute a professional secret of the village midwives";[34] "the spells are kept in great secrecy by midwives and handed down by word of mouth, with the command that they not be told to outsiders."[35] b

The midwife's stay in the new mother's home was not confined to delivery and rendering first aid. According to the most widespread tradition, for three days after the birth she lived with or spent the greater portion of the day with her.[36] In some places this period was extended to seven or nine days.[37] Her principal duty during this time was to bathe the mother and child (thus the often-encountered statement that "the midwife may leave only after three baths"),[38] and also "keep watch" so that no one "blights" the mother or child. This is understandable, since the child before baptism (which was to be arranged as soon as possible), as well as the mother, were considered unprotected against all misfortune [porcha]. Therefore, the midwife stayed with the mother and child in the steam bath (a very impure place, according to peasant notions), remained at their side when others visited, etc.[c]

Furthermore, the midwife provided practical assistance to the mother. She did not often come empty-handed to the mother's home: "she brought bread and a couple of eggs,"[39] "something for the child—clean swaddling clothes, a braid, a bonnet, some mint leaves and soap"[40] and so forth. The kind and extent of assistance depended on both tradition and the need for assistance. Zelenin, characterizing the midwife's role in the family that invited her, writes: "The village midwife not only helps the woman deliver, but also lifts her from the bed if necessary, tidies her up, takes her and the child to the steam bath, and even cooks her meals, milks the cow, and so forth. In cases where there is only a single adult woman in the peasant family, the midwife also plays the role of mistress of the house, i.e., she will perform essential household chores until the new mother is able to work by herself."[41] These descriptions are confirmed by reports from other Russian provinces.[42]

In the 1920s, as mentioned, the amount of assistance to the new mother decreased. Even so, "the midwife bakes this or that and brings pancakes, lard, and swaddling clothes, if she has any."[43]

In an emergency, the midwife could baptize the newborn. In reports from various places we read that "if the newborn is very weak, the midwife baptizes him in a pot in her own way";[44] "the midwife baptizes the baby, taking holy water and diluting it with plain water in an ordinary plate. She then pours this on the baby three times, saying each time: 'In the name of the Father, in the name of the Son, in the name of the Holy Spirit, Amen' and gives the child a name."[45] This was especially common in remote Old Believer settlements. After the revolution, baptizing of babies by midwives became even more common in connection with the destruction of churches. Women who gave birth during those years recall that "the midwife sprinkled holy water and named [the child]."[46] As we see, the foundation of a midwife's actions was purification with water, prayer recitation, and (especially) naming. Such a baptism, performed "to ward off great harm," as the peasants said, did not replace church baptism.[47] If the child survived, the priest completed the rite without immersion in water, giving the name that had been bestowed by the midwife.

The church rules not only did not forbid such activities, but imposed as a duty on priests to explain "to all laymen, and especially midwives," that in cases of danger to a child's welfare they were supposed to baptize "by immersing in water or pouring water three times, pronouncing certain words."[48] Of course, the church was forced to entrust christening to the midwife (according to church rules, women did not perform religious rites) in order to avoid death of unbaptized children. It is possible, however, that naming and performing certain religious rituals were part of midwifery duties in pre-Christian society, gradually assuming the nature of a Christian rite as the idea of the necessity of Orthodox baptism took hold in people's minds. In this case, evidently, the church sought to control the midwife's ritual actions, to prevent the meaning of the church sacrament from being distorted. And such cases were evidently not rare. It is reported, for example, that a midwife "christens" a child before birth to facilitate delivery "holding the crucifix over the belly three times" and sprinkling holy water. Such a child was believed to have "received the cross," and would be buried in accordance with common practices.[49] Midwives frequently gave a name to stillborn children, which was categorically prohibited.

In relations between the peasantry and midwives, a large part was played by belief in the magic bond between midwives and the children they delivered.[50] This was expressed, first and foremost, in the choice of the midwife, whose personal qualities were supposed to conform with prevailing opinions. Not every woman could become a midwife. The village midwife was always an elderly woman; often it is specified that "she should no longer have monthly cleansings"[51] and "should not herself bear children."[52] Maidens, "even though very old, should not be midwives."[53] There were also behavior requirements: "The midwife should be of irreproachable conduct and never implicated in unfaithfulness to her husband."[54] In certain places, it was considered that only widows, and not married women, could be midwives, i.e., the possibility of sexual relations was excluded.[55] A midwife's immoral behavior, in peasant belief, meant that "the children she delivered would not live" or they would be born sick: "the yellow sickness will come on the child for forty days, they are often pigeon-toed."[56] We encounter the same belief among Belorussians: "The midwife must be an elderly woman, unmarried or not living with a husband, and of good conduct; otherwise, she is considered impure and unworthy to be a midwife."[57]

Violation of a given locality's accepted behavioral norms could destroy a midwife's reputation and deprive her of her community's trust. In this connection, the report of a correspondent from Kaluga Province is interesting. He writes that "all old women here hold a meat fast on Mondays, so that their hand is more nimble during childbirth. One midwife, who long practiced throughout the district here, forgot and ate meat in front of people on Monday, and as a result no one invited her and she lost her entire practice."[58]

The midwife's professional art was infused with a definite ethic: she was supposed to exert all her knowledge and ability exclusively to preserve the life of the child. As elderly women recall, during the 1920s and 1930s there were women "who knew how to perform abortions, but never midwives."[59] Mere suspicion of violating the professional ethic could deprive a midwife of her community's trust. For example, it is reported that "certain midwives are invited to those who have become pregnant by illicit cohabitation; to these the children are born dead, while to legitimate wives the children are born alive. The people regard this as chance, but even so the neighbors of these midwives do not call upon them."[60]

Sometimes the choice of a midwife depended on "whether she was happy in her family."[61] People avoided calling upon childless women or those whose children had died, since it was believed a child delivered by such a midwife would be born dead.[62] Much importance was also placed on whether children delivered by a midwife were living; if they had died, it was believed that "a newborn delivered by her would also die."[63] In such cases, women preferred to "deliver alone, rather than invite such a midwife."[64] Viability of the newborn testified that the midwife had a "nimble hand," and that everything essential—both magical acts and medical care—had been done properly. This was implicated in the custom, prevailing in certain places, of inviting the same midwife to a family. Thus, it is reported that "the men would do whatever they could to have the same midwife deliver their children, and even if they were at odds with her they would still ask; only if she refused would they call on another." If their "own" midwife were temporarily absent, superstitious dread of harming the infant by inviting a different midwife led to "not tying the umbilical cord for ten or twelve hours or even longer."[65]

It was widely believed that all the midwife's words and actions could be reflected in the newborn. Thus, for example, in Tver' Province, only the midwife was supposed to answer the priest's question as to whether it was a boy or girl, and "if she answered the priest's question wrong, the household mourns for the child as though lost, and the midwife loses her profession. Woe to her if the child should die: she must give up her occupation forever."[66] This extended to actions not directly related to childbirth and the infant. According to popular belief, a midwife was not supposed to wash the dead, as this would bring about the death of the children delivered by her. There is an interesting report from Perm' Province, illustrating the attitude of the church to such superstitions. An elderly woman came to a priest, complaining that she "not be commanded to wash the dead, since I am a midwife." The priest tried to explain to her that there is no such ban in the rules of the Orthodox church.[67]

Peasant beliefs as to the midwife's retribution beyond the grave are interesting, revealing the ambivalent attitude toward her profession. On the one hand, the midwife continually dealt with the "impure" (according to the community) act of childbirth. In a legend cited by S. V. Maksimov, a husband warns his wife, a midwife: "You are wrong to go among these headdresses [povoi], woman, anything might happen there, perhaps you will even commit a sin."[68] The ritual "impurity" accompanying childbirth extended to the midwife. At the same time, she was the protector, chiefly through prayers and incantations, of the mother and child. The complexity of the attitude toward the midwife came from diverse and conflicting beliefs as to the magical link between midwives and children they delivered, as well as the mothers themselves, in the other world.

We present several examples. In Smolensk Province, it was believed that "women performing a midwife's duties would carry about the umbilical cords of the children they delivered in an apron in the other world, and therefore each woman during her life had to give away at least one sack to a beggar, which she could use after death to carry the umbilical cords."[69] In Moscow Province it was believed that the midwife "would not even suffer those terrible punishments in the next world that were reserved for us sinners. The children would pray for her and God would accede to their prayers."[70] An ambivalent attitude also arose sometimes at a midwife's burial. It is reported that "it is considered a sin to be a midwife in Shenkursk *uezd*." The midwife "must harvest a whole field of thorns in the next world. Therefore, each mother she has helped should lay a mitten in her grave, so that she doesn't prick her hand."[71] In Saratov Province, "when a midwife dies, the women whom she delivered wind ribbons about her hands, so that the dead children may recognize and serve her."[72]

The midwife's stay at the home of a new mother, the nature of her activity, her "impurity" after birth and that of the new mother required an obligatory cleansing, according to peasant belief. In most of the territory inhabited by Russians—at least in the central, southern, and western provinces—this was achieved by the ritual of "washing the hands." The ritual had no fixed deadline. According to the most widespread Russian tradition, it was performed on the third day after birth and ended the midwife's stay in the house.[73] Local traditions also dictated other time frames: "after the third day,"[74] on the ninth day,[75] or on the twelfth.[76] In western Russian districts as well as among neighboring Belorussians, the ritual was often done immediately after christening.[77]

The ritual's essence was as follows: the mother and the midwife poured water, to which various objects carrying a symbolic meaning were frequently added, onto each other's hands three times, asking each other's forgiveness. After this, the midwife could go and deliver another child. Completion of the ritual made it possible for the mother to return to everyday existence (total cleansing, according to the church and often the local beliefs, was performed by a prayer on the fortieth day).[d] According to eyewitnesses, "among villagers this rite is held to be so holy that even after the priest reads the purificatory prayer, neither the one nor the other will touch a candle or an icon until this strange ritual is performed."[78] As frequently happened, the peasants sought to corroborate the tradition and universality of an existing custom in a reinterpretation of evangelical themes. Thus, it is reported from Kursk Province that local peasants are convinced that "the Mother of God herself, after giving birth to the Savior, washed her hands with the midwife

Solomoneia in the same way." It was also believed at times that failure to perform the ritual would result in "the hands being bloody up to the elbow in the next world."[79]

The washing ritual was performed either in the steam bath or the home; sources sometimes specify that participants were supposed to stand beneath a beam,[80] beneath the saints,[81] or on the hut's threshold.[82] Usually only the midwife and the mother took part in the ritual; sometimes it is specified "no one besides them should be in the hut."[83] In other cases, tradition did not demand the isolation of the main ritual participants and purification was extended to "everyone present and taking part in the birth."[84]

In the eastern section of Pskov Province, as well as in Tver', the ritual took place the first day after the birth, along with the washing of the mother in the steam bath: "Upon entering the bath, the midwife goes and throws hops on the stone," after which they all wash themselves. Then the midwife "washes the mother's shirt, the mother pours water on the midwife's hands, which are held over a pan on which three small stones are placed."[85]

Although the symbolic content was the same, local versions of the rite's performance differed considerably. As a general tendency, the rite was more saturated with magical actions in southern and some western provinces, having much in common with the Ukrainian version.

Generalizing the available descriptions, we discern an approximate invariant of the ritual in these places. The midwife poured water into a vessel while whispering something; three hot coals, "holy water and some grains" were added to this; then the midwife and the mother stood on an axe and a broom,[86] an axe, or a candle.[87] After this, the midwife poured water onto the mother's hands so that the water flowed to the elbows; the mother caught the water from the right elbow with the left hand and drank it, and then she poured water onto the hands of the midwife, who did the same.[88]

The ritual necessarily included the mother asking pardon three times "for troubling you with the birth" and thanking the midwife for the service rendered. In other cases, the ritual prescribed mutual begging of pardon: in Roslavl' uezd, "the mother, bowing low before the midwife, begged: 'Goodwife, forgive me, and again, and again.' The midwife answers: 'God forgives you, and I forgive.' Then, with the same words of apology, the midwife pours water on the mother, but without bowing down."[89]

Hand washing might be limited to the mother and midwife pouring water on each other. But the use of attributes of protective (axe, coals) and productive (oats, wheat, hops, noodles, egg) magic broadened the symbolic meaning of the purification ritual. Productive meaning was sometimes strengthened by the midwife's spells. Thus, for example, while washing the mother with water in which oats, eggs, and hops were placed, the midwife says: "As hops are light yet strong, so too will you be; as the egg is full, so too will you be; as oats are fair, so too will you be."[90] The hand-washing ritual ended with the mother giving the midwife an obligatory gift.

Where no special purificatory ritual existed, the idea of necessary purification was often realized by giving the midwife an obligatory gift of soap (soap and a towel are the usual, if not exclusive components of the gift presented during hand washing). According to V. M. Martynov, who investigated Russian life on the Pechora, "no matter how poor the woman, each house necessarily gave the midwife a piece of soap weighing one pound: 'You have become soiled by us, midwife, here is soap for you.' "[91]

We shall now examine a very important topic, leading us into the realm of traditional relationships within the village—the forms, extent, and necessity of remuneration of the midwife for her labor.[e] Neither juridical nor customary law regulated this. We have not found a single mention of midwives appealing or being able to appeal to any body with complaints of inadequate payment or refusal to pay. The accepted norms of behavior on this point may be included in the broad area of ethical norms of village life, "governed not by juridical rulings, but almost exclusively by public opinion."[92]

The sources are not entirely consistent in describing the extent and forms of remuneration. This depended on local tradition and the nature of the service provided, the wealth of a family, and so on. Analyzing our available data, we may regard child delivery as a profession demanding both skill and considerable time. Furthermore, the midwife could not refuse to come by claiming urgent business of her own. With such an occupation, of course, she could not entirely run her own farm. According to peasant notions, the midwife was even supposed to be at home often, in order to render assistance and not distract other women from their daily chores. As one elderly woman recalled: "Of course, the mother-in-law was there and could help, but she has her own chores."[93] Perhaps the reason midwives were mostly widows was not only the demand for purity, but also the desire of women left alone to find an additional source of livelihood. The documents frequently emphasize that midwives prized their reputation in the community, striving to preserve their practice and also their income. We find confirmation that child delivery brought some income to midwives indirectly—for example, the tale of how a midwife went to the devil to deliver says that "an old woman, not having work, wanted to be a midwife even for the devil if only she could earn something."[94]

Payment for midwifery on almost the entire Russian territory consisted of individual remuneration from the mother and collective payment. What was peculiar about the form of payment was that both individual (more often) and collective remuneration were cloaked in ritual form. As we have already mentioned, the hand-washing ritual ended with a compulsory gift for the midwife. We emphasize that not only in the nineteenth and early twentieth centuries, but also later on, in the 1920s and 1930s, according to peasant terminology, which reflected the corresponding ideas, the midwife was not paid but rather given a *gift*. According to the most common Russian tradition,[95] the gift necessarily included articles that would serve for purification—soap and a towel—as well as bread. In the second half of the nineteenth and especially in the late nineteenth and early twentieth centuries, the gift was supplemented with a small monetary sum.[96] We present several examples: in Kungursk *uezd* the entire remuneration was confined to soap and several yards of cloth;[97] in Saratov Province "the mother falls at the midwife's feet and bestows on her soap and a jacket, or thirty to forty kopecks in money";[98] in Novgorod "the mother gives the midwife a handkerchief or calico cloth for making sleeves";[99] in Smolensk "canvas basting four to five arshins long to wipe the hands,"[100] in Kursk "cloth, bread, a salt cellar, and three silver kopecks,"[101] in Orenburg "1 lb. soap and some money,"[102] and so on. The joining of the ritual and the gift in such cases was so traditional that if the ritual was not performed, no gift was given.[103]

Where the washing ritual was not adopted or (as observed in the early twentieth century) disappeared, remuneration was still expected, usually consisting of the same articles. In such cases, the midwife received gifts from the mother either at the baptismal dinner, usually at the end of the meal (this did not exclude gift-giving during hand washing), or at the end of her stay at the mother's house. But even this time frame could be changed, especially in the 1920s and 1930s. An indirect form of payment adopted in particular by well-to-do families was the "treating" of the midwife: she is "given the best food to eat and tea with sugar to drink, since the midwife is a welcome guest in every home."[104]

We have seen how the midwife was paid by the family that invited her. The relationship between the midwife and the family where she delivered a child was dependent exclusively on custom. Traditional norms of behavior determined the necessity of a gift—"it is an unforgivable sin not to give a gift." At the same time, the midwife was not supposed to demand more than the family could afford. The sources usually point out that each family gave the midwife "what they could."[105]

We shall now consider the collective payment of the midwife, which usually took place at the christening. The celebration of the christening (*krestiny, krez'biny, kstiny*) involved many magical actions whose semantics were linked to the act of birth. It is likely that this also explains the role of the midwife, the main personage in the birth ceremony, in the christening cycle. From the information available, we may conclude that on christening day the midwife acted as mistress of ceremonies for a considerable number of ritual (nonecclesiastic) and nonritual actions taking place in the home. She bathed and swaddled the child before christening, said parting words to the godparents, received the christened child from the godparents, and so forth, often accompanying all of these procedures with incantations.

The midwife had various duties at the christening meal itself. Occasionally she would take over the entire management of the meal: "she prepares the oven, the food, invites the guests, and is a perfect hostess to all."[106]

The midwife and the godparents were the primary actors or officiants in various rituals, and at the same time focal points in certain of them. The central place, given the number and diversity of actions and their importance in people's minds, was held by rituals involving a special ritual food—porridge, which was cooked (or at least served) by the midwife— "baba's porridge."[107] These customs were known over almost the entire territory of European Russia, being absent or less common in northern and northwestern provinces. In these areas, the christening meal was simplified. No ceremonial features are reported, even when describing the ritual food—porridge, or sometimes eggs. Customs similar to the Russian "baba's porridge" existed among Belorussians[108] and Ukrainians—those living in northern provinces of the Ukraine.[109] In certain provinces, such as Tver', the terminology of the main ritual food was transferred to the entire christening meal, which became known as the "porridge."

We do not propose in the present article to examine all customs associated with the "baba's porridge." We shall dwell on only two items, since they have an immediate bearing on the midwife's ritual and social characterization.

The christening meal ceremony is permeated by magic and wishes spoken to ensure the life and health not only of the newborn child but of all the living. Analyzing the corresponding rituals among Ukrainians, N. Gavriliuk writes that "in the people's conception, human vitality and procreation were associated with the earth's fertility, especially grains, and livestock."[110] At the christening meal, all rituals, all formulas of wishing characteristic of fertility magic, associating birth ceremony with agrarian festivals, center around the "baba's porridge," with the midwife as customary officiant (although sometimes these functions devolve upon the godfather). These rituals are especially characteristic of the southern and western Russian provinces. Lifting a pot with porridge, the midwife intones: "Let there be children on the bed, calves under the bed, piglets under the oven, chicks on the floor. And let my grandson grow tall."[111] Or: "As much as there is in the marketplace, let there also be in this house; let the grain grow, the cattle thrive, and the child become strong and happy."[112] Following which, the midwife usually broke the pot. Similar wishes: "Produce, God, rye, wheat, and every grain of my grandchildren,"[113] accompanied by breaking of the pot, also characterized the Ukrainian and Belorussian christening ceremony.

The custom of the "baba's porridge" necessarily included a collection of money, known in many places as the "selling of the porridge." Different variants of the custom—judging from the descriptions, each locality had its own nuances—do not prevent us from grasping the meaning of what is taking place: this is beyond doubt an ancient form of collective payment of the midwife. Nor is it an accident that the custom of "selling the porridge" took place at the christening dinner. With sufficient foundation, scholars regard the collective christening celebration, with invitations to relatives, neighbors, and acquaintances, as a "residual form of the family-clan meal (*trapez*, later than the communal meal)."[114] In fact, the midwife received the bulk of her monetary remuneration "for porridge" from the guests and household members (except the mother, who even if attending the christening did not take part in collecting money). The size of the contributions depended, of course, on the class of those present. For example, it is mentioned that "the midwife collects as her portion for the porridge as much as one ruble from the godparents and guests, even more when they are wealthy. Yet the mother pays her only a dress and meat pies."[115] A correspondent from Smolensk Province mentions that "even at the poorest christenings the midwife collects thirty kopecks in money, which goes to her profit, for which she comes to the mother."[116] The collection of money "for porridge" may be seen not only as remuneration of the midwife for her trouble in respect to a particular child, but also as a collective payment for her past and future activity, since all or nearly all of those present made use of her services. At the same time, this is a reflection of family, neighborhood, and community bonds into whose sphere the newborn is admitted, and which are realized in gratitude toward the midwife for her efforts on behalf of the new member of the collectivity. In her turn, the midwife, having assimilated the norms and notions of village life from childhood, pronounces the opinion of the peasant society on the future of the newborn in the ceremonial sayings and parting words; the content of these sayings reveals the great importance attributed to public opinion in the peasant milieu: "Grow up to be an ornament to your father, a consolation to your mother, and the pride and honor of the entire community";[117] "let my grandson grow tall, be happy, a joy to father and mother, and respected by people."[118]

The ritual format of the money collection was so traditional that it was preserved even in those cases when the christening was confined to entertainment of the godparents and the midwife.[119] In this connection, the recollection of a Smolensk Province resident is interesting. During the war, it fell to her to deliver a child for a Polish family in the west of the province. When the talk turned to thanksgiving, this woman explained to the hosts that where she came from, "it was customary to thank the midwife over the porridge." The hosts made porridge, over which she spread a handkerchief, and everyone threw money [onto it].[120]

Collective midwife payment sometimes had a different ritual expression. For example, on the Bilimbaevsk estate (Perm' Province), the collection of money occurred not during the christening, but when the village women came to visit the new mother, as was the custom among all Russians. Each of those who arrived brought "money between the teeth for the newborn, whatever each one could afford, and this money went toward the midwife."[121]

Frequently the gratitude for services rendered at childbirth was not confined to the aforesaid methods of payment. The midwives, especially those enjoying popularity, were also helped when they were no longer able to work. Such help might be both individual (women brought food and meat pies on holidays) and collective. As residents of Barkanovsk village, Vozhegodsk Region, recall, "the men plowed the midwife's acre—she could not do it herself, you know—and they were all grateful to her"; "whoever had a birth, whomever she helped, they did not forget her goodness, they fed her during the hungry years." And help came not just from those whose children she had delivered. This indicates the preservation of traditions of collective help, a characteristic of the Russian community.[122]

The delivery of a child created certain, albeit minor (in everyday life) relations among the midwife, the children delivered by her, and their parents. As reported from the towns, "the midwife is treated with great respect. If there is a wedding or some other feast at a house where she delivers, the midwife is always invited as an honor, that is, for hospitality."[123] There are scattered reports that after a midwife's death, at weddings of children delivered by her she was replaced by her daughter or another woman "from the hut."[124] Terminologically, this link was expressed by the fact that the midwife called the children delivered by her, and often also their parents, "grandchildren," and they called her "grandmother." Perhaps these are vestiges of ancient notions about an artificial form of kinship with the midwife.

But there was one day in the year when a special holiday was arranged for the midwives—the so-called *babiny*, or "baba's porridge." This was the second day of Christmas—December 26 (according to some reports, it also fell on the Mother of God's birthday—September 8).[125] Genetically, this holiday was connected with ancient Slavic beliefs.[126] Regarding childbirth and the fertility of nature as a single phenomenon explains why the "midwife's days" coincide in time with the two major agrarian festivals of the Eastern Slavic calendar. It was of primary significance that "in both cases, even in Christian mythology, the childbearers are childbearing goddesses."[127]

Although the holiday owed its origin, according to B. A. Rybakov, to pagan [*iazycheskii*] "childbearers," nevertheless in the nineteenth century it was not related to ancient goddesses either semantically or in the celebrants' conception. In peasant consciousness, Mary's divine delivery was accepted as an entirely genuine act; the church worship related to the icon "Help in Childbirth," which took place on the second day of Christmas, had the meaning of gratitude for a successful delivery. For this reason, the midwife—the person providing genuine assistance during the birth—was at the center of attention on this day.

There are not many descriptions of the celebration of "midwife's day." In Surgut territory, after worshipping in church, "the mothers invite the midwives to their houses, give them money and serve them porridge, which it is essential to cook on this day, wherefore the holiday is known as "baba's porridge."[128] In Kursk Province on the evening of this day "many of the peasants who have children go with their wives to the midwife and bring her vodka, food, meat pies or pancakes, and whatnot, and eat and drink there often until early dawn."[129] Even more festive and redolent with rituals was this day in Smolensk Province. V. N. Dobrovol'skii wrote a detailed description of midwife's day, *babiny*, in Roslavl' *uezd*. The midwife thoroughly prepares for this day: "She gets vodka, makes sausage, prepares jellied mincemeat, pudding, and porridge, fries potatoes and chicken, cooks pancakes and meat pies, and makes the filling for the pies out of porridge." "The grandchildren, for their part, also bring refreshment: a loaf of bread, a piece of lard, a string of sausage, a piece of raw meat, and the obligatory porridge." On midwife's day, the midwife herself visits all her grandchildren and invites them, who have already begun to prepare themselves. Curiously, she invites everyone out of courtesy, but only those delivered by her show up. At the end of the entertainment, the midwife brings a pot of porridge and "the guests, instead of eating the porridge, place money on the porridge for the midwife. Whoever gives the most has the right and duty to smash the pot of porridge. The midwife collects the money for herself."[130] Despite varying ritual expression, "midwife's day" has a number of common elements indicating a genetic relationship with the rituals of "midwife's porridge" at the christening. This connection is especially vivid in the description cited from Roslavl' *uezd*. In both cases, there is a collective meal, associated with childbirth and involving a collective gathering of money for the midwife. (In the Kursk variant, the refreshments brought to her have the same meaning.) At both the christening and the meal on "midwife's day," those giving money do not receive any simultaneous service from her. The ritual food—porridge, the symbol of fertility—testifies to the unity of the birth rituals and christening cycle with Russian agrarian rituals.

We have presented the principal beliefs, rituals, and customs associated with the midwife. Her primary function was to deliver and care for the child. But she was not merely an obstetrician: the village midwife was also an essential helper in the busy peasant family, and a protectress, the custodian of mother and child. Ancient magical notions permeate the attitude to her, being especially evident in the rituals associated with her.[131]

The life and health of the next generation depended largely on the midwife's skill. Therefore, gratitude and respect are the primary sentiments toward her. At the same time, the importance of successful childbirth to the peasant family is the reason for the requirements that were placed on the woman delivering the baby.

Midwifery may be regarded as a professional craft in the Russian village. In village society, midwives occupied a definite social position, which led Zelenin to identify them as being in "a special class of village midwives and herbalists."[132] Midwives' social characteristics are the same over the entire territory considered, local variants appearing mainly in the different ritual performance. It is not our purpose to discuss the many local variants of rituals and superstitions. We have set forth the main aspects (in our view) constituting the Russian ethnic tradition. Comparison of materials of the mid-nineteenth and early twentieth centuries with our field materials, covering the period from approximately the early 1920s or earlier on occasion (thanks to the handing down of information), suggests that, associated with village socioeconomic changes, two tendencies may have emerged from an identical process. On the one hand, there is a definite curtailment of the midwife's magical actions, while preserving all the practical activities. On the other hand, household members or neighbors, instead of the midwife, are invited with increasing frequency to render the necessary assistance to the mother and child, especially as midwives became fewer. However, it was still preferable to appeal to a midwife. Many women aged seventy or eighty recall that they were invited to attend a mother. In such a situation, "you have to wash the mother, take her to the steam bath, wash the dirty cloths, and wipe her belly." Yet this performance, which they subsumed under the general term *babit'sia*, according to their own notions, in no way made them a *babka*, a special midwife. The period and extent of help offered the mother by the woman "midwifing" the child were reduced—the visit was usually limited to one or two days; if requested, she might bring swaddling clothes and food, help around the house, and so on. On the whole, it may be said that an unwritten code of conduct existed for the midwife, violation of which would be censured by the community, while this tradition did not extend to the invited woman. Nevertheless, the basic rituals and customs associated with the midwife were often transferred to the person acting in her stead. Age and conduct restrictions were observed, though not always; the custom of "hand washing" and porridge rituals at the christening dinner were preserved. It was also considered impolite to refuse to attend a birth.

Field studies in a number of regions have shown that, as the network of hospitals and maternity clinics expanded, midwives and customs associated with them simultaneously vanished from village life.[133] Almost, but not everywhere. For example, in western Smolensk oblast, despite the gradual disappearance of midwives, many customs and rituals were preserved by arbitrary appointment of certain women to function as midwife. First and foremost are the elements characterizing the midwife as a person concerned not so much with birth as with the infant. Thus, in Krasninsk and Roslavl' regions, after returning from the maternity clinic, an elderly woman, on occasion the grandmother, is invited for the child's first bathing.[f] The person invited will bring a belt, swaddling clothes, handkerchiefs, "and as she washes, she will also bring soap and a towel, and leave all of this behind."[134] The woman chosen as midwife was necessarily invited to the christening dinner, where she performed the rituals previously acted out by the genuine midwife. Thus, one woman reported how she went "in place of the midwife": she sat in the corner, bestowed a dress on the mother, three diapers, handkerchiefs, and a winding ribbon on the child, and the mother gave her two kerchiefs. And at the christening she jumped up and down in the corner, and waved the fabric given to her, and they stole the fabric from her, and she ransomed it back, i.e., she did everything in keeping with the prevailing tradition of the christening dinner.[135] Even young women are today invited to play the part of midwife. There are no traditions of any kind in respect to the choice of this person, and certain modern "rules" are literally arising as we speak. Thus, a resident of Krasnoe village reported that a neighbor called on her to be midwife, since two months previous she had come and bathed the neighbor's newborn son, but she refused. The reason for the refusal was that the neighbor already had a "midwife" for her first daughter, one even younger than she was, so she should call on her for the boy.[136]

The playing of the part of midwife creates certain relationships between the midwife and the child, whom she calls "grandchild" from that time onwards, and he calls her "grandmother."[g] Every year, such midwives bring presents to the child on Christmas, and they are invited to all the major events in the life of their "grandchild"—"such women will occupy the corner seat at the wedding and when a boy is inducted into the army."[137]

In the present instance, the old rituals and customs have no real foundation; the reason for their preservation is simply tradition and the persistence of religious culture.

Study of the contemporary life of the Russian village may reveal other variants of transformation of traditional rituals and customs.

Editor's notes

a. The phrase *nechistaia sila* refers generally to all aspects of "impure power" or supernatural force used for evil. Still in use today in both villages and towns, the concept dates back to pre-Christian times. As it was appropriated by Russian Orthodoxy and adapted by the peasantry, it became associated with Satan and witchcraft. Midwives were believed able to counteract these evils through Christian symbols and actions: incense, holy water, and prayer. But during childbirth they acted beyond the bounds of standard Russian Orthodox practice, positioning themselves as mediators between a newborn and benevolent spirits defined as saints. In this, they functioned as a kind of "white shaman."

b. This passage indicates there was sometimes extensive midwifery training in esoteric knowledge, despite statements in some of Listova's other sources to the contrary. The contradiction derives from differing definitions of knowledge and training.

c. The Russian concept of *porcha* covers different kinds of willed misfortune, or "spoiling," for example cursing and the evil eye. *Porcha* was especially likely at times of vulnerability, for example after childbirth, during lovemaking, and during menstruation. Russian ideas of "impurity" were linked to these times of vulnerability, and it is noteworthy that the "impure" steam bath (a place of cleansing and shedding impurities) was where licit and illicit lovemaking often took place. For more on concepts of spoiling and impurity, see Linda J. Ivanits, *Russian Folk Belief* (Armonk, NY: M. E. Sharpe, 1989); Mary Douglas, *Purity and Danger: An Analysis of Concepts of Pollution and Taboo* (London: Routledge & Kegan Paul, 1966); and Thomas Buckely and Alma Gottlieb, eds., *Blood Magic: The Anthropology of Menstruation* (Berkeley: University of California Press, 1988).

d. Similar timed ritual cleansing, or purification, are known in many cultures and religions, including Judaism, where the fortieth day was also significant.

e. The topic is particularly important to Russian scholars whose legacy of Marxism makes them sensitive to abuse of position through economic exploitation. Indeed, folk curers and even midwives were accused by Soviet zealots of the 1920s and 1930s of exploiting communities for economic gain. But this was rare indeed for midwives, as Listova's account reinforces.

f. This kind of compromise, using European medicine but calling in a symbolic midwife for ritual purposes, is also known in other areas of the former Soviet Union, for example Siberia and Central Asia.

g. The male gender designation of the child is in the original, although clearly both male and female children are included in the practice.

Notes

1. The most complete information on our subject has been assembled in the collection of the Ethnography Bureau of V. N. Tenishev (Manuscript Department, State Museum of Ethnography, Collection 7). These are correspondents' replies to a questionnaire on popular customs and beliefs of Russian peasants of European Russia in the late nineteenth and early twentieth century.

Similar material is contained in the replies from the towns to the program of the Department of Ethnography, Geographical Society, issued in 1948. Some of the replies were published in the proceedings of the *IRGO*. Valuable information, some of it published in *Etnograficheskoe obozrenie*, has been gathered by the Society of Amateur Natural Philosophers, Anthropologists, and Ethnographers, founded in 1864 at Moscow University.

2. M. Smirnova, "Rodil'nye i krestil'nye obriady krest'ian sela Golitsyna Kurganskoi volosti Serdobskogo u. Saratovskoi gub.," *EO*, 1911, no. 1/2, p. 253.

3. AIE, "Vostochnoslavianskaia ekspeditsiia. Pskovskii otriad, 1982 g.," d. 8064, tetr. 1, l. 25-ob., "Pskovskia obl., Velikolutskii r-n, d. Zakharovo"; d. 58, d. Safonovo; "Permskii otriad, 1982 g.," d. 8594, l. 62, "Permskaia obl., Cherdynskii r-n, d. Cherepanovo."

4. GME, f. 7, op. 1, d. 384, l. 2, Vologodskaia gub., Ust'-Sysol'skii u.; d. 240, l. 2, Vologodskaia gub., Kadnikovskii u.; d. 141, l. 3, d. 15, l. 17, Vladimirskaia gub., Viaznikovskii u.; TsGIA, f. 1024, op. 1, d. 20, l. 33-ob., Tverskaia gub., Kaminskii u.

5. GME, f. 7, op. 1, d. 1366, l. 2, "Penzenskaia gub., Nizhnelomovskii u."

6. AIE, "Pskovskii otriad, 1982 g.," d. 8064, tetr. 1, l. 51, 58, Velikolutskii r-n, d. Safonovo; Smolenskii otriad, 1984 g.," d. 52, l. 1, Sychevskii r-n.

7. S. V. Martynov, "Pechorskii krai (St. Petersburg, 1905), p. 263. The famous Russian ethnographer S. V. Maksimov wrote that "Her (the midwife's—T.L.) origin is very simple: she is almost always the daughter of another midwife" (S. Maksimov, *Lesnaia glush': Kartiny narodnogo byta* (St. Peterburg, 1871), vol. 2, p. 11. Perhaps this was also the case when a single person combined the functions of midwife and herb doctor, as the skill and knowledge of the village herb doctors were often inherited. We have encountered no information on inheritance of midwifery.

8. GME, f. 7, op. 1, d. 1518, l. 84, 1897 g., Simbirskaia gub., Ardatovskii u.; "Etnograficheskie nabliudeniia po puti po Volge i ee pritokam," *Izv. IOLEAE* (Moscow, 1877), vol. 28, bk. 4, p. 59; GME, f. 7, op. 1, d. 548, l. 17, Kaluzhskaia gub., Meshchovskii u.

9. GME, f. 7, op. 1, d. 1341, l. 4, Penzenskaia gub., Krasnoslobodskii u.; d. 676, l. 6, Novgorodskaia gub., Belozerskii u.; d. 264, l. 2, Vologodskaia gub., Kandikovskii u.; d. 438, l. 57, Viatskaia gub., Orlovskii u.; d. 1554, l. 3, Smolenskaia gub., Viazemskii u.; d. 1411, l. 8, Pskovskaia gub., Porkhovskii u.; d. 1222, l. 1, 1898 g., Orlovskaia gub. i u.

10. V. N. Kharuzina, "Neskol'ko slov o rodil'nykh i krestil'nykh obriadakh i ob ukhode za det'mi v Pudozhskom u. Olonetskoi gub.," *EO*, 1906, no. 1/4, p. 89; GME, f. 7, op. 1, d. 890, l. 9, Olonetskaia gub., Vytegorskii u.; AGO, r. 5, op. 1, d. 7, l. 67, Vitebskaia gub., Sebezhskii u.

11. AIE, f. OLEAE, d. 170, l. 12, 1890 g., Permskaia gub., Bilimbaevskii zavod.

12. GME, f. 7, op. 1, d. 1726, l. 15, Tverskaia gub., Zubtsovskii u.

13. Ibid., d. 1442, l. 1-ob., 1900 g., Riazanskaia gub., Zaraiskii u.

14. Ibid., d. 445, l. 8, 1899 g., Viatskaia gub., Sarapul'skii u.

15. "Byt krest'ian Tverskoi gubernii Tverskogo uezda," *Etnograficheskii sbornik* (St. Petersburg, 1853), issue 1, p. 185.

16. AGO, r. 5, op. 1, d. 7, l. 67.

17. V. N. Dobrovol'skii, *Smolenskii etnograficheskii sbornik* (St. Petersburg, 1893), pt. 2, p. 3.

18. "Byt krest'ian Tverskoi gubernii Tverskogo uezda," p. 183.

19. D. I. Uspenskii, "Rodiny i krestiny, ukhod za rodil'nitsei i novorozhdennym," *EO*, 1895, no. 4, p. 73.

20. GME, f. 7, op. 1, d. 445, l. 9, 1899 g., Viatskaia gub., Sarapul'skii u.

21. Ibid., d. 948, l. 3, 1899 g., Orlovskaia gub., Bolkhovskii u.; d. 970, l. 2-ob., Orlovskaia gub., Brianskii u. Sometimes it is pointed out that "the witch-women are not invited to the birth" (GME, f. 7, l. 97, op. 1, d. 211, Vologodskaia gub., Griazovetskii u.).

22. Ibid., d. 743, l. 4, 1898 g., Novgorodskaia gub., Tikhvinskii u.; d. 970, l. 2-ob; d. 1078, l. 32, Orlovskaia gub. i u.; d. 1506, l. 64, 1899 g., Simbirskaia gub., Alatyrskii u.

23. Ibid., d. 1078, l. 32, 1898 g., Orlovskaia gub. i u.

24. Solomeia, or Solomonida, according to the popular aprocryphal Protoevangelium of Jacob, was a midwife summoned by Joseph during the divine birth of Mary. In the iconography of the Birth of Christ, she is depicted in white clothing preparing to wash the Infant Jesus. Sometimes an appropriate inscription was placed above the image of Solomeia: See, e.g., the icon "Birth of Christ" [Rozhdestvo Khristovo] from the GTG collection, inventory no. 14550.

S. I. Dmitrieva, without sufficient proof (in our opinion), assigns the "old woman Solomoneiushka" of northern incantations to pagan goddesses. Cf. S. I. Dmitrieva, "Slovo i obriad v mezenskikh zagovorakh," *Obriady i obriadovyi fol'klor* (Moscow, 1982), p. 38. In the present case, the personality in the Evangelium, having no pagan prototypes to our knowledge, has passed into popular beliefs.

25. GME, f. 7, op. 1, d. 1198, l. 1-ob. Orlovskaia gub. i u.

26. Ibid., d. 141, l. 2, Vologodskaia gub., Vologodskii u.

27. Ibid., d. 676, l. 6, 1899 g., Novgorodskaia gub., Belozerskii u.

28. Ibid., d. 869, l. 60, Novgorodskaia gub., Cherepovetskii u. See also similar incantations in: "Byt Tverskoi gubernii Tverskogo uezda," p. 184; Dmitrieva, "Slovo," p. 38.

29. GME, f. 7, op. 1, d. 840, l. 16-ob., Novgorodskaia gub., Cherepovetskii u.

30. Ibid., d. 1198, l. 1-ob., 1897 g., Orlovskaia gub. i u.

31. Ibid., d. 307, l. 18, Vologodskaia gub., Nikol'skii u.

32. Martynov, "Pechorskii krai," p. 264. See also: GME, f. 7, op. 1, d. 240, l. 2, 1897 g., Vologodskaia gub., Kadnikovskii u.

33. V. Magnitskii, "Pover'ia i obriady (zapuki) v Urzhumskom u. Viatskoi gub. (Viatka, 1883), p. 19. See also: GME, f. 7, op. 1, d. 1732, l. 9, Tul'skaia gub., Bogoroditskii u.

The mentioning of Solomonida in the role of midwife is found in incantations having no connection with childbirth. Thus, e.g., in Orlovskii province there was an incantation against wolves:

On the Ocean-sea,
On the Island Kurgan,
Mother Solomonida
Delivered Christ our Lord,
She struck one stone against another,
As the stone hardens,
So the wolf's lips and teeth
And liver and spleen will harden.
(GME, f. 7, op. 1, d. 1075, l. 1, 1987 g.).

34. GME, f. 7, op. 1, d. 799, l. 7-ob., 1899 g., Novgorodskaia gub., Cherepovetskii u.

35. Ibid., d. 1078, l. 32, 1898 g., Orlovskaia gub. i u.

36. "Byt krest'ian Tverskoi gubernii Tverskogo uezda," p. 23; GME, f. 7, op. 1, d. 440, l. 80, Viatskaia gub., Sarapul'skii u.; d. 540, l. 3, Kaluzhskaia gub., Medynskii u.; d. 1470, l. 34-ob.,

Sankt-Peterburgskaia gub., Novoladorzhskii u.; d. 1341, l. 4, Penzenskaia gub., Krasnoslobodskii u.; TsGIA, f. 1024, op. 1, d. 20, Tverskaia gub.; D. K. Zelenin, *Opisanie rukopisei IRGO*, issue 2, p. 271, Nizhegorodskaia gub., 1850 g.; AIE, Pskovskii otriad, 1982 g., d. 8064, tetr. 2, l. 9, Pskovskaia obl., Porkhovskii r-n, d. Borovichi.

These lines have also found a reflection in folklore:
> And godfather was a good young fellow,
> And godmother the distiller's wife,
> And the midwife spun for a living,
> She was three days delivering me.

(A. Sobolevskii, *Velikorusskie narodnye pesni* (St. Petersburg, 1902), vol. 7, p. 57.)

37. GME, f. 7, op. 1, d. 1366, l. 4, Penzenskaia gub., Nizhnelomovskii u.; d. 141, l. 6, Vologodskaia gub., Vologodskii u.; AGO, f. 12, op. 1, d. 12, l. 42, Orenburgskaia gub., Orenburgskii u.; N. A. Ivanitskii, "Materialy po etnografii Vologodskoi gub.," *Izv. OLEAE*, 1890, vol. 1, issue 1/2, p. 108; AIE, Permskii otriad, d. 8594, l. 49-ob.; l. 56, Permskaia obl., Cherdynskii r-n, d. Tulpan.

38. GME, f. 7, op. 1, d. 699, Novgorodskaia gub., Belozerskii u.; d. 434, l. 5, Viatskaia gub., Orlovskii u.

39. AIE, Pskovskii otriad, 1981 g., d. 7780, tetr. 9, l. 12, Ostrovskii r-n; tetr. 2, l. 17; tetr. 5, l. 10, Sebezhskii r-n.

40. GME, f. 7, op. 1, d. 1647, l. 7, Smolenskaia gub., Roslavl'skii u.

41. Ibid., d. 445, l. 9, 1899 g., Viatskaia gub., Sarapul'skii u.

42. See, for example: ibid., d. 175, l. 3, 1899 g., Vologodskaia gub., Griazovetskii u.; d. 1392, l. 1-ob., 1900 g., Penzenskaia gub., Saranskii u.; AGO, f. 12, op. 1, d. 12, l. 42, 80-e gody XIX v., Orenburgskaia gub. i u.

43. AIE, Smolenskii otriad, 1982 g., d. 8303, tetr. 1, l. 4-ob., Smolenskaia obl., Dukhovshchinskii r-n.

44. TsGIA, f. 1024, op. 1, d. 20, l. 43, Tverskaia gub.

45. V. I. Stepanov, "Svedeniia o rodil'nykh i krestil'nykh obriadakh v Klinskom u., Moskovskoi gub.," *EO*, 1906, no. 3/4, p. 227.

46. AIE, Smolenskii otriad, 1982 g., d. 8303, l. 49-ob., Dukhovshchinskii r-n, d. Berlizovo; Pskovskii otriad, 1981 g., d. 7780, tetr. 8, l. 4, Gdovskii r-n, s. Remda; tetr. 9, l. 17, Ostrovskii r-n, d. Gorshki.

47. In Roslavl' uezd, Smolensk province, such children were called "dipped," in Velikolutskii u., Pskov' province, "those who were prayed for." The midwife's christening eliminated the terrible (in the mind of the peasant) danger of dying unbaptized and nameless, and permitted the church to perform a burial in the common graveyard.

48. S. V. Bulgakov, *Nastol'naia kniga dlia sviashchennotserkovnosluzhitelei* (Kiev, 1913), p. 976.

49. E. P. Kazimir, "Iz svadebnykh i rodil'nykh obychaev Khotinskogo u. Bessarabskoi gub.," *EO*, 1907, no. 1/2.

50. This may be connected with the saying "he takes after the midwife" (TsGIA, f. 1024, op. 1, d. 20, l. 34, 80-e gody XIX v., Tverskaia gub.).

51. GME, f. 7, op. 1, d. 1389, l. 4, 1899 g., Penzenskaia gub., Saranskii u.

52. Ibid., d. 699, l. 11, Novgorodskaia gub., Belozerskii u.; d. 1497, l. 52, Saratovskaia gub., Khvalynskii u.

53. This was evidently due to the widespread belief that the presence of a girl during childbirth or even her knowledge of the event had a particularly negative effect on the course of the labor. This was connected with the reluctance to employ the help of young female accoucheurs (see above).

54. GME, f. 7, op. 1, d. 1389, l. 4, 1899 g., Penzenskaia gub., Saranskii u.; d. 1518, l. 5, Simbirskaia gub., Ardatovskii u.; AGO, r. 38, op. 1, d. 19, l. 20, 1898 g., Smolenskaia gub.

55. Ibid., d. 434, l. 5, Viatskaia gub., Orlovskii u.; d. 1222, l. 2, Orlovskaia gub. i u.

56. Magnitskii, "Pover'ia i obriady," p. 20; GME, f. 7, op. 1, d. 29, l. 16, Vladimirskaia gub., Melenkovskii u.; d. 1222, l. 2, Orlovskaia gub. i u.

57. "Byt belorusskikh krest'ian (Vitebskaia gub.)," *Etnograficheskii sbornik* (St. Petersburg, 1854), issue 2, p. 147.

58. GME, f. 7, op. 1, d. 540, l. 5, 1899 g., Kaluzhskaia gub., Medynskii u.

59. AIE, Smolenskii otriad, d. 8303, l. 102-ob., 1982 g., Smolenskaia obl., Roslavl'skii r-n.

60. GME, f. 7, op. 1, d. 1470, l. 20, Sankt-Peterburgskaia gub., Novoladozhskii u.

61. Ibid., d. 384, l. 2, 1898 g., Vologodskaia gub., Ust'-Sysol'skii u.

62. Ibid., d. 29, l. 16, Vladimirskaia gub., Melenkovskii u.; d. 1389, l. 4, 1899 g., Penzenskaia gub., Saranskii u.; AGO, r. 5, op. 1, d. 7, l. 67, Vitebskaia gub., Sebezhskii u.

63. Ibid., d. 283, l. 32, 1898 g., Vologodskaia gub., Nikol'skii u.; d. 29, l. 17, Vladimirskaia gub., Melenkovskii u.; d. 699, l. 11, 1898 g., Novgorodskaia gub., Belozerskii u.; d. 1392, l. 1-ob., 1900 g., Penzenskaia gub., Saranskii u.; d. 1389, l. 4.

64. Ibid., d. 1389, l. 4, 1899 g., Penzenskaia gub., Saranskii u.

65. GME, f. 7, op. 1, d. 1597, l. 8, Smolenskaia gub., Krasninskii u.

66. TsGIA, f. 1024, op. 1, d. 20, l. 35, 80-e gody, Tverskaia gub., Kashinskii u.

67. PEV, 1885, no. 33, p. 461. See also: Zelenin, Opisanie rukopisei IRGO, issue 1, p. 293, Volynskaia gub.

68. S. V. Maksimov, Nechistaia, nevedomaia i krestnaia sila (St. Petersburg, 1903), p. 517. This is the only instance found in Maksimov when Paraskeva-Piatnitsa appears as midwife.

An indirect testimony of the attitude toward midwifery as an "impure" trade are the taunting sayings about the midwife, e.g., "The midwife's daughters are trollops, her sons homeless drunkards" (GME, f. 7, op. 1, d. 1470, l. 23-ob., Sankt-Peterburgskaia gub., Novoladozhskii u.).

At the same time, it is often pointed out that "the midwives enjoy great respect in the village" (ibid., d. 970, l. 2-ob., Orlovskaia gub., Brianskii u.; d. 1518, l. 1, 1897 g., Simbirskaia gub., Ardatovskii u.).

69. GME, f. 7, op. 1, d. 1643, l. 6, 1894 g., Smolenskaia gub., Porechskii u.

70. Stepanov, "Svedeniia," p. 14. The opposite notions are also found among Ukrainians. Thus, e.g., in Kupianskii u., Khar'kov province, a poppy was placed in the grave of the midwife. Remember that the poppy in Ukrainian beliefs was a popular magical remedy, protecting against evil power. The local explanation of the custom is that "in the next life, the midwife will give the poppy as a gift to the welcoming children, who will come toward her demanding presents." Moreover, "in the next life, the grandchildren will come to meet the midwife with by no means friendly intentions, but rather a desire to revenge themselves on her, since she was partly to blame for their earthly sufferings, helping bring them into the world. The midwife throws the poppy to them so that while they are busy gathering the poppy seeds she may slip away and hide" (I. Ivanov, Ocherk vozzrenii krest'ianskogo naseleniia Kupianskogo u. na dushu i na zagrobnuiu zhizn' [Khar'kov, 1909], p. 6).

71. AGO, f. 12, op. 1, d. 12, l. 39, 80-e gody, Arkhangel'skaia gub., Shenkurskii u.

72. Smirnova, "Rodil'nye i krestil'nye," p. 253.

73. GME, f. 7, op. 1, d. 1331, l. 36-ob., Penzenskaia gub., Kerepskii u.; AGO, f. 12, op. 1, d. 12, l. 42, Orenburgskaia gub., Sterlitamakskii u.; Zelenin, Opisanie rukopisei IRGO, issue 1, p. 355, Voronezhskaia gub., Valuiskii u.; Selo Viriatino v proshlom i nastoiashchem (Moscow, 1958), p. 91; "Byt krest'ian Kurskoi gub. Oboianskogo u.," Etnograficheskii sbornik (St. Petersburg, 1862), issue 5, p. 22; "Selo Golun' i Novomikhailovka Tul'skoi gub. Novosil'skogo u." Etnograficheskii sbornik (St. Petersburg, 1854), issue 2, p. 102.

74. "Byt krest'ian Kurskoi gub. Oboianskogo u." Etnograficheskii sbornik, p. 22; "Selo Golun' i Novomikhailovka," p. 103.

75. Stepanov, "Svedeniia," p. 227; Smirnova, "Rodil'nye i krestil'nye," p. 254.

76. GME, f. 7, op. 1, d. 1085, l. 11, 1898 g., Orlovskaia gub. i u. Materials discovered by M. M. Gromyko.

77. Ibid., d. 1628, l. 6, Smolenskaia gub., Porechskii u.; d. 1647, l. 1, Roslavl'skii u.

78. AGO, r. 29, op. 1, d. 75, l. 4-ob., 1848 g., Permskaia gub., Kungurskii u. This concerns a tradition of purification in the same religious and ethnic group. In those cases when the midwife delivered children among the unorthodox (including Old Believers) and in families of different nationality, the ritual cleansing was not deemed sufficient and, to all appearances, was not performed. In these cases, the midwives preferred church purification. As reported by church functionaries, the midwives demanded "reading of the purifying prayer to assuage their conscience," which caused the priests to ask for an explanation, since there was no special prayer for cleansing of the midwife (Bulgakov, Nastol'naia kniga, p. 935). According to our information, during the 1920s and 1930s in mixed Old Believer/Orthodox towns of Russian settlement the midwife's delivery of a child in a family of different religious group did not require additional cleansing.

79. "Byt krest'ian Kurskoi gub. Oboianskogo u.," p. 22; GME, f. 7, op. 1, d. 1506, l. 70,

1899 g., Simbirskaia gub., Alatyrskii u.
  80. GME, f. 7, op. 1, d. 743, l. 9, Novgorodskaia gub., Tikhvinskii u.
  81. Ibid., d. 1085, l. 11, 1898 g., Orlovskaia gub. i u.
  82. Ibid., d. 972, l. 6, Orlovskaia gub. i u.
  83. Ibid., d. 1085, l. 11, Orlovskaia gub. i u.
  84. Uspenskii, "Rodiny," p. 78.
  85. AGO, r. 32, op. 1, d. 19, l. 10, Pskovskaia gub., Kholmskii u.
  86. "Byt krest'ian Kurskoi gub. Oboianskogo u.," p. 22; GME, f. 7, op. 1, d. 972, l. 6, Orlovskaia gub. i u.; Zelenin, *Opisanie rukopisei IRGO*, no. 1, p. 375, Voronezhskaia gub., Valuiskii u., 1853 g.
  87. GME, f. 7, op. 1, d. 1647, l. 4, Smolenskaia gub., Roslavl'skii u.
  88. "Byt krest'ian Kurskoi gub. Oboianskogo u.," p. 22.
  89. GME, f. 7, op. 1, d. 1647, l. 4, Smolenskaia gub., Roslavl'skii u.
  90. Uspenskii, "Rodiny," p. 78.
  91. Martynov, "Pechorskii krai," p. 263.
  92. M. M. Gromyko, "Problemy, metody i istochniki issledovaniia eticheskikh traditsii vostochnykh slavian (XVIII–XIX vv.)," in *Istoriia, kul'tura, etnografiia i fol'klor slavianskikh narodov* (Moscow, 1983), p. 108.
  93. AIE, Pskovskii otriad, 1982 g., tetr. 2, l. 9, Porkhovskii r-n, d. Borovichi.
  94. AIE, f. OLEAE, d. 170, l. 24, 1890 g., Permskaia gub., Bilimbaevskii zavod.
  95. The accounts of the sources on this subject reflect the tradition adopted in the given locality. But it must be realized that tradition is not an obligatory norm, and the kind and extent of remuneration also depended on the family's wealth and the gift-giver's sentiment.
  96. Sometimes money came to the midwife indirectly as an element of ritual. For example, the mother would place "a certain quantity of metallic money" into the bathing water, which then went to the midwife (Kartoteka Drevnerusskogo slovaria, Institut Russkogo Iazyka, Akademii nauki SSSR/Arkhangel'skaia gub. Podvin'e; AIE, Pskovskii otriad, 1981 g., d. 7780, tetr. 5, l. 18-ob., Sebezhskii r-n, d. Zamoshan'e).
  97. AGO, r. 29, op. 1, d. 75, l. 4-ob., 1848 g., Permskaia gub., Kungurskii u.
  98. Smirnova, "Rodil'nye i krestil'nye," p. 254.
  99. GME, f. 7, op. 1, d. 743, l. 8, 1888 g., Novgorodskaia gub., Tikhvinskii u.
  100. Ibid., d. 1597, l. 11, Smolenskaia gub., Krasninskii u.
  101. "Byt krest'ian Kurskoi gub. Oboianskogo u.," p. 22.
  102. AGO, f. 12, op. 1, d. 12, l. 43, Orenburgskaia gub., Orenburgskii u.
  103. GME, f. 7, op. 1, d. 743, l. 9, 1898 g., Novgorodskaia gub., Tikhvinskii u.
  104. Martynov, "Pechorskii krai," p. 263.
  105. As recollected by women who delivered with midwives, "if they had nothing, nothing need be paid—she would still come" (AIE, Smolenskii otriad, 1982 g., d. 8303, l. 46 ob., Krasninskii r-n). This, of course, is an exception that only emphasizes that the midwife could not refuse to perform her duties.
  106. A. Sobolev, *Svadebnyi obriad v Sudogodskom u. Vladimirskoi gub.* (Vladimir, 1912), p. 50. Also concerning this see Maksimov, *Lesnaia glush'*, vol. 2, p. 9.
  107. In places it was customary to make two porridges, one from the hosts and one from the midwife, but the primary ritual actions involved the midwife's porridge.
  108. E. R. Romanov, *Belorusskii sbornik* (Vil'no, 1912), issue 8, p. 323–36; P. V. Shein, "Belorusskie narodnye pesni (St. Petersburg, 1874), p. 12; *Pamiatnaia knizhka Vitebskoi gub. na 1865 g.* (St. Petersburg, 1865), p. 77.
  109. N. K. Gavriliuk, *Kartografirovanie iavlenii dukhovnoi kul'tury* (Kiev, 1981), p. 142.
  110. Ibid., p. 144.
  111. GME, f. 7, op. 1, d. 970, l. 3, 1898 g., Orlovskaia gub., Brianskii u.
  112. AGO, r. 15, op. 1, d. 41, l. 5, 1854 g., Kaluzhskaia gub., Masal'skii u. Materials discovered by M. M. Gromyko. Also compare similar incantations on Vasilii's Day: the eldest male in the family, lifting up a piglet, intones: "May the swine produce pigs, and the sheep lambs, and the cows calves" (Maksimov, *Nechistaia, nevedomaia i krestnaia sila*, p. 331).
  113. Romanov, *Belorusskii sbornik*, p. 238.
  114. G. A. Nosova, *Iazychestvo v pravoslavii* (Moscow, 1975), p. 86.
  115. GME, f. 7, op. 1, d. 1714, l. 47, Smolenskaia gub., Iukhnovskii u.
  116. Ibid., d. 1539, l. 7, Smolenskaia gub., Bel'skii u.

117. Ibid., d. 1085, l. 7, 1898 g., Orlovskaia gub. i u.

118. Ibid., d. 1660, l. 9, Smolenskaia gub., Krasninskii u.; also: AIE, Smolenskii otriad, d. 8303, l. 160-ob., 1982 g., Smolenskaia obl., Krasninskii r-n.

119. The custom of giving the midwife a gift "for porridge" was accepted at the christening dinners in various social milieux. In the early eighteenth century it is recorded that "the sovereign Empress Ekaterina Alekseevna [Catherine the Great] gave the midwife two pieces of gold for the porridge" at the christening feast ("Kartoteka drevnerusskogo slovaria. Arkhivnye bumagi Petra I." See also: M. G. Rabinovich, *Ocherki etnografii russkogo feodal'nogo goroda* [Moscow, 1978], p. 248).

120. AIE, Smolenskii otriad, 1982 g., d. 8303, l. 86-ob., Dukhovshchinskii r-n.

121. AIE, f. OLEAE, d. 170, l. 14, 1890 g., Permskaia gub., Bilimbaevskii zavod.

122. AIE, Vologodskii otriad, 1986 g., d. 8336, l. 10-ob., 24, Vologodskaia obl. For the traditions of mutual help, see M. M. Gromyko, *Traditsionnye normy povedeniia i formy obshcheniia russkikh krest'ian XIX v.* (Moscow, 1986).

123. GME, f. 7, op. 1, d. 1600, l. 3, Smolenskaia gub., Krasninskii u.

124. Iu. F. Krachkovskii, *Byt zapadnorusskogo selianina* (Moscow, 1874), p. 23.

125. Among the Bulgarians, a similar midwife's holiday—"Midwife's Day"—was observed on January 8 (*Kalendarnye obychai i obriady v stranakh zarubezhnoi Evropy: Zimnie prazdniki* [Moscow, 1973], p. 279).

126. B. A. Rybakov, *Iazychestvo drevnikh slavian* (Moscow, 1981), pp. 469, 470; V. I. Chicherov, *Zimnii period russkogo narodnogo zemledel'cheskogo kalendaria XVI–XIX vv.* (Moscow, 1957), p. 60.

127. Rybakov, *Iazychestvo*, p. 470.

128. Chicherov, *Zimnii period*, p. 60.

129. "Byt krest'ian Kurskoi gub. Oboianskogo u.," p. 23.

130. GME, f. 7, op. 1, d. 1648, l. 1, Smolenskaia gub., Roslavl'skii u.

131. *Selo Viriatino v proshlom i nastoiashchem* (Moscow, 1958), p. 91.

132. GME, f. 7, op. 1, d. 445.

133. However, even in the forties, their help was sometimes sought more readily than that of the doctor. Certain of the factors mentioned above continued to operate. Perhaps the presence of an experienced midwife had positive psychological effect on the woman giving birth. Even the doctor's assistants, especially the young ones, in villages far from hospitals and qualified help, would call the local midwife for help (AIE, Vologodskii otriad, d. 8336, l. 24, 1986 g., Vologodskaia obl., Vozhegodskii r-n).

134. AIE, Smolenskii otriad, 1982 g., d. 8303, l. 19-ob.

135. Ibid., l. 161, 168.

136. Ibid., l. 168-ob.

137. Ibid., l. 19-ob.

"She Entered a Nunnery . . ."

Iu. Kuz'mina

"I want to enter a nunnery. Don't ask why. I can only say that the nunnery is my age-old dream." Svetlana Sh., Krasnodar.

Our editors received the above letter. Yes, even today, certain women choose the lot of a nun.

Our correspondent spent some time at the Kuremiae (Pukhtitskii) Nunnery (100 kilometers from Tallin, on the border of Pskov Oblast), talked with its prioress and its residents, familiarized herself with their way of life. She shares her experiences from this trip.

Ding, dong, ding, dong. The bell of the nunnery summons the residents to the morning service. The hands of the bell-ringer have turned red—it is chilly out. The nuns hurry to the Church of the Assumption, the central point of the nunnery. From the open door of the vestibule a sweet scent of incense comes. The faces of those entering the church are bright and friendly.

"God be with you, sisters!" they say to the novice Lidiia and Mother Aleksandra, who have spent the night on watch [*dezhurnym*]. They bow their heads. All night, without resting, they have been guarding the enormous grounds of the nunnery with dogs, but they do not look tired. It is their work of obedience, having received the blessing of Mother Varvara, and therefore it must be done willingly and joyfully.

Ding, dong, ding, dong.

New arrivals come through the open gates of the nunnery. Despite the early hour (6:30), there are a lot of them. The nunnery attracts people not only with its special sanctity of worship, its beautiful church, but also its nearby "holy" spring, half a kilometer away. There is a legend that if you dive into the holy font you will be cured. I asked Sister Agniia whether it really works. "People think so," she eagerly explains. "And surely there is no harm in it. No one has fallen ill, no matter how cold it is outside. We ourselves take a dip all winter long, even on Christmas. The hole in the ice does not freeze over."

The cathedral is bright, clean, delicately pierced by the first sunbeams.

Russian text © 1988 by "Nauka i religiia." "Ushla v monastyr'," *Nauka i religiia*, 3 March 1988, pp. 45–48. A publication of the All-Union Knowledge Society.

The high, pure voices of the chorus respond to the fine, resonant baritone of the deacon.

The morning prayer is finished, but the assembly does not disperse. They wait. In an hour, the solemn liturgy will begin. No talking is heard, everyone is immersed within themselves, having renounced the world. Nuns fix the guttering candles without disturbing the deep silence. They lift the trays with the communion bread closer to the altar.

Yet the industrious monastic life began long before the first bell.

The farmyard workers have set out to do their work; the cloister has six horses, cows, chickens. Nor are those who are working today in the hothouses at the morning service. The cooks are occupied in their work, the shift changes in the boilerhouse. At the flour mill, the bakery, the sewing rooms—everywhere the novices are at work from the crack of dawn.

Yes, the Piukhtitskii Nunnery is an industrious place. The farm—75 hectares of land (plowed fields and hay meadows)—requires strenuous year-round physical labor from 148 novices. The farm has a tractor, automobiles, farm machinery, but much still has to be done by hand. Just the winter supply of wood, berries, and vegetables takes a lot! And it is not easy to manage the beehives, a short distance away behind a hill. In the autumn, each resident receives one or two jars of fragrant linden honey. As a general principle, everything here is shared equally. The residents perform whatever work is directed by the Mother Superior. And it is not simply work, but "obedience," receiving the blessing of the mother. Each novice firmly believes that the mother knows best how one is to live and what occupation to perform. The difficult work of the nunnery is constantly accompanied by prayer.

"The most physically strenuous obedience need not be a burden," I am told by Mother Georgiia, the right hand of Mother Superior (for thirty-two years they have been living in adjacent cells). "What work is more difficult is a worldly question. The difference between work and obedience is enormous. Obedience is fulfillment of God's will, transmitted through the mother to the novice, whose own will is no longer a part of the decision."

Mother Georgiia lets me understand that there are things that the "non-chosen," those who are in the world, cannot grasp. In fact, I was given this to understand many times in the nunnery. For example, a person of the world cannot understand the joy of strenuous physical labor, done with constant prayer, to fulfill the supreme will.

But frankly, this element of the life of the cloister is perfectly understandable to me, a nonbeliever, who does not admit any "cutting off of the will." I also feel that a lot depends on this very fact. How many of my friends and acquaintances are languishing from a wrongly chosen occupation, from having got onto the wrong track! And there is no one to blame—they themselves made the choice, they are the ones responsible, and thus in constant spiritual discomfort.

Working at the nunnery

Residents of the nunnery go on an
"official visit" to Jerusalem

Also obedient

The nunnery provides an opportunity to test oneself in simple physical labor, the outcome of which is always evident and cannot fail to please: plowed ground, mown hay, carefully stacked firewood, the granary, bulging barrels of pickled cabbage. And no one's self-pride is wounded, for *everyone* is doing the same. What is more, the work relies on a spiritual underpinning, and in this a creative principle is doubtlessly present.

"Work for our brother is charity," says Monk Svat, the hero of A. Platonov's novel *Iamskaia sloboda*.[a] "In work, brother, the soul is lulled and unexpectedly finds itself comforted." And these words are now particularly clear to me.

Without the comfort of oblivion, perhaps, the soul would not endure within the walls of a nunnery. You cannot live by imagination alone. But work is genuine, and the joy from work is real, whether in the world or in the nunnery. In the cloister, however, it does not matter if you are gifted, dexterous, strong, or even lacking in any talent whatsoever. Here, a person necessarily "exists" as a novice, since she performs the task chosen for her by the mother: the Mother Superior Varvara, a keen psychologist, knows the kind of task or work that each particular "daughter" of hers will feel capable of doing, and always provides them with such an opportunity.

There is a piano in the cell of the novice Natal'ia. Nonetheless, she prefers to play in the hall and sing in the evenings. Natal'ia is writing music for the psalms.

Her long, delicate fingers have become rough from farm work. Her excellent, "heavenly" voice has been made slightly hoarse from frequent colds. Yes, she is gifted, and for that reason the mother has made a "personal" instrument available to her. But in other respects, she is the same kind of novice as all the others: she has lived through both the cattle yard and the fields.

"Natal'ia," I venture an indiscreet question. "Couldn't you have lived in the world, worked and spent your time with music?"

She looked me straight in the face, not shifting her eyes as formerly:

"Do you remember Tarkovskii's [film] *Stalker*? 'The organ is lost.' It is hard, if not impossible, for those who are not chosen to understand us."

I understand, indeed, I do. From the sidelines, much is visible. Natal'ia in the world would have lacked this feeling of personal selection. I feel that, behind her self-conviction, there is a certain judging of those different from and those like her. I have noticed it in the residents here; they seem to say "We are redeemed, the grace of God is upon us, while as for you. . . ."

Ding, dong, ding, dong. The evening bell rings. The windows of the church shine, yellow lights come on in the cells. Everyone has returned from a hard day's work; the "personal time" now begins. One of them is learning the acathistus,[b] others are simply praying. The blue courtyard of the cloister grows empty, soon the gates will close.

"Bless the night watch, mother!"

"Go with God, daughters. . . . "

Lida has been living in the convent for eleven years. She left the "world" a fully grown and educated person. By training she was an architect. She worked at a research institute. Her life was smooth, with no special adventures or vicissitudes. Most of those here are like that: Mother Varvara is extremely careful in selecting her future "daughters." She is usually very scrupulous in the preliminary interview.

Do you want to leave a small child behind in the world? It's forbidden. Bear your cross. Has your lover abandoned you and you dream of escaping your grief? No. The convent is not a refuge—it is a Cloister. Is your impetuous nature uncomfortable around people? Again a refusal. Reform yourself in the world, and then be welcome; we are not a house of correction, but a service to God.

History gives us a lot of information about convent morality, of how unworthy wives and dishonored maidens were sent to a nunnery for the rest of their days. How many passions, tears, tragedies, blasted destinies have the convent walls concealed! In this respect the modern monastery has little in common with the former kind, except for the name. No one will injure the reputation of the cloister nor bring discord into its inner life. Those entering the convent are usually well aware of the life here: basically, they are all women who have been raised in the faith; many of them have or used to have nuns in the family.

As I became familiar with the convent, I noticed that most of the novices were from incomplete families. In one case, the parents were divorced; in another, there was only the father; in a third, only the mother. Life has not pampered them.[c]

But then there is Lida. Her father is a serviceman. Her mother was always home with her and her brother. They were not poor. There are no religious members of her family. Yet Mother Varvara accepted her eagerly. It was clear to her that Lida was decent, humble, and had not become pregnant out of passion.

Everything was normal in her family. In their own way, the parents were concerned for the spiritual welfare of the children.

"We often moved. And wherever our new home was, the first thing father would do was to hang a map of the world over my brother's bed, and over mine a quotation. I still remember it by heart: 'In science there is no broad, well-marked highway, and only he may reach its glistening summits who clambers over its rocky paths, heedless of fatigue. K. Marx.' I became used to my quotation, but never took it to heart. It was simply an interior furnishing." Lida smiles, and pretty dimples appear in her cheeks.

Lida is exceptionally nice. Small, fragile, a tiny freckled face with no eyebrows. Large, clear eyes, a fresh, smiling mouth. Such an open, trusting, intelligent girl. She shows me a psychology test (the scientific approach that she absorbed as a child is still with her!): in six squares, complete the drawings of various lines and circles to produce a completed shape, and your calling in life will be revealed. I produce a house with chimney, an apple, and a flower. Lida is satisfied. It works. Her nun friends, it seems (whom she also tested), all attempted to draw a starry sky in the squares. To each her own.

Lida became a believer when still a student, studying to be a rural architect. She often spent time in the outdoors, drawing the cathedrals of Troitsa and Sergievaia Lavra and going inside them. In the atmosphere prevailing there, she always felt tranquility in her heart. She was pleased by everything she saw. The "Lives of the Saints" made a great impression on her. "Those were people! Duty, conscience, decency, a willingness always to take up another's burden!" (At this point, for some reason I with disappointment think of her father: one may hang up a quotation, and that is all well and good, yet something was certainly lacking in her spiritual upbringing, if the "Lives of the Saints" can produce a moral revelation in an eighteen-year-old girl. Duty, decency, sacrifice, forgetting oneself for the sake of others—with all due respect to the "Lives," there are more impressive models, both in life and in literature.)[d]

Clearly, Lida had an inborn readiness for heroism, for self-sacrifice. But her parents shielded her from the unpleasantries of life. Should they be blamed for this? If something tragic had occurred in her life, something that demanded an exertion of effort, self-dedication, surely, the best side of her nature would have been revealed—she might have saved another's life at the cost of her own. The opportunity did not present itself.

Perhaps this is what prompted Lida to join the convent, where she saw a chance to serve the higher good. This was the burden that she invented for herself.

The motto "If not me, then who?" she learned from religious books.

And now, having lived in the cloister for eleven years, she is preparing to take the tonsure of the nun. At the Piukhtitskii cloister, the novices wait many years for this. "The convent needs the novices more," one nun explained to me with candor. "They can work more. After all, the nuns also have the duties of daily worship, reading of the Psaltery, and praying, and this takes up more time."

Lida's ideal is the eighty-eight-year-old Varsonofiia, who has taken the vows of schema and prays day and night for the entire world.[e]

"Are not all of us in the cloister like a family?" Lida wonders. "And what a family! Friendly, loving. We love all people. We are doing a noble thing: there are so few of us, and so many sins. Our lot is not the easiest, believe me. But a family, children—these are so little compared to eternity. Vanity."

She is happy and sincere.

I try to put myself into Lida's place. No, not quite like that. But what if I suddenly found myself here, within the walls of Piukhtitskii Convent? There would be no more crowded public transit, where people are not so congenial any more, no more quarrels at the editor's briefing sessions, which also do not make for calmness; no more husband's shirts and daughter's lessons, her crying, our heated arguments and sudden reconciliations. It would not be necessary to stand in the endless lines of the stores, listening to the news of the city, then rush across town after a hard day's work to visit a friend in the hospital. There would be no explanation of the complex relationships that occur at the crossroads of many people's lives, no concern for the many people with whom I am connected and for whom I am responsible. I would walk in the early morning through the dew-covered grass, flowers around me, the sun shining, knowing exactly what I would be doing and how, even how tired I would become. And in the evening, no need to go to pieces, trying to help everyone I want to help. Prayer for all would be all the help from me. Work and prayer. Work and prayer. And this every day. Without end.

I do not want such a life! I do not want this happy destiny. As soon as I tried it on myself, the idyllic picture that had begun to take shape in my consciousness—work in the outdoors, to the sounds of the piano and singing, a pastoral existence, and everyone happy—immediately fell apart.

The thirty-seven-year-old Lidiia thinks of the second tonsure, the one to become a nun, as the highest happiness. She remembers the first one down to the smallest detail. She tells me about it with delight. When she came to the part where the mother firmly grasped the tresses gathered in a knot with her strong yet tender hand and clipped with the scissors—meaning that all the novice's private thoughts and mental distractions were "cut off"—her voice trembled. I saw that she was indeed excited. This was a great and happy moment in her life. I remember my own great and happy moments: when I suddenly noticed how like my father was my child. When I first saw an article signed with my name in a newspaper. The first steps of my father in the hospital corridor after three weeks between life and death! There was also a lot of grief. I would not surrender any of it.

"The taking of the nun's vows is a height that must be taken and held firmly," Lida finishes her story with elation, bringing me back from reminiscences to her sparkling clean cell.

The day will come when Lida will fall, sprawling, to the floor—for such is the ritual—and crawl from the confessional to the holy gates, wearing only a white shirt beneath the mantle of her spiritual mother. She will be happy, because "only the schema is higher than nunhood, and few attain that." Lida will greet her mother, who visits on rare occasions (her father does not come), meekly, but also with pride: she will maintain her height. And what will the mother think, who raised her daughter to be decent and good, and always told her what was right and wrong? What more was needed? I don't know what she will think at these meetings. She probably doesn't understand what was lacking in her daughter's life, which began as properly as everyone else's, even better than most. I think that good and decent people sometimes think that their qualities will not be properly appreciated in the world and they hope to find acceptance in the cloister, this exalted and mysterious world.

Or perhaps, isn't Lida happy here because she has found in Mother Varvara, Mother Georgiia, and Mother Aleksandra wise and good counsellors, such as she needed and yet did not find, either when studying or when she began to work? These mentors of hers are ready to look into every quarrel, to make peace with everyone.

"Why have you come, sister, falling before the holy altar and this holy assembly?"

And Lida's quiet reply will be barely audible, falling like a weightless yellow leaf to join the pile of other autumn leaves:

"Wishing a pious life, your holiness."

The main role in her life will be played out, her soul will attain its desire, the not quite conscious thirst to feel herself at the center of a celebration, which women somehow always seem to not feel enough, will be satisfied. The "moment in the stars" will pass, and the weekday chores will resume.

Lida, Olia, Larisa, Inna. I talk to many and in almost each one I notice a kind of inner, inborn meekness. I wonder whether they have not abandoned worldly life because the convent is the best abode for those whose nature is fearful of the complexities of life, who tremble before the inevitable "revelation of lowly truths." Perhaps they were brought here by an instinct of self-preservation—in search of a guarantee? Some of them were born with eyes blinkered to the world from the start, others are stricken by a redemptive Daltonism, preventing them from seeing the many colors of life.

However it may be, the Mother Superior testifies that the woman who has once tasted the monastic life and learned its warmth, sanctity, unity, and protective halo, will never be able to return to ordinary worldly existence. In the 1930s, when the cloisters were closed and disbanded, even the nuns who received a blessing to return to the world (they had nowhere else to go) could not find a place in it.[f]

"There was a longing in the soul, a longing," explains Mother Superior Varvara, shaking her head. "Even though they founded families and bore children, nothing in their life was more pure than the cloister."

I made the acquaintance of a woman who had left Piukhtitskii Convent ten years ago. The person on whose behalf she decided to return to the world was a widower, the owner of a small stone house and a well-tended garden near the monastery. He was welcome in the cloister, being a jack of all trades, with skillful hands, a clear head—part driver, part electrician, part carpenter. And reticent. He told the sorrowful story of his life to her alone, and her heart was moved with pity. This decided everything.

Both mothers tried to dissuade her from the marriage, fervently crossing themselves before the icons, covering their burning faces in bitter understanding of this step. "You will lose your soul." But she had resolved on it, and they were married.

The former nun was forbidden even to attend the church. She merely gazed at it from her home, from which the entire convent was visible and the ringing of the bell could be heard.

"But why forbidden?" I asked Mother Georgiia. "Since she only took the first tonsure, wearing the cassock. Is it really such a sin to start a family, without yet having renounced the world?"

"Well no, not especially grievous," she agrees. "But a disgrace. A disgrace to the entire cloister. And her life has not worked out. She is not happy, nor will she be, even though God is merciful and has forgiven her. But because having once tasted the monastic life. . . ."

Yes, yes, I know. There is no happiness and no peace. And this very woman, at our next encounter, bitterly smiled:

"There is nothing to say. The past cannot come back. I submitted to temptation and am bearing my cross. Outsiders cannot understand this. . . . O God, what a life it was!"

Mother Superior Varvara was probably right. The monastic system strongly reshapes human nature to its own form. The personality changes irreversibly. The natural attitudes of life are broken, sometimes forever. And then the main dream becomes, for example, as in the case of the nun Liuda, to learn the acathistus of Michael the Archangel in one month.

"Without predicting, of course—as God wills," she tells me.

The days follow each other, the seasons of the year change, one task of obedience follows another. The words of the prayer become habitual, necessary. The only event to occur is that, three or four times a year, the residents "transfer" from one cell to another. Such is the procedure. Each of them should come closer to the others, so that distant souls become familial in this small, closed world behind the wall of the convent.

A year has passed, and with it the tender girlish expression has vanished from one of their faces; wrinkles have appeared in another, who counts herself in middle age; the very old ones, looking back, see an ever more uniform path composed of identical days. A devout path, outside of time.

In the cold early morning, I bid farewell to Lida and Mother Aleksandra (they are just coming off duty), and took a last look at the sleeping cloister from a bus window. The doors closed, and several hours later I was in Tallin. The cloister was wiped from my memory with each new face in the noisy crowd, with each turn of the busy streets. In Town Hall Square, the clock struck noon. A different life, a different keeping of time.

Editor's notes

a. Andrei Platonov, "Iamskaia sloboda," *Povesti i rasskazy* (Leningrad: Lenizdat, 1985), pp. 38–84.

b. In Russian, *akafist*, or eulogistic hymns and prayers to Christ, Mary Mother of God, and the saints.

c. This is reflective of the divorce rate prevailing in the society at large, which is about 50 percent, roughly comparable to U.S. divorce rates in recent years. See Marilyn Rueshchemeyer, *Professional Work and Marriage: An East-West Comparison* (New York: St. Martin's Press, 1986); William Moskoff, "Divorce in the USSR," *Journal of Marriage and the Family*, 1983, vol. 45, pp. 419–42; Gail Warshofsky Lapidus, ed., *Women, Work and Family in the Soviet Union* (Armonk, NY: M. E. Sharpe, 1982), especially part 2.

d. Examples of the "Saints' Lives" are in *Medieval Russia's Epics, Chronicles and Tales*, ed. Serge A. Zenkovsky (New York: Dutton, 1974), pp. 153–66.

e. Schema refer to the strictest vows of the Russian Orthodox Church.

f. This is the only allusion in the article to the harsh treatment endured by the Russian Orthodox church, including its monasteries, in the Soviet period. See, for example, Paul Miliukov, *Outlines of Russian Culture: Religion and the Church* (New York: Barnes, 1960 [original 1942]), pp. 151–212; Boleslaw Szczesniak, ed., *The Russian Revolution and Religion: A Collection of Documents Concerning the Suppression of Religion by the Communists 1917–1925* (Notre Dame: University of Notre Dame Press, 1959); Michael Bourdeaux, *Patriarchs and Prophets: Persecution of the Russian Orthodox Church Today* (New York: Praeger, 1970). For contrasting positions, review the journals *Voprosy nauchnogo ateizma* and *Religion in Communist Lands*.

Customary Law, Daily Life,
Medicine, and Morality

The Living Past

Daily Life and Holidays of the Siberian Village in the Eighteenth and First Half of the Nineteenth Centuries

N. A. MINENKO

Maintain honor from youth onwards

The Siberian peasants had clear ideas about honor and dishonor, and a reputation as an honest person meant much in the eyes of agriculturalists: "poor but honest," "naked but not a thief," "honest people take one's word," they would say. Interesting are the words of the Dalmatovsk peasant A. N. Zyrianov in response to an insult by a government official: "You cannot take away honor, which I will rightfully defend and will seek justice." "Honor, honor! What is your honor to me? Is your honor so grand? . . . I will show how much your honor is worth!" shouted the official. To demonstrate his power over the peasant, he ordered him to be sent under escort to the registration center in Verkhno-Iarsk village. The peasant stubbornly defended his right (making appeals to the authorities of his *volost'*, to the *okrug*,[a] and to the minister of state property) and ultimately a special investigatory commission made a decision in his favor—thus, he was successful in defending his honor.[1]

An honest person, in the mind of the peasant, was first and foremost an industrious one. "Everyone laughs long and hard," wrote A. Tret'iakov about the inhabitants of Shadrinsk district [*uezd*] in the mid-nineteenth century, "over those who from laziness do not finish plowing in good time or do not complete the threshing in the wintertime."[2] Peasants were proud of children who successfully grasped all the details of the economy. "At the age of fourteen," N. Chukmaldin remembered about his village childhood, "I was already able to make a simple chair from start to finish. My grandfather

Russian text © 1989 by "Nauka" Publishers. *Zhivaia starina. Bydni i prazdniki Sibirskoi derevni v XVIII–pervoi polovine XIX v.* (Novosibirsk: Nauka, 1989), pp. 91–147, 154–59. A publication of the USSR Academy of Sciences, Siberian Division, "Pages from the History of Our Motherland" series.

Nikifor, an artist and craftsman, would praise my work, saying: 'Well, brother Nikolakha, you will indeed be a master when you grow up.' "[3] The highest praise for a woman was the phrase: "*Zaryvnaia* (i.e., diligent) *baba . . . robit'.*" A hard-working peasant, according to the observer N. Popov, "attracted the respect of others, so that he was the first to be called on for advice, elected head of the *volost'*, and so on."[4]

The idea of virtue to the peasant was closely connected with thrift and with disapproval of wastefulness, carousing, and drunkenness. "Drink to the bottom, and you will not know good times," "a fiddle and a horn lost the whole house," according to field toilers. "Out of 500 people no more than 3 can be said to carouse on workdays for love of vodka," concluded an observer. "Such people generally suffer universal contempt and are given an abusive street nickname."[5] Whenever anyone was "commended" by the community, it would be said: "Neither a rogue, nor a wastrel, nor a drunkard, suspected of no crime and zealous in farming." And here is a disapproving characterization of one peasant by inhabitants of Legostaevsk village in 1820: "Vasilisko Konovalov's wife, Avdot'ia, Alekseev's daughter, in the absence of her husband lived in an unseemly way, was often drunk, and did not exert herself in work, as was often noticed."[6]

The village lad who forgot "his trade—the plow," who "managed to acquire a tattered frock coat, combed his hair to the side in order to set himself apart from the common peasant, and became acquainted with the pipe and the bottle," was in the opinion of the peasants "an unlucky Matrena, or neither a peacock nor a crow."[7] "Have a care," Nikolai Chukmaldin was instructed by his aunt Anis'ia when he was sent to the town of Tiumen' to work for a rich relative, "Do not dream of drinking wine or smoking tobacco there! I will scratch out the eyes of whoever teaches you this."[8]

A system of priorities in the sphere of moral values may be judged, for example, from the parable of "The Monk and the Salvation of the Soul." This tells of a monk who prayed "twenty years in a hermitage" and finally decided "that he was saved." But once he dreamed of someone who said: "Even though you have thought a lot about yourself, go into the world and see there how a man and wife are saved, although they have children."

The monk went out "into the world" and, "coming to a place where a man and wife dwelt," he asked if he could spend the night. He noticed that these people "lived like everyone else, with no devotion at all, not as they lived in the hermitage." Nevertheless, to his surprise, the monk saw "angels around them" at night. "He left them in the morning and prayed another ten years, not leaving his cell or setting eyes on anyone," all the time waiting for "angels" to arrive. But the popular wisdom left no hope for the ascetic: "In the world, you see, it was easy for them to be saved, because even though they sinned all the time, in the midst of work they did not think about themselves, whether they were sinful or free of sin." It is necessary to think about work, about one's family, about life, rather than about the salvation of the soul, and then "freedom from sin comes of itself, without our concern"— such is the main idea of the story recorded by A. N. Zyrianov in Shadrinsk *uezd*.[9] On the same subject are sayings that were popular in Siberian villages in the first half of the nineteenth century: "sweat and work overcome all"; "without work you will not find salvation."

The peasants considered an attempt against another's property—thievery—as dishonorable. To call a person a thief without justification was to offer extreme insult. "On this second day of January 1726," complained the peasant P. Elistratova from Kulakov village, Tiumen' *uezd*, to the court commissioner, "Ogrofena, the daughter-in-law of Leontii Larivonov, and his son Kondratei, both from the same Kulakov village, accused her, Palageia, of stealing cloth and called her a thief, yet they found this cloth in their home and thus defamed her." The village community Ikonnikov, Biisk administration, in 1781 requested the rural court [*zemskaia izba*][b] to penalize the peasant Stepan Mal'tsev, who "called his neighbor a thief and a scoundrel through the window" without any proof and in the presence of witnesses.[10]

"Thieves are beaten and given no rest"; "a thief steals not for profit, but for his ruination"; "a thief's hat burns"—these proverbs were very popular among peasants at this time.

Respect for another's property and thrift were natural virtues for the village working class. They were coupled with generosity and hospitality, which held a foremost place in village ethics. Not to receive guests or to refuse an invitation was considered a sign of rudeness. "Why don't you come to visit me, Guliaev," asked an offended V. Zagrivkov (a resident of Tulinsk village, Berdsk administration, in 1760) "or are you mad about the old debt?"[11] There was a saying: "The chicken would not come to the feast, but they dragged it by the feathers."

Both host and guest were required to be courteous and respectful to each other. There was an elaborate ceremony for greeting guests. Among Ialutorovsk peasants, for example, in the mid-nineteenth century, the host greeted them on the porch, "or at the entrance to the porch, or even at the gate, depending on the status, family, and importance of the guest." They greeted each other with low bows. In Tarsk *uezd*, the host met the guest in the yard. "Men doffed their hats," reported T. Popov, a resident of Takmytsk settlement, "grasped each other by the hand, and courteously bowed to the women, while women took each other by the hand and exchanged kisses. After these greetings and inquiring about the health of the others, the entire group entered the parlor, the host last."[12] Various Siberian regions evolved their own verbal formulas that were pronounced by the guests and hosts during the welcome. Thus, in Enisei province during Yuletide "mummers" would visit all the houses "with a star," performing a song of greeting: "Hail, host and hostess and all the guests. . . . The host in his house is like Adam in paradise; the hostess in the house is like a raspberry bush in the garden; young children in the house are like bees in honey! Greetings, hosts!" The hosts received them with the words: "Be so kind, be so kind. Come talk with us."[13]

A guest may not be "arrogant": he was supposed to be moderate in eating and drinking. "For an arrogant guest, the door is as good as the floor"; "a stuffed guest is easy to manipulate"; "it is no shame to leave another's table without overeating," they said in the villages. The story "The Dinner," recorded in Shadrinsk *uezd*, is full of sarcasm. It tells of a government official, a boyar (noble), who came to call on a "peasant," demanding refreshment: "What do you have for me to eat?" "Well," answered the peasant, "we have cabbage soup, peas, beans, . . . and stewed turnips." "Well then, my little host, bring me some turnips," ordered the guest. They brought turnips on a plate and the boyar began to eat. He ate them up and asked: "Do you have a lot of this wonderful fare?" "Fifteen cartfuls." "Oh! Oh! God was kind to you. Well then, give me some more." They brought the boyar more turnips. He ate and ate. He ate so much that he was bloated like a cow. . . ."[14]

It was necessary to give thanks for hospitality. For example, G. N. Potanin writes: "Among stoneworkers, upon leaving the table one thanks each relative thus: 'God save Aleksandr, God save Malan'ia' and even the youngest in the family: 'God save Alenka'; each one responds: 'Thank God'; in the village community, one says 'Thanks for the bread-and-salt,' to which the reply is 'Thank the Holy Ghost.' In a village at the foot of the Altai mountains, in response to the thanksgiving one says: 'Please do not sin.' Sometimes in jest they reply to the bread-and-salt greeting: 'The highway goes past the table, please follow it.' " Another observer, V. Verbitskii, reported that the thanks " 'For bread-and-salt!' not only follows hospitality but also is the greeting for a next encounter."[15]

In certain cases, when seeing off guests it was necessary to give them gifts.[c] Gift giving was generally widespread among the peasantry. They had the saying: "Never look a gift horse in the mouth"—a gift should not be overly examined. Custom demanded that the person receiving the gift should give one in return. Those who "Didn't give, but took" lost the respect of fellow villagers. To be prudent did not mean to be miserly. When a newborn was given a steam bath, the midwife would say: "Do not cry, do not howl, be a quiet baby, don't be greedy, don't be stingy. . . ."[16] Liberality was a means of strengthening one's prestige.

Without mutual support and mutual obligations, the individual peasant economy could hardly withstand the daily struggle against social and natural calamities. "The lending of agricultural and other implements and livestock for breeding," writes N. Kostrov of the Tomsk peasants, "almost always occurs under the condition that the person receiving the loan of a particular article or animal will render a similar service to the giver when necessary, so that nothing is loaned to an outsider and when the need has passed the loan is returned in its entirety to the owner."[17] Observers have noticed similar situations in other regions of Siberia. It is important to be prompt in offering assistance: "an egg is dear on Christmas Day"; "alms are dear in time of need."

Chukmaldin recalled that in Kulakov village, where he lived in his childhood, all contracts in such cases were oral. "There were no bills or notes; everything was trusted to one's conscience or, in the extremity, an assurance was required that 'Let God or the holy martyr Nikola be your guarantee.' Throughout my childhood I do not recall a single instance of a dispute between debtor and creditor. All accounts were settled in the stipulated terms, always honestly and faithfully."[18]

To deceive one's fellow peasant was dishonorable. Sibiriaki despised a tanyga—a swindler or fraud. "If you lose confidence in the ruble, neither will they believe in the needle [spire]"; "if you gave your word—keep it, if not— stand firm"; "order governs the world"; "an agreement is better than money" went the sayings. "You will find no truth in him, nor legs on a snake," was said of a person who was caught in a lie. However, sincerity was required only in relations with "one's own." "The village world in general and each peasant individually," writes Chukmaldin, "maintained good Christian relations only among themselves in their daily life and dealings. This moral, generally . . . harsh simplicity was pure and expressed by the commandment of physical work." As for the "masters," the government officials, and the clergy, the peasants felt that God himself commanded that they be deceived. In the peasant world, according to Chukmaldin, it was believed altogether impossible to form a relationship with the "masters" without deceit and cunning.

Chukmaldin recounts a "secret war" successfully conducted by Kulakov villagers, who concealed the location of a gravel deposit from the authorities. "It was clear to all the villagers that a fearsome forced labor would ensue—hauling pebbles for the road," he relates, "and therefore it was necessary to conceal it from the authorities in any way possible. They even dug pits in areas where there was no gravel or where the gravel lay only a couple of inches deep and filled them in again with dirt, in order to sink shafts in this location in the presence of the authorities and prove that there was little or no gravel. . . . No one among the peasants proved a traitor and not even wealthy peasants [miroedy] risked telling the authorities what was going on."[19] A person who did not want to be considered dishonest was simply obliged to deceive the government. It was apparent to the writer S. Turbin, traveling through all of Siberia, that "according to the notions of the Siberian people, the human race is mainly divided into two classes— people and government officials."[20]

The true attitude of agriculturalists to the "masters"—government officials—found a reflection in the story "The Peasant and the Stranger," which circulated among Siberian villages in the first half of the nineteenth century. The hero of the tale, a woodcutter, is telling the tsar where the money goes that he earns cutting wood: " 'With the first 50 cents I pay back a loan, the second I give in loan, and the third just goes away.' 'How is that?' asks the tsar. 'Whose loan are you paying back?' 'Your Highness! Father and mother fed me, so I am now feeding them with the first 50 cents, paying back a kind of loan; with the other 50 cents I feed my children, giving them a kind of loan, and they will feed me later on, paying it back.' 'Now tell me,' asks the tsar, 'where does the third 50 cents go?' 'The third 50 cents I throw away.' 'How is that?' 'Well, Your Highness: the third 50 cents, you see, I give to the clerks and masters. . . .' 'Why do they take this money from you?' 'Who? The clerks and the masters? Well, how do I know what they take it for, how they live is not your way nor our way, tsar.' "[21] Here there is an evident desire to place the "masters"—government officials—outside the realm of the logical (from the peasant's standpoint) social hierarchy: they are a useless burden on the shoulders of the people, and do not live like other folk. And such an attitude toward the "masters" was fully deserved.[d]

One had to put up with the government as an inevitable evil, but it should never be trusted, in the opinion of the peasants: the duty of honor required that it be deceived whenever convenient. In the same story, the tsar himself recommends that the peasant adopt this stratagem: "Then the tsar bade farewell to the woodcutter, saying to him: 'Will you be at home this week?' 'If I am healthy I will be home.' 'Then look here, a hundred geese will come to you, pluck their feathers as you are able.' 'Who are these geese, Your Highness?' 'Well, brother, you will recognize them; but for now, farewell, woodcutter!' "

The geese that were to be "plucked" proved to be the "service princes and barons and the clerks of the boyar's council"—in other words, government officials, whom the tsar sent to the woodcutter in order to solve the riddle "that I myself heard from him" (threatening, should they fail, to deprive them of "life and estate"). " 'Greetings, worthy sirs!' the peasant welcomed them mockingly. 'Where are you going in such a group?' 'Why, we have come to you, woodcutter. Tell us your riddle, as you did the tsar.' 'I know nothing, honored sirs.' 'Take what you will from us, only tell it to us.' 'Very well, honored sirs, I will think about it; but my riddles will cost you dearly.' "
For his riddle, the woodcutter took three thousand rubles each from "a hundred men." "The barons then went straightaway to the tsar"— thus concludes the story of the clever peasant and the stupid officials—"and explained the riddle to him, as they had been told and had written down. The tsar dismissed them alive and well; he sent a messenger to the peasant, summoning him to his presence, and asked: 'Well, woodcutter, how did you

pluck the geese with no swans?' " The tsar, participating in the joke against the "masters," sanctions from above not only the behavior of the peasant, the hero of the tale, but also other such actions of the peasant.

T. Popov, a priest at Takmytsk settlement, reported that the peasants' desire not to tell the truth to officials ("you will not live to a hundred on truth") became their daily custom. Such was their practice, for example, when the administration was gathering information on the extent of their crops: "The peasants told me personally," writes Popov, "that they declare only half of the crops or slightly more, and conceal the rest out of fear or by habit."[22]

At the same time, peasants saw no dishonor in flattering the authorities on occasion if an advantage could be gained. Sometimes this flattery took on such dimensions that an attentive person could easily discern a shade of irony in it. As an example, we present a fragment of the petition written by peasants Ivan Popelin and Maksim Krivonogov, acting on behalf of the Chistoozern *volost'*, Ishimsk *okrug*, and addressed to the senators V. K. Bez-rodnyi and B. A. Kurakin. "The fame of your incomparable virtues, of your most excellency and radiance, not only rumbles through the distant regions of Siberia, but also in the most royal cities of Russia; its thunderous sound has also reached the ears of our principals, downtrodden by fate in various circumstances and begging the patronage of the law and your gracious protection. Believe us, your excellency and your radiancy, this is not flattery on their part or ours, nor hypocrisy, but the true voice of our melancholy soul, which dares to cry out to you and beg for the wellsprings of happiness and consolation. . . . We are of course aware that any insignificant request of the subservient disturbs the peace and troubles the heart and soul of the authorities, who are occupied with high state commissions. But only think, your excellency and your radiance, where will the subservient find protection, if not from the authorities, the patrons, the fathers and architects of the happiness of the subservient."[23]

These unctuous sentences form an excellent contrast with the words about the "geese" in the story "The Peasant and the Stranger." Incidentally, as emerges from the story, even in his dealings with the tsar the village laborer was allowed to maintain his dignity. The very beginning of the tale is interesting: "A peasant was cutting wood in a particular place. Suddenly, an unknown stranger came up to him and said: 'May God help thee, worthy man! Tell me true, do you earn much money from this wood?' 'And why should you know this? Are you the state inspector, to come to me in the woods? Did you come here to stop my work? Leave me, worldly sinner.' 'Please be kind'—the stranger again coaxed—'show me fatherly mercy, enlighten me, how much do you earn a day? For my part, I seek no harm, for I am your tsar.' " True, after these words the peasant was "dumbfounded" and began to excuse himself for his curtness, but thereafter continued to speak to the tsar without the slightest groveling—a working man, in the opinion of the peasants, should respect himself and demand a respectful attitude from others.

"Among the personal verbal insults," N. A. Kostrov writes about Tomsk peasants, "is a reproach for a past, long-settled misdemeanor, . . . calling someone 'heartless,' 'an old woman,' 'a deathless evil spirit' [*koshchei*]."[24] It was considered offensive to call someone a "devil," "murderer," "Judas," "robber," "blood-sucker," or other "unseemly" words. A. Berezhnov, a resident of Loktev village (Altai), complained in 1782 to the Biisk rural court about the peasant Gileva, who "abused him and called him a rogue, a scoundrel, a beast, a thief, and a dog." The peasant M. Mal'tsev in 1781 appealed to this same body against the retired public servant N. Khlystov, who had told the plaintiff, in particular, "you are a true godless creature." Pautov, the headman of the Biisk community, accused of having beaten the peasant I. Klepikov, justified his actions by saying that Klepikov had called him a busybody [*khlopusha*]. In 1827 peasants of the Abatsk settlement, Ishimsk *okrug*, complained to the authorities against the police officer himself, saying that he had called them "fools" [*duraki*] at a meeting (even though, as the petitioners declared, "they were the best people in the community").[25]

It was considered a serious humiliation to cut off a man's beard or a woman's braid. Questions of female honor in general occupied a special place in peasant ethical traditions. It was considered "slighting" a girl's honor to accuse her of "illegitimate relations" with a fellow villager. To accuse a married woman of cohabitation with another man was even more humiliating. For such defamation of a woman, the community court usually sentenced the guilty party to severe physical punishment. It was also considered a "defilement" to pull the kerchief from the head of a girl or woman. This is explained by the fact that, in the opinion of the peasants, for a female to appear in the presence of a man with uncovered hair was tantamount to going naked in the street. In February 1791, for example, the peasant Vasilii Kovrigin of Tropina village (Altai) petitioned "against the peasant Iakov Nekrasov of the same village for insulting his maiden daughter by pulling off her shawl in the street," for which Nekrasov was punished, by sentence of the community court, "with cudgeling by the community collective [*mir*]."[26] Not a few such instances could be mentioned.

Any kind of physical violence against a woman on the part of "outsiders" was declared a disgrace. Thus, the peasant Avdot'ia Berezovskaia of Agafonikha village, Kailinsk *volost'*, complained to the *volost'* authorities against her village foreman, who, being sent by the community to invite her to the meeting and receiving a refusal, grabbed her "by the hand, fastened a withy around her hand and led her from the house disgracefully." The foreman later justified himself, saying that he and his companion "first politely asked the said Berezovskaia" to come to the meeting, "exhorting her considerably," but she did not yield to persuasion. A similar complaint was brought in 1762 before the Tobol'sk clerical consistory by the archbishop's peasant Ivan Rychkov against the headman of Voskresensk village.[27]

Not even a husband had the right to violate the human dignity of his wife, "her person." As the saying went, "you cannot force love." "A woman in Siberia," according to Chukmaldin, who grew up in a peasant family, "is not a man's slave; she is his companion. If the husband dies, the home and household started by him will not perish. The widow will continue to manage it with the same energy and dedication as the husband." The exceptional importance of a woman's work in the peasant economy assured her the respect of the family and society. "The Siberian peasants," declared A. P. Stepanov, governor of the Enisei (1830s), "are very courteous in their dealings with each other. The women hold the first place among them at banquets, and if the room is crowded all the men stand."[28]

P. I. Nebol'sin in his travel notes reported: "Speaking about Siberia, I employed the terms '*muzhik*' and '*baba*.' You will never hear these expressions in Siberia, unless in swearing."[29] This refers in fact to the use of these words in direct speech. In peasant letters, memoirs, and records of songs and conversations that have been preserved from the eighteenth century and the first half of the nineteenth, the husband addresses the wife in various ways: *khoziaika* [mistress], *zhena* [wife], *mat'* [mother] (if there are children present), by name, by name and patronymic, etc., but never *baba*.[e]

The communal nature of the organization of the life of the peasantry required that all members of the *mir* protect its interests. Betrayal of the *mir* was one of the most dishonorable actions, and to call someone a traitor to the *mir* was to offer him the most serious disrespect. "The *mir* is a wave, as one goes so do they all," said the peasants. Whoever did not support the community in time of need would lose his dignity and right of respect in the eyes of fellow villagers. On October 29, 1763, for example, the peasant Mikhailo Eremov of Bobrovsk village "deposed" at the Tobol'sk Metropolitan's house that, "last September . . . , the peasant foreman Mikhailo Koz'min Zubov . . . came to him and summoned him to a village (Preobrazhensk—N.M.) council of peasants to organize an uprising, . . . but he did not go. After this foreman left, . . . the peasants Flor Eperin and Afonasei Iakovlev Petukhov soon came to his house, and having banners with them they broke down the thatch doors, went into the hut, grabbed him by the hair, dragged him into the street and took him to the village of Preobrazhenskoe, beating him on the way . . . and chastising him for abandoning the people and not being united with them in peaceful agreement." The fellow-villagers of another such "renegade," Kirill Alemasov of Voskresensk village, threatened to "uproot him and his entire house," telling Fedor Stolbikov, who agreed with Alemasov, "that he had a soul worse than a dog's."[30]

The honor of the family and the entire community depended on the behavior of each of its members. It is no accident that sayings like "a bad sheep spoils the flock" and "a pig will not bear a beaver, but only another pig" were popular in the Siberian village. According to the village priest, T. Uspenskii, street nicknames ("little noodle" [*lapshonok*], "little fellow" [*maliuk*], "little buckwheat" [*krupenok*], etc.) in Shadrinsk *uezd* passed "from father to children, grandchildren, great grandchildren, etc."[31] Thus, a person's honor depended on the reputation of the "clan." It was not enough to be free of all "qualities" (qualities among the peasants meant bad traits, vices); one also had to come from "honest" parents. This is explained by the fact that, during the time in question, the process of personality individualization and its liberation from regulating familial authority, the community, the familial "nest," had not been completed. "Preserve your honor from childhood" admonished folk wisdom. If a person had not become accustomed to observing the norms of village morality from childhood, the peasants believed that the situation could only grow worse.

Social stratification of the Siberian village introduced certain changes in the traditional ethics. The peasant consciousness absorbed the idea that wealth entitled one to greater freedom of behavior than allowed by tradition: "the rich man does what he wishes, the poor man what he can"; "the miser has his navel in lard"; "the rich man is like a dove—he flies where he will."

But even well-to-do peasants tried to live according to the norms set by tradition. Violation of these norms led to loss of respect from the majority of the villagers, and under the socioeconomic conditions of the feudal order this deprived one of the much-needed feeling of security and stability of existence.

Village book-lovers

Studies of recent years have shown that the Russian village in Siberia during the time of feudalism was far more literate than previously thought.[f] True, the surviving sources do not provide detailed statistical information; no special investigations of literacy were conducted at that time. It must be borne in mind that peasants frequently concealed their ability to read and write from the authorities. There were several reasons for this: the desire to avoid additional burdensome duties with respect to the elective nobility, the belief that an appeal to "illiteracy" could save them from punishment in an emergency, and a general desire "not to stand out." "In the eyes of the authorities," notes the historian T. S. Mamsik, "literacy was a characteristic that distinguished a peasant from his class, which did not always suit his interests. Therefore, the peasantry as a whole . . . were prone to conceal the actual level of their cultural development. In conflicts with the officials, they played their customary role of simple-minded, illiterate villagers. . . ."[1] Claiming "illiteracy," the peasants would refuse to "lay hand" to documents, fearing undesirable consequences. "Sometimes it was necessary to send for a village clerk from a distance of at least thirty or forty versts from the village where I was holding an inquest, in order to write down testimony," reports G. Z. Eliseev about Tobol'sk province.[2] Based on such facts, he drew the incorrect conclusion that literacy was not common among the local peasantry. However, even on the basis of official data, it may be concluded that elementary literacy was possessed by no small portion of village residents as early as the seventeenth and eighteenth centuries.[3] And by the middle of the nineteenth century, as observed by students of Siberian history, nearly a quarter of the peasant population east of the Urals was literate.[4]

The communication of written culture to the Siberian village was facilitated by the fact that the overwhelming majority of the population was descended from the common [*chernososhnyi*] peasantry of the Russian North, who had a relatively high level of literacy. It was from the north of European Russia that the tradition was brought to Siberia of parents or private "masters of letters" teaching peasant children in the home. Not uncommonly, among home-seekers fleeing from central regions of the country to Siberia were some who could read and write. Finally, the Siberian peasantry was continually replenished by members of the service class, who were quite educated for those times. A number of teachers were banished to Siberia, and many of the exiles began to teach village youth. In time, many exiles became part of peasant society—yet another source of replenishment of the Siberian peasantry with literate people. In 1833, for example, the Tomsk general provincial administration stated that "in many villages the deportees include literate people. . . . Having married local peasant girls and purchased homes, they now live like the locals."[5]

The need for literacy stemmed primarily from socioeconomic conditions. The development of commercial-monetary relations in Siberia, according to Mamsik's accurate conclusion, meant that "mastery of such elements of culture as the ability to read and write became an urgent necessity for all rural strata."[6] A certain level of literacy was required for the peasants to engage in commerce and trades. Nikolai Chukmaldin, for example, who was born in Kulakov village, Tiumen' *uezd*, recalled that the question of sending him to school was decided in 1843 at a family conference, to which were invited his maternal aunt Anis'ia and his "intelligent maternal uncle Semen, a worldly-wise man who had ridden as far as Kazan' as a carrier." Uncle Semen's comment is interesting: "It will be altogether better for the child if he can read and write. . . . For I am able to 'work the abacus' but cannot read. And so what? My associate Aleksei, who can read, was writing the whole trip, and when the account was settled it turned out that I had less money and he more. How could I prove that he wrote incorrectly?"[7]

Yet the desire of Siberian peasants to read and write was also due in no small measure to their spiritual needs. "This Nikolai Kozhev as a sign of friendship hands over this book to the peasant Mikhail Menshchikov of Barabinsk *volost'* for reading and the profit of the soul, in 1818," attests the inscription on a collection of 1779, including the "Christian School" of Ieronim Rokis, the "Tale . . . of Macarius the Egyptian, How an Angel Appeared to Him," and the story of the angel who disobeyed God.[8] The peasant fully understood the edifying value of the handwritten and printed word. For this reason books were esteemed among the peasantry; they were carefully preserved, copied, and bequeathed to the children. From the pages of an early-nineteenth-century manuscript collection of religious materials, for example, we read: "This holy book upon my death I bless to my son Dimitri, one of my relatives, as a keepsake. Koz'ma Algazin puts his hand hereto. I also instruct after my death that the chamber room be held in common with daughter Paraskov'ia and grandson Egor, and the hut for grandson Andrei, that they may all live together . . . and not move away."[9] This same peasant Algazin bequeathed to his son Dimitri yet another book—"The Life and Praise, Wonders and Service of Nikolai Mirlikiiskii." As we see, the book is here equated in value with the dwellings; no mention is made of household articles, clothing, livestock, tools, etc., in the written will—evidently, Koz'ma Algazin was not very concerned about who would get them after his death.

In speaking of how peasant household libraries were formed, one may assert with confidence that they included, in particular, books brought by the first settlers from European Russia. Even runaway serfs would on occasion take books along with other property. Thus, it is reported in a document concerning the clerk A. Vareev Savva Ivanov, "a bondsman," that he ran away in the 128th year (1619–20), "stealing money and clothes, and books" to the value of 180 rubles.[10] The Siberian peasants also acquired books by purchase "from peddlers" and at fairs, in bookstalls in the towns. Sometimes it was necessary to make sacrifices. Chukmaldin recalls that when it was necessary to buy him a psaltery for school, his father was worried: "Alas," he said, "the book costs five rubles, and where will I get them, now that it is tax time?" Mother found a solution: "Well, it can't be helped. I do not need a dress for Christmas. Here is the money for the psaltery."[11] Such incidents confirm the observation that absolute materialism did not prevail in the peasant system of values during the period of feudalism.

The copying of books by peasants was a widespread practice in Siberia. Mikhail Kuznetsov, a resident of Tugozvonova, Tobol'sk province, was an experienced copyist. In one week—from July 1 to 7, 1774—he "wrote down" a book of forty-eight pages, and also in July he made a collection of extracts of twenty-two pages "from the book of Efrem Sirin."[12] Koz'ma Algazin also transcribed books. The collection dated 1816, bequeathed (as noted) to his son Dimitri, has the inscription: "This holy and God-inspired book is copied from the printed translation, known as the *Tsvetnik*, selected from religious books, written by the peasant Koz'ma Algazin, and whatever I have overlooked, forgive and correct in a spirit of meekness, for it is due to my meager understanding."[13]

The copyist thus excused himself before the reader for possible distortions, omissions, and mistakes (the manuscript numbers 445 pages). As a matter of fact, absolute adherence to the original was one of the requirements for a copy. The Old Believers were especially strict on this point. The peasant Mikhailo Menzelin of Suersk fort (Ialutorovsk jurisdiction), for example, in 1782 confessed to the provincial chancellory that he had met with Father Pakhomii, "a teacher of the schism, in the village Ankraky, Beliakovsk settlement, at the house of the girl Matrena, Mikhailov's daughter, of Tiumen' jurisdiction, who was living there" and spent two days with them, "in the course of which Pakhomii read him books, one the Apocalypse, the other John Chrysostom, and he explained . . . that whoever leaves out or adds something to the book will be anathema."[14] This, however, does not mean that peasant copyists did nothing but copy all the time: they would make changes in the text, prompted by considerations of both ideological and artistic character. Versions of "peasant exegesis" were even found among religious productions circulating in Siberian villages.

Collections produced by a copyist's pen also on occasion included original masterpieces of Siberian peasant literature. A famous name is that of the peasant writer Miron Ivanovich Galanin, an Old Believer, who lived in the eighteenth and early nineteenth century, the author of numerous journalistic writings, as well as an extensive historical work on the Russian schism.[15] In 1754, the sixty-five-year-old Semen Tavdintsev, a native of Shadrinsk settlement, "schismatic and fragmenter," was arrested. Besides other articles, found on his person was "a large book, with the title of Efrem the Elder, printed 7161" [1761?], several manuscripts, thirteen sheets of foolscap, a clean notebook, and a copper ink stand.[16] Chukmaldin tells us of another talented Old Believer writer— Artemii Lazarev, a native of Kulakov village, Tiumen' jurisdiction, nicknamed "Skrypa" [Violin]. In the 1820s, Artemii was recruited as a soldier, but shortly thereafter fled back home. "The fact that Skrypa, the runaway soldier, was living at his brother's in a separate cabin," writes Chukmaldin, "was known by the entire village and many in the surroundings and town of Tiumen'. The local priest knew of this, as did the regional police, yet they could never capture him, because all residents of the village took pains to hide him, warning of the slightest hint of a search and capture." Lazarev was very well read and possessed a superb talent for words; he belonged to the Old Believers of the philippic [denunciatory] school and composed polemical epistles denouncing other persuasions; these epistles circulated among his lettered followers. Chuk-maldin states that Skrypa had "a tremendous moral influence on all in-habitants of Kula-kov village," not only the philippians, but also the Old Believers of other persuasions and the Orthodox peasantry.[17]

Village writers wrote both religious and secular works: regional history, journalistic prose, herbals, etc. The outstanding role that peasant writers could play in village life is evidenced by the example of Aleksandr Nikifor-ovich Zyrianov (born 1830), a native of Verkhne-Iarsk village, Shadrinsk *uezd*, the son of a poor peasant who died during his childhood. He attended the Dalmatov religious academy for only a few months. Already at the age of thirteen the orphan was expected to earn his education—he served as a clerk, first at the Dalmatov *volost'* office, then at the offices of the Uksiansk, Baturinsk, Kargapol'sk, Mekhonsk, and other *volosty*. This continual wan-dering from one job to another is explained both by his desire to learn more, see more, acquaint himself more closely with the life of his people, and also by peculiarities of his character—Zyrianov was unable to flatter, he had the habit of telling the truth to one's face (including his superiors), he valued his human dignity highly and never compromised his conscience. He openly condemned the greed of wealthy villagers, ministers of the church, and gov-ernment officials. The deputy chief of Dalmatov *okrug* called him nothing less than an "informer" and "mutineer." Understandably, *volost'* ad-ministrators wished to rid themselves of such an unaccommodating clerk as soon as possible. Eventually leaving the service, Zyrianov settled in Dal-matov, where he earned his livelihood writing petitions for others. Through-out his life, in the words of D. D. Smyshliaev, who knew him well, Zyrianov "struggled with poverty."[18]

"The passion for reading," writes one of his biographers, "had become a distinguishing feature" of Zyrianov since childhood. Already at the age of twelve to fifteen he was seriously interested in the history of his region. "We see in his papers various comments," reports this same biographer, "jotted down in the 1840s."[19] To the pen of Zyrianov belong more than forty excellent works on the regional history of individual settlements ("On the Town of Shadrinsk," "A Survey of the Former Administrative Center Dalmatov," "Materials for a Description of Shadrinsk *Uezd*," "Materials for a History of the Settlement of the Land beyond the Urals" and others), on the peasant movement ("The Peasant Movement in Shadrinsk *Uezd*, Perm' Province, in 1843," "Pugachev's Rebellion in Shadrinsk *Uezd* and Its Sur-roundings," "The Legend of Ulugushsk Fortress," "Shadrinsk *Uezd* in April 1842"), on handicrafts ("Crafts in Shadrinsk *Uezd*," "The Making of Brick by the Peasants of Shadrinsk *Uezd*, Perm' Province," and others), on peasant customs and rituals ("Wedding Rituals in Shadrinsk *Uezd*, Perm' Province," "Materials for a History of the Legal Affairs of the Land beyond the Urals during the Time of Its Settlement").

The historian of Dalmatov region carefully kept abreast of published historical and other literature. In his works, he acted as a defender of ordinary peasants. We know that his articles on Pugachev's "rebellion" earned a positive appraisal from N. A. Dobroliubov.

The self-taught peasant [Zyrianov] was actively involved in making collections. He captured the oral creativity of the people: songs, fables, parables, riddles. A sizable number of the stories he recorded in Shadrinsk *uezd* were sent to the Russian Geographical Society, which handed them over to A. N. Afanas'ev, the well-known expert in Russian folk poetry, for study. A major portion of the second edition of *Russian Folk Tales*, published in 1859 in Moscow under Afanas'ev's editorship, consisted of stories sent by Zyrianov. Many oral folk creations collected by Zyrianov were published in two books of the "Perm' Collection."

In 1860, Zyrianov became interested in excavation of burial mounds and archeological settlements—first on Smyshliaev's instructions, and then on his own initiative as member and colleague of the Russian Geographical Society. He sent his finds, including ground plans and a description of the course of the work, to the Petersburg Archeological Commission. The results of his archeological investigations appear in his published articles and notes.

Zyrianov also conducted meteorological observations (on instruction from the Geographical Society, which gave him the necessary instruments): among his works are "On the Climate of the Village of Ivanishchevsk, Shadrinsk *Uezd*" and "Meteorological Observations in the Village of Ivanishchevsk."

He spared neither energy nor funds in acquiring manuscript and antiquarian books and documents. In time, he amassed a large library. After his death, his family were almost paupers, and his wife was compelled to sell the deceased's library and archive as scrap paper to the merchant Deriushev, who, according to reports, hauled away three cartfuls of books. Shortly after his death, A. Dmitriev visited the home of the regional historian "in order to acquaint myself with the interesting collection of manuscripts and old books." "It is a great pity," he writes, having learned that the collection was sold, "that many of the pillars of the seventeenth century that the deceased had collected may now be lost forever to scholarship."[20]

Zyrianov founded a school for peasant children in Ivanishchevsk village (1859) and managed to have publishers send textbooks to this school, usually free of charge. Thanks to his exertions, a girls' school was opened in Dalmatov. In 1859, he began working actively to create a public library in Ivanishchevsk. Having himself experienced the power of the printed word, Zyrianov wanted his compatriots to take up books as soon as possible. He turned for help to the writer and historian Smyshliaev. "I gave him some of the books from my library," recalls Smyshliaev, "and he then appealed to several learned societies and publishers of newspapers and magazines in the capital to send their publications free of charge and met with the same sympathy on their part."[21] In his note "The Ivanishchevsk Library," published by Smyshliaev in the second book of his "Perm' Collection," he says of this library: "Thus far, it has only thirty book titles, but all of them carefully selected, matched to the understanding and needs of the peasants and distin-guished by the most popular presentation possible. . . . The worthy Aleksandr Nikiforovich informs us that the project is going successfully, it has attracted readers, and only the schismatics stay away from the library. . . . We consider it our duty to express deep gratitude to Mr. D. V. Polenov, permanent secretary of the Imperial Archeological Society, who donated a copy of the "Transactions" [*Izvestiia*] of the society and the first volume of the "Notes" [*Zapiski*] of the Department of Russian and Slavic archeology."[22] By 1861, the library already had 940 books and 825 newspapers. The books were given free of charge for the peasants to read and, in Smyshliaev's words, "circulated throughout the district."

To Zyrianov's way of thinking, books were priceless. As his wife would later recall, when leaving home temporarily he would order "that the books and manuscripts be saved first of all in event of fire, leaving everything else—clothing, household goods, etc.—to the whim of fate."[23] The peasant-enlightener was remembered gratefully by his fellow Dalmatovians.

During this period, we know of no other public libraries in the Siberian countryside. Yet there were evidently a large number of community libraries here. These include, first and foremost, the libraries of the Old Believer groups and communes. "Bought . . . by the Tarbagataisk community in Nadeino . . . ," "1857 . . . by the community from Amel'ian Trifonov,"—such inscriptions are found, for example, in the "Oktoikha," 1594 edition, acquired by Novosibirsk archeographers in the Buriat ASSR.[24] A rather complete idea as to the Old Believer book collections may be gathered from the library of the "philippic" group in Kulakov village, Tiumen' *uezd*. This was kept in the home of the group's chief, Artemii Lazarev ("Skrypa"), "in a secret place behind the stove." "This secret alcove," reports Chukmaldin, "was concealed by an upright board or step, turning on an unseen inner shaft. The board, studded with mock brackets and nails, looked so natural that . . . it never betrayed its secret. Here were kept Black Letter books and handwritten illuminated collections [*tsvetniki*] with gorgeous painted pictures of religious content, starting with the life of St. Feodora and ending with the Apocalypse of John the Baptist." Skrypa regularly organized group readings, attended by Old Believers and by peasants adhering to Orthodoxy. The Chukmaldins, for example, were "true Orthodox," but frequently listened to edifying readings from the Chet'i-Minei, the Prologues, the Resurrection Evangelium, the Apocalypse, and even the Nomo-kanon [*Kormchaia kniga*] among followers of the once radical creed of the *popovshchina*.[g]

The reading of the Kormchaia, the Stepennaia, and the "Olonetskie Responses" of Simeon Denis'ev always aroused long and heated disputes. "In the summer," recalled Chukmaldin, "an audience of thirty men and women would gather outdoors, at the foot of a hill, beneath a tent. A table covered with a cloth was placed in a convenient place and the books to be read were brought. . . . Grandfather Artemii was an excellent reader and an even better interpreter of what was read." It is here where disputes arose. "Grandfather Artemii would patiently hear his opponent out and then clearly and convincingly set forth his arguments, quoting books and even citing pages where a familiar text was printed or written. Sometimes there would be a group singing of the Old Believer verses. . . . All of these verses were contained in handwritten collections and had been set to music in the old style. Grandfather Artemii knew the music well and, having trained some of his followers to sing, would amaze the listeners with this skill."[25]

The collective readings became a kind of village tradition in Siberia. The denunciation of the priest Vasilii Mashenov and the clerk Zakhar Vavilov, submitted in 1783 to the Tobol'sk church consistory, portrayed a scene similar to that recreated in Chukmaldin's memoirs: "The aforesaid clerk Vavilov, having come to the home of the peasant Miron Galanin, and hearing that he was speaking aloud in his cabin . . . without going into the cabin, but opening the window shutter slightly, he noticed that he, Galanin, was seated centrally on a chair and holding a book in his hands, from which he could be heard reciting . . . and at the same time with him, Galanin, in the room were around twenty or thirty people, male and female."[26] Prokopii Zaikov and Ivan Varlakov, residents of Beliakovka village, Ishimsk *uezd*, as follows from a denunciation of the priest Il'ia Karpinskii, also submitted to the consistory in 1799, would read to their fellow villagers and show them "a picture book, with a painting of paradise on the cover, depicting birds of paradise and rivers of milk and honey."[27] About the peasants of the Altai Burlinsk *volost'*, Shkoldin reports that "both sexes have literacy and read various church books, but their reading and interpretation may not be correct, since the readers and listeners, dividing into two opposite sides—schismatics and official orthodoxy [*kulundinsk*] followers—each understand the same passage of the books in their own way."[28]

Generally speaking, it is clear that theological, church worship, and homilectic literature occupied the main place in the Siberian peasant repertory. This is evident not only because such literature is predominant among the surviving books of that time, but also given inscriptions and marginal notes indicating peasant ownership. A similar conclusion is suggested by the testimony of contemporaries: N. Chukmaldin, P. Shkoldin, E. Kuznetsova, N. Abramov, and others. At the same time, there is reason to believe that the range of reading by villagers in the eighteenth and first half of the nineteenth century was in general rather extensive. Siberian manu-

scripts [*letopisi*] and other historical accounts, the works of the historians
G. F. Miller and N. M. Karamzin, plus fiction stories were popular among
the local peasantry. Literature of secular content was very widely represented in Zyrianov's Ivanishchevsk library, as mentioned. There was quite an
inclination for worldly reading among the peasants. Chukmaldin recalled
how, when still a village lad, he was given *Eruslan Lazarevich*, purchased in
Tiumen': "How glad I was to read the first town-printed book to come my
way! My impatience to know what it contained was so great that I read it
straight through from first to last page in the wintertime, while walking. . . . I
then took it home and often reread it in the evenings, becoming excited and
admiring the hero of the tale, deeply engrossed."[29]

Usually, however, a book would be read aloud, in the presence of friends,
acquaintances, and relatives. And thus the circle of peasants who enjoyed a
book was not limited to those who "could read and write," but was much
more extensive.

"To My Dear Friend . . . "

During the feudal epoch the Siberian peasants were quite familiar with com-
municating long distance through frequent correspondence. Unfortunately,
not many peasant letters have been preserved in archives—no one made it a
point to collect them. However, analysis of the content of the letters confirms that they were a customary thing in the Siberian village as early as the
eighteenth century. "I am very surprised at you and am continually crying
because you have not written me, while I have already written four letters
from across the sea, from Tomsk,"—the peasant Ivan Khudiakov, whom circumstances placed in the town of Verkhneudinsk, "beyond the Baikal Sea,"
reproached his wife and children, living in Sekisovka village in the Altai
mountains, in 1799. "Please, I humbly beg you, write," he urged. Khudiakov,
by the way, spent slightly more than half a year away from home. The fact
that an answer was expected from the addressee and that its delay aroused
criticism ("Well, my friend, you write me nothing," declared in 1764 the
peasant Sergei Kazakov from the Chaussk fort to his acquaintance Matvei
Galantsov, who did not reply promptly enough, "perhaps you will tell me
why"), testify that Siberiaki regarded frequent letter writing as an ordinary
thing.[1]

Also worthy of note is the everyday, trivial nature of the specific goals of
letter writers. "Our dear mother, we ask you sincerely, do not forget your
son if you hear that his shirts are worn out and also his pants. Also, our gracious mother Okulina Onisimovna, do not forget us entirely, come if only
for a short time . . . , we will be glad of it"—such is the main content of a letter received from her son by Akulina Eremina, a resident of Ilkova village,
Berdsk *volost'*, in September 1795. "My friend Nikifor Kalinich, you do not

know that I am in distress," hastened to explain the betrothed woman [*zhenka*] Mar'ia Kirillova from Atamanova village in 1787, "do not abandon me, a poor orphan, send me a ruble in money. . . ." The peasant Fedor Baskin asks his correspondent—"my good friend Ivan Semenovich Tikhobaev," serving as the elected headman's clerk, to help arrange that the investigation of the case of the humiliation of Baskin's wife be conducted not at the *volost'* center, but where it occurred, in Cheremushkina village, not forgetting to "thank" him in advance: "And with the bearer of the letter, Egor Kuznetsov, I am sending two kopecks and shoe soles, promising in other respects to remain your servant." "Please, dear grandfather and mother," wrote Iakov Meshcheriakov to Kirga settlement in January 1723, "send my wife Oksin'ia and daughter Anna to visit me in Tobol'sk, if only for a short while, until the great fast, and I will send her back to you, to Kirga, on the day of the fast with attendants and with Oleksei. . . . And let her, Oksin'ia, bring several hundred pounds of malt, and if you have unsold mutton, let her bring that, and gray cloth to make a suit . . . , and let her bring a fresh slaughtered pig, the best one there, and slaughtered geese."

The purpose of letters for Sibiriaki, however, did not reduce solely to the transmission of specific requests. They served as a means of sustaining familial and friendship ties and exchanging information. The peasant considered it a continual obligation to share personal and familial information with close friends. On occasion, all of this would be put in a single paragraph: "As of [the writing of] this letter, we are all healthy and well at home, and trust in God for the future. Also my father Ivan Demidych remains healthy and well, and all our parents (relatives—N.M.) are still living: Mikhailo and his wife, Andrei with his wife, Osip with his wife, and also their children are well." Iakov Meshcheriakov wrote more frankly and in greater detail to his family "in Kirga": "And let me tell you of myself, mother and grandfather, as of the forthcoming date, thanks to the will of God and your parental blessing, I and my son Aleksei remain in good health in Tobol'sk, as long as God remembers to keep us so in future. As for my grandfather Danilo Petrovich, let me tell you that we received tidings on Vasilii Day, this January 1, the year 723 [1723?], that he is living in the town of Eniseisk in good health, although they say he is drinking, and when he will arrive home we really do not know. My aunt Avdot'ia Grigor'evna and her son Petr and daughter Natal'ia Danilovna are extremely sad, but still alive, although often tearful, as are my aunts Mar'ia and Ofim'ia Petrovna, first, because our grandfather Danilo Petrovich has not been home for a long time, and another sorrow is that my brother, Ivan Danilovich, has not really mended his ways."

Ivan Khudiakov from Sekisovka, who was forced to part with his wife and children for a certain time, told of his wanderings in detail by letter. The candor and subtlety of feeling of the Altai peasant are striking: "Let me also tell you that as of the sending of this letter we remain alive, while only trusting to the will of God for the future . . . I expect by God's grace we will be able to see each other somehow. But even if distance continues to separate us, my heart is always with you, for I pass the time in misery and sorrow and each hour cheer myself with bitter tears, yet through such joy I hardly see light, especially since I have not seen a single line from you for such a time. If I were to describe everything to you in detail, I could not hold the pen in my hand. . . ."

The grain-growers were saddened in parting with their intimates and impatiently awaited news of them. "Find out about my family and brother, write a letter," asked the peasant Sergei Kazakov of his countryman M. Galantsov, even though he immediately added: "I will soon set out for home." Quite a few facts could be presented to corroborate that the letters reflected genuine immediate life situations. "My heart was heavy at the thought of leaving home, father, mother, sister . . . ," recalled N. M. Chukmaldin, born in Kulakov village, whom the family decided to give "in service" to a wealthy merchant in the town of Tiumen'. This same Chukmaldin reproduces the scene of parting of recruits in Kulakov in the mid-nineteenth century: "The recruit candidate experienced, first of all, at his house, in his room or parlor, in the last hour of separation from his family, a terrible bidding of 'farewell.' In the front corner of the room before the icon, sobbing inconsolably, his father and mother said goodbye, blessing him "along all of your roads, to the farthest point" and expecting never to see him again. Then the "brave lad" would be taken by his comrades to the yard and street, along which an entire crowd would advance to a gathering point at the hill, the pasture gate of the village. The recruit would go, or rather be led by his comrades, dressed in his Sunday attire, with a shawl about the shoulders, occasionally waving a bundle of colorful handkerchiefs over his head. Sometimes he would stop to say goodbye "for the everlasting centuries" [na veki vechnye] with a close friend and then resume his path. His mother, overwhelmed with grief, would walk behind if she could stand, lamenting, while at the same time the young people would sing parting [razukhabistye] songs one after the other. All of this, taken together, presented a deeply dramatic scene from village life."[2] The peasant Egor Tropin of Chaussk volost', who was recruited into the "mining service," during Fomin's Week returned to his native village "with the intention of seeing my wife," "not bearing the unaccustomed loneliness" that "came over him" away from her. After seeing his wife, Egor himself went to the volost' court "to report the matter."[3]

A temporary departure, of course, was not accompanied by such tragedy, but even in this case it was very desirable to receive news from the family. The same Sergei Kazakov went from the Chaussk fort to Tomsk for a very short time, yet nonetheless managed to become severely homesick.

With the help of letters, an historian is able to penetrate into the most secret areas of peasant spiritual life. Analysis of their content confirms an elaborate culture of interpersonal relationships among village laborers. Invariably, the correspondent would be addressed by first name and patronymic.

The peasant letters are replete with epithets. "My dear, darling mother, my dear Fekla Kipriianovna," carefully traced the hand of a man more accustomed to other pursuits, "I send you, mother, great respect, a humble bow, and I ask your parental blessing in my absence, and my dear, lovely daughter Ovdotiia Timofievna I send you, my dear daughter Ovdotiia, parental blessing, and my dear brother Onton Petrovich, and your spouse Marina Stepanovna, and Iakov, Ovdotiia, Okulina, Orina, Marfa, Ovdotiia Egorovna I send great respect, a humble bow to the very ground. . . ." Ivan Khudiakov was able to find words of extraordinary meaning for his wife: "My most gracious and dear spouse and guardian of our honor, and most special protectress of our health, and most special comfort of our shared family, and most honored keeper of our household Anna Vasil'evna, I send . . . my most humble bow. . . ."

Usually, the best wishes of the author, considered an obligatory epistolary element but also an expression of genuine human relationships, would follow. It is important that the formulas in this case were not standard. "To my most dear friend and warm-hearted companion Nikifor Kalinin from your most dear companion Mar'ia Kirilovna. I hope you prosper for many, many years," wrote a *zhenka* from Atamanova in 1787. Other versions could be presented: "Dear gracious sir and father Luka Afonas'evich, may you prosper over many and countless years" (a letter from the peasant Iakov Korotkov, Berdsk, 1782); "I wish you many years of health and spiritual salvation" (letter from Ivan Khudiakov); "I ask that the most supreme creator give you happiness in livestock and life, and also health and well-being for all the days of your life" (letter from Konstantin Eremin, Krasnoshchekov village, 1795).

Letters had an important role in the upbringing process. Through them, parents tried to instill in children certain rules of conduct and a proper (in their opinion) view of various aspects of existence. "Please, live in our home like good people live, with no disobedience or excuses," Iakov Meshcheriakov tells his daughter in 1723, when business forced him to live in Tobol'sk (his grandfather, parents, wife and daughter remained, as already noted, in Kirga settlement); "I heard the following saying from good folk: 'A well-behaved person is received better than a naughty complainer.' Indeed, as you live in our home, in the home of our most dear mother, and our other people, they will not teach you wrong. For you should live so as not to offend God or make good people laugh at you. . . . And we shall never forget you, by God's will. . . ." "I beg you, my dear children and daughters-in-law—the missive of the peasant Khudiakov chimes in with Meshcheriakov's letter—honor your mother and obey her in all respects, and commence nothing without her blessing, wherefore you will be praiseworthy of God and people, and live on good terms with the neighbors, and whatever is unwholesome to you, do not that to other people."

Correspondence allowed the master away from home to help his family with economic advice: "Let me also tell you, my grandfather Danilo Ivanovich," wrote Iakov Meshcheriakov, "to please have the grain ground by good people at the proper time, according to your discretion . . . so that the grain is not needlessly wasted. And if grain is now expensive there, sell as much of it as you like, only put some away for your own needs, for food and sowing."

At times letters conveyed frank opinions on various events, people, and actions of the government. For example, Khudiakov in his letter calls elected peasant agents [*vybornye*] and military commanders [*sotniki*], who helped officials of the rural court deal with unruly peasants, "traitors" and "false Christians." The officials, in Khudiakov's estimate, were harsh extortioners; when he was himself "captured" by Cossacks under command of the manorial assessor Borisov ("a relative, who is known as Borisov the Lame in our town" he clarifies), "it is not possible even to say how great was the tyranny and they milked me for 300 rubles and let me go." Khudiakov found the government decrees regarding passports of leave "very strict" ("And I have much sorrow and grief, since I am told that the passport will soon run out, and the decrees are very strict: old men with overdue or no passport are put to labor, and young men sent to the soldiers").

The authors' frankness was largely encouraged by the fact that they usually skirted official channels in sending letters, making use of the services of acquaintances or happenstance. Thus Meshcheriakov sent his letter "with Russian people" traveling from Tobol'sk to the Irbitskaia fair. ("Good and true people will be sent to you"—he warned his relatives in Kirga. "See that they are treated well, with every courtesy." These people, incidentally, were killed en route, and the letter did not reach its destination, but ended up in the papers of the Tiumen' military governor's chancellory, which investigated the murder.[4]) Khudiakov, in writing to his wife and children, availed himself of the help of Verkhneudinsk bailiff, Evsei Bondyrev, whose father, an old peasant, was a neighbor of Khudiakov's family in the Altai mountains.[5] Aleksei Kirgintsev, a resident of Chernolessk village, Ust'-Kamenogorsk jurisdiction, in 1765 sent a letter to his wife by an acquaintance, the peasant Miron Glazyrev. Upon his return, however, Glazyrev told Aleksei "that your wife did not accept your letter, saying that her husband, Kirgintsev, was dead, and the letter forged."[6] The peasant Fedor Baskin turned for help to his fellow villager Egor Kuznetsov in sending his letter. Several more examples of this nature could be given.

The peasants did not use envelopes; the sheet of paper was simply rolled up and the address indicated on the blank side: "Deliver this letter to

Okulina Onisimovna Eremina, Legostaevsk settlement, Ilkova village. From Krasnoshchekov village"; "To my dear spouse Anna Vasil'evna Khudiakova in the home of the peasant Ivan Khudiakov in Sekisovka. From her husband from beyond the Baikal sea, from the town of Verkhneudinsk." Sometimes only the addressee was given: "To my dear master Luka Afonas'evich, his worthy family Iushkov." An unfamiliar person could not obtain letters addressed in such way.

The private correspondence of Siberian peasants was not subject to influence by normative models represented in Russian manuals of letter-writing style. On the other hand, official documents exerted some influence on the peasant letters. "To my grandfather Mikhailo Vasil'evich and your spouse, may you thrive for many years, from Grigorii Uskov, a bow. I humbly ask you, Mikhailo Vasil'evich, having gotten a brown mare from me for the price of 6 rubles, and having received from you 1 ruble 50 kopecks, I instruct you to give the remaining 4 rubles 50 kopecks to Prokopii Voronov with a receipt. . . . January, the 22nd day of 1774"—this is not the only time a letter writer borrowed certain elements from the petition style.

It is instructive that a private letter itself might be treated by the peasants as a document. For example, Ivan Dolganov, of Tavdinsk settlement, having arrived in 1749 in Kundussk village, where he found his "runaway" daughter-in-law Ovdot'ia, asked the peasant Petr Popugaev (the second, "illegitimate" husband of Ovdot'ia) "to send a letter about her to her parents in Tavdinsk, to the effect that she, Ovdot'ia, was dead and no longer among the living, so that his son, Iakov Dolganov, could marry another, and she would be the wife of Popugaev forever." The peasant Mariia Alekseeva from Kadoshnikov village, accused of having left "a living husband" (he was "in military service") to marry a widower in her village, justified herself at a hearing in the consistory (1769): "She . . . lived four months in the Ukovsk land holding [zavod] with her father Aleksii Poludnitsyn, and from there she went to Betiukovsk zavod, where she lived for five years in the home of her uncle, the peasant Vasilii Pishchagov, and during all these years received no letters" from the first husband.[h] But now, she added, he "writes to her, Mariia, that she should go to whomever she pleases."[7]

It is evident that indication of an address and date of writing (or sending) came into personal letter style from official documentation. Here also, there were different versions: "The peasant Fedor Baskin. 1793, July 12"; "Your servant Sergei Kazakov. 1784, August 14;" "July 12, 1782. Your most obedient servant, the peasant Iakov Korotkov of Bersk"; "Your acquaintance, Ivan Vasil'ev Khudiakov. April 26, 1799"; "In other respects wishing you well, Ivan Openyshev. Sunday"; "Your obedient servant Aleksei Bogomolov. February 16, 1781." Sometimes the letter would have no signature or date, ending with "bows": "A bow from your grandchildren Ovdot'ia Kostentinovna and Mavra Kostentinovna. We send a bow to all of our relatives"; "A most humble bow from Ovdot'ia Petrovna."

The wide occurrence of private correspondence in the Siberian village was possible because the local peasantry, as already stated, included many who could read and write. All the letter writers whose names are given above were able to write.

Those in the village who could read and write came to the help of their neighbors in organizing correspondence. Thanks to their efforts, historians today have a unique source that conveys in undistorted form the thoughts, feelings, and attitudes of the village working class and the structure of peasant speech.

Folk curers and sorcerers

Even in the second half of the nineteenth century the medical needs of the Siberian peasant population were generally met by self-taught healers and folk medicine. This was even more true of the previous period, since medical institutions and qualified physicians in Siberia, even by the middle of the nineteenth century, were scarce. Nor did the peasants themselves willingly resort to doctors for assistance. "Here, as almost everywhere else among Siberian villagers," wrote K. Golodnikov about the Ialutorovsk *okrug* of Tobol'sk province (1840s), "there is a disinclination toward doctors. Only in major and predominantly external illnesses and injuries . . . do they occasionally resort to medical aid, and even then with distrust and even fear."[1] This report is corroborated by other sources.

The peasants' behavior is explained by various motives. First of all, a doctor's treatment involved no small expense. The Tiumen' regional doctor I. Sokol'nikov in 1829 observed that, when he came to Reshetnikova village, Lipchinsk *volost'*, "to take the proper steps" in halting "an epidemic of purulent nervous fever" that was raging there, many patients refused to take medicine from him, so that they would not have to pay for it later.[2] Payment for medication, in fact, was always exacted from the peasant "community." The Siberian administration gave the local doctors, according to their own testimony, too "few funds for service free of charge, especially among the peasantry."[3]

The unconscientious attitude of some medical service members to their duties was also significant here. In a report to governor A. Belikov by the rural court on July 29, 1800, the Chaussk *volost'* authorities stated, for example, that several people "overcome by a wind-borne infectious disease" died from "resorting to the medical apprentice Solodovnikov, who was sent out by the Suzunsk office, and who being in a drunken condition during these efforts and thus placing the inhabitants in such a state of despair that they would not admit him, Solodovnikov, into their homes and were even afraid to report cases of infection."[4] It is no accident that the Siberian peasants viewed vaccination as, in the words of the priest T. Popov, "if not the seal of the Antichrist, then at least a needless pricking of the child"; the vaccinators for the most part used vaccine that was no longer effective (because of lengthy storage). " 'Of what disease did the child die?'—you will ask at the burial service (writes Popov). 'From smallpox.' 'Was he not vaccinated?' 'Of course, three times, but clearly it did not work.' "[5]

That the physicians resorted to the administration for help did not win them respect. Such a physician would come to a village with the assessor, and the peasants would be gathered at a meeting. The assessor, as usual, would threaten the assembly: "I will thrash you all, scoundrels, unless you listen to the doctor." Yet the peasants' behavior would not change.

A conscientious doctor in time would gain the trust of the villagers, even the Old Believers. The physician Sokol'nikov reports that at first many of the inhabitants of Reshetnikova did not want to "avail themselves of him because of a comical prejudice that sickness could not be cured, for one can live only as long as God has written for his birth in the book of fate. . . . The falseness of this opinion . . . I proved by terse and well-reasoned persuasion, and then by trials in fact, for I cured those who were very sick, whom nearly all the villagers . . . had consigned to death while still alive."[6] This referred to the Siberian Old Believers themselves.

The attitude of the peasants toward doctors was also influenced, of course, by popular views as to the cause of disease. A whole range of diseases was easily explained to the villagers by obvious natural causes ("strain," "chills," bruises, etc.), and in such cases they would resort to the doctors. But infectious, nervous, and many internal diseases, according to popular beliefs, were either "the punishment of God" or the result of malicious doings of "sorcerers." Here, the peasants thought, medicine could do nothing. "He wants to cure God's doing! He wants to be greater than God," they would say of a doctor who thought to cram a patient with medicine. Peasants tried to buy off the doctors sent to a village to deal with an epidemic; those who would not agree were boycotted and patients hidden from them. "I witnessed one such very sad case in Kamyshevsk *volost'* around five years ago," recounted the regional doctor Nadezhdinskii. "It happened thus: on the first day I examined the patients, handed out medicine, and promised to return again the next day; but on the morrow, I found the cabins everywhere empty and to my question, 'Where have the patients gone?' received the same reply, that 'One is tending the horses, another has gone for the hay. . . .' In one cabin, a storeroom caught my attention, the door being half ajar. I went in and found here four patients. . . ."[7]

In the opinion of the villagers, either God himself or "God's *ugodniki*"—the saints—could "punish" by illness. In one village, for example, an elderly peasant told Nadezhdinskii: "We never knew [experienced] anything as long as we were celebrating Saint Vlasii and Medosii; but then they assigned us to Spas. Since that time, it has been one calamity after another: first a plague among the people, some kind of cholera, and then the livestock were slaughtered. We already asked the authorities to let us honor Vlasii and Medosii—God's saints—in the old way, but they refused, saying it was all the same on which day we got drunk; but clearly it is not all the same—God's saints are displeased with us."[8]

Another cause of disease in the peasant mind was "blight," sent by sorcerers having dealings with the "devil." "Among the people are legends, probably started by sorcerers . . . to scare them," reports Nadezhdinskii, "stating that sorcerers sell their soul to the devil under condition that he supply them with wealth for a certain term. . . . The people distinguish the sorcerer from the fortuneteller [*vorozheia*] and the folk curer [*znakhar'*]. In the people's conception, the sorcerer is in command of demons. . . . When in public, these charlatans always adopt certain mannerisms. For example, I heard that they walk with the head down, whispering and at times shoving away unseen devils who are pestering them for work. . . . In Siberia, there are *koldun-vezhdivtsy* (or *vezhlivtsy*, as the common folk pronounce it).[j] These wretches are primarily involved in weddings and, indeed, sometimes do no good, scaring the horses and beguiling young people. It is said that these scoundrels usually provide themselves with fresh animal fat, most often bear fat, the odor of which can be sensed by horses . . . from afar. To frighten the horses, sorcerers usually smear this fat on the gate posts or rub it into a rawhide thong that they stretch on the gate. Once the horses catch wind of the smell they go wild, and on more than one occasion there have been tragic outcomes, where people were even killed as a result of such a sorcerer's prank. Yet the peasants, knowing this custom of these rogues, feel obliged to invite the well-known pranksters and so conciliate them. At the wedding, such scoundrels are usually treated with deep reverence, given the first place at table, and served first with wine and beer. The duty of the sorcerer at the wedding is to ward off any trouble during the bridal procession. For this purpose, before the procession starts, the sorcerer will usually go among the horses, whispering and gesticulating, then sit by himself in the sled and slowly drive toward the church, inspecting anything suspicious on the road. For example, if he finds a wood chip, the sorcerer dismounts, picks up the chip, whispers over it, spits on it, and then throws it over his head. If he finds a stone, he does the same with it. After the road has been surveyed in this way, the procession starts and moves confidently to the church. Before leaving the church, the sorcerer repeats the same procedure. With almost an identical ceremony the sorcerer ushers the young people into the house and even places them on the bridal bed. However, this custom has already been long abandoned in many places, especially where people are more refined, such as along highways and in villages on the outskirts of towns; but in the hinterland, where the people are more savage, all of this continues in its original form. There one may often hear stories and complaints about the pranks of sorcerers, and more than once parents have come to me . . . saying that a sorcerer was being spiteful with their child. Not uncommonly sorcerers also harm crops and livestock there . . . ; old women, as though in conspiracy with sorcerers, further strengthen belief in the sorcerer's acquaintance with evil power by screaming during attacks of 'blight' [*porcha*] by a particular sorcerer and naively confessing that he has put the 'evil' [literally "unclean," *nechistyi*] in her belly."[9]

The Siberian village had both sorcerers and sorceresses. People would generally keep their distance from them. On occasion, peasant communes requested that a person suspected of sorcery be moved to a different village or *volost'*. For example, in 1833, the inhabitants of Berezov village, Kolyvansk *okrug*, gathered to request the authorities to move Praskov'ia Kungurtsova and Mar'ia Shmakova to another settlement, since they "were suspected of throwing a bundle tied with red thread at the door of the peasant Matrena Anferova at night, this bundle containing woman's hair, a small piece of brocade, and the head of a snake." The villagers believed that this bundle was placed there to "ruin" [*isportit'*] Anferova, "because Kungurtsova and Shmakova have already boasted more than once that they would ruin her." In 1842, the Kazan' *volost'* authorities reported to the rural court that Ust'-Tandova community requests the peasant Luker'ia Malysheva be moved elsewhere, accusing her "of ruining women and children."[10]

Sometimes more decisive steps were taken against sorcerers. Thus, in 1848, during a cholera epidemic, an incident of mob justice occurred at a meeting in Kulakov village, Tiumen' *okrug*, with the local tailor, Iakov.

> In our Kulakov, in Lugovsk, Kamensk, and other hamlets, there were a lot of cases of death from cholera. The summer heat was scorching, such as few could remember in those parts. The water in the river Tura took on an unusual reddish color. No singing or laughter could be heard, and it was even considered inappropriate to wear flowers during this time. Everyone was in a somber mood, awaiting the coming disaster "sent by God for our sins," in the opinion of the villagers, or sent by an evil man, perhaps "through the wind," "through the water," "for see how red it has become." At the village meeting, someone said that it was necessary to "look into" what kind of red-colored balls the tailor Iakov had and why he was singing songs at such a time. Everyone became aroused, as though suddenly discovering something important, and they began to recall how Iakov went fishing and always cast the line "over the left shoulder"; how he drank wine in the tavern and again splashed the dregs "to the left" and every evening for some reason walked in the sunset. The people became very incensed against Iakov and demanded that he appear before them at once. Within a quarter of an hour, the tailor Iakov, brought by force, was standing before the meeting, shouting something loudly and waving his hands, but his words could not be understood over the crowd's noise. Someone

pulled a red ball from his pocket and placed it on a log lying in the street. From the heat of the sun, the ball began to melt, releasing a kind of vapor and giving off a smell. The crowd then became enraged, accusing Iakov of sorcery, and several of them began to beat him with whatever came to hand, not listening to the exhortations of those who still kept their senses. . . . At this moment, Karp Lazarev, old and gray, came up to the wild and noisy crowd and, after learning the cause of the mob action, threw his hat on the ground and shouted:

"What are you doing, fools? What do you know of Christ's cross? Bring water at once."

The crowd fell silent, and several of them went for water. "Now see what you wretches have done," continued the old man, touching Iakov and loosening his collar, revealing a copper crucifix.

"Here is the reproach to your wickedness," added Karp, pointing to his cross.

The crowd was hushed, apparently struck by the words of the old man. Many of them began to pour water on Iakov's head and give him some to drink. The unfortunate man began to groan and get up from the ground. He was helped home to his room.

Chukmaldin recalls yet another case "from the world of superstition." At the home of Vasilii Pimnev, "his son became ill with a swelling of the legs during a lunar eclipse." For some reason, his mother insisted that both the moon and her son Fediusha had been ruined by none other than their neighbor Shcherbikha. Because of this, it was absolutely essential to have the *volost'* examine the witch Shcherbikha to see if she had a tail, and if so, she must be placed in a hole in the ground up to waist level for three days, with an aspen stake driven in before her. Otherwise, she "will utterly ruin the moon and the people." During the course of the evening, Vasikha went among all the neighbors with this tiding, arousing everyone against the poor witch Shcherbikha. Fortunately, sensible people were present who said they should wait until the next evening to see "what would become" of the moon and Fed'ia. It turned out that the moon shone without eclipse and Fed'ia became better, and Shcherbikha was left in peace. Even so, Vasikha said: "Remember my words, Shcherbikha let alone the moon and Fediusha's sickness only out of fright. If not for this, we would still have no moon today."[11]

There were some illnesses that the peasants believed were "God's punishment" and could not be treated—God himself had foreordained their outcome. Those suffering from such illnesses received almost no assistance from fellow villagers; their relatives only provided them with food and water. For all other cases, folk medicine provided the most diverse remedies, both rational and magical. Illnesses caused by a natural, visible source were usually treated by the peasants themselves; each person and family carried a certain amount of medical knowledge that was handed down as a legacy.

The government and the Siberian administration actively tried to influence this area of folk culture. Peasant behavior during an epidemic was set forth in legislation. The Law Code, as a contemporary observed, "contained whole chapters on public health and loss of livestock, relating the causes of such evils and explaining the measures against them, but . . . these chapters were not assimilated by the people."[12] Various instructions and manuals written in Petersburg and the Siberian provincial centers were distributed among the *volosty*: on first aid in accidents, on methods of treating the Siberian ulcer [*iazva*], on the curative properties of herbs, etc. It was usually recommended to read them aloud to the peasants "during each meeting annually," so that the information bestowed upon them would become part of village life.

One can imagine how such injunctions would be interpreted at the scene: the people would gather in the presence of an official from the *uezd* (usually the assessor) and a clerk would read the text. "This person pronounces almost every word wrong, halts at every letter and entirely loses the meaning," reported an observer, "and mumbles whatever occurs to him. Apart from this, the piece was not written very comprehensibly for the peasant, and since every word is also garbled, the peasant is fully convinced he is hearing a sermon by the priest. The community quietly raises a collection—a farthing from each—and gives it to the elder in token of gratitude to his worship, saying 'Well enough, we have heard.' The elder timidly approaches the assessor from behind, tugs at his sleeve and almost in a whisper asks him to 'Please come inside.' The assessor answers, 'Let him finish reading,' but the elder persuades him: 'That is all right, let him finish here.' The assessor goes inside, receives without haggling the 'gratuity' for teaching the fools common sense, and has the peasants sign a paper to the effect that they have heard the instructions. . . ."[13]

Medication was also distributed among the towns by order of the treasury, with instructions as to the methods of its use during illness. This medicine was purchased with funds collected from the peasants. The Ialutorovsk *okrug* doctor Nadezhdinskii reports that during his regional rounds he "occasionally encountered medicine chests at the *volost'* offices: all the contents were mixed up, spilled, moldy, and transformed into chemical substances of unknown nature." And when he asked the functionaries "whether anyone was treated with these medicines," he saw on their faces such a smile "as though they had heard an indescribable piece of silliness for the first time." "We keep this to show the authorities," they told Nadezhdinskii.[14] Thus, although governmental measures proved inefficient, nevertheless they influenced in some degree the peasant's knowledge in the field of medicine.

There were also medical "professionals" among the peasantry—folk curers—who were consulted in more serious cases, especially "blight." "In Ialutorovsk *okrug*," writes an observer, "several persons have become famous for their practice among the peasants, some of them therapists, others surgeons. They include men and women, the women being somewhat more numerous."[15] Female curers were generally old women. There were also horse doctors. The *znakhar'* differed from other people (in the opinion of the peasant) simply by having more knowledge of medicine, in particular an acquaintance with various magical procedures for treatment of disease.[k] There was never any question of a relationship between the curer and "unclean strength." The curers would attempt to conceal their "professional" activities [literally "baggage"], but they would tell them not only to their successors but also to acquaintances, and even (for payment) to anyone else.

We may learn about the biography of a typical curer from an inquest concerning the peasant Iakov Ploskikh of Ialutorovsk *okrug* (in the 1760s).[16] He was born in 1710 in Iarensk *uezd*, Vologda province, to a family of "black earth" peasants. When he was three years old, his father took him to Siberia, and the Ploskikh family settled in Ialutorovsk *uezd*, Tobol'sk province. Here, Iakov buried his parents, got married, and had children. At the inquest, he stated that "every year with his wife and children he would attend confession and take communion at the Sretensk parish church." Chance led Iakov to the local peasant Ivan Pnevskii, who gave him an herbal (this book Pnevskii himself had taken down "by word" from the peasant Vasilii Savinov, who lived in Mysovsk village in the home of Matvei Krivonogov "to teach his son Feodosii to read and write"). After this, Ploskikh turned to "medical" practice. The retired soldier Semen Novikov—a fellow villager—taught him incantations and several magical operations. By 1766, when Iakov Ploskikh was arrested, he already had experience in treating the most diverse illnesses and was rather famous in his *uezd*.

The peasants felt no superstitious dread of curers. Their gesticulations could become an element in a theatricized village presentation. Thus, the inhabitants of Grachevaia village, Isetskoe jurisdiction, decide to "rechristen" Ivan Grekhov during a holiday. As the merry company was going from the house of Grekhov to the nonpeasant [*raznochinets*][l] Gurii Kaigorodov, the *zhenka* Ekaterina Krivonogova picked up in the road "a chip, to which a thread was tied, and calling this chip . . . a cross, she gave it . . . to Grekhov," and then said: "Here is a cross for you, godfather, and let you be my godchild." Grekhov tied "that chip to his belt." In the home of Kaigorodov, and then also "to the people standing in the street," he showed his "cross," "lifting up his shirt tails" ("now the child has been brought into the Christian faith," joked Grekhov) and called Ekaterina Krivonogova his own "godmother." During the celebration, yet another "amusement" happened: "sitting" at Kaigorodov's, Grekhov began clowning and "cried like a baby in fun," saying that he, "a small child," was "hexed" by Fedor Mel'nikov. The women that were here, "laughing at this," told Mel'nikov that he should "charm the spell with water and heal Grekhov." ("For he, Mel'nikov," the peasant would later testify at the inquest, "had been invited formerly to many homes to charm away spells.") Mel'nikov, deciding to play along, took water in a "skull" and, "turning toward the wall, he whispered and spat on this water . . . and then laid Grekhov down on the bench with his belly up and doused him with this water." The "cured child," to the laughter of the women and other guests, "jumped up and said, 'like water off a bird, the illness has fallen from me, the spells and chants of the dark woods.' "[17]

If the intervention of the curer did not bring recovery, he was refused the promised payment and mocked.

Physiotherapy and pharmacotherapy held a major place in folk medicine. T. Uspenskii wrote that inhabitants of Shadrinsk *uezd* (mid-nineteenth century) "seldom resort even to household medicine remedies and all of their diseases are treated with a bath."[18] The situation was similar in other regions. Often the bath would be combined with other forms of healing—medicinal, physical, psychological. Thus, the peasant P. Shkoldin of Burlinsk *volost'* wrote of his community: "They have no colds, nor fevers, nor other minor complaints . . . they take steam baths each week, usually whole families or even several families together, without distinguishing age or sex, and so hot that after leaving the bath they fall on the snow, or into a hole in the ice or the water above an ice crust and, heedless of the crackling frost, wash themselves until their hair freezes and their body becomes scarlet. And they suffer no ill effect from being so long in the frost in their ancestral clothing, only covering themselves with the *venik* [switch of birch twigs]."[19]

The peasants also exploited the curative properties of certain bodies of water. "On the shore of the Chanov, I passed by Kliuchi village, famous for its curative waters, with its lake," wrote N. M. Iadrintsev in his travel diary. "Mineral lakes are not rare in Baraba. Of the curative ones, there is Ust'-Ianovskoe, twenty-five versts from Kainsk; the lake at the new village, fifteen versts from Iudina, and Lake Kliuchi. All of these waters, it is said, are especially effective against shingles and rashes. The bitter Lake Kliuchi is around five versts in circumference. . . . The water is so dense that a person stays afloat on the surface."[20]

The peasants made extensive use of showering with cold water, scorching, massage, heating in a stove ("where rye bread is baked") and in hot sand.

All these procedures were usually accompanied by mysterious gesticulations, incantations, and prayers. "When Osip, our neighbor, took ill," said one of the inhabitants of Dolgoiarsk village (Tobol'sk *okrug*, 1848), " . . . everyone began to say: 'they have put enemies (devils) in him' and they began to whisper on wine, on water, to sprinkle and wash [him with it]."[21] In Ialutorovsk region the word *pukhtat'* was even coined, meaning "to cure by whispering on water and sprinkling with it." The water that was "whispered" was to be taken, in certain cases, from three rivers, "in the direction of the current," "at three dawns," and the patient was to be showered with it on a door threshold. The threshold also appears in descriptions of massage procedure. For lumbar and hemorrhoid pain—it is reported of the Western Siberian peasants by N. Abramov, for example—"they chop up a whip-like branch [*vitiun*]." The patient is not supposed to eat or drink for a full day and night, after which "he lies with his belly across the threshold, a besom branch is placed on his naked loins and is chopped up with a blunt hatchet, while the patient says: 'Cut, cut, grandfather.' " The "cutting of the *vitiun*" was also known in the Altai mountains; the locals also attributed special importance to a chicken roost: the patient was often doused with water "in the animal pen, beneath the chicken perch."[22]

Nor was the curative action of fresh air overlooked by villagers, although again various verbal formulas (the meaning of which had been lost by this time) were included. "For inflammation of the throat," observed the same Abramov, "the cure is as follows: at dawn and at twilight the patient comes outside and says: 'Morning twilight Mareia, evening twilight Marem'iana, take away my quinsy [angina]; if not, I will eat the pine and the birch with the roots and branches,' he opens his mouth, takes in air and says: 'Kham, kham, I eat them.' " "For dropsy," he continued, "they rub the entire body in the bath with sliced cucumbers. . . . For spells (the evil eye), they take water in a pitcher, add hot coals from the stove, whisper over the water, sprinkle it and give it to the afflicted to drink."[23] When a child began to suffer from the "English disease" (scrofula, known among the peasants as "dog's old age"), they make a *karal'ka* (a large ring) of wheaten dough, smear sour cream on the sick one, "and after placing the child through this ring in the bath, they bring in a dog, who eats the ring and then is allowed to lick off the sour cream."[24]

Folk physiotherapy had a rational basis on the whole, and doubtlessly played an important part in the fight against disease. Irrational components associated with it may also have helped cure by affecting a patient's psyche; an identical function was played by magical procedures and formulas adopted when taking medicine.

Every peasant knew the curative properties of certain herbs; the curers had the most extensive knowledge in this area. They would make decoctions, infusions, and juices from herbs, using the leaves, seeds, roots and stalks. Frequently medicines of vegetable origin would be used in conjunction with chemical substances, remedies of animal origin, etc. In particular, St. John's wort [*zveroboi*]—the meadow (or blue) and the stone (or cross) variety—enjoyed broad popularity. The blue variety was used as tea for coughing and chest pain. The stone variety would be made into a decoction, to be taken (along with honey) for coughing, intestinal diseases, etc. The geodesist I. Shishkov, who made a survey of Tomsk *uezd* in 1739–41, reported: "The peasants treat fever thus: they drink the dried leaves of St. John's wort warm in a concoction from a hollowed tree trunk or a fish cavity."[25]

The herb called Mother-of-God [*Helchrysum arenarium*] was used for many illnesses; decoctions of it were drunk for colds, coughing, headache, and various hysterical and convulsive fits; the crushed herb was applied to wounds and used to treat toothache. The peasants also knew of the curative properties of Siberian windflower (*vetrenitsa* or Altai anemone). "Our entire day was made pleasant by the clumps of Siberian windflower growing everywhere," P. S. Pallas wrote in his travel diary. "This is very well known to the peasants . . . they praise a decoction of this herb for colic in young children."[26] Blackhead [*skorokopytochnik* or *Actaea spicata*], Valerian root, and the herb tsar's eyes [*pereloinaia* or *Parnassia palustris*] were used as binders. "For convulsions and hysterical fits" they used a decoction of Marina's root [*Paeonia tenuifolia*] "for red hernia" a decoction of wolf's eye berry [*voronets* or *Paris quadrifolia*].[m]

Also widely used in the folk medicine of Siberia in the eighteenth and first half of the nineteenth century were red, blue, and yellow *deviatil'nik* [*Achillea nobilis*], horses' mane, *zhabrei* ["chicken herb" or *Galeopsis tetrahit*], saffron milk cap, *zmeevka* ["heart root" or *Polyganum bistorta*], chamomile, hellebore, *starodubka* ["hare's poppy" or *Adonis appenina*], and marjoram. "Red *deviatil'nik* is useful for blood-spitting; it is used . . . as a tea. Blue *deviatil'nik* is also useful in the above case; its herb is used for chest disease. A decoction of yellow *deviatil'nik* is used against worms; the juice squeezed from the fresh herb is applied to broken skin on the legs and cleans the wounds," declared Abramov.[27] Horses' mane was used to "clean" the lungs and kidneys. The juice of *zhabrei* was helpful in treating wounds. The seeds of saffron milk cap were boiled "in water with admixture of honey" and used "for poisons ingested, for jaundice and coughing." Its seeds ("resembling cotton") also helped "against asthma." The techniques for using the herbs were sometimes rather complicated. "If there is pain in the ear from wind getting in," wrote Abramov, "they will take an onion, cut it in half, remove the core and in its place put a chamomile bud; the onion is put back together and placed in the stove in hot water until it is baked, and then the warm chamomile bud, removed from the onion and impregnated with its juice, is placed in the ear. This is a sovereign and well-tested remedy."[28] Chamomile was also used successfully for "fevers" and "wind in the stomach."

Used in the folk medicine of Siberia were common mustard ("the crushed seeds with various kinds of sour dough and salt are used as a plaster"), George's lance ("a decoction . . . is used for headache and weakness"), [the boletus mushroom] *kazak* ("a diuretic and useful in bladder disease"), *kashnik* [sheep's herb] or *mokhnatik* ("for pain in the stomach"; "the boiled herb is applied warm to an inflammatory swelling"), hops ("a decoction mixed with whey purifies the stomach, causes urination, and cleans the blood"), raspberry paste ("externally in poultices for inaccessible hemorrhoids and old wounds"), wild asparagus ("causes urination, purifies the lungs and kidneys"), and other herbs. There was not always a rational meaning for the use of a particular herb: "For fever, they use a medicine from the sonchus, the flower thereof, tying it in a rag, fastened to a person's neck chain with its cross," reported I. Shishkov (1740s) about the peasants of Kuznetsk *uezd*.[29] There were herbs that were truly a universal remedy. The "Statistical Description of Ishimsk *Okrug*" (1841) states: "Another universal medicine is sarsparilla, or, as they call it here, the 'dear herb,' which is steeped in ordinary wine."[30]

The Siberian peasants also used the curative properties of vegetables, berries, the bark and leaves of trees, various products of animal origin, and minerals. These were frequently used in combination with each other. Thus, children suffering from "scrofula" were given a decoction of currant leaves to drink. "In fevers" they used cowberry or cranberry water; they also made compresses—"they bind moist gray clay to the head, legs, and arms; they soak the head in vinegar." For constipation, they drink heavily salted water or pickle and sauerkraut juice. "For pain and aching of the bones" they apply "birch leaves blanched in water to the sore spots." "Whitlow" was treated by applying salty *kvas* [low-alcohol beer] lees to the sore finger, or hemp seeds boiled in milk or oil; for furuncles, they applied a baked onion, cobbler's wax, or a plaster "of pine wax, taken from the tree." In event of "inflammation of the eyes," they made compresses of beaten eggwhite with ground alum. For those suffering from Siberian ulcer, they cut open the "swollen callus of the affected area down to the quick" and applied to the wound "lint or a rag, soaked in a mixture of tobacco and sal ammoniac, steeped together in ordinary wine." Salves made "from bay oil, verdigris, mercury, and copperas, dissolved in bay oil or sour cream, were popular. The Siberian curers made active use of corrosive sublimate, camphor, copperas, gunpowder, and bay oil (cajeput oil).

Healing was also done with mineral water. Iadrintsev wrote about Lake Kliuchi in Baraba: "The salubrity of the lake is subject to medical evaluation; what concerns us is how the people heal themselves. They use this water for many diseases. According to local inhabitants, it was useful in the following cases: a drunken cart driver fell off a horse and his side became ill; he then drank the water and was relieved. It drives away itching and pimples as well as scratches; a Karasuksk peasant with an eye disease washed with the water and the disease went away. It is also helpful against scrofula. They say it is necessary to drink a glassful, washing it down with vodka or tea since it has a bitter taste. I took samples of the water from the mineral lakes. The village of Kliuchi is very poor and considered by its neighbors as a den of thieves. At any rate, we were warned of this as we passed through the neighborhood. It turned out subsequently that the inhabitants of Kliuchi, although they make the roads unsafe, do not molest those who come to be cured, as they obtain from them the advantage of their sojourn."[31]

Medicinal agents of mineral origin were generally not as effective as herbs; their use often involved a risk to the patient's life. The same may be said of surgical intervention: "As for obstetric surgery, there is nothing to say," wrote an observer. "This branch of quackery each year conducts a large number of mothers in the villages to the other world."[32] Self-taught surgeons performed the most diverse operations: they lanced abscesses, removed tumors and affected bones, let blood, cut out "cancerous proliferations in all parts of the human body," etc. Their implements were the scalpel and probe. Women were particularly involved in this "trade."

The Siberian peasants personified certain diseases. For example, Siberian ulcer was imagined to be a huge, fleece-covered person with horse's hoofs who lived in the mountains. It was believed that he "would come with a whistle" or pronouncing the conjuration "come canker," "come assail," "come bespot." "Fevers" (twelve varieties were counted) took the form of women—daughters of King Herod—in peasant consciousness. It is reported for Burlinsk *volost'* inhabitants that "all diseases usually appear in the form of a woman."[33] A common belief was that such diseases could be countered by deception, intimidation, etc. Thus in the Altai, guns were fired in a field to prevent Siberian ulcer from coming into the village. "Fevers," as the peasants believed, usually appeared to a person in a dream and posed various questions; if "the unfortunate, waking up, should inadvertently reply to them, he immediately contracts the disease, but if he is smart and keeps silent he will remain sound." "The very treatment for fever," wrote Shkoldin, "is a consideration of absurdity. For this, they employ every kind of filth inside and out, in order to drive off Herod's children with the foul odor. On the day of the paroxysms, early in the morning, the patient leaves the house, walking backwards, and hides, so that Herod's daughters lose his track; this means that their victim has ostensibly come home, and they look for him, do not find him, and give up. Another technique is for the patient to leave home and cover himself with a trough. Herod's daughters, although they find him, think he is dead and in a coffin, and thus their business is over; usually there is an alleviation."[34]

In Tobol'sk region, to drive away "fever" they would drag a felled birch tree along the road, raising dust. G. N. Potanin was told an interesting story about the "fevers" in the mid-nineteenth century by the elderly Petr Markych. In all, as the peasant said, "there are twelve aunts; the twelfth, internal one, who oppresses the heart, is the most dangerous. They all sit chained up and in spring are released by the will of God. Once they were going to town through a field where a peasant was plowing, talking among themselves. One of them said: 'there is a merchant in the town, I will beset him, cause him some grief, and then go away.' But the inner one, the wicked one, answered her: 'and I will become a fly and make sure to fall in the porridge, and when he swallows me I will oppress him.' The peasant immediately ran to town to the merchant and told him what he had heard. The merchant sat down to dinner; just as he was scooping out the porridge, a fly landed in his spoon. Quickly he wrapped it along with the porridge in a rag, tied it with a knot, and hung it over the *dymnik* [round wattle stove]. At that time, they still had *dymniki* instead of ovens. The next day, this same peasant was plowing in the same field and he saw the fevers. They were walking along and conversing. One of them said: 'I will cause a little grief and go away; they will like me for this and feed me.' But the inner one answered: 'no, I will not even go to this town; just see how they have tortured me, only one shoe is left.' "[35] Such ideas about disease gave rise to corresponding methods of treatment, and therefore the irrational in Siberian folk medicine was very significant. Magical operations and incantations were the usual means of treatment among the peasantry. "There are various remedies against warts: they tie as many knots in a thread as they have warts, measuring around each with the knot before it is tightened, and this thread is buried in manure. When the thread decays, the warts will disappear. As the moon is waning, they pass their hand along a wall where the moonlight is shining and smooth this hand over the warts from top to bottom, repeating this for several days. They wash the warts with water from the washing of the cooking table," Abramov wrote of the Ialutorovsk peasants.[36]

To remove a sty from the eye, they made a reproving gesture with the fingers toward the sty, chanting: "Sty, beware, whatever you wish, that shall you buy. Buy yourself a hatchet and cut yourself in two." They then passed a finger over the sty. They also pierced the sore spot with a barleycorn [*iachmen'* meaning both "barley" and "sty"], passed a wedding band around it, etc. For chronic headache, they "howled greatly": "winding the hair around two fingers at the sore spot, they pull with all their might." Those suffering from jaundice were made to stare fixedly at a live pike placed in a container; it was believed that the illness would gradually "go over to the fish." In the case of a burn, a red cloth was placed on the sore spot. "For a strain of the navel" (as the peasants say)—continued Abramov—they place a pot on the navel [*pup*] or drink a decoction of the herb known as *pupovnik*. Or lying on their back, they press against the navel with a blunt stick, saying that the navel will jump back in place."[37]

Shingles and boils were "cured" thus: spitting on a "nameless finger," they would use this finger to trace out a knot of wood found in the wall, and then this same finger would be used to trace around the shingles or boils, chanting: "No longer, no further stay in this place, here you shall perish."[38]

It was thought that if a child cried incessantly he had been touched by the evil eye. In such a case, when all were going to bed one of the adults went outside the gates and, "turning toward the dawn," repeated up to three times, "while spitting, the following phrase: '*Zoria-zarnitsa* [Dawn, dawning], lovely maiden, take the crying from God's slave' " (saying the child's name); or one went in the evening to the graveyard and, standing at a grave, repeated, again spitting, up to three times: "Gray *kochetok* [cock spirit], spotted *kochetok*, red *kochetok*,[n] take the crying from God's slave" (say the name).[39]

If a child suffered from "griping" or "colic," they took him into the woods, found a young oak, slashed it at the root, and then, as M. F. Krivoshapkin wrote (1860s), the man and wife, standing on different sides of the oak, pushed the child into the crack up to three times. The sapling was then tied together and, if it grew back, this was taken as a guarantee of recovery. "Such a method of healing is called passing through the oak." "Colic is also cured," continued Krivoshapkin, "by having an old woman chew on the child's navel, while the mother asks: 'What are you chewing, grandmother?' 'I am chewing the griping.' 'Chew well then!' This is said up to three times. It is done at the time of the new moon."[40] For insomnia, children were splashed in the face with water through the door latch, allowing the water to "drip off the face onto the threshold, convinced that the insomnia will fall upon whoever is the first to step on the threshold."[41] Such means of curing were widely practiced in feudal Siberia.

Incantations pronounced against various illnesses are sometimes strikingly poetic. "On the ocean sea, on the mountain hill, there sit thirty-three maidens, in their hands are golden needles, silken threads; they are sewing, they are sewing up the young white body of God's slave (say name). To this I say amen. A tsar is riding, the horse beneath him is chestnut brown; I know him; you, red one, stop, and you, wound, heal up"—thus, for example, the Altai peasants conjured bleeding.[42] As has already been rightly observed in the ethnographic literature, such spoken formulas and magical rituals in general had, "especially given the whole-hearted belief of the patient, a considerable psychotherapeutic effect, which sometimes in itself could exert a positive curative action, and given a propitious combination with effective medicinal remedies occasionally brought about a rapid cure."[43]

Despite its negative effects (leading some doctors to insist on a quite negative appraisal), folk medicine provided help to the rural population in curing many diseases and played a positive role in feudal Siberia.

Popular amusements

In the epoch of feudalism, the labor of an individual peasant family on its plot of land was generally isolated in character, giving rise to a closed type of rural family life and economically isolated households. At the same time, life itself imperiously dictated the need for peasant families to come together in a neighborhood organization—the community was one of the guarantees of normal functioning of a small private establishment. Yet the stability of the community organization depended on the degree of development of various forms of social relationships and contacts within it. In an environment of isolated work, recreational activities took on great importance.

The distribution in time of peasant "merriments" was dictated primarily by the calendar of agricultural work. By mid-September, the gathering of the harvest was mainly completed in Siberia, and it was then that the "joyful season" began in the life of the village youth: they began to organize parties, which were one of the favorite forms of village recreation. There were neither territorial nor class distinctions among those attending a party: both the invited and the uninvited could attend.

Parties were arranged in both the evening and the daytime at a participant's home. A room might be rented from one of the villagers for a small sum (or treat). Sometimes they would coax an elderly spinster to "let the party come to her" for an entire season. Such gatherings of young people were usually confined to feast days, although parties also occurred on weekdays and even during the time of fasting. "Though I was traveling during the great fast," marveled I. Belov, who visited Western Siberia in the mid-nineteenth century, "the young people were gathering in *besedy* or *posidelki* not only in the evening, but even during the day"[1] (this refers in fact to parties).

Young men did not always attend parties on weekdays, but girls would go to them "with work, usually spinning or sewing." Once assembled, they would sing long and loud songs. The historian of the Barnaul region, S. I. Guliaev, wrote (in 1848) that these songs "consist for the most part of a girl, woman, or young man telling of some bitter lot in life. The verses . . . of these songs are delivered in melodies and are distinguished by the same sadness that imbues nearly all melodies of the Russian people."[2]

> Farewell, farewell, o foreign land,
> O foreign land, Uspenska settlement.
> Far-famed Tomsk town stands in its splendor,
> Stands in its splendor, above the river Tom'.
> On the river Tom', Mashen'ka went for water, Mashen'ka
>   went for water, for cold spring water.
> How our Masha's eyes are red from crying,
> The poor girl vowed, she vowed to love a married man.
> The married man has a full-toothed wife,
> A full-toothed wife, sharp-tongued and chatty.
> It is better, pretty Masha, to love a bachelor,
> A bachelor has neither home nor livelihood,
> Neither home nor livelihood, only his dear mother;
> His mother sent Van'ka to wander all night long,
> To wander all night long, to visit all the parties,
> He came to all the parties, and Masha was not home,
> Masha was not home, I waited on the porch—

they sang, for example, at the weekday parties in the villages along the Irtysh.

Lengthy preparations would precede the holiday parties. The organizers, "especially bold and clever young men," from noontime on went to houses of unmarried daughters to invite the girls to the "merriment." After this, they harnessed a horse to a sledge and rode through the village "singing and playing the accordion," thereby announcing their project to the other villagers. In certain localities—for example, in the Altai and in Ust'-Nitsinsk *volost'* of Tiumen' *uezd*—the girls had the role of party organizers, even on feast days. At such gatherings of young people, there was usually no refreshment: the time was spent in singing, playing games, and dancing to the balalaika, fiddle, accordion, and tambourine.[4] Often they danced to song alone. "The dancing songs," writes Guliaev, "are those to whose melody they dance at parties where there is no musician."[5]

> Spir'ka of Kolomna,
> Has a short thin coat,
> A shirt one finger thick,
> Breeches of the same coarse cloth.
> He is raging, he is splitting,
> At the window he is grieving,
> The orphan he is called.
> Who, oh who, will pity the orphan.
> Who, oh who, will have him spend the night,
> I will gild the sore spots

—G. N. Potanin cited the texts of this and other ribald dance songs popular in the south of Siberia in the mid-nineteenth century.[6]

The dancers would "repeatedly bestow kisses on each other." Kisses also accompanied almost all games at the parties. Each of these games was "connected" with a particular song. "Everyone takes part in the songs," observed Guliaev of the Altai peasants, "but usually only a pair takes part in the game: a boy and girl, representing, judging from the content of the game and song, a husband and wife, or bride and groom."[7] A similar situation existed in other regions. In most games a chorus had to form a living circle, within which the "drama" was enacted. For example, to the melody of the song:

> Just look, good people,
> How my wife does not love me,
> How my life and my heart hates me.
> I will go to Kitai town,
> I will buy some things,
> I will buy her a wonderful jewel.

Take it, wife, don't be proud.
Just look, good people,
How my wife does not love me,
How the evil, wicked one hates me.
I will go to Kitai town,
I will buy some things.
I will buy for her a silken lash.
Take it, wife, don't be proud.
Just look, good people,
How my wife loves me now—

the couple portraying the spouses would slowly "walk in a circle"; the fellow [*molodets*] would caress his girl [*zhenushka*], gazing "in her bright eyes," but she would stubbornly turn away from him, even after he gave her a present. Only at the words "I will buy her a silken lash" would her "haughtiness" disappear, and she herself "pursued" the boy, hugging and kissing him.[8]

Observers were struck by the diversity of peasant party games. In some of them, active participants were numerous. "The reindeer game," reported, for example, Guliaev, "is played at almost every party. . . ." In this case, a chorus performed a song about the reindeer ("The reindeer is sitting under a bush, under a broom bush. Are you warm, reindeer? Are you cold, reindeer? I am not warm. I am not cold. Put me on, wrap me around . . . "), and one of the boys would sit in the center of the "circle" on a chair, collecting forfeits—rings and bands—from the others. This person would then invite the "Council of Boyars," asking them: "Whose forfeit is picked, what are they to do?" The "Boyars" would think up a task for each.° "The performance of the Boyars' instruction," concluded an observer, "sometimes makes the entire company laugh, sometimes embarrasses the performer, or sometimes pleases him, if the task involves the liberty of a kiss."[9]

Young people's relations at parties were generally quite free. The church tried to oppose the parties, but according to the admission of the priests themselves, this form of merrymaking "has taken such deep root in society that neither sermons nor strict injunctions of the pastors" achieved the required effect.[10]

Although parties could be held even during the great fast, the main "party-going season" lasted from mid-September until mid-November (Phillip's Fast) and from December 20 until the end of February or beginning of March (end of Shrovetide), i.e., autumn/winter. The time from December 21 to January 5 was especially significant, when young people of both sexes would gather for games and parties day and night.[11] The number of such youth gatherings varied in the different regions: as a rule, parties were frequent, but in certain villages there were no more than five per year. This form of peasant recreation is attested not only among the adherents of official Orthodoxy, but also the Old Believers. One traveler reported that, in Iuzhakov village, Tiumen' *okrug*, he and his companions came upon a party "of schismatics, and at first without any intention we caused much alarm with our tobacco. Fortunately, the matter ended with friendly explanations. . . . The girls were crowded on benches against the walls, and gray beards could be seen on sleeping bunks. . . . One game followed another, representing drama in its original, youthful form."[12] Thus, as spectators even older generations attended parties, which were primarily recreation for unmarried boys and girls (who began to go to them at the rather tender age of eight to ten years old).

For married women, specific social forms of recreation when not laboring in the field were the *kapustki, supriadki, kopotukhi (kopotikhi)* and *posidenki (besedki)*.[13] All these gatherings permitted attendance of "maidens," and also boys in certain regions. Women gathered for the *kapustki, supriadki,* and *kopotukhi* on the initiative of a particular housewife requiring help in her work. It was obligatory to provide refreshment for all the guests at the end. Women and girls were invited to the *kapustki* in the middle or latter half of September. The *kopotukhi* were held in October–November in Siberian villages for the purpose of dressing the flax. The most crowded were the *supriadki* (for spinning the flax)—as many as fifty people would be invited to a single house. The hostess would distribute the raw material to the spinners in advance, and then invite them to her house for refreshment on one of the days of autumn or (more commonly) at Christmastide, when the guests would appear in their best finery with the skeins of yarn already spun. If the hostess also invited boys, after the refreshment there would be dancing, singing, and games resembling those of the parties.

The *posidenki* or *besedki* (evening and daytime) were held from the second to the last week of the great fast. Males were not allowed to attend. Ordinary *posidenki* were attended by women of the same village, in everyday clothing, with work to spin or sew. "Special *posidenki*" also occurred, when women gathered "on specific invitation, even from distant villages, at the home of a young woman just married before Lent." At such gatherings, the guests would show off their attire and abundance of victuals; conversation was the only activity.[14] The women and girls, according to an observer, "chat about this or that, tell what is new, and gossip about their friends and most of their absent acquaintances."[15] Only a woman who knew how to receive her guests at the *posidenki* and entertain them in the proper manner was considered a true hostess.

Women also had "gatherings" on feast days during the off season of the year. The refreshment here was not only "victuals" but also a honey drink [*medovukha*], beer, and herb tea. They assembled in small groups of relatives or friends; the term *posidenki* did not apply to these meetings.

Entertaining during the holidays—from October until the beginning of

March (but also at other times)—was the most important pastime for all villagers, especially the middle-aged and elderly. The "great" feast days within a *volost'* were celebrated at all villages in turn: the people in the vicinity converged on the village whose turn it was for the merrymaking (hence the term visiting holiday [*s"ezzhii prazdnik*]). The order of progression was dictated by tradition. "These holidays are days selected by each village from among the holidays of the year," declared the priest T. Popov from Tat'mytsk settlement, Tarsk *uezd*, "to be celebrated, as they say, at their convenience. There is not a trace of religious purpose here."[16] In particular, in the Tat'mytsk settlement jurisdiction, holidays were held on Whitsunday, Epiphany, the [Mother of God's] Entrance, the days of the Kazan' Mother of God, the Prophet Il'ia, the Apostles Peter and Paul, St. Nikolai, and the Great Martyr St. Dimitrii.

In Burlinsk *volost'* in the Altai, visiting holidays occurred in villages on Nikola's Day, Peter's Day and Peter's Fast, Il'ia's Day, Mikhail's Day, Phillip's Fast, Christmas, Epiphany, and the Day of Protection [*Pokrov*]. "The visiting holiday," wrote P. Shkoldin, a Burlinsk peasant, "is a social forum, the occasion for a particular village to hold a feast for its neighbors. . . . On the holiday, people drive to the designated village. . . . Around noon, arrayed in their best clothing, the guests assemble with the hosts at one end of the village, by evening making up a multicolored crowd of 100 to 300 people or more, of both sexes." According to him,

> there is no difference between rich and poor in holiday clothing: luxury and a desire to flaunt is evident in all. Men's summertime holiday clothing consisted of a loose shirt of local cloth, cloth or hempen baggy pants, a robe of thick silk, tricot, skins, or other material; a girdle of spun silk, worsted, or cotton; a tricot cloth cap, a wool felt hat, chamois gloves, and high boots; many wear frock coats and the like. The clothing of the women is a loose jumper [*sarafan*] of various fabrics, a silken belt with tinsel tassels, white linen and calico sleeves, a head scarf of silk, tinsel, and cotton, with a ribbon in the girls' braids, or a cap, embroidered with tinsel or simply of silk, for married women; on the legs, shoes and cotton stockings; in winter, a coat [*galanka*] of *satin-du-pli*, broadcloth, sateen, velveteen, etc., with a fox or squirrel fur collar, and a lining of linen, rabbit fur, or sheep fleece.[p] But to this must be added, in the case of certain show-offs, all the wardrobe of a lady or demoiselle, except for the hat and parasol. Besides the Russian *sarafan*, many girls wear dresses tailored according to the fashion borrowed from the gentry. In general, female attire reveals excessive luxury beyond their condition. Watching the strolling crowd on Easter or a visiting holiday, one is led to ask, where do they get all this? To which it may be answered, that much comes from work, and the rest from their wits, i.e., their behavior. From the salesmen who travel among the villages and dispense their masters' goods, loaning them to friends without hope of recovering them. And that is why the poor do not lag behind the rich in respect to clothing. But I have not spoken of male clothing in winter during the holiday; this

comprises a long, loose jacket [*tulup*], cloth on the outside and lined with sheepskin or lambskin, with a collar of Crimean or Russian lambskin, Tiumen' boots or Kungur shoes, a velvet or cloth hat with squirrel, muskrat, beaver, or other brim.[17]

In Ust'-Nitsinsk settlement, Tiumen' *uezd*, each village also had its own visiting holidays. In the settlement itself were five such holidays: Epiphany (January 6), Trinity, Assumption (August 25), *Pokrov* (October 1) and Winter Nikola (December 6). Each host would try to "recruit" guests. "The young host, hostess, or other member of the family," wrote Shkoldin, "picks out from the crowd those whom he or she wants to entertain and sends them to the house, while staying to recruit more guests. . . . At the house, the guests are welcomed joyously, seated at table, and given refreshment."[18]

"Preparing for the holiday," testified Popov, "each hostess would begin to brew beer and cook various dishes a week or more in advance. . . . The guests were met in the yard. The men, removing their hats, shake each other's hand and courteously bow to the women while these in turn take each other's hands and kiss each other. After these greetings and asking about the health of the others, the entire crowd enters the parlor, the hosts last. The samovars stand ready, the plates and victuals have been set out. . . ." Without fail, there were be "rectangular or tray-shaped strawberry or cranberry *shanishki* . . . , various pies, fancy loaves, honey, vegetable oil or butter . . . ; the more meticulous the peasant, the more complex the table."[19]

In Ialutorovsk district in the 1840s, arriving guests were met on the porch or at the gate. They were welcomed with low bows, the hosts saying: "Kindly accept our humble fare." The guests expressed gratitude "on this occasion for the previous refreshment (even if this were more than a year ago)," and the hosts responded: "Oh please, do not sin [by praising overmuch]!" The guests were then ushered into the parlor and seated at the table. The dishes were already on the table, with the only utensils being spoons and forks ("but even these are on a separate plate, and if used, it is only for ceremony; they are usually replaced by two or sometimes all five fingers"). "After the table," wrote K. Golodnikov, "the host takes a tray with glasses, fills them with beer and brings them to the guests, while other family members, standing in a row at a distance from the table, bow to each guest and ask that he not spurn their hospitality."[20] Those who arrive later " . . . usually wait for the previous arrivals to leave the table; after eating their fill at one house they go to another."

The lowest pauper strove to keep up with others in "preparation of refreshment." Guests strove to visit all houses in the village organizing the holiday "reception" of its neighbors. The young people abandoned the receptions right after refreshment at the first house. Since a peasant gathering was often accompanied by a fair, the boys and girls would first visit it and then, if the weather was favorable, stroll until late "in the streets," or the young hosts would invite the guests to a party. "At this time," observed Shkoldin, "intimate relations are established among the young people, ending in marriage."[21]

In the meantime, the adults would "amuse themselves" with conversation, songs, dances, and games. When members of the indigenous population were present at a holiday gathering, not only Russian but also Ostiak and Tatar songs were heard.[22] Anyone was free to attend the peasant holiday gatherings: local officials, the middle class, priests, exiled settlers, occasional travelers, the native non-Russian inhabitants—all could expect entertainment befitting the means of the host. This was conditioned by the specific situation of Siberia—that is, an absence of sharp class differences and the strength of customs handed down from the past, especially the custom of hospitality.

The wide diversity of people attending village holiday gatherings promoted an active exchange of information, knowledge, rumors, and socially meaningful experience. "The Siberians," wrote A. P. Stepanov, "love gossip and the spreading of rumors. . . . From Tiumen' to Iakutsk, everything that happens and even that which does not happen is known."[23] Of course, news was also exchanged on weekdays, but the holidays with their large gatherings played a special role. Another factor was the holiday spirit of "heartfelt conversation." "External political events echoed dimly in Kulakov village," recalled Chukmaldin. "Thus, the Hungarian campaign of 1849 looms in my memory in the narrative of an invalid, whose leg had been cut off and replaced with an iron-tipped wooden one. On a holiday, I remember, the invalid sat on a dirt mound outside the house and told his listeners, gathered in a circle, the following tale: 'Bah! It is strange how wars sometimes happen. See here, not long ago the Hungarians rebelled against their tsar. Their tsar, a German, saw that the situation was bad, so he goes and sends our tsar a letter: such and such, do help me, dear fellow. And our tsar thought awhile, pondered the situation, and consulted with the senators as to what they should do. Today they are rebelling here, and tomorrow, who knows, they will rebel somewhere else, so he sat down and wrote. Well, he thought, I will teach the Hungarians a lesson, and he sent our army to help the German tsar. As soon as the Russian soldiers arrived, what happened to the Hungarians? We scattered them like feathers. . . . And what a thank-you did the German tsar send our tsar! 'Were it not for you,' he said, 'I would be completely *kaput.*' "[24] Thus, he reported not only the facts, but also a social appraisal of them. Another source of information disseminated among those attending the holiday gathering was books and periodicals. N. A. Kostrov, for example, left a description of Christmas *posidelki* among Minusinsk peasants.

> Christmas evenings are perhaps the happiest time in the monotonous and toilsome life of the peasant here. By this time, he has taken care of his grain, sold

it, sent it where he should and paid the tax for the second half of the year; by this time, he has managed to lay in fish and pine nuts for the entire winter, produce hops for beer on the holidays and on long winter evenings; finally, by this time, if there is an adolescent in his family, he has managed to marry him and thus acquired one more worker in the house. In a word, by Christmas the peasant here has managed to complete all his important tasks; he can now rest a little from his labors and perhaps even make merry....

Evening.... Lights appear here and there in the village. At times in the street a merry song can be heard, or a carriage will rush by with jingling horses. It is probably a rich peasant driving with his wife.... They are now returning home because it is a holiday and they will have guests, or they will themselves visit others to while away the evening. It is now totally dark; the entire village is lit with lights; the streets have become noisier and more crowded.

Let us enter the first house of any prosperous peasant and see what goes on there. The entire log house of almost every peasant home is separated by a short hall into two halves—the kitchen, with a huge Russian oven and shelves along the walls, and the parlor, sometimes with a Dutch oven, appointed with chairs, occasionally even sofas. In the kitchen, fire burns brightly in the stove and the samovar is boiling loudly; the guests must be given food and tea. Already several old men and women have gathered in the parlor, sitting sedately around the table covered with a clean white cloth. Here is the host himself... a stout peasant with roguish gray eyes. But do not think that he is really a rogue. God forbid! Of course, it is not easy to dupe him; he will instantly grasp that something is wrong and say: "No, friend, tell this to someone else." For that matter, neither will he try to dupe anyone else.... After the third and fourth cup of tea, the conversation gradually becomes more lively. The old women talk about their household affairs, the old men about their own. Among the latter, the voice of the host is especially audible, a man who can read and who even receives newspapers.... What important political news one may learn here! After tea, four glass plates, the product of a certain factory in Krasnoiarsk, appear on the table: one with biscuits, another with raisins, the third with dried apricots, and finally the fourth with the indispensable accessory of any party—pine nuts. All of this is for the women, the men will not touch it, for they require something more substantial.... Soon there appears on another table a large tray with a carafe of wine, a bottle of Madeira and two wine glasses.... Alongside are pies with fish, pressed caviar, and salmon. The wine is given properly to the men, the Madeira to the women. The entertainment begins. The glasses are passed among those present, two or three times each. Tongues become looser, the heart even more merry. One of the old women, slightly tipsy, tells a riddle, and then another one. The old men also listen to the women.... And as the riddles are told, time flies. Voices and loud songs are heard in the street. Someone has driven up to the gate with noisy jingling. In a minute, the door to the parlor is flung open and mummers appear. These are the local youth, fifteen men and women. They have arranged to assemble this evening at one house and masquerade [*mushkorovat'sia*]. Some of them are costumed as Jews, Gypsies, and bailiffs. They even have their own music—a balalaika, sometimes a fiddle and accordion.... The guests bow and, without saying a word, separate into two groups: the men on one side, the girls on the other. The balalaika and the accordion play. The men come up to the women, bow low, and sing as they slowly walk backward:

Princesses, we have come to you; young ones, we have come to you.
Boyars, why have you come; young ones, why have you come?
Princesses, to see the brides, young ones, to see the brides.
Boyars, show the groom, young ones, show the groom.
Princesses, in here, in here is the groom, young ones, in here, in here
    is the groom.
Boyars, show the caftan, young ones, show the caftan.
Princesses, in here, in here is the caftan, young ones, in here, in here
    is the caftan.
Boyars, show the shoes, young ones, show the shoes.
Princesses, in here, in here are the shoes, young ones, in here, in here
    are the shoes.
Boyars, show the cap, young ones, show the cap.
Princesses, I forgot it on the pillow, young ones, I forgot it on the pillow.
Boyars, show us the gloves, young ones, show us the gloves.
Princesses, the bride will bring them, young ones, the bride will bring them.
Boyars, you have not finished tying, young ones, you have not finished
    shaving.
Princesses, tie us quickly, young ones, tie us quickly.
Boyars, whom do you love, young ones, whom do you love?
Princesses, we love Annushka, young ones, we love Ivanovna.
Boyars, open the gates, young ones, open the gates.

The man on the right is usually the groom. He takes the hand of the opposite person and forms a gate. The girls pass through one after the other, but the gate closes in front of the bride. The groom takes her by the hand and kisses her. The game is repeated and by the rules of the celebration should be repeated as many times as there are men. But the host sees that this is boring, and therefore after the second kiss he courteously asks the guests to rest a bit, have some pine nuts and biscuits, eat and drink a little. The mummers sit down; the old men and women get up from their seats, go over to them, look in their faces and try to guess who they are. It is not very hard to guess, since the entire village is well known. The masquerading girls again start to sing:

Young one, young one,
Whom you love, whom you know,
That one kiss.
I love my beloved,
I will kiss her—
And stay for as long
As I will.

At the start of this song, one of the masquerading men goes into the middle of the parlor and begins to dance to the girl's voice. At the end of the song, he goes up to the girl of his heart, kneels before her, and kisses her . . . but time flies, especially between the amusements and various refreshments, which the cordial host does not forget to offer his guests. They must also visit several other houses, where the same merrymaking and refreshment await them. Therefore, they bid farewell to the host and hostess and go their way. Only the old men and women remain. As the masqueraders depart, loud singing is again heard in the street. It is now almost midnight. Time for the old ones also to go home. After sitting awhile and chatting a bit more, finally they also prepare to depart. The hosts sometimes walk them to the gates. These old folk will arrive home, go to bed, and manage to get a good sleep, even though they are quite intoxicated, and every now and then in the street comes the sound of a rushing sleigh on the snow and the noise of bells; the loud songs of the wandering youth are still heard; in the windows of houses still shine welcoming lights, indicating that lingering guests still sit beneath the warm roofs of these houses, despite the late hour.[25]

The mummery and the scenes enacted by the mummers at the Christmas holidays and in early January were the most important element of the "carnival" folk culture. In Surgutsk *uezd*, partial enactments of the folk dramas "King Maximilian" and "The Lazy Baron" enjoyed the greatest popularity. In Samarov village, Tobol'sk *uezd*, the mummery was known as "listening." "Villages of both sexes, chiefly boys," wrote a local, "garb themselves in various costumes and put on sometimes bizarre masks. These are the 'listeners' (masqueraders). In the bitter frost, they run from one house to another, where they are welcomed, and changing their voice, gait, and manners, amuse the hosts and try to remain unknown, although this happens seldom."[26]

During Yuletide in all Siberian villages there was sumptuous feasting and "joyous movement in the houses and in the streets." The oldest women would climb down from the stoves and stove ledges and around them would form "circles, amused by the old wives' tales." The young people would play at *imal'tsy* or blind man's buff (one of the participants, chosen by lot, had his eyes covered, and was supposed to catch "his companions running around, who make themselves known by the sound of their movement and by snapping their handkerchiefs"). "They would like to continue the game but a dozen noisy mummers enter. One of them is a bogeyman: his face is covered with soot, there are horns on his head, rags on his ears, in his mouth a cigarette with the lit end inside; another is an actual devil—with horns, with tail, covered entirely in black calico; another is a shaman in Tungus clothing, carrying a drum, and covered all over with bells, tambourines, models of loons and other birds and fish; and here is Death himself, tall, all in white, with a beet instead of a nose, with fangs carved from turnip and radish; here is one who has sewn himself in a bearskin and moves on all fours, stopping to rest on his hind paws; and here a harlequin, but with a mask so frightening and repulsive that it is impossible to look at. And the others are also disguised. They dance to the beat of the drum and peculiar whistling, chirping, clapping, etc.," reported M. F. Krivoshapkin, a resident of the Eniseisk region.[27]

The celebration of Christmas and New Year also involved other amusements. At Christmas, the young people would "give praise." "Eight of us gathered," recalled Kh. Loparev, "and we made a big, many-colored star, and after matins we walked around the entire village until mass, giving praise to Christ, and turning the star about its axis. After the singing, one of us 'gave a sermon'; there were several of these. I remember the shortest of them, which we said in childhood: 'I, a young peasant, jumped on the table, played the flute, greeted Christ; May the host and hostess prosper for many years!' "[28]

Krivoshapkin gave a detailed description of the star carried through the streets during the holiday by "a merry crowd of singers." It was one and a half arshins [one arshin = 28 inches] across. "The first mask, of thin paper soaked with vegetable oil, is usually half an arshin across. It is fastened to horns that are glued together from paper with two walls, between which are cross bars with two candles. Around them are aspen fillets. The horns are fastened to the masks and fringes, made from pink sugar paper. On the inner fringe around each horn there is a star of red paper. The outer mask has a fringe around it. On this mask are portrayed a ship, with a bow in the form of a snake, the hero Polkan at the stern, and on the deck Dobrinia, Il'ia Muromets, and Alesha Popovich;[q] then three churches, the sun, the moon, and a star; a Turkish town, a sea, where the Turks are in boats, flags at the helm. Such star is fastened to a long pole, by means of which it is lifted high."[29]

Children of both sexes "not older than twelve years," according to P. Shalabanov, a priest from Kainsk, "on New Year's Eve at twilight or after darkness" would rush to the windows of the houses and sing "a holiday greeting song [kaleda] in the loudest voice, according to the heathen custom."[30]

Certain rituals were reflected in the games with which adults amused themselves during holidays. Thus, in the home of the coachman Aleksei Khozianinov of Tiulina (Tobol'sk uezd, 1759), in the presence of guests a mock wedding of Iakov Soskin was held "according to church rite": they set up "several wooden puppets, around which they performed the rite . . . selecting . . . as bride a Samarov coachman, living in this village of Tiulina." The role of the priest was played by a local resident, Fedor Gubin ("learned in Slavonic-Russian writing and able to read"), that of the master of ceremonies [tysiatskii] by the host's brother, Tikhon; the best men were the host himself and his other brother Semen. "Parental characters" were played by a relative of Aleksei, Semen Ivanov Khoziainov and the widow Kseniia Chukrieva. The matchmakers were the wives of Aleksei and Tikhon.

"At the end of this wedding that they performed, following the custom the groom with the bride were placed in a special chamber, whereupon the bride ... at their (the Khozianinov's) command, beat the aforesaid ... Soskin with a horse whip." "And thereafter," a relative of Soskin concluded his report to the religious authorities, "they, the Khoziainovs, in the same way performed the same operation on Ivan Andreev Kuznetsov, the Samarov coachman." Soskin himself at the investigation declared that his wedding at the Khoziainov home "was done for buffoonery [*blagoshpakurstvo*]."[31]

Many different kinds of "merrymaking" were especially evident in the Siberian village at Shrovetide, occurring in the latter half of February and beginning of March. Besides the usual holiday diversions—gatherings, hospitality, etc.—they organized a street "carnival," the central event of which was the appearance of "Lady Shrovetide." "They make Shrovetide as follows," reported Shalabanov, "they harness horses to a sleigh or wood sledge, around which they hang braces and coarse matting." Musicians are seated in the sleigh, who play "fiddles, balalaikas, accordions, and tambourines, standing upright and amusing the onlookers." In the middle of the sleigh is "fastened" a long log, on which is placed a cartwheel (this is securely tied to the log), and on the wheel is placed "Lady Shrovetide" herself—a person dressed in the most ridiculous clothing, smeared with soot. The holiday "train" rides from house to house, receiving "money and wine as recompense" from the hosts.[32]

In the Altai, *enaraly* ["generals"] and *fet'marshaly* ["marshals"] took part in the Shrovetide holidays. "Invested with the titles of *enaraly* and *fet'- marshaly*," wrote A. Shirokov of Suzunsk, "these heroes dress in motley old- fashioned uniforms. The three-cornered hats and ribbons of honor that they wear across both shoulders they make themselves from elegant wallpaper, gluing mica to them to make them shine. Instead of orders, the *enaraly* decorate themselves with painted tobacco-box lids, the housings of pocket watches, etc. The *enaraly*'s usual parade equipage consists of four or six large boxes, a fathom tall, in which coal is usually hauled from the houses for factory work. All these boxes, firmly fastened together, are covered on top with boards to accommodate the *enaraly* and an orchestra of musicians: several pine fiddles, homemade trumpets, tambourines, and drums. In the middle of the equipage, like a mast, is fastened a tall thick pole, at the upper end of which a wheel is placed horizontally, serving as a seat for a masked clown. From the height of his perch, the clown amuses the venerable public by making strange faces and singing various songs, first beginning with a rooster call, the barking of a dog, and the meowing of a cat. Several pairs of skinny horses, harnessed one behind the other and hung with wreaths, brooms, and similar decorations, slowly drag this monstrous chariot from one place to another."

The scenario of the Shrovetide procession in the villages of the Altai was carefully worked out in its main features—certain of its elements came down from past times, others were inventions of the first half of the nineteenth century. The dramaturgical talent of several generations was enacted, at the same time leaving ample room for improvisation and the participation of all who wished in the creative and artistic action. Shirovov related:

> The procession begins with two deformed characters, representing an old man and an old woman. The man, in a high Kirghiz headdress [*malakhai*] and a shaggy costume hung with dead rabbits, sparrows, and crows (a parody on the shaman's costume—N.M.), is armed with a bow of remarkable construction: one end of the arrow is tied to the bowstring, and at the other end, where the tip should be, there is attached a small tin funnel. With this weapon, the old man permits himself every possible foolishness, exploiting the curiosity of the peasants, who stop in the street with open mouth to watch the glorious uniforms and proud faces of the *enaraly*; he steals up behind them and, filling the funnel with snow, shoots the unwary right in the face with it; before they have a chance to wipe their eyes, the nimble rogue has concealed himself in the crowd, to the accompaniment of general laughter. And the old woman, dancing, twirls a straw doll in her arms, representing a suckling babe. Next come a whole squadron of paper grandees, striving to assume the gait and appearance of magnificent importance, arousing the involuntary laughter of the onlookers. After these come a row of singers and, last, the ceremonial chariot on a wood sledge, holding the musicians and, on occasion, the *enaraly* themselves; a large and noisy crowd concludes the procession. When this ceremonial procession begins, the sound of music is immediately heard accompanying the singers, who with their hats aslant and one hand placed on the cheek shout a merry song with all their might. . . . But now the heroes of the holiday have stopped at a wealthy house, and the accompanying crowd forms a large circle around them. Here a new spectacle is presented. The imaginary grandees begin to speak in a tongue that they themselves do not understand; the talk grows heated and finally turns into a feud. They instantly separate and, drawing swords, accost their opponents. . . . Suddenly the voice of the main singer is heard: "Stesha walked in the yard . . . " and, when the words are repeated by the general chorus, with music and deafening whistles: "I will not obey the father but will comfort the brave lad. I will comfort him, because he is the only son of the father"—the angry faces of the feuding parties instantly assume a happy expression; with no further ado, unsheathed swords in hand, they crouch down and begin to dance in the Russian manner, literally until they drop. Next, the old woman with her straw baby comes on the scene and, wriggling in front of the old man, begins to dance with him, singing about her costume:

> *Sarafan* my *sarafan*,
> The buttons are shiny.
> You, my *sarafan*,
> Are fit for everything:
> A cloth for fine horses,
> A veil for pretty girls . . .

The master of the house sends the *enaraly* wine and money, and they move off with the same noise and the same shouts of glee.

"It is needless to say," Shirokov concluded, "how great is the mirth that overcomes Sibiriaki watching these amusements."[33] A doll made of rags, straw, and hay was present in the Shrovetide processions in other regions of Siberia, and at the end of the "carnival" it was torn apart in public.[34]

Other scenes were also enacted during the celebration of Shrovetide, verses composed by the peasants themselves were delivered, and *starinki*—songs of epic [*byliny*] type—were performed. At Charyshk station in the Altai, a "boat with rowers, archers, and other comedians" mounted on wheels was driven through the streets during Shrovetide week.[35] The holiday program also included the capture of a snow town, as attested by observers in various parts of Siberia. The "town" was taken on the last day of Shrovetide, the so-called day of absolution. The fort was usually built on the ice of a river or lake. "Several tall, thick columns of snow, joined at the top by arches and doused with water for strength," wrote Shirokov, "comprise the base of the fort. Boards are placed on the arches, and at the corners of the fortress are very tall poles, crowned with straw. Add to all this a whole row of snow statues placed along the ramparts—the work of Siberian sculptors, and you will have the entire fortress, or town, as Sibiriaki call it."[36] The priest T. Popov recalled his childhood in Medvedevsk village, Ishimsk *okrug*, where they also enacted a capture of the fortress on Shrovetide[r]—the walls here were decorated with figures of dogs, cats, rabbits, etc., molded from snow.[37] Shirokov has left a detailed description of the storming of the "town":

> The day of absolution, so famous among Russians, arrives, and before the onset of evening the shores of the pond cannot contain all the curious of both sexes. The ice, two arshins thick, crackles under the weight of the sleds and spectators, who impatiently direct their glances to where the heroes of the celebration are to appear. Finally, the sound of music and song heralds their approach, and a murmur of impatient anticipation is heard in the crowd. After several more minutes, the gay procession of Shrovetide grandees comes into sight and halts near the fortress. All around the excitement of the people is stilled, and all that can be heard are the occasional instructions and commands of the *enaraly*, who at this time separate into attackers and defenders, and one of them is made the commandant. Suddenly, songs and music are heard at the top of the fortress, while at its gates a garrison of volunteers is arrayed in defensive position. At some distance away, a squadron of twenty daring horsemen, commanded by one of the *enaraly*, suddenly hurls itself with a furious cry against the bastion, but being met by a multitude of hats, snowballs, and blank gunshots, it withdraws in disorder; forming up again, the squadron attacks the besieged with greater force. This is repeated several times with increasing fury. . . . The assault continues until finally one of the bold fellows, heedless of himself and his horse, breaks through the ranks of the garrison and, coura-

geously reaching the gates of the fortress, gallops on his steed beneath the snow arches. Shouts of approval are heard everywhere. . . . There now begins such turmoil that the eye and ear of the observer must become fatigued. Hundreds of children with a deafening shout hurl themselves against the fortress and in several minutes raze it to its foundation. The large crowd of on-lookers instantly is set in motion and disperses in every direction.[38]

In Eniseisk province, reported A. P. Stepanov, "footmen and horsemen were used in the assault. The former climb onto the walls, the latter rush the gates. Brooms and whips constitute the weapons."[39] After taking the town, the victors are celebrated.

Other Shrovetide amusements were riding horses through the village and riding sleds down ice hills. "During Shrovetide," wrote N. A. Abramov of the Ialutorovsk peasants, "they ride through the village with songs, while the young men, girls, and children also sleigh down hills that are made of snow and iced with water."[40] "Here," exclaimed another observer, Shirokov, "there is a bazaar of mutual compliments and passionate glances."[41] All these Shrovetide amusements (and also the others) helped produce a holiday feeling, an emotional uplifting, and a distraction from daily chores. The holiday amusements gave the peasant a relief from the strain built up over the difficult working days. "The merrymaking and pleasures of the holi-days serve as a distraction in the harsh yearly existence of the ordinary per-son," wrote Kh. Loparev.[42] "If you ever decide to witness the time span from Christmas until Shrovetide," reported P. A. Slovtsov through the words of one of the characters in "A Walk around Tobol'sk," "you would be amazed at how quickly the locals here of both sexes dash from foolishness to prankishness, so that at Shrovetide they slide about, heedless of the current understanding of proper behavior."[43]

Holiday "foolishness" and "prankishness" and celebratory laughter were essential to the peasant. Clearly, V. Ia. Propp is correct in declaring that holiday "revelry and laughter were an expression of protest against the op-pressive, ascetic morality and restraint imposed by the church and the entire social order."[44] Holiday customs and rituals contained a temporary denial of class inequality, class barriers—"generals," "field marshals," and the other peasants were on an equal footing here. This conclusion is confirmed by I. Bedniakov, a priest from Dolgoiarsk village, Tobol'sk region: "On a holiday, the priests revel so much that you cannot tell who is the priest, who the clerk, and who the peasant; they are all equal."[45] Consequently, calendri-cal holidays gave the peasant not only psychological but also social relief, transporting him in time "to the Utopian kingdom of universality, equality, and abundance."[46] There was a temporary vacating of the hierarchical class relationships of feudal society. This temporary social respite helped the agri-culturalist support the harsh reality of everyday existence.[s]

In the autumn and winter season the peasants often visited each other, even on work days. They would usually pay visits in their village "to chat"—"about birth," "about marriage, "about neighbors"—in the evenings (and not without cause was this time of the day known as the "sitting" in Siberian villages). Male, female, and more often mixed groups would gather. The number could vary from two to five or more people. On weekdays, they drove to other villages to visit relatives, in-laws, and acquaintances. They generally showed up uninvited, but sometimes the hosts issued a special invitation. Conversations during such weekday visits were of the most diverse content; the peasants shared the latest news, afflictions, hopes, and plans, received and gave advice, and "judged" their fellow villagers. The weekday visits might be accompanied by a "feast" [*pirom*]. In 1766, Fedos'ia Zamiatina, a resident of Novoeniseisk village (Altai region) stated at an inquest that, on September 18 (by "invitation of her husband" Nikita) the peasants Trofim Berezovikov and Petr Poklonov from Peshchansk village came to her house. Nikita was away from home, and Fedos'ia gave the guests beer "and they sang songs." Soon, however, Nikita's brother, Danilo Zamiatin, who lived nearby, deeming it "unseemly" that the bride "had thrown a banquet without her husband," evicted the visitors with the help of his nephew Afanasii.[47]

The peasants had other amusements in the time free from field work. "Much pleasure on winter evenings," wrote T. Uspenskii of Shadrinsk *uezd*, "is provided by an old storyteller to the assembled family."[48] And such was the case not only in the villages beyond the Urals. On such occasions, they also told *byval'shchiny* [worldly tales] and *pobasenki* [tall tales]; the children tried to figure out riddles; and the literate peasants passed their time reading books and organized collective readings for the others.

With the onset of the spring warmth, the young people gathered in the open air. According to S. I. Guliaev, from the first day of Easter week until Trinity the girls and young women sang songs in the streets together with the boys "from evening until late at night."[49] At Easter, they set up rope swings on scaffolds or garden gates—swinging was one of the favorite amusements of young people everywhere. "By the end of the week after Easter," reported one author, "the swings are for the most part taken down and not put back until the following Easter."[50]

Easter was observed rather modestly in most Siberian regions; among the older people, it was confined to "hosting" and refreshments. However, in certain villages, on this holiday the women, dressed in their best clothing, went "on a promenade." "During Easter week they carry the icons of the resurrection, the crucifixion and the Virgin Mother to the houses," reported Popov of Takmytsk settlement residents, "and though not all, the greater portion attend prayer services. The icons are set in wheat bread, crumbled in a sieve or screen, and a table is set with various kinds of pies and eggs. Everyone in the house—from the young to the old—exchange the triple kiss with the clergy. On Palm Sunday, those who have gone to church and those who have not make palms [willows] in each house and decorate the icons with them."[51]

A traditional pastime of girls and young women (preserving a certain religious meaning) was the collective walk into the woods on *Semik* [the Seventh Thursday after Easter] and Trinity. "The young people pass *Semik* with much celebration," observed I. Zubov (1848) of the peasants of Sladkovsk, Akmolinsk province. "On this day, the girls dress in various clothing, sometimes even male attire, walk to the woods with songs and other amusements, and there deck birches with wreaths, leaving them here until Trinity Day, when they again assemble in a circle dance and go to remove these wreaths, with which they sing songs and dance."[52] The "maidens and young women" of Kainsk went into the woods "beating on frying pans."[53]

Trinity (Whitsunday) was observed by peasants of all ages. In certain villages, there were visiting holidays on Trinity. "Making merry" with beer and wine, the men and boys turned to "gymnastic amusements": fighting and wrestling with poles. In a petition submitted in 1737 to the Chaussk court (Tomsk *uezd*), the peasant Luka Rudnev reported that, on May 29, he and his brother Savva were in Iunsk village "on the holiday of Trinity Day" in the home of Iakov Mal'tsev, and when he came "out from the house into the street, he was called to fight" by Aleksei Glukhikh, a Cossack idler. The petitioner continued: "And I did not go to fight with him, Glukhikh, and refused, saying, 'I do not know how to fight and will not fight,' but that Glukhikh for this struck me in the eyes with his fist and said, 'the five rubles are no loss to me' "[54] (to pay the fine for fighting—N.M.). Government clerks, the local middle class, and the village priests could take part in peasant "gymnastic amusements" ("all of them try to fight or grapple on poles"). Men of all ages would fight and grapple "on poles" both on Trinity and on other summer holidays.[55] Chukmaldin recalled that in the mid-nineteenth century, in Kamensk village, twenty-eight versts from Tiumen', a large group of people assembled on Prokopii's Day: "a row of temporary tents was set up at the riverside, with places to make fire, where they roasted food and where the young people made merry and sang songs. . . . Dense crowds marked the 'circles,' where they were wrestling 'under the belt' and where the hero of the day was often Antoshka Lazarev, who would vanquish as many as seventy people in a row and, having no more competitors, carried off the circle."[56]

F. Zobnin has described a village fight in detail. It involved the entire male population of the village, or occasionally that of several villages. "Usually fighters from the upper end fight in turn with those from the lower end. But on major annual holidays, usually both ends unite to fight against those from other villages and hamlets. Only two men fight, while the others surround the scene with a thick living ring of onlookers. The fight is always started by the smaller fighters. Each fighter entering the ring must be bound with a belt across one arm and around the waist. The purpose of the fight is to throw one's opponent to the ground three times."[57]

A popular form of revelry for young people, on holidays and Sundays starting with Trinity, was the circle dance. "In the evenings," reported Iv. Meves, who journeyed through Siberia in 1858–61, "we often encountered circle dances in the villages. Siberian women's songs are distinguished by their monotony; they sing in a half-tone, and the shrieks that form a part of our village melodies are not heard in them. The sturdy, broad-shouldered girls, linking arms in the dance, exchange glances with the boys and just as boldly reward their admirers with slaps for a clumsy clasping of the hand or some other offense."[58]

Circle dances were held either beyond the village—in a field, in meadows, at the outskirts, or in a special "free" area—on the village green or sometimes simply in the street ("at the gates of the girl who is the queen of the circle dance"). Girls, boys, and young women and men took part. The "players" would clasp hands, form a circle, and begin to "move in one direction or another, fast or slow, depending on the song."[59] Many Sibiriak dancing songs have been recorded.

> My true love and I walked in the garden,
> We plucked an apple,
> We broke it up,
> We ate it together.
> We came together, bowed, greeted:
> Hail, dark-eyed beauty.
> Greetings, my sweet,
> Greetings, my dear,
> Kiss me, my lovely—

sang Samarov peasants in a favorite circle dance song. "At these words," recalled Loparev, a fellow villager, "I involuntarily laughed and asked the singers: 'How is this? First they ate and then greeted each other?' But they paid no attention to my comment: 'And could we change that which is handed down almost with mother's milk?'—I seemed to read in their eyes."[60]

Many of the dancing songs involved games. They would play "the pillow": one of the girls danced with a kerchief in her hand inside a closed circle, while the others sang:

> Oh young one, oh young one,
> You are truly young!
> Oh pillow, oh pillow,
> You are truly soft!

> Whosoever you like,
> Him shall you kiss,
> To him shall you give the soft pillow.

The girl would give the kerchief to one of the boys and kiss him.[61] Sometimes the circle dance was divided into female and male halves. "Each half," reported an observer, "would sing in turn, with the song of one half composed of questions and that of the other the answers; during the questions and answers the two halves would come together and then draw apart."

Circle dance games were varied. These were distinguished by genuine mirth and absence of constraint, primness, or tension. "We encountered the population on a holiday," wrote N. M. Iadrintsev of Verkhne-Katunsk village (Altai), "the men in town suits, the women in red calico dresses, shoes, collars and silk kerchiefs. . . . In the crowd we saw a lad who was wearing a very original brocaded vest. In the boisterous streets, they were playing at circle dances, and a reed pipe was heard. One could say that this was a Katunsk idyll."[62] "Stay, my dear circle dance, stay, all the happy people, stay, do not go. I would like to jump and dance in this merry circle dance. I would like to jump and dance, drop the wreath, I would drop the wreath, and find my dear one. My darling is going, there goes the pretty one, she is carrying the wreath. I take the wreath, I place it on my arm, on my arm I place it, three times I kiss," the joyful dancing song would echo all around.

The young people found other amusements on the summer holidays. "Skipping" was popular: on a wooden platform they would place a board "five arshins in size," the girls would stand at either end of this board and "jump" in turn. This was a very old game. Even in the mid-seventeenth century the military governor of Verkhotursk wrote that "women and girls jump on boards" in Siberia.[63] Another girls' amusement was "tag": the participants gathered in a circle would shout "Catch us if you can!" and run in various directions, "twisting and turning," except for one of their number, who was supposed to catch them. Whoever she caught would take her place.[64]

Girls played "separation" together with the fellows. The participants formed a long line of pairs, with one of them standing in front at a certain distance from the line. At a signal, the boy and girl in the last position were supposed to run along opposite sides of the line and clasp hands before the "separator" caught or tagged one of them. If they succeeded, they became the front of the line and the whole process repeated itself. But if the "separator" caught one of them, he formed a pair with that one, and the other took his place. "The separator, if a boy," wrote Loparev, "tried mainly to catch the girl, in order to form a pair with her, and vice versa."[65]

Boys and young men usually played knucklebones, leapfrog, toss, skittles, and various ball games. Chukmaldin wrote:

I recall several of my friends and companions of youth. There was our neighbor's son Iliusha, quiet, modest, thoughtful beyond his years. He was two or three years older than me. We would be playing a game and everyone would be happy, shouting loudly, laughing uncontrollably, and he would laugh quietly, or only smile, and so sadly that you could almost look into his heart. . . . He liked to sing songs sometimes and sang wonderfully. . . . I had another companion, Fedia Pimnev, the same age as I, a bright and happy boy. He was always the first to start a game.

"Today we will play knucklebones," he would say. And we played knucklebones.

"Let us play ball," he would say another time, and the whole gang of lads played ball.

I remember another companion, Semka Kozhan. This was a sullen boy; he liked to fight and chase. . . . I had other friends, two brothers—Stepa and Vasilii Pimnev. . . . Vasilii shouted during games without rhyme or reason, louder than anyone else; but Stepa played quietly, calmly, and strictly observed the rules of the game.[66]

Knucklebones were made from pasterns, which were first boiled. The largest and heaviest bone was chosen for the striker, and sometimes was cast in lead. The players, after setting up their knucklebones, paced out a certain distance and took turns "knocking down" the bones with the strikers. The bones that were knocked down or out by a player became his property.[67]

To play leapfrog, two groups were formed. Those in one group assumed the following position: the first propped his head against a wall, the next behind him "placed his head beneath the arm of the first," and all the others behind in the same fashion. The players of the other group took a running start and jumped one after the other "on the stooping team." In the Altai, Iadrintsev also saw girls taking part in this game: "In one of the villages," he wrote, "we found the peasant youth playing games. The girls were playing ball with the boys with huge clubs, hitting the ball so hard that it was lost from sight; their physical development was strong. These girls also play leapfrog, first putting on trousers before running and jumping."[68]

One of the ball games played was "sparrows": they dug a hole in the ground, placed a wooden board in it, and on the board a ball, and then hit the board with a bat ("the first to hit is chosen by lots"). Whoever caught the ball replaced the player. Another game was known as "hidden friends are more dangerous than snakes": one half of the players went into the field, taking positions there ("some standing in the middle and others at the sides")—they were supposed to catch the ball. "One of the fielders pitches the ball," reported an observer. "Whoever misses with the bat three times is out, whoever hits every time continues until he misses three times." Another name for this game is *lapta*. The swinger waits until the ball is thrown so far that it is possible to run through the field "one time or there and back" as it is being caught. But if "those standing in the field hit the runner and themselves run to the boundaries, then the teams switch: the other half begins to take the field and pitch the ball, while the first half bats the ball into the field."

There was also the game "ball against the ground" (and against a wall): "Two players measure off a bat, and whoever's hand is on top becomes a *matka*, to begin the game. One throws the ball against the ground so hard that it makes high bounces, and catches it using his arm or leg during the bounces, continuing until he misses." In the latter case, the ball is thrown against a wall, instead of the ground.[69]

The game of toss was played using an iron spike with a large head. An iron ring was placed on the ground, the spike was taken by the sharp end and thrown, with the goal of landing mid-ring, with the spike sticking in the ground. It was all the better if the ring was pushed to one side. The distance from the spike to the ring was then measured by span, and this measurement was called "pies." If the spike did not stick in the ground, the player was eliminated. In the words of an observer, "whoever did not stick the spike after ten times was forced to give each player a spike and tell him, in jest, you have put the yoke on father."[70]

The game of skittles [*chugi*], popular throughout Siberia, was played as follows:

> Two squares, or kitties, are traced out on the ground at a certain distance from each other, the lines of the kitties being known as *vereii*. On the front line of the kitties are placed approximately ten skittles, and on the back line a single skittle, known as the priest. When the skittles are set up, the players divide into two groups: first, the two main players, known as *matki*, will be chosen and then pairs will approach them and ask: '*matki, matki*, which will it be? Earth or stone? Fire or water?' And so on, thus being divided. After the players are divided into two teams, the *matki* throw lots to determine which kitty the first will knock down. At first, the *matka* from the front line of one kitty throws a stick at the other kitty, and if he knocks out at least one skittle from the kitty he continues to knock down skittles, but from half the distance between kitties. A skittle that falls within the line is known as lying; but a skittle that stays on the line is stood up and called a priest. It is clearly easier to knock down a standing skittle than a lying one, so that often there is an argument as to whether a particular skittle should be considered lying or promoted to a priest. Whoever judges incorrectly in such case is said by the other team to flounder. . . . When the last skittle is knocked down, the team triumphantly shouts: 'enough of bats!' and the opponents must be content with the rejected bats. If they do not judges incorrectly in such case is said by the other team to flounder. . . . When the last skittle is knocked down, the team triumphantly shouts: 'enough of bats!' and the opponents must be content with the rejected bats. If they do not knock down their kitty, they are considered losers and must set up both kitties (place the skittles on both lines of the kitties).[71]

The ingenuity of the children knew no bounds—they constantly invented new games. A detailed description of these games ("king," "pike," "academy," "bear," "sorcerer," "burying gold," "neighbors," "needle," etc.) has been left by an official, who lovingly (in his words) watched the daily life of the common people "during official trips in various regions."[72] All of these games were doubtlessly very important—they promoted both the socialization and the physical development of young people.

The characteristics of rural production during feudalism resulted in leisure not being fully separated from work occupations: a vivid example of this is help sessions [*pomochi*] and varieties thereof.

Peasant "amusements" played an important role in the eighteenth and first half of the nineteenth century: they were aimed at restoring the strength of the peasant, helped consolidate the communities, and were one of the ways the commune functioned as transmitter of public opinion and custodian of cultural and work traditions.

In lieu of a conclusion

The work and struggle, joy and sorrow, aspirations and hopes of the everyday existence of the Siberian village have not, of course, found full expression in the pages of this book. Many of the realities of peasant life, family holidays, and rituals have not been examined. There were significant peculiarities among Siberian peasants in this area. It is no accident that so-called runaway marriages were popular east of the Urals. By the mid-nineteenth century, the opinion was prevalent among peasants in certain localities that the only proper way to marry was to "steal a girl." And Siberian brides themselves proved exceedingly discriminating. . . .

The historical and geographical knowledge and various aspects of the social consciousness of the peasantry deserve special attention—in particular, their judgments of the most important events and actors of the past and the role of the masses in history. Also extremely interesting is the question of the relationship of Siberian farmers toward the supreme government and local bureaucracy. Modern journalism often mentions the tsarist illusions about Russian peasantry in explaining the sources of certain views and ideas of the working class, even in the Soviet era. But these references can acquire the force of argument only after close familiarization with the sources. Indeed, the documents make one ponder. . . .

Relations between peasantry and clergy, the attitude of Siberian farmers toward the church, church duties, the celebration of religious holidays, and the very phenomenon of the people's orthodoxy are all subjects that deserve special treatment.

The sources contain a wealth of information on the attitude of Sibiriaki toward the natural environment and centuries-old weather omens. Of these omens, the Russian peasants were especially interested in precursors of rain, frost, snow. And this is quite understandable: it is extremely important for agriculturalists to predict a temperature drop, onset of frost, rain, or fair weather, so they watch the external symptoms that herald changes in the weather.

The author hopes to give special treatment to all these topics.

Editor's notes

a. Regional administrative hierarchies are reflected in the terms *volost'*, *okrug*, *oblast'*, *uezd*, and *guberniia*. *Volost'* jurisdiction often coincided with the *mir* in Siberia. *Volost'*, *okrug*, and *uezd* can all be properly translated as "district" but this homogenizes them, masking the complexities of regional administration. The *oblast'* and *guberniia* levels can be glossed as "provinces." A relevant reference is Sergei G. Pushkarev, *Dictionary of Russian Historical Terms from the Eleventh Century to 1917* (New Haven: Yale University Press, 1970).

b. *Zemskaia izba* is sometimes glossed as the town or village hall, being the rural center for tax collection and local court cases. The word *izba* literally means hut, while *zemskaia* comes from the root *zemlia* or land. For social-historical analysis, see Cathy Frierson, "Crime and Punishment in the Russian Village," *Slavic Review*, vol. 46 (Spring 1987), pp. 55–69; idem, "Rural Justice in Russia: the Volost' Court Debate, 1861–1912," *Slavonic and East European Review*, vol. 64 (October 1986), pp. 526–45; and Stephen P. Frank, *Cultural Conflict, Law, and Criminality in Rural Russia 1861–1907* (forthcoming). Frierson argues that strong local allegiances influenced customary law and its administration.

c. Hospitality in rural Siberia and Russia has remained a strong value. I saw food "for the road" urged on visitors during fieldwork in Siberia in 1976 and 1986. The word for hospitality, *khlebosol'stvo*, stems from the words "bread-and-salt," the traditional symbols of a proper reception.

d. Minenko exhibits a rare editorial comment here, reflecting her Marxist training, which encourages generalizing about a whole group of people as an exploitive socioeconomic class.

e. Respect for women in Siberia came not only from their strong economic role in the peasant household, but also from their social and spiritual role, which was reinforced when husbands went on long hunting and trading trips. Cf. N. A. Minenko, *Russkaia krest'ianskaia sem'ia v zapadnoi Sibiri (XVIII–pervoi poloviny XIX v.)* (Novosibirsk, 1979).

f. The Western historian Ben Eklof has made a similar argument for a later period in his *Russian Peasant Schools: Officialdom, Village Culture, and Popular Pedagogy, 1861–1914* (Berkeley: University of California Press, 1986); and idem, "Peasants and Schools" in *The World of the Russian Peasant: Post-Emancipation Culture and Society*, eds. Ben Eklof and Stephen P. Frank (Boston: Unwin Hyman, 1990). Jeffrey Brooks, *When Russia Learned to Read: Literacy and Popular Literature, 1861–1917* (Princeton: Princeton University Press, 1985) makes a somewhat more functional argument, and places any extensive peasant interest in literacy quite late.

g. The *popovshchina* are those Old Believers who adhered to the validity of priests, as opposed to the even more radical *bezpopovskie* Old Believers, who rejected priests entirely. See N. A. Kazakova and Ia. S. Lur'e, *Antifeodal'nye ereticheskie dvizheniia na Rusi XIV–nachala XVI veka* (Moscow: Nauka, 1955); A. I. Klibanov, *Reformatsionnye dvizheniia v Rossii v XIV–pervoi polovine XVI vv.* (Moscow: Nauka, 1960); idem, "Fifty Years of Scientific Study of Religious Sectarianism," *Soviet Sociology*, vol. 8, no. 3–4 (Winter–Spring 1970), pp. 239–78; and idem, *History of Religious Sectarianism in Russia (1860s–1917)*, trans. Ethel Dunn, ed. Stephen P. Dunn (Oxford: Pergamon, 1982), pp. ix–xv and 1–66.

h. Women in some areas were automatically allowed to remarry when their husbands were drafted, for military service was for life in much of the eighteenth century, and reduced to twenty-five years in 1793. See Jerome Blum, *Lord and Peasant in Russia from the Ninth to the Nineteenth Century* (Princeton: Princeton University Press, 1971, original 1961), pp. 466–68.

i. This description fits a process called in the medical anthropology literature "hierarchy of resort," which is often combined with ideas about different kinds of problems being appropriate for different levels of attention. A major "folk" distinction is between natural and supernatural causes, with a mediating category of illness brought on by moral transgression. These latter illnesses are believed resistent to cures by European-style doctors. Some religious groups, like Old Believers and Christian Scientists, expand this category in a reliance on God-determined fate. See Lola Romanucci-Ross, Daniel R. Moerman, and Laurence Tancredi, eds., *The Anthropology of Medicine: From Culture to Method* (Westport: Bergin and Garvey, 1991, revised).

j. *Koldun-vezhdivtsy* probably refers to sorcerer-hermits, living on the edge of some Sibiriak villages. The root *vezh* means tent or hut. Sorcerers were invited to weddings in part to assure they would not curse the families involved in the wedding for not inviting them. Buying their goodwill was an insurance policy.

k. The Russian word here is *bolezn'*, approximating our medical science term for disease. In medical anthropology literature the term "illness" is used to describe a more patient-generated definition of medical problems, often combining psychological and biological symptoms. See Arthur Kleinman, *Patients and Healers in the Context of Culture: An Exploration of the Borderland between Anthropology, Medicine, and Psychiatry* (Berkeley: University of California Press, 1980). In Russian the distinction between disease and illness is blurred by using *bolezn'* for both, although *toshnota* approximates our word "sickness," with overtones of feeling nauseous.

l. The term *raznochinets* reflects an interesting residual social category, most often defined negatively as one who is neither a peasant, a noble, nor a guild member. The case described here landed in a 1754 inquest over malpractice, due to the appeal to non-Christian forces for healing.

m. Many medicinal plants mentioned here have multiple and poetic names, varying regionally. For instance, to combat the symptoms of *pereloi*, or gonorrhea, Russian villagers used the herb *Parnassia palustris*, called tsar's eyes, fall color, golden drop, one-leaf, *velozor*, and *gorlianka*. Many of the plants and plant combinations used in concoctions were indeed curative.

n. This suggestive incantation, evoking a *kochetok*, or spirit taking the form of a cock, may be a part of an older ritual in which a cock or chicken was sacrificed for curative purposes.

o. The tradition of such games, especially at weddings, is reflected in some of the current wedding celebrations of young Sibiriaki. In the 1980s, the Komsomol in some Siberian villages was encouraging variations on traditional games at weddings. In 1986, this became part of the anti-alcohol campaign, with games viewed as more healthy than drunken binges.

p. Elaborate traditional peasant dress is displayed in numerous Russian art books. See, for example, I. Ia. Boguslavskaia, *Russkoe narodnoe iskusstvo v sobranii Gosudarstvennogo Russkogo Muzeia* (Leningrad: Khudozhnik, 1984).

q. These are folk heroes that continually appear in the most venerated Russian tales (*skazki*) and legends (*byliny*). See, for example, the collections of A. N. Afanas'ev, *Russian Fairy Tales*, N. Guterman, ed. and trans. (New York: Pantheon, 1974); idem, *Narodnye russkie skazki* (Moscow, 1957), 3 vols.; *Narodnye russkie legendy* (Kazan', 1914). See also A. E. Alexander, *Bylina and Fairy Tale: The Origins of Russian Heroic Poetry* (The Hague, 1973).

r. Medvedevsk translates as Bear village. The Shrovetide ritual of capturing a snow fortress was made famous by the 1891 painting by V. I. Surikov, "Vziatie snezhnogo gorodka," kept in the Russian Museum of Leningrad.

s. Minenko branches from description here into analysis, relying on the well-known works of V. Ia. Propp and M. Baktin, and focusing on the more reductive and functional aspects of their arguments. Also relevant, merging symbolic, processual, and functional analysis of masquerade, is Natalie Zemon Davis, *Society and Culture in Early Modern France* (Stanford: Stanford University Press, 1975), pp. 97–123.

Notes

Maintain honor from youth onwards

1. I. A. Ivancha and M. S. Koshevarov, "Aleksandr Nikiforovich Zyrianov," *Isetsko-Pyshminskii krai* (Shadrinsk, 1930), pp. 2–3.

2. A. Tret'iakov, "Shadrinskii uezd Permskoi gubernii v sel'skokhoziaistvennom otnoshenii," *ZhMGI*, 1852, pt. 45, no. 12, p. 193.

3. N. Chukmaldin, *Moi vospominaniia* (St. Petersburg, 1899), p. 60.

4. N. Popov, *Khoziaistvennoe opisanie Permskoi gubernii* (Perm', 1804), pt. 2, p. 338.

5. Tret'iakov, "Shadrinskii uezd," p. 193.

6. GANO, f. 100, op. 1, d. 22, l. 631.

7. P. Shkoldin, "Khoziaistvenno-statisticheskoe opisanie Burlinskoi volosti," *ZhZMOSKh*, 1863, bk. 1, p. 41.

8. Chukmaldin, *Moi vospominaniia*, p. 66.

9. *Permskii sbornik* (Moscow, 1860), bk. 2, p. 179.

10. TF GATiumO, f. 181, op. 1, d. 45, l. 7; TsGADA, f. 1402, op. 1, d. 33, l. 429.

11. TsGADA, f. 1401, op. 1, d. 22, l. 427-ob.

12. K. Golodnikov, "Ialutorovskii okrug gubernii Tobol'skoi," *ZhMVD*, 1846, pt. 16, pp. 516–17; Popov, "Sloboda Takmytskan," *Tobol'skie gub. vedomosti*, 1866, no. 9, p. 58.

13. M. F. Krivoshapkin, *Eniseiskii okrug i ego zhizn'* (St. Petersburg, 1865), vol. 1, p. 44.

14. *Permskii sbornik* (Moscow, 1859), bk. 1, p. 126.

15. V. Verbitskii, "Piataia sotnia oblastnykh slov, upotrebliaemykh prialtaiskimi zhiteliami," *Tomskie gub. vedomosti*, 1863, no. 26, p. 149.

16. F. Zobnin, "Ust'-Nitsynskaia sloboda Tiumenskogo uezda Tobol'skoi gubernii," *ZhS*, 1989, no. 2, p. 152.

17. N. A. Kostrov, *Iuridicheskie obychai krest'ian-starozhilov Tomskoi gubernii* (Tomsk, 1876), p. 53.

18. Chukmaldin, *Moi vospominaniia*, p. 59.

19. Ibid., pp. 53–54.

20. S. Turbin, *Strana izgnaniia i ischeznuvshie liudi* (St. Petersburg, 1872), p. 36.

21. *Permskii sbornik*, bk. 1, p. 123.

22. Popov, "Sloboda Takmytskaia," no. 6, p. 34.

23. TsGIA, f. 1376, op. 1, d. 35, l. 1–1-ob.; *Permskii sbornik*, bk. 1, p. 123.

24. Kostrov, *Iuridicheskie obychai*, p. 81.

25. TsGADA, f. 1402, op. 1, d. 34, l. 382–82-ob.; d. 33, l. 311; TsGIA, f. 1376, op. 1, d. 29, l. 52–52-ob.

26. GANO, f. 110, op. 1, d. 7, l. 192-ob.

27. Ibid., f. 101, op. 1, d. 24, l. 15–17 ob; TF GATiumO, f. 156, 1762 g., d. 177, l. 196.

28. Chukmaldin, *Moi vospominaniia*, p. 99; A. P. Stepanov, *Eniseiskaia guberniia* (St. Petersburg, 1835), pt. 2, p. 110.

29. P. I. Nebol'sin, "Zametki na puti iz Peterburga v Barnaul," *Otechestv. zap.*, 1849, vol. 64, p. 178.

30. TF GATiumO, f. 156, 1762 g., d. 177, l. 195–95-ob., 197; 1763 g., d. 134, l. 77.

31. T. Uspenskii, "Ocherk iugo-zapadnoi poloviny Shadrinskogo uezda," *Permskii sbornik*, bk. 1, pp. 38–39.

Village book-lovers

1. T. S. Mamsik, "Iz istorii razvitiia gramotnosti v zapadno-sibirskoi derevne (po materialam sudebnykh del pervoi poloviny XIX v.)," *Kul'turno-bytovye protsessy u russkikh Sibiri XVIII–nachala XX v.* (Novosibirsk, 1985), p. 106.

2. Gryts'ko, "O Sibiri," *Sovremennik*, 1858, vol. 72, p. 190.

3. See *Krest'ianstvo Sibiri v epokhu feodalizma* (Novosibirsk, 1982), p. 415; Iu. S. Bulygin, "Nekotorye voprosy kul'tury pripisnoi derevni Kolyvano-Voskresenskikh gornykh zavodov XVIII v.," *Krest'ianstvo Sibiri XVIII–nachala XX v.* (Novosibirsk, 1975), p. 66; N. A. Minenko, *Istoriia kul'tury russkogo krest'ianstva Sibiri v period feodalizma* (Novosibirsk, 1986), pp. 5–22.

4. Gryts'ko, "O Sibiri," p. 189; AGO, razr. 61, op. 1, d. 6, l. 56-ob.

5. TsGIA, f. 1264, op. 1, d. 206, l. 4–4-ob.

6. Mamsik, "Iz istorii razvitiia gramotnosti," p. 105.

7. Chukmaldin, *Moi vospominaniia*, pp. 6–7.

8. E. I. Dergacheva-Skop and E. K. Romodanovskaia, "Sobranie rukopisnykh knig Gosudarstvennogo arkhiva Tiumenskoi oblasti v Tobol'ske," *Arkheografiia i istochnikovedenie Sibiri*

(Novosibirsk, 1975), p. 118.
9. Ibid., p. 126.
10. A. A. Preobrazhenskii, *Ural i Zapadnaia Sibir' v kontse XVI–nachale XVIII veka* (Moscow, 1972), pp. 127–28.
11. Chukmaldin, *Moi vospominaniia*, p. 7.
12. Dergacheva-Skop and Romodanovskaia, "Sobranie rukopisnykh knig," pp. 100, 132.
13. Ibid., p. 126.
14. D. Smyshliaev, "Lzheuchitel' Menzelin," *Sbornik statei o Permskoi gubernii* (Perm', 1891), pp. 185–86.
15. *Ocherki russkoi literatury Sibiri* (Novosibirsk, 1982), vol. 1, pp. 162–63.
16. Bulygin, "Nekotorye voprosy kul'tury," p. 69.
17. Chukmaldin, *Moi vospominaniia*, pp. 16–18.
18. D. Smyshliaev, *Sbornik statei o Permskoi gubernii* (Perm', 1891), pp. 280–83.
19. A. Dmitriev, *Pisatel'-samouchka Aleksandr Nikiforovich Zyrianov* (Kazan', 1885), p. 4.
20. Ibid., p. 15.
21. *Permskii sbornik* (Moscow, 1860), bk. 2, pp. 38–39.
22. Smyshliaev, *Sbornik statei*, p. 282; *Permskii sbornik*, bk. 2, pp. 38–39.
23. Dmitriev, *Pisatel'-samouchka*, p. 15.
24. N. D. Zol'nikova, "Opisanie knig kirillovskoi pechati XVI–XVII vv. (sobranie IIFF SO AN SSSR)," *Pamiatniki literatury i obshchestvennoi mysli epokhi feodalizma* (Novosibirsk, 1985), p. 183.
25. Chukmaldin, *Moi vospominaniia*, pp. 6, 17.
26. N. N. Pokrovskii, *Puteshestvie za redkimi knigami* (Moscow, 1984), p. 45.
27. TF GATiumO, f. 156, 1799 g., d. 102, l. 9–10.
28. Shkoldin, "Khoziaistvenno–statisticheskoe opisanie," p. 41.
29. Chukmaldin, *Moi vospominaniia*, p. 28.

"To My Dear Friend . . . "

1. All quotations from letters cited in the chapter are taken from the following archive files: TsGADA, f. 1401, op. 1, d. 32, l. 881–881-ob., 884-ob.; d. 31, l. 122; d. 36, l. 83; d. 38, l. 284–284-ob.; d. 43, l. 73–74; d. 48, l. 904–906-ob.; d. 44, l. 118–a-ob.; TF GATiumO, f. 156, 1797 g., d. 99, l. 58-ob.–59-ob.; GATiumO, f. 47, op. 1, d. 4738, l. 3–5; GANO, f. 109, op. 1, d. 8, l. 153–153-ob; f. 105, op. 1, d. 30, l. 22.
2. Chukmaldin, *Moi vospominaniia*, pp. 45–46.
3. GANO, f. 110, op. 1, d. 12, l. 122–123-ob.
4. GATiumO, f. 47, op. 1, d. 4738, l. 3–5.
5. TF GATiumO, f. 156, 1797 g., d. 99, l. 57.
6. Ibid., 1787 g., d. 41, l. 2-ob., 11.
7. Ibid., 1750 g., d. 104, l. 1–3-ob.; 1769 g., d. 65, l. 1–6-ob.

Folk curers and sorcerers

1. K. Golodnikov, "Ialutorovskii okrug gubernii Tobol'skoi," *ZhMVD*, 1846, pt. 15, pp. 511–12.
2. TF GATiumO, f. 152, op. 41, d. 50, l. 39–41-ob.
3. [No initials in Russian text] Nadezhdinskii, "Narodnoe zdravie," *Tobol'skie gub. vedomosti*, 1863, no. 44, p. 375.
4. GANO, f. 78, op. 1, d. 2, l. 33.
5. T. Popov, "Sloboda Takmytskaia," *Tobol'skie gub. vedomosti*, 1864, no. 7, pp. 39–40.
6. TF GATiumO, f. 152, op. 41, d. 58, l. 42.
7. Nadezhdinskii, "Narodnoe zdravie," *Tobol'skie gub. vedomosti*, 1863, no. 48, p. 418.
8. Ibid., no. 21, p. 160.
9. Ibid., no. 20, pp. 153–55.
10. N. A. Kostrov, "Koldovstvo i porcha mezhdu krest'ianami Tomskoi gubernii," *Zapiski Zap.-Sib. otd. RGO* (Omsk, 1879), bk. 1, pp. 5–12.
11. Chukmaldin, *Moi vospominaniia*, pp. 47–50.

12. Nadezhdinskii, "Narodnoe zdravie," *Tobol'skie gub. vedomosti*, 1864, no. 21, p. 164.
13. Ibid., 1863, no. 44, pp. 375–76.
14. Ibid., 1864, no. 24, p. 187.
15. Ibid., 1863, no. 48, p. 420.
16. TF GATiumO, f. 156, 1767 g., d. 82, l. 2–15-ob.
17. Ibid., 1754 g., d. 72, p. 1-ob.–24.
18. Uspenskii, "Ocherk iugo-zapadnoi poloviny Shadrinskogo uezda," p. 12.
19. Shkoldin, "Khoziaistvenno-statisticheskoe opisanie," p. 37.
20. N. M. Iadrintsev, "Poezdka po Zapadnoi Sibiri i v Gornyi Altaiskii okrug," *Zapiski Zap.-Sib. otd. RGO* (Omsk, 1880), bk. 2, pp. 31–32.
21. AGO, razr. 61, op. 1, d. 10, l. 7.
22. G. N. Potanin, "Polgoda v Altae," *Russkoe slovo*, 1859, no. 12, p. 298.
23. N. Abramov, "Gorod Ialutorovsk s ego okrugom," *Tobol'skie gub. vedomosti*, 1864, no. 27, p. 219.
24. V. Verbitskii, "Predrassudki i sueveriia prialtaiskikh krest'ian," *Tomskie gub. vedomosti*, 1863, no. 12, p. 55.
25. LO AAN, f. 21, op. 5, d. 150, l. 17-ob.–18.
26. *Puteshestvie po raznym mestam Rossiiskogo gosudarstva* (St. Petersburg, 1786), pt. 2, bk. 2, pp. 24–25.
27. Ibid., p. 10.
28. N. Abramov, "Reka Tobol s ee pritokami," *Tobol'skie gub. vedomosti*, 1863, no. 3, p. 11.
29. LO AAN, f. 21, op. 5, d. 150, l. 70.
30. N. Cherniakovskii, "Statisticheskoe opisanie Ishimskogo okruga Tobol'skoi gubernii," *ZhMVD*, 1843, pt. 2, pp. 241–42.
31. Iadrintsev, "Poezdka po Zapadnoi Sibiri," p. 32.
32. Nadezhdinskii, "Narodnoe zdravie," *Tobol'skie gub. vedomosti*, 1863, no. 48, p. 421.
33. Shkoldin, "Khoziaistvenno-statisticheskoe opisanie," p. 42.
34. Ibid.
35. Potanin, "Polgoda v Altae," p. 299.
36. Abramov, "Gorod Ialutorovsk," p. 219.
37. Ibid., pp. 218–20.
38. Ibid., p. 219.
39. Krivoshapkin, *Eniseiskii okrug i ego zhizn'*, vol. 2, pp. 2–3.
40. Ibid., p. 3.
41. Ibid.
42. Verbitskii, "Predrassudki i sueveriia," p. 56.
43. Iu. V. Bromlei and A. A. Voronov, "Narodnaia meditsina kak predmet etnograficheskikh issledovanii," *SE*, 1976, no. 5, pp. 13–14.

Popular amusements

1. I. Belov, *Putevye zametki i vpechatleniia po Zapadnoi Sibiri* (Moscow, 1852), p. 11.
2. S. I. Guliaev, "Etnograficheskie ocherki Iuzhnoi Sibiri," *Biblioteka dlia chteniia*, 1848, vol. 90, p. 60.
3. Potanin, G. N., "Iugo-zapadnaia chast' Tomskoi gubernii v etnograficheskom otnoshenii," *Etnograficheskii sbornik* (St. Petersburg, 1864), issue 6, p. 81.
4. AGO, razr. 55, op. 1, d. 53, l. 2–2-ob.; razr. 62, op. 1, d. 4, l. 2; d. 8, l. 22-ob.; Guliaev, "Etnograficheskie ocherki," p. 60; M. M. Gromyko, *Trudovye traditsii russkikh krest'ian Sibiri (XVIII–pervaia polovina XIX v.)* (Novosibirsk, 1975), p. 328.
5. Guliaev, "Etnograficheskie ocherki," p. 60.
6. Potanin, "Iugo-zapadnaia chast' Tomskoi gubernii," pp. 60–61.
7. Guliaev, "Etnograficheskie ocherki," p. 63.
8. Ibid., pp. 65–66.
9. Ibid., pp. 69–70.
10. AGO, razr. 55, op. 1, d. 53, l. 2-ob.–3.
11. Ibid., razr. 62, op. 1, d. 8, l. 22-ob.
12. "Zhivopisnoe puteshestvie po Azii (Moscow, 1839), vol. 1, p. 30.

13. Gromyko, *Trudovye traditsii*, pp. 79–80; Guliaev, "Etnograficheskie ocherki," p. 60, 62–81; AGO, razr. 61, op. 1, d. 23, l. 47-ob.; Potanin, "Polgoda v Altae," p. 266.

14. N. P. Grigorovskii, "Krest'iane-starozhily Narymskogo kraia," *Zapiski Zap.-Sib. otd. RGO* (Omsk, 1879), bk. 1, pp. 16–17, 25; D. K. Zelenin, *Opisanie rukopisei uchenogo arkhiva RGO* (Petrograd, 1916), issue 3, p. 1039.

15. Grigorovskii, "Krest'iane-starozhily," p. 17.

16. Popov, "Sloboda Takmytskaia," *Tobol'skie gub. vedomosti*, 1866, no. 9, p. 58.

17. Shkoldin, "Khoziaistvenno-statisticheskoe opisanie," pp. 46–47.

18. Ibid., pp. 40–41.

19. Popov, "Sloboda Takmytskaia," p. 58.

20. K. Golodnikov, "Ialutorovskii okrug gubernii Tobol'skoi," *ZhMVD*, 1846, pt. 15, pp. 516–17.

21. Shkoldin, "Khoziaistvenno-statisticheskoe opisanie," p. 41.

22. AGO, razr. 61, op. 1, d. 10, l. 3–3-ob.

23. Stepanov, *Eniseiskaia guberniia*, p. 102.

24. Chukmaldin, *Moi vospominaniia*, p. 59.

25. N. A. Kostrov, "Sviatki v Minusinskom okruge Eniseiskoi gubernii," *Zap. Sib. otd. RGO* (St. Petersburg, 1858), bk. 5, pp. 26–33.

26. Kh. Loparev, *Samarovo selo Tobol'skoi gubernii i okruga* (St. Petersburg, 1896), p. 120.

27. Krivoshapkin, *Eniseiskii okrug i ego zhizn'*, vol. 2, pp. 39, 47.

28. Loparev, *Samarovo selo*, p. 142.

29. Krivoshapkin, *Eniseiskii okrug*, pp. 41–42.

30. AGO, razr. 62, op. 1, d. 8, l. 22–22-ob.

31. TF GATiumO, f. 156, 1761 g., d. 67, l. 1–2.

32. AGO, razr. 62, op. 1, d. 8, l. 22 ob–23.

33. A. Shirokov, "Sibirskii karnaval," *Maiak*, 1844, vol. 17, pp. 51–55.

34. Gromyko, *Trudovye traditsii*, pp. 100–11.

35. Potanin, "Polgoda v Altae," p. 259.

36. Shirokov, "Sibirskii karnaval," p. 53.

37. Popov, "Sloboda Takmytskaia," p. 58.

38. Shirokov, "Sibirskii karnaval," pp. 53–54.

39. Stepanov, *Eniseiskaia guberniia*, p. 114.

40. AGO, razr. 61, op. 1, d. 23, l. 49–49-ob.

41. Shirokov, "Sibirskii karnaval," p. 50.

42. Loparev, *Samarovo selo*, p. 136.

43. P. A. Slovtsov, *Progulki vokrug Tobol'ska* (Moscow, 1834), p. 39.

44. V. Ia. Propp, *Problemy komizma i smekha* (Moscow, 1976), p. 140.

45. AGO, razr. 61, op. 1, d. 10, l. 5-ob.

46. M. Bakhtin, *Tvorchestvo Fransua Rable i narodnaia kul'tura srednevekov'ia i Renessansa* (Moscow, 1965), p. 12.

47. TsGADA, f. 1402, op. 1, d. 18, l. 87; d. 19, l. 327–28.

48. Uspenskii, "Ocherk iugo-zapadnoi poloviny Shadrinskogo uezda," p. 36.

49. Guliaev, "Etnograficheskie ocherki," p. 60.

50. Kh. Mozel', *Materialy dlia geografii i statistiki Rossii. Permskaia guberniia* (St. Petersburg, 1864), pt. 2, p. 540.

51. Popov, "Sloboda Takmytskaia," p. 58.

52. AGO, razr. 66, op. 1, d. 1, l. 4.

53. Ibid., razr. 62, op. 1, d. 8, l. 23.

54. GANO, f. 105, op. 1, d. 8, l. 186.

55. AGO, razr. 61, op. 1, d. 23, l. 49; TsGIA, f. 1290, op. 4, d. 1, l. 21.

56. Chukmaldin, *Moi vospominaniia*, p. 87.

57. F. Zobnin, "Iz goda v god (Opisanie krugovorota krest'ianskoi zhizni v s. Ust'-Nitsynskom Tiumenskogo okruga)," *ZhS*, 1894, issue 1, p. 53.

58. I. Meves, "Tri goda v Sibiri i Amurskoi strane," *Otechestv. zap.*, 1863, vol. 148, bk. 5, p. 258.

59. S. Guliaev, "O sibirskikh krugovykh pesniakh," *Otechestv. zap.*, 1839, vol. 111, no. 5, p. 58.

60. Loparev, *Samarovo selo*, p. 130.

61. AGO, razr. 55, op. 1, d. 36, l. 3 ob–4.

62. Iadrintsev, "Poezdka po Zapadnoi Sibiri," pp. 65–66.
63. Kostrov, *Iuridicheskie obychai*, pp. 8–9.
64. AGO, razr. 65, op. 1, d. 36, l. 1–1-ob.
65. Loparev, *Samarovo selo*, p. 136.
66. Chukmaldin, *Moi vospominaniia*, pp. 28–30.
67. Loparev, *Samarovo selo*, p. 134; AGO, pazr. 55, op. 1, d. 36, l. 2-ob.
68. Iadrintsev, "Poezdka po Zapadnoi Sibiri," p. 101.
69. AGO, razr. 55, op. 1, d. 36, l. 1 ob–2.
70. Ibid., l. 2–2-ob.
71. Loparev, *Samarovo selo*, p. 136.
72. *Tobol'skie gub. vedomosti*, 1866, no. 1, pp. 2–4; no. 2, pp. 3–5; no. 3, pp. 3–5.

Traditional Norms of Behavior and Forms of Interaction of Nineteenth-century Russian Peasants

M. M. Gromyko

Community and reputation. Public opinion

The solving of a number of problems at community meetings depended on the reputation of the peasant. The otherwise latent mechanism of public opinion appeared in blatant form during discussions of the misdeeds of community members at the meeting. Thus, when appointing a ward for an orphan, the question of the moral character of a candidate was raised. The choice of the ward depended entirely on the community. "The community collective [*mir*] has the right to remove from the wardship not only close relatives, but even a mother, when a mother or relatives are 'unreliable' or 'worthless' people," wrote a correspondent from Viazemsk *uezd*, for example.[75] The same appraisal by the community can be found in a report from Poshekhonsk *uezd*:[a] if there is a close relative, but "he is an unreliable person," another person may be appointed ward "by order of the community and the *volost'* authorities."[76] Poor peasants were chosen as wards at the rural gathering "if the community was sure of their incorruptible honor," reports an informant from Vologodsk *uezd*.[77] V. V. Tenishev, summarizing the information about wardship sent to his agency from various provinces, noted the importance in the eyes of the community of the moral character of the persons selected as guardians. A. A. Lebedeva found that the community exercised control over the behavior of the guardian among Russian peasants of the eastern Baikal area.[78]

According to a report from a correspondent in Ust'-Pudozhsk parish (Vel'sk *uezd*), during an examination of theft at a community meeting, a person who had stolen for the first time and under the influence of another person was treated leniently by the peasants. Furthermore, the treatment of

Russian text © 1986 by "Nauka" Publishers. *Traditsionnye normy povedeniia i formy obshcheniia russkikh krest'ian XIX v.* (Moscow: Nauka, 1986), pp. 105–13, 115–17. A publication of the N. N. Miklukho-Maklai Institute of Ethnography, USSR Academy of Sciences.

the victim also depended largely on his reputation in the village.[79]

An opinion declared openly and definitely at the meeting had taken shape gradually in the community. The everyday routine of the *mir* provided sufficient material for neighbors to form their judgments. In this respect, evidently, the community was a rather flexible mechanism: a reputation, even one fixed by documents at a meeting, could be changed: "If it were noted that a guardian is making use of the estate in some way, this would be reported to the community, which would immediately remove him and select a new guardian."[80] A change in the reputation that one had established in the community was also reflected in meeting verdicts (in the language of the documents themselves, the "commune verdicts" or *"mir* verdicts"), involving the removal of previously elected persons. The election of any official person or group of persons was accompanied by the delivery of a verdict (occasionally an "election"), including the reason for the selection—a positive description of the elected person, a kind of "formula of confidence."[81] The term "formula" is appropriate here in view of the recurring stereotypical characteristics found in one document after another. Being conventional, the formulas of confidence do not provide information on the specific reasons for the preference given to one peasant or another. Yet they are of certain interest as a generalized expression of the qualities deemed essential to an elected official: "Of good behavior, thrifty in his household, experienced in grain-growing, never punished or fined, and able beyond doubt to fulfill the duty entrusted to him"; "of wholly good and sober behavior, never brought to trial"; "not younger than twenty-five and completely honest, never arrested or brought to trial";[82] and so on. Not uncommonly the formulas of the verdicts would be copied from specimens of official documentation, but the latter (in turn) represented the views of the peasants.

Each person elected received a formula of confidence of this type, but when certain of them were replaced (the headman, for example, was replaced frequently) the commune would find itself compelled to hold special elections "on account of untrustworthiness" of the previously elected person, or "because of ineptitude in management" or "inactivity in duty," and so on. These deficiencies became evident during the term of office of the elected person, and the commune responded appropriately. "Of course, these motivations do not always reveal the true causes of reelections; however, their wide distribution indicates a kind of tradition."[83] Another aspect of this was the practice of "honorary reelections of the headman to a new term and incentives in the form of salary bonus."[84]

Another incentive was the flattering description drawn up in a certificate and issued to elected officials their term of office was completed. We present one such document in its entirety: "This certificate issued by the Biisk *volost'* administration to Leontii Fedorov Fefelov, headman in the *volost'* in

1820, in view of the fact that he conducted himself properly in the exercise of this function, behaved graciously, respectfully, and indulgently with his subordinates, observed the duty of the oath in trials, presented to the government the recruits designated from this *volost'* and handed over both the recruits themselves and the appropriate clothing and footwear for them and other sums assessed in due order, offered offense to no one and no one has made a complaint against him, wherefore he has earned the rightful gratitude of the community, and will henceforth be accepted as a man of worthy honor in the *mir* communities, in affirmation of which we affix our seals, January 8, 1821."[85]

The opinion of the community regarding certain of their members active in civil affairs is also attested in warrants issued in connection with the need to solicit or exert oneself in a certain matter on behalf of the community. These documents also expressed the fact that a particular person was entrusted with acting on behalf of the community in a particular matter, and usually the nature of the affair.

The relationship with the person entrusted was expressed, for example, as follows: "We trust you in everything, and what you do in future, we shall not dispute or deny, your obedient servants, as we subscribe hereto."[86]

The functions of the person trusted (commissioned) by the community were often vested for a lengthy time in certain people by virtue of their literacy, activity, ability to handle themselves in a strange environment, willingness to sacrifice for the community, etc. They would be called to this duty for different reasons. In any case, the same persons entrusted by the community usually handled the same affair for several years (repeatedly submitting petitions, pleading in various courts, etc.). The affairs in which peasants enjoying the appropriate reputation submitted petitions on behalf of the entire community could be of the most diverse kind—from questions of land use to authorization to build a church with community funds.[87] If authorities found the behavior of a community to be seditious, it was the entrusted persons who were first called to account.

The reputation of the peasant was also judged in the authorizations for a *pokormezhnyi* [local rule] passport, issued by the community (the passport itself was issued by the *volost'* authorities on the basis of the authorization). He was attested "of good condition and behavior, not heretofore punished or fined, a quiet neighbor and a person worthy of every trust."[88]

The peasants clearly understood the importance of public opinion. Immoral actions were brought before the judgment of the *mir* not only by direct discussion at the gathering,[89] but also in other forms of appeal to the neighbors. We shall take up several of these below in connection with youth assemblies. Basically, any kind of large gathering in the village (from a christening to a wake and from a circle dance to a help session) could serve as a forum for an appeal to public opinion. Artistic forms were widely used to present a claim; most peasants were adept at many folklore forms and were able to improvise within a particular genre. A claim presented in the traditional folklore form, appropriate to the circumstances, would be suitable where a direct attack "in public" was entirely impossible.

Of great interest in this respect are the materials involving wailing or lamenting [*vyt'e*] for the deceased. Not only the relatives, but also the neighbors wailed (keened). Wailing was considered a tribute of respect and love for the deceased. From the number of wailing women who were not relatives, one could determine the relations of the deceased with his neighbors. "There are times when the entire village wails, but also times when no one will open her mouth."[90] But not only was a reputation long formed and now culminated presented at the funeral: it was also possible to act directly on public opinion regarding the living. "Sometimes a lamentation for the deceased serves as a pretext to discomfit one's enemies 'in public'; this is done especially often by young women suffering real or imagined offenses in the family of the husband, from her mother-in-law, etc. A woman may come to a wake, stand beside the deceased, mourn, gather her courage, and begin to tell the entire god-fearing community (it must be remembered that the cabin is full of people) in the presence of her enemies everything that has built up inside her, and they can only squirm with anger and silently swallow the bitter pill." A correspondent presented the text of one such keening. It is noteworthy that the observer described this as a common occurrence.[91]

The reputation of young men and women found a reflection, in particular, in the vaunting songs performed in the circle dance, and these songs in turn created and strengthened certain elements of reputation. For example, in a number of *volosty* of Orlovsk and Karachaevsk *uezdy*, the dancing songs [*khovorody*] singled out a girl who was able to *lead* the dance—to go in front as the dance was moving through the streets: "Who among us, who among us will lead the circle dance? Who among us will go in front? There is here, there is here, oh!, the pretty girl Arina Alekseevna! She it is, she it is who will lead our circle dance; go through the entire street";[92] and so on. Other songs of the circle dance expressed more serious aspects of public opinion, e.g., the attitude toward a choice of a bride or groom (we shall discuss this below).

The degree of mastery of work skills played an important role in reputation forming. We have already touched on this matter in speaking of the ethical traditions in work processes. Individual capabilities—cleverness, dexterity, strength, talent in certain operations—were displayed at the communal hay mowing, *pomochi*, and other collective chores. Furthermore, an opinion as to the ability of almost every community member in household affairs in general or in a particular aspect was also formed on the basis of labor performance. This prevailed not only in major economic matters but also in secondary (yet important to the reputation) affairs. Thus, an opinion of a girl as a hard worker, invariably relevant in the choice of a bride,[93] was formed both by watching her work and indirectly from the product—everyone could behold her homespun clothing, her intricately embroidered holiday dress. In some places, community women attended special viewings of needlework, especially at "exhibits" of potential brides, and also at the *perebaski*—competitions in fine attire at a girl's home.[94]

Adolescents were early taught various kinds of work. Those who did not possess skill appropriate to their age (according to local opinion) were scorned. The continual exercise of public opinion in this form is indicated by mocking nicknames for the maladroit, which became a permanent part of common speech. Those unable to weave bast sandals [*lapti*] were laughed at and called *bezlapotniki* (boys began to learn this skill at age sixteen— materials from the villages Radomin', Savinok, and Melovoi, Orlovskii province). A peasant who could not weave sandals was considered the lowest of humans.[95]

Girls who did not learn how to spin at the proper time (eleven years old in this locality) were called *nepriakhi*; those who could not weave *krosny* (taught at age fifteen or sixteen)—*nitkakhi*; those who could not set up a loom [*stan*] by themselves "without prompting from their mother" (at age seventeen)—*bespodstavochnye*.[96] Those who were last in performance of certain kinds of collective chores also received mocking nicknames. Thus, the last to carry manure into the field was known as the "laggard" [*kila*], "old woman-cabbage" [*babushka-rozhenitsa*], "leftovers" [*poskrebenia*], or "mop" [*pomelo*]; sometimes the nickname would remain the entire year: "This year's *kila* are you—you will be last the whole year."[97]

"In demanding from each person certain personal aptitudes, public opinion exalted those who brought favor not only to themselves, but also use to others," observed L. M. Saburova, who investigated the culture and daily life of the Russian population of Angara Region. "This can be seen in community attitudes toward those who knew and preserved the precepts of the folk calendar, which was an essential guide in the productive life of the peasants. . . . All peasants knew the most general facts from the popular calendar, but only a few had systematic knowledge in this area. Such people were widely known to the surrounding population, who resorted to them in cases of need."[98]

Attendance at church and appropriate performance of all religious prescriptions played a major role in the formation of individual reputations. Not only the elders in a family but the entire community would watch to see that youngsters did not miss especially important church services. The neighbors would tell a mother if her son "was lazy" in going to mass.[99]

In the system of individual reputations in the countryside, some people were known to display a tendency and aptitude to play permanent parts in calendrical or familial rituals, holiday entertainments, etc. Thus, in Salomykova village (Oboiansk *uezd*, Kursk province), two peasants had a reputation as jokers and tellers of tales [*okazniki, vygadniki*]. At Shrovetide, one of them would put on an old woman's *sarafan* or *saian*, a crone's sheepskin jacket and kerchief; hitching up a horse to a toboggan, he stretched an old horsecloth across them and drove down the street, sometimes giving a ride to children. The other made a dummy [*maiak*] of straw—"like a man"; he clothed this anthropomorphic doll with a *saian*, shirt, and kerchief, and drove with it through the street, acting out scenes and fighting with the *maiak*.[100]

G. S. Vinogradov also wrote about such fooler-buffoons [*chudiki*] and clown–tale-tellers [*balagury*]:[b] "In the holiday and ordinary existence of the people they play a remarkable role: they help to fill the idle hours, they brighten the winter housework."[101] In each community, the actors of the main roles in the Shrovetide carnival, the leaders of the Christmas processions, and the leaders of the circle dances were well known. "To perform the main role in the Shrovetide ritual they usually invite a peasant who is experienced in work and has a good knowledge of all details of the rite," wrote N. A. Gorodtsov about the Russian peasants of Tiumen' *uezd*. "Such a peasant should be a good folk curer, teller of tales, and singer of popular songs and verses."[102]

The assignment of a ritual role to a particular person was most prominent in the case of the wedding *druzhka*. "The *druzhka* is especially proficient in all rituals in their customary sequence. It is incumbent on him to direct the entire course of the wedding; he should be a kind of folk curer in the good meaning of this term, i.e., know how to ward off evil spells. He is an extremely lively person, and his various unexpected actions and pranks should inspire fear and respect for him. He considers everything possible," remarked M. F. Krivoshapkin on the basis of observations in Enisei Region in the 1860s.[103]

The *druzhka* was usually a gifted person, possessing acting talent, organizational abilities, a knowledge of many folklore texts and, in certain localities, the reputation of a witch [*vedun*].[104] Not only did he guide the performance of all elements of the wedding ritual over several days and himself play the leading role, but he also possessed in the eyes of the peasants of his community a kind of supernatural power, allowing him to work magic and protect the bride and groom, and afterwards the newlyweds, against possible attacks of evil forces (in particular, the workings of sorcerers).

Sometimes the performance of the functions of a bride's and groom's matchmaker (one or two of each), or that of *poludruzhka* (the *druzhka's* helper) and certain other wedding officiants was assigned to certain people in the village. In some regions, special verse-leaders [*stikhovodnitsy*] or dance-leaders [*khorovodnitsy*], who knew the entire program that was to be performed by the bride and her maids, were invited to the weddings. "The verse-leader is an ordinary (married) woman, smart and experienced, who had attended many weddings in her time and, therefore, knew the subtleties in all the rites of weeping and verses, i.e., how the bride should bewail forfeiting her maidenhood, her free life, and what kind of tirade should be pronounced on this occasion."[105] Such a woman—an expert in local folklore and rituals—would service several villages. For example, in the 1870s, there were no more than three or four verse-leaders "for the entire Onega."[106] The matchmakers, verse-leaders, and wedding directors essentially exercised community control over the observance of traditions in familial rituals.

The stable personification of roles in calendrical and familial rituals was one of the means by which the community preserved its ethical traditions. Such peasants were a living embodiment of tradition, the wardens of custom and custodians of standards.

One of the individual carriers of ethical traditions in the community was, beyond question, the "community nanny," whose characterization as pertains to the Russian North was given by K. V. Chistov. He remarked that, in many villages, this title was carried by "women who considered it their duty to help everyone in need—orphans, the sick, a family that had suffered a calamity, a recently widowed young woman, a recruit going off to the army. Often these were lonely old women, but not exclusively; some were young women with their own families, burdened with their own concerns. The community repaid them in the same way, sharing earnings with the nannies—fish, fresh meat, mushrooms or berries, mown hay, sometimes just a bowl of milk or a scrap of bread. These offerings were not intended as payment for service or as a handout; such treatment of the nanny was considered impolite. What she did was done selflessly, and her recompense was a voluntary offering. Those who could not afford to, gave nothing."[107]

Among the personal carriers of tradition were the midwife[108] and the dream-interpreter. "Dream books are not popular among the peasants," reported an informant from Chal'sko-Darsk *volost'*, Gzhatsk *uezd*, "since each village has an old woman who interprets dreams. Some of these fortunetellers enjoy much popularity not only in their own village, but also in the entire surrounding area."[109]

Public opinion enduringly assigned to certain people the reputation of folk curer, witch, or sorcerer. The sorcerer was considered to be a bearer of evil power, who was able to blight a person, cause sickness in animals, and damage grain. In peasant conception, a sorcerer contrasted with the curer, who was an expert in folk medicines and a veterinarian, using herbs and other means of curing accompanied by prayers or incantations (often improvising on familiar prayers). It was commonly believed that the folk curer was able to resist evil forces.[110] Such a reputation usually went beyond the village.[111] The reputation of the virtuous peasant-hermit, dwelling on the edge of the village, spread far and wide. Leading a virtuous life, according to popular opinion, he gave advice and religious-moral instruction to those who consulted him, and conversed on these themes.[112]

Local civil and church authorities were at times alarmed by the degree of influence held by such peasants in their role of popular preacher. The situation might come up for discussion at the synod. For example, the question of a peasant in Kaluberov village, Cherepovetsk *uezd*, Novgorod province, brought up by the local police officer and the priest, was first examined by the governor, who in turn consulted the Ministry of Internal Affairs, which in turn gave it to the synod.[113] This peasant, Fedor Ivanovich Serov—as is evident from the records—was extremely popular in the district, converting dissenters to the Orthodox faith. In his *volost'* alone, he converted thirteen people, "to say nothing of outsiders." The synod, troubled by widespread schism in Cherepovsetsk *uezd*, resolved not to interfere with Serov's activities. Archpriest Petr Fedotovskii of Cherepovetsk Cathedral was instructed to "test" the peasant in his moral qualities and knowledge of the religious dogma,[114] after which Serov was authorized to convert the schismatics, but in the form of "private admonition," and not publicly. He was sent books of theological content that he had requested, as he could not find them at the local priest's.[115]

The reputation of the storyteller [*skazitel'*] was firmly rooted in the community and beyond. Considerable material has been gathered on this, since the "issue of the personality of the storyteller, first raised by P. N. Rybnikov in 'Observation of a Collector,' and then by A. F. Gil'ferding in the article 'Olonetskaia Province and Its Rhapsodies' (1873), has not been overlooked by a single collector or student of folklore. N. E. Onchukov, D. K. Zelenin, Iu. M. Sokolov, and B. M. Sokolov have presented a vivid picture of this issue and provided copious material for observations."[116]

Thanks to biographies of renowned storytellers, it is possible to trace a series of steps whereby a peasant endowed with a poetic gift was assigned to the steady permanent enactment of this function in the community. For example, I. A. Fedosova was first noticed among the other girls for her ability to make up songs. The songs would be remembered and became popular. At gatherings where young people acted out weddings, Irina began to hold forth "for the fun of it." When it happened that the neighbors had no one to perform the function of "lamenter" at a wedding, they thought of Fedosova, as she had "made herself known" (in her own words) at the gatherings, i.e., her reputation as a performer was first formed there. It was necessary for the community to exert pressure on her parents in order for her to perform the function at a genuine wedding. "Mother does not dare allow it," she told E. V. Barsov. "The *volost'* scribe was a relative of the bride, and he came to me and said: 'If you consent, we will convince your father, we will not let you be scolded or punished.' I consented and the wedding was held. Next spring, they invited me to another wedding. Father said: 'Why invite her? She doesn't know anything.' 'What do you mean? She performed for a neighbor in the winter.' Father became angry: 'Who allowed it?' 'The clerk Petr Kondrat'evich,' answered Mother, 'and the headman Aleksei Andreevich.' 'Well, if such people request it, let it be so, it is their business.' From that time on, the girl, still very young, was given 'honor and a place in the great corner,' and her fame soon spread throughout the land beyond the Onega."[117] In the 1860s and 1870s, P. N. Rybnikov still found stories in Kizhsk *volost'* about how a gathering (sometimes even a *volost'* gathering rather than simply a village gathering) asked a storyteller to recount the old ways.[118]

Along with the reputation of an individual in the community, and sometimes beyond its borders, there was also the reputation of a family, which was firmly preserved and sometimes handed down from one generation to another. A factor in selecting a bride, along with her other positive qualities, was that "she was from a good clan, known in the district for its honesty and other good qualities."[119] In Buninsk *volost'*, Bolkhovsk *uezd*, Orlov province, a young man could select his own bride, but the elders tried to undo the marriage "if the bride was from a poor clan or was lazy."[120]

Finally, the community itself had a reputation among the surrounding villages. Characterizations such as "no one is a better host than a Meshkovskii peasant"[121] or "one is reluctant even to talk to your peasants, they stand in church like merchants"[122] would point out features in the traditions of a particular village. But apart from this, there was the evaluation of the village as a whole according to a commonly held scale of moral attributes, and the community often expressed concern about this issue during certain discussions at meetings. In this regard, parents of a girl who had misbehaved were admonished with the following characteristic argument: "the reputation of the other girls in the village will suffer."[123] In the petitions sent to the consistories and synod for construction of new churches (these petitions were sent via the meeting, even in cases when the church was supposed to be built not with community funds but with the money of certain rich peasants) one finds formulations of community duty as concern over the religiosity and morality of its members.[124]

Editor's notes

a. See note a in the excerpt by N. A. Minenko translated here (page 218) concerning administrative regions. Gromyko's endnotes begin with number 75 because this selection is part of a larger work.

b. The fools and clowns described here come from a rich Russian tradition of minstrel-clowns called *skomorokhi*. See Russell Zguta, *Russian Minstrels: A History of the Skomorokhi* (Philadelphia: University of Pennsylvania Press, 1978). For a recreation of a *skomorokh* in action, see the Russian movie *Andrei Rublev*, directed by Andrei Tarkovskii.

Notes

75. GME, f. 7, op. 1, d. 1533, l. 4.

76. Ibid., d. 1762, l. 1.

77. Ibid., d. 121, l. 2.

78. V. V. Tenishev, *Pravosudie v russkom krest'ianskom bytu, svod dannykh, dobytykh etnograficheskimi materialami pokoinogo kniazia V. N. Tenisheva* (Briansk, 1907), pp. 56–57; A. A. Lebedeva, "K istorii formirovaniia russkogo naseleniia Zabaikal'ia, ego khoziaistvennogo i semeinogo byta," in *Etnografiia russkogo naseleniia Sibiri i Srednei Azii*, 1969, p. 164.

79. GME, f. 7, op. 1, d. 105, l. 10–11.

80. GME, f. 7, d. 121, l. 6 (Vologodskii u.). For the replacement of a guardian who has come under suspicion of the community, see d. 1533, l. 2 (Viazemskii u.).

81. M. M. Gromyko, "Territorial'naia krest'ianskaia obshchina Sibiri (30-e gody, XVIII–60-e gody XIX v.)," in *Krest'ianskaia obshchina v Sibiri XVIII–nachala XX v.* (Novosibirsk, 1977), pp. 35–36.

82. GATO, f. 56 (Biiskoe volostnoe pravlenie), op. 1, d. 16, l. 15–16, 18–19-ob. (Tomskaia gub.).

83. G. A. Alekseichenko, "Prigovory sel'skikh skhodov kak istochnik po istorii krest'ianskoi obshchiny v Rossii vtoroi poloviny XIX v.," *Istoriia SSSR*, 1981, no. 6, p. 121.

84. Ibid.

85. GATO, f. 56, op. 1, d. 16, l. 28-ob.

86. TsGIA, f. 383 (Pervyi departament Ministerstva Gosudarstvennykh Imushchestv), op. 4, d. 3121, l. 8–10-ob. (Ialutorovskii u.).

87. TsGIA, f. 796, op. 103, 1828 g., d. 783, l. 1 (Stavropol'skii u., Kavkazskoi gub.); GAOO, f. 3, op. 3, d. 4070, l. 49, l. 69-ob., 79–79-ob. and elsewhere (Sebezhskii u. Vitebskoi gub. and Tarskii okrug Tobol'skoi gub.); Gromyko, "Territorial'naia krest'ianskaia obshchina," pp. 37, 54–55, 83.

88. GATO, f. 61 (Tutal'skoe volostnoe pravlenie), op. 1, d. 18, l. 48–48-ob. (Tomskaia gub.).

89. N. A. Minenko, "Obshchina i russkaia krest'ianskaia sem'ia v iugo-zapadnoi Sibiri (XVIII–pervaia polovina XIX v.)," in *Krest'ianskaia obshchina v Sibiri*, p. 117.

90. GME, f. 7, op. 1, d. 1549, l. 9.

91. Ibid.

92. Ibid., f. 7, op. 1, d. 1082, l. 2–3.

93. Ibid., f. 7, op. 1, d. 510, l. 9 (Zhizdrinskii u. Kaluzhskoi gub.); d. 907, l. 7 (Bolkhovskii u. Orlovskoi gub.), *MGSR*, Kostromskaia gub., p. 501.

94. GME, f. 7, op. 1, d. 104, l. 2 Esiutinskaia ((Vel'skii u. Vologodskaia gub.); d. 117, l. 3–4 (Fetin'inskaia vol. Vologodskii u.).

95. Ibid., f. 7, op. 1, d. 1086, l. 3.

96. Ibid.

97. N. N. Tikhonitskaia, "Sel'skokhoziaistvennaia toloka u russkikh," *SE*, 1934, no. 4, p. 86.

98. L. M. Saburova, *Kul'tura i byt russkogo naseleniia Priangar'ia* (Leningrad, 1967), p. 238.

99. L. A. Anokhina and M. N. Shmeleva, *Kul'tura i byt kolkhoznikov Kalininskoi oblasti* (Moscow, 1964), pp. 237–38; GME, f. 7, op. 1, d. 1563, l. 18; d. 1467, l. 5.

100. GME, f. 7, op. 1, d. 630, l. 44–45. On the deliberate wearing of old things by the driver and the horse in Shrovetide ceremonies in Siberian provinces see M. M. Gromyko, *Trudovye traditsii russkikh krest'ian Sibiri (XVIII–pervaia polovina XIX v.)* (Novosibirsk, 1975), pp. 100–4.

101. G. S. Vinogradov, "Otchet o rabote v Tunkinskom krae letom 1925 g.," *SZhS*, 1926, issue 5, p. 169.

102. N. A. Gorodtsov, "Prazdniki i obriady krest'ian Tiumenskogo uezda," *EGTM*, 1915, issue 26, pp. 20–21.

103. M. F. Krivoshapkin, *Eniseiskii okrug i ego zhizn'* (St. Petersburg, 1865), p. 77.

104. AGO, r. 29, op. 1, d. 12, l. 13, 22, 32-ob., 63; r. 62, op. 1, d. 2, l. 2; r. 57, op. 1, d. 2, l. 11-ob.-31; d. X, l. 12–30-ob.; d. 7, l. 1–22; S. I. Guliaev, "Etnograficheskie ocherki iuzhnoi Sibiri," pp. 2–47; I. Kashin, "Svadebnye obychai priarguntsev," *VRGO*, 1860, pt. 30, pp. 147–82; Gromyko, *Trudovye traditsii*, pp. 331–34; N. A. Minenko, "Svadebnye obriady russkikh krest'ian Zapadnoi Sibiri v XVIII–pervoi polovine XIX v.," *SE*, 1977, no. 3, p. 99.

105. P. S. Efimenko, "Materialy po etnografii russkogo naseleniia Arkhangel'skoi gubernii," pt. 1, *Izv. OLEAE*, 1877, pp. 121–22.

106. Ibid., p. 122.

107. K. V. Chistov, *Russkie skaziteli Karelii. Ocherki i vospominaniia* (Petrozavodsk, 1980), p. 131.

108. T. A. Listova, "Chiny v rodil'no–krestil'noi obriadnosti russkikh severnykh i zapadnykh oblastei RSFSR," in *Vsesoiuznaia sessiia po polevym etnograficheskim issledovaniiam 1981-1982 gg.* (Nal'chik, 1983).

109. GME, f. 7, op. 1, d. 1558, l. 10.

110. Dm. Zelenin, *Russische (Ostslavische) Volkskunde* (Berlin and Leipzig, 1927), pp. 395–96; Gromyko, *Trudovye traditsii*, pp. 334–36; E. V. Pomerantseva, *Mifologicheskie personazhi v russkom fol'klore* (Moscow, 1975), pp. 140–42.

111. GME, f. 7, op. 1, d. 120, l. 13.

112. GME, f. 7, op. 1, d. 947, l. 8 (Bolkhovskii u. Orlovskoi gub.); d. 1466, l. 1–3 (Skopinskii u. Riazanskoi gub.).

113. TsGIA, f. 796, op. 111, 1830 g., d. 497, l. 1–3.

114. Ibid., l. 4–6.

115. Ibid., l. 22 ob.-23.

116. R. P. Matveeva, *Tvorchestvo sibirskogo skazitelia E. I. Sorokovinkova-Magaia* (Novosibirsk, 1976), p. 8.

117. Chistov, *Russkie skaziteli*, pp. 20, 127–28.

118. V. I. Chicherov, *Shkoly skazitelei Zaonezh'ia* (Moscow, 1982), p. 26.

119. *MGSR*, Kostromskaia gub., p. 501.

120. GME, f. 7, op. 1, d. 907, l. 7.

121. Ibid., d. 911, l. 25 (Meshkova Bolkhovskogo u. Orlovskoi gub.).

122. Ibid., d. 1045, l. 7 (s. Alekseevskoi Maloarkhangel'skogo u. Orlovskoi gub.).

123. Ibid., d. 1809, l. 4–5 (Rostovskii u., Iaroslavskaia gub.).

124. TsGIA, f. 796, op. 103, 1828 g., d. 783, l. 1; op. 102, 1821, d. 530; d. 531, l. 1–7; d. 1420, l. 1–10-ob.; d. 1421, l. 1–10 and elsewhere. GAOO, f. 16, op. 1, d. 7.

The Commune and Customary Law among Russian Peasants of the Northern Cis-Urals

Seventeenth to Nineteenth Centuries

I. V. Vlasova

The northern Ural Russian peasantry formed a part of European North rural population since the time of settlement along the middle and northern Kama River from the late sixteenth to the early seventeenth century and the Upper Pechora River from the late eighteenth to the early nineteenth century. As early as the sixteenth century, the northern Ural region had become a transshipment point for the peasantry between the Russian North and Siberia. The socioeconomic development of this region followed the same course as other territories along the White Sea coast and fostered continuous development in newly settled Siberian territories. Administratively the towns along the Kama and Pechora in the second half of the eighteenth century formed part of Perm' Province. In terms of natural resources and economic and social conditions of development, these regions are part of northern European Russia, while within the European North we identify them as the northern Cis-Urals, the connecting link of the European North with the Trans-Urals and Siberia.

During seventeenth- to nineteenth-century settlement and economic exploitation, state ownership of land developed in most places along the northern reaches of the Kama and the Upper Pechora. Some land fell into the hands of large landowners [*votchinniki*] such as the Stroganovs and other Perm' landowners and mining operators. A quite insignificant portion of land went to monasteries.

Among state peasants of the Kama, like all state peasants of the North, a hereditary homestead system of land use existed with right of free plot disposition. Private transactions for land plots were widespread. In these cir-

Russian text © 1989 by "Nauka" Publishers. "Obshchina i obychnoe pravo u russkikh krest'ian severnogo priural'ia (XVII–XIX vv.)," in *Russkie: semeinyi i obshchestvennyi byt* (Moscow: "Nauka" Publishers, 1989), pp. 24–44. A publication of the Order of Friendship among Peoples, N. N. Miklukho-Maklai Institute of Ethnography, USSR Academy of Sciences.

cumstances, the activity of the peasant commune [*obshchina*] took on special importance, regulating both peasant farming practices and every possible redistribution of land. In commune land distributions an egalitarian tendency came into conflict with the norms of customary law that survived a long time in northern Russian regions.[a]

Examination of community life particularities among Kama peasantry reveals not only general northern Russian features in the commune and in the customary law norms, but also how they were manifested in the local setting.

Various sources have been used to answer these questions. Primary are archive materials pertaining to different periods in Kama history: the beginning of settlement in the 1570s; the period of intense development from the 1620s to the early eighteenth century; the time of the General Land Survey in the 1780s to the early nineteenth century; the development in the nineteenth century before and after the reform.[b] The nature of these sources varies. For the sixteenth and seventeenth centuries, the principal ones are the census books of 1579, 1623, and 1672–82,[1] containing data about Kama economic development, the formation of the commune land fund, large estate ownership, and the constitution of the hereditary homestead system for peasant land use.

Analogous material for the later period of the eighteenth century is contained in the 1707 census books for Solikamsk and Cherdynsk *uezdy*,[2] in the "Descriptive Portraits" of the northern Ural districts, and in questionnaires with "Economic Comments" compiled during the General Land Survey.[3]

For the nineteenth century, the main sources were descriptions of various aspects of peasant life in answers to the well-known Russian Geographical Society [RGO] questionnaires. These are materials from the 1840s to 1870s on individual *volosty* or settlements of the northern Ural districts, compiled by RGO Ural correspondents, among whom were village priests, local scholars of regional history, and public officials. Some of these descriptions are in the Geographical Society archive;[4] others have ended up in provincial and district archives.[5] Town archives preserve materials with statistical information on land ownership and land use in the Kama districts and descriptions of everyday life or settlement sanitary-epidemiological situations, presenting data on land usage in the territory.[6]

The most complete statistics on land ownership and land use in Perm' Province districts is provided by Central Statistical Committee documents, with listings of population points and documents on peasant land occupancy by district and *volost'* during the 1860s to 1880s.[7]

The nature of commune land use and the operation of the peasant customary law standards are recorded in special Free Economic Society questionnaires in the 1870s. This information contains two types of document—"A Program for Gathering Information on the Rural Land

Commune" and "A Questionnaire on the Agrarian Movement."[8]

Contrasts between peculiarities of land use and commune practices among peasants belonging to large estates and mine operators as compared to state peasant land use was reflected in various sources—for example, documents of the Lazarev collection at the TsGADA [Tsentral'nyi gosudarstvennyi arkhiv drevnikh aktov SSSR][9] containing numerous data on land holding and estate [*zavod*] management in Chermoza.

Material on various government steps to regulate peasant land use in the territory is held in the collections of the Central Resettlement Authority and the Chancellory of the Minister of Land Use, describing in detail how land was provided to the peasants during resettlement, homesteading, etc.[10] Many field materials come from the East Slavic Expedition Perm' detachment of the Institute of Ethnography, USSR Academy of Sciences, which studied Perm' oblast and the Komi ASSR in 1978–84. Data on community life, activities, land reallotment, customary law, and commune collective labor among northern Ural peasants in these materials pertain to the late nineteenth and early twentieth century.

Little attention has been given to the northern Ural peasant commune, either by prerevolutionary or Soviet scholars. An exception is V. A. Aleksandrov's work on the rural commune in Russia,[11] where the question of peasant commune activity in conditions of large estate ownership is examined on the basis of materials in the collections of the estate offices, including Perm' estates.

In the prerevolutionary period, aspects of peasant community life, land use, and customary law norms were clarified in studies devoted to Kama Region history and ethnography, to which local scholars and students of regional history contributed. Works by P. N. Krylov[12] and I. Ia. Krivoshchekov[13] include information on the topic of the present article. A fundamental description of Perm' Province undertaken by the General Staff in connection with an investigation of all Russian provinces, covering geography, history, and statistics, treated aspects of the Perm' commune and peasant customary law norms.[14]

Active study of Ural history began in the 1950s and 1960s. A number of works appeared in which questions of the commune and customary law among northern Ural peasants were examined in connection with the problem of Ural socioeconomic development—first and foremost the works of A. A. Preobrazhenskii,[15] P. A. Kolesnikov,[16] N. N. Pokrovskii,[17] and V. A. Oborin.[18] There are valuable publications on socioeconomic history in collections of articles appearing in the 1960s and 1970s.[19]

The present article examines the functions of the northern Ural commune in regulating village land relationships, as well as certain elements of the commune life and collective peasant activity along the middle and northern reaches of the Kama and the Upper Pechora. Materials from different districts from the former Perm' Province are used—Solikamsk, Cherdynsk, and Perm'. In these places, two forms of land ownership came into being: state and large estate. The northern Ural peasant commune and its activity in places with state and estate land ownership had certain differences.

State land ownership throughout the European North was characterized by a juxtaposition of state land ownership, hereditary usage, and free peasant disposition of plots. In towns along the Kama with state land ownership, from the sixteenth to the first half of the nineteenth century the hereditary homestead system of peasant land use was combined with the right of free disposal of homestead land. Essentially, this system of land use meant that the peasant *volost'* communes had a certain quantity of land at their disposal, used by individual homesteads. The plots assigned to the homesteads corresponded to the amount of tax levied on each homestead. The tax was determined by family economic and labor capacities, and therefore each homestead had its own tax assessment.[20]

The commune determined the economic capacities of peasant families and made land available accordingly. Usually this was done separately for each homestead. But there were instances when land was assigned for joint use by relatives comprising several families, or labor partners [*skladniki*]. Not uncommonly, a particular plot of land would be assigned for use by several settlements. In such cases, contiguous land was created.[21]

The peasant *zhereb'i* [assigned plots of land] in the North, owing to the customary law norms in practice, became hereditary and were handed down, for they were often created from pieces that came into peasant possession by right of homestead and were then cultivated and became farmlands. The peasantry expressed the hereditary nature of the *zhereb'i* by the term *votchina* [estate], especially when emphasizing the fact that a *zhereb'i* could not be divided among relatives. Yet the peasants, in calling the *zhereb'i* their *votchina*, never forgot that the owner of the land was the state ("your queen," "the sovereign's land"). And the state, in turn, regarded the peasants merely as holders or users of its land.[22]

Since peasants made use of the land "in practice," "by lots cast," "by *zhereb'i*," which were not equal, some acquired surplus land and others a shortage. This inequality violated the principle of correspondence between land and tax, and frequently in such cases the peasants demanded an equalization of plots from the commune. In the seventeenth century, when there was a shortage of arable land along the White Sea coast, the communes began carrying out equalizations—a simple assignment to individual family members or partners of the portion in the common land fund to which they were entitled. The prevailing homestead (customary) law of this time led to partial ownership of the village plowed land with three-field crop rotation and individual ownership of squatter's land with slash-burn clearings, in neither case preventing free plot disposition.

With the change to a population poll tax in the early eighteenth century, land reallotment became an issue since plots remained unequal with this form of taxation, everything depending on the number of men in peasant families. In the second half of the eighteenth century, insufficiency of land for peasant families became more acute throughout the North, due not only to increasing population and overworking of arable land, but also the complexity and confusion of land relationships between and within communes. More and more frequently, the inequality of peasant shares in "patrimonial holdings" was the primary motive for their reallotment. But only in the late eighteenth century were regular land reallotments introduced in the White Sea *volosty* to correct land share inequality. Here the communes came up against the prevailing norms of peasant customary law regarding ownership of cleared, purchased, and other kinds of land. The northern peasants' farming practices indicate that their use of land plots was almost unlimited from the seventeenth century on, despite government edicts against free alienation of peasant plots. Introduction of reallotments restricted peasant independence but did not eliminate free land disposition and, hence, the inequality of land among the peasants. All of this was also characteristic of the communes and peasant land use along the Kama, where state land ownership existed.

Major changes in peasant land use in the North, including the Perm' communes, took place in the latter half of the nineteenth century and were connected with implementation of the peasant reform of 1861. At this time, an equalization-reallotment land use system was introduced in the North. Peasant seizure of land was definitely forbidden, a survey was made of Exchequer lands and the peasant communes, with standards set for peasant allotments. Peasant acquisition of new land amounted to leasing or purchasing it from the Exchequer. Yet the commune remained as a land organization and its activity in regulation of peasant land use continued.[23] Despite government prohibitions, certain customary law practices had not yet disappeared.

The commune itself at this time was no longer the *volost'* commune organization that existed formerly among the "black plow" [*chernososhnyi*] peasantry. Now the commune generally consisted of several rural societies [*obshchestva*], each society primarily uniting peasants of one village.[c] The rural societies had their own separate executive bodies and their own meetings in each village.[24] On occasion, several nearby villages constituted a single rural society.[25] For example, on the upper Kama, in Bondiuzhsk *volost'*, Cherdynsk *uezd*, the villages of Pal'niki, Moskali, and Vortseva, lying at a distance of 6–10 km from each other, were united into a single rural commune.[26] Certain *volosty* were spread out over dozens of kilometers, making village rural societies too far from the center. In the thinly populated Tulpan *volost'*, rural communes were spread 85–100 km from Tulpan village. In such rural communities, meetings and gatherings took place on the spot; an elder was chosen in the village and performed his duties for two years.[27]

Each rural society was given a certain amount of land from the common fund. In the separate village lands, the society distributed plots to homesteads. Prior to the land surveys and the peasant reform, peasant "holdings" and Exchequer land were not delimited (they formed "a single mass"), and thus peasants could enlarge their plots at the expense of government land. This "seizure" of government land gave rise to confusion and strip holdings within each former *volost'*-commune and each rural society. In the late nineteenth century, Votskova, a hamlet in Cherdynsk *uezd*, Anisimovsk *volost'*, had "holdings" consisting of woodland plots near the neighboring village of Anisimovo and the village of Kushmangort "with hamlets," government land "from one place" of Anisimovsk *volost'*, a seasonal plot of hay meadows, Naromida, village of Anisimovo, with villages and hamlets, seasonal hay meadows at Lake Krivoe and the river Visher, and plots in Glebovaia hamlet.[d] All this space consisted of thirty-one separate sectors in a radius as large as twenty versts.[28] There was such a "patchwork" land use in Iurlinsk *volost'*, Cherdynsk *uezd*, where the peasants of Ziuzdino hamlet had allotments in fifty piece-strips in different places.[29]

After the law was issued preventing peasants from expanding their lots into government land or during "planned" rearrangement of hamlets, Exchequer lands were separated from the peasant land and boundaries were drawn between them; within hamlets, fields and meadows were bounded off, and neighboring hamlets were not in their purview.[30] Furthermore, in certain cases additional "sectors not yet seized by the peasants were allotted to their holdings and handed over to the rural communes as forest plots for common use." But the former *volost'* land-strip arrangement was not eliminated since various pieces of land still remained in peasant hands—cleared, purchased, etc., situated in different places that had not yet come under jurisdiction of the rural communes, and used by them in the former way on the basis of customary law. In one Cherdynsk *uezd* community, for example, peasant clearings were enclosed in Exchequer borders during the survey work in 1869. Upon petition of these peasants, the Ministry of State Properties was compelled to leave their rights of clearing unchanged.[31]

Later on, in the early twentieth century, these peasant lands were absorbed by wealthier peasants [*kulaki*], who bought up smaller plots.[e] Thus peasant seizure of land was replaced by purchase of former peasant land by *kulaki*, who increased their holdings at the expense of commune and peasant land.[32]

The economic use of the land and every conceivable reapportionment after the reform continued to be under commune control. During this period, land reapportionment was now universal, and this was the chief means of regulating commune and peasant land use. The basic principle of reapportionment was a *per capita* land distribution, cutting out strips of land from blocks of various quality and distributing them among peasant households according to the number of males in a family. These shares were generally situated in nearby fields. The household [*udvornaia*] fields consisted of such small plots, belonging to peasant families.[33] The rural commune determined the amount of tax on the males and the portions of land were cut out accordingly "by eye: using bushes, hummocks, and other objects."[34] If certain households had too much or too little land, the commune regulated land use by giving additional land or taking away the excess. This principle was known as "allowance-balance" [*skidka-nakidka*].[35] When land was scarce, permission was often granted to work the forests.

Only commune land was reapportioned. The peasant clearings were not subject to reapportionment and remained in individual use, given continuance of customary law.[36]

A characteristic of the commune-reapportionment organization in Kama Region was the rarity of reapportionment. Quite often, border areas were divided rather than the fields themselves (in Iurlinsk *volost'*), and the reapportionment came down to adding on or cutting away land so that the same plots were in constant use by each proprietor.[37] In Kama Region, land left fallow was not reapportioned. This was due to the fact that the territory was developed later than the other regions of the North and land scarcity was not immediately felt here. The same thing occurred in the settlement of Siberia, where there was more land.

Reapportionment was quite recent in areas of Kama Region, and there were places where it did not exist at all.[38] In most areas within Cherdynsk and Solikamsk *uezdy*, scarcity did not appear for a long time, and permanent plots of plowed land and hay meadows remained in the use of peasant homesteads until the 1870s. In Vil'gort village, reapportionment of hay meadows began only in the late nineteenth century. In effect, meadows were changed to a square measure, which was supposed to remain unchanged for twelve years, and this "reapportionment" was stretched until 1922. Prior to this, the meadows in the village were laid out "by the allocators, sighting on carts and using markers."[39] In the hamlet of Dii, fields were never divided and were constantly used by the same proprietors. New settlers were given the opportunity to divide up new lands. For hay meadows, they occupied areas "seized" during settlement of this locality. Some of them had more than enough hayfields. They enjoyed the use of their unpartitioned hayfields until 1936, when collective farms were organized here and all plowed land and meadows went to them.[40] To the North, along the Upper Pechora, farming was poorly developed, yet even here the commune exercised its land-regulating functions. True, it did not engage in reapportionment, as "there was no need for this." Each proprietor also had an allotment here, which remained in the same hands. And although, as it was said, "everyone lived the same," there would be times when someone would lack for land. In such cases, the commune permitted clearing plots in the forest.[41]

The standards of customary law in land distribution continued to be observed after the reform. The principle that each household had the right to use land according to its capacity to work it was not applied equally to all kinds of land. The foundation for holding household land continued to be the number of taxpayers ("tax" or "poll" land). The rural commune divided this according to its quality and determined the standard for each household (per male member). Clearings and purchased land were not submitted to this distribution. The commune could dispose of such land only after the death of its owners who had no heirs. Such land was included in the commune reapportionments in the Iurlinsk and Upper Kama hamlets in the late nineteenth and early twentieth centuries. The commune dealt with vacated land in the same way. After the deportations to Siberia from Ziuzdino and Lopva hamlets (Iurlinsk *volost'*), Pianteg village, and Ambor hamlet (Pianteg *volost'*) in the early twentieth century, evacuated proprietors' portions came under the commune's jurisdiction.[42]

In the postreform period, shortage of allotted land among peasants was compensated by the rural communes permitting not so much clearing of forests as purchase and leasing of land.[43] This took place in a number of Kama hamlets beginning in the late nineteenth century. Hayfield purchase by Ziuzdino hamlet residents from their neighbors is well known. Sometimes these residents would lease land from wealthy peasants for the season. Bondiuzhsk *volost'* peasants leased land from the Exchequer. Iumskie peasants (Iurlinsk *volost'*) sold lots to those without land or purchased land from widows who could no longer work it themselves.[44] In Solikamsk hamlets of Polovodsk *volost'*, peasants also leased land from the Exchequer.[45]

Such land use survived in Kama hamlets until the revolution, after which the principle of land allotment, as everywhere else, was changed to a distribution "by mouths" (both males and females). After the revolution, the individual right to make use of clearings was also infringed, and many slash-burn clearings and meadows came under the new land distribution and reapportionment. In Ziuzdino hamlet in 1918–20, the clearings of Volodiatsk fields were reapportioned, having been in personal use since settlement of these localities. In Osokino village (Polovodovsk *volost'*, Solikamsk *uezd*), slash-burn clearings were divided.[46] These plot reapportionments were facilitated by the fact that they were close to the hamlets and could be added easily to nearby common fields.

State peasant propriety over the northern Urals remained low after all the changes and reforms. At the end of the nineteenth century, the peasant allotment was 1⅓ to 2⅓ *desiatina*.[47 f] In Stolypin's time, the situation scarcely changed, despite the development of leaseholds and the possibility of buying land. In Kama Region as a whole, land shortage was less acute than in other northern regions, yet almost everywhere land was leased from the Exchequer. Throughout the province, up to 500 to 600 *desiatina* were leased each year, including 200 *desiatina* from the Exchequer.[48] As a result of such deals, peasants often received land ill-suited to farming, and were not able to acquire more suitable and expensive land. Land purchase (including peasant allotments) intensified during Stolypin's time, ending up in the hands of *kulaki*.[49]

Despite changes in commune practices, customary law survived in the second half of the nineteenth century. After the reform, land use by seizure continued in places. "Free land is readily seized," it is reported in answers to the VEO [Vol'noe ekonomicheskoe obshchestvo] program for Solikamsk *uezd* in 1879.[50] Another outcome of customary law was collectivism in the community among northern peasants. In Kama Region, this was expressed in various forms until the end of the nineteenth and beginning of the twentieth centuries. Collectivism of work in the North grew out of former cooperative enterprises.[g] These developed during settlement of the territories, when it was necessary to open up land and bring it into cultivation, which could not be done by the efforts of single families. Such "unions" or artels of common labor and common ownership of the fruits of labor existed almost everywhere and always in northern regions.[51] Echoes of this phenomenon were found in the late nineteenth and early twentieth centuries. Such, for example, were the holdings by several proprietors of common hayfields and forest clearings and farm buildings (barns, threshing floors). There was a similar occurrence in Cherdynsk hamlets in the nineteenth century; common land use existed in the hamlets of Anisimovsk and Piantezhsk *volosty*.[52]

Collective labor continued in the communities. One type was the *pomochi* [joint help], when often the entire rural society took part. Perm' peasants were known to work the land "by universal *pomochi*":[53] as many as seventy people gathered at the hayfields at Murty and Pianteg and the Ziuzdino meadows; up to fifty people participated in carting manure to the fields and harvesting at Ium village. Most often, the *pomochi* was organized to bring in the harvest. The principle of the *pomochi* was, first, to help one owner, then another, and thus the entire hamlet, although more often such *pomochi* were organized by wealthy peasants.[54] After the collective work came refreshments and merrymaking. *Pomochi* were used to build houses, when it was necessary to "raise" a house or "break" an oven. "You cannot raise a house alone" was a saying at Pianteg.

In the hamlets on the Obva, *pomochi* were usually held by the rich or by single individuals who were not able to gather the harvest. Such work ended in carousing with a *kandrel'*. On the Obva there were also such forms of collective work as plowing, sowing, and carting manure to the fields in turn. Locals considered this duty a "debt." It was done without monetary remuneration. Work for which money was received (for hire) was known here as a "collection" [*sborishche*]. Mowing and threshing were done at the *sborishche*. As many as twenty or thirty people were assembled, receiving forty kopecks apiece per day. This work also ended with carousing.

Housebuilding was done here not only by *pomochi*, but also by day labor.

In Cherdynsk and Kolvensk hamlets, *pomochi* "caravans" were employed for hauling manure to the fields ("at portages"), collective mowing for families with few members (as many as five or six families would gather), house construction, and harvesting. Yet here, as on the Obva, milking was done as a form of "loan"—working for each other.[55]

In the Upper Pechora hamlets, *pomochi* also took place. They always "raised houses," "felled trees" (to clear fields), and cut wood in common.[56]

There were also common female chores in the hamlets. First and foremost, the *supriadki* and *kopotikhi*, when they gathered in autumn to spin flax or hemp in a party.[57] In Ium village, the tow was usually distributed among neighbors and spun by each at home; after the work was done they would gather at someone's house for refreshment—a "merriment" [*vesel'e*]. In Polovodova village, such *supriadki* were held when there were few females in a family: tow was collected from the families, spun at home, and the finished product returned to the owners, holding a common "feast." In Obva hamlets, flax was combed and teased together, and then each woman did the spinning by herself, even though they gathered in a common place for this. On the Kolva and Upper Pechora, the common combing and spinning of flax was known as *otrabotka*.[58] In certain hamlets of Perm', after the *supriadki* and *kopotikhi* they would ride singing through the villages, and at night "they played and danced."[59]

There was a division of labor in *pomochi*: men plowed, women harrowed, and the elderly sowed. The children (boys) helped in carting manure to the fields and harrowing: they usually guided the horses and were known as "harrowers." Children also helped during harvest, carrying in the sheaves.[60]

People in the hamlets eagerly made use of the *pomochi*, as it was an inexpensive method of performing work. It was only necessary to spend money on the dinner during the "merrymaking," which was acceptable to the wealthy, who organized *pomochi* more often.[61] *Pomochi* always existed in the hamlets. Village life was inconceivable without this. In responses to the VEO program for Perm' Province, it is reported that the *pomochi* was used to cut down forests, build houses, gather the harvest, clear virgin land and plow it, haul manure and lumber, plant potatoes, i.e., the basic chores in the hamlet.[62] In addition, Perm' hamlets also had special collective chores—the gathering of hops in the forest. The places where hops grew were owned by the commune. Collective hops gathering was considered a holiday. The hops were also sold by the commune to hops wholesalers who appeared in the villages to barter with the commune for its purchase.[63]

* * *

Commune organization also existed among Cis-Ural peasants who belonged to the large landowners and mining operators in the prereform period. Yet its sphere of activity on the estates was limited, compared to that of the commune among state peasants.[64] The peasants of landowners were supposed to perform various manorial chores: on the agricultural estates to work the "master's fields," on industrial estates to work in the plants and perform other tasks. The commune was also involved in meting out these responsibilities.

Yet commune land use of private landowners' peasants was on the whole similar to that of the state peasants, albeit on more limited scale. The land fund of such a commune was in fact encompassed by the manorial holdings. And although land in peasant communes was distributed, as among state peasants, by head from lots assigned by the commune, peasant land use on the estates was comparatively slight. On average, the *per capita* share of plowed land in the second half of the nineteenth century was 1½ *desiatina*.[65]

It was common for peasants to lease land from estate owners. Government peasants at this time also had land that they used by customary law (purchased, cleared). Landowners' peasants were deprived of this and could not sell land. Their only method of increasing allotments was leasing. The Lazarev estate's peasants on the Obva leased land from their masters; the Stroganovs' peasants in Solikamsk *uezd* leased plowed land and hayfields from the counts.[66]

Nor did the shares of landowners' former peasants increase at a later time. In the early twentieth century, the former Stroganov peasants of Kuvinsk and Koz'modem'iansk *volosty* of Solikamsk *uezd*, who were allotted land after the reform, used up the forest lands and meadows, resulting in unauthorized cutting in the count's forests and seizure of meadows.[67]

Reapportionment was rare among landowners' peasants, and involved parceling out land or cutting off excess. Meadows, like fields, were seldom divided. Forests were exploited with the permission of estate overseers. Peasants of Kopal'no village, Perm' *uezd*, enjoyed the use of the forest belonging to the Princes Golitsyn. At the end of the nineteenth century, the owner sold his shares along the river Chusova to the Franco-Russian society, who were building a factory there. A forest warden was then appointed to regulate peasant usage of the forest.[68]

Collective work and *pomochi* survived among landowners' former peasants, as among government peasants. They were organized during the field work, chiefly by the wealthy or by single individuals not able to reap the harvest alone.[69]

There were many Old Believers among government peasants, especially those of the private landowners in Perm' districts. But there were no special Old Believer communes separate from the peasant *mir*, with the exception of religious communities.[70] Although the village *mir* sometimes had special "elected officials" whose duty it was to collect a double tax from Old Believers, the authorities preferred to deal with the regular commune administration, especially as mutual responsibility in collection of this tax did not extend to adherents of the official faith.[71] Since the boundaries of the schism were fluid and indistinct among the peasantry, special Old Believer communities were not defined. Yet *mir* traditions lived on among Old Believers. In cases of their oppression by the authorities, everyone rose to their defense, including those who lived in the same commune with them who were not of their faith.[72] On the whole, the life of community members was the same regardless of religious persuasion. Yet there were more wealthy persons among schismatics, and in the late nineteenth century they formed a merchant class, owing to their more enterprising spirit and the better organization of Old Believer households.[h]

Certain features distinguished the commune among the northern Ural population of larger enterprises [*zavody*]. Both government and privately owned peasants worked at and for these enterprises. The commune regulated not only their agricultural chores, but also work related to other enterprises, especially in the case of government peasants, since a special administration was involved with *zavod* work on estates.

Northern Ural peasants were occupied with *zavod* work to varying extents. The peasants of the mining estates themselves performed *zavod* work, and their share in agriculture was minimal. Peasants attached to *zavody* (both government and private), although largely occupied with agriculture, were compelled to devote a considerable amount of time to other *zavod* activities. Only government peasants in agricultural regions primarily worked the fields, even though subsidiary chores at the *zavody*, trades, and temporary labor elsewhere were common for them.

The hiring of government peasants for *zavod* work took place through the commune organization—the *volost'* authorities and special recruiters. For such work, the commune assigned peasants whose payment was in arrears, or "volunteers" were selected to go to the *zavody* and negotiate work contracts.[73]

On mining and other estates, peasants' "work duties" were determined by the *votchina* administration and by the peasant commune in terms of the number of officially counted heads, "judging by their physical strength and condition." This "condition"—in other words, work capacity, fitness for performing responsibilities—depended "on the quantity of grain and number of livestock, and only partly on the extent of cultivated land." On the Lazarevs' estates in the first half of the nineteenth century, peasants were obligated to perform "work duties" on the following basis: a peasant rated as a single taxpayer worked 100 days, two taxpayers 133 days, and three 166 days.[74]

In respect to land, the *zavod* population had the least, and their agriculture was poorly developed due to their employment in the *zavody*. This applies to the mining population of the government and private establishments. The *zavod* population received land allotments from *zavod* managers. Prior to the peasant reform, the government *zavod* population had an average allotment of barely 2 *desiatina* per person,[75] consisting mainly of strips.

The *zavod* population kept livestock, since oxen were needed to perform the *zavod* work, along with domestic animals for their own use.

Unlike estate peasants, the *zavod* population had their own clearings in addition to allotments; like government peasants, they enjoyed these for life, according to customary law, and even sold them. Only after the death of an owner with no successors did the clearing come into the possession of the *zavod*;[76] as in the case of government peasants, a "forfeited" clearing passed to the commune. "Proprietory" rights of the *zavod* population were restricted during implementation of the 1861 reform. To bind this population to the *zavod*, they were given smaller allotments than their lots prior to the reform.[77] Before the end of the nineteenth century, they had no legal title to their own clearings but instead received "tickets" entitling them to lease the clearings from the *zavod* managers.[78] Real land endowment began in 1877. The population themselves demanded that they be given land to own (Chermozsk, Iugokamsk, Lys'vensk *zavody*), be exempt from payments, be transferred to government peasant rank, and be given a farmstead and clearing to own (Tagil'sk and Shaitansk *zavody*).[79]

In 1877, on the basis of "charter deeds" defining their land use by agreement with *zavod* authorities, this population was granted ownership of all lands being worked by them, including leased and cleared land, and the extent of the pasture was determined. But only in 1901 were government *zavod* peasants allowed to buy up their allotments (like government peasants), eliminating their time-dependent status with respect to the Exchequer.

Peasants assigned to government *zavody* had clearings, in addition to their allotment of plow land, which made up for their land shortage; they were permitted to lease these clearings.[80] By the early twentieth century, their allotment included land being worked by them, in addition to the land of the charter deeds.[81]

For the estate landowners, no single legislation concerned providing land to the privately owned population. This population had the lowest standards of allotment before the reform. Their allotments included only strips that were unequally divided among the population. Thus, the Lazarev *zavodchiki* divided their people according to condition into "first class," "average," "needy," and "poor" peasants.[82] The owners of the *zavody* held up the land apportionment. The former Lazarev peasants of Lenvensk village, Solikamsk *uezd*, received "poor-quality plots" by the charter deeds and felt the "burden of the quitrent exacted from them."[83] At Vsevolozhsk *zavody* in Solikamsk *uezd*, peasants were classified as craftspeople rather than agriculturalists, and nothing was to be given to them. Moreover, they themselves refused an allotment of hayfields due to their high price. Only by 1907 at certain *zavody* were the former serfs of private landowners given allotments.[84]

Yet actual land use was not uniform since the population of the *zavody* held clearings, which they used by customary law. There were also leased and purchased lands. In the late nineteenth and early twentieth centuries, a stratification took place in the population of the *zavody*. *Kulaki*, merchants, and contractors began to appear, especially in settlements where the *zavody* ceased operation and their residents turned exclusively to agriculture.[85]

* * *

The commune life of Kama Region peasants reveals that commune traditions survived among the northern Ural peasantry from the time of settlement of Perm' lands until the end of existence of the commune in Russia. Many elements characteristic of the northern Russian commune appeared and thrived among peasants inhabiting the Siberian territories, especially collective work—"side-by-side" joint labor, ownership and use of lands "with comrades," and the long free disposal of land by customary law. Peasant use of land in Siberia repeated the path that it had taken among the northern peasants. In addition to direct echoes of these traditions surviving in the European North and the Urals, Siberian peasants developed their own traditions in the local setting.[86]

Thus, examination of aspects of northern Ural peasant community life indicates that the population of the Urals preserved traditions that had developed among the peasants of the European North. The activity of the commune and peasant customary law norms took on specific features in Kama Region, connected with the socioeconomic development of its individual areas.

Editor's notes

a. The article focuses on a special form of community organization, the commune, or *obshchina*. The concept is tricky because the same word also can be glossed as community; the form *obshchnost'* is also used for community, and *obshchestvo* translates as "society." The commune organization is similar to the peasant *mir*, but that word was less used in the area Vlasova focuses on. Vlasova seems to restrict her use of *mir* to specific peasant meetings.

b. This refers to the reform of 1861, under Alexander II.

c. This passage clarifies Vlasova's use of the term "commune," *obshchina*, depicting a multilayered society that evolved with different amounts of land under control of various peasant groups. Thus specific administrative regions, *volosty*, were once more congruent with communes than they became.

d. Vlasova uses the words *selo* (village), and *derevnia* (hamlet) here, to communicate differences in size. Both are usually translated as "village," but *derevnia* is also used to contrast a rural territory with a township.

e. Vlasova's approach to *kulaki* is clearest here, for her language implies they were something other than true peasants, and were in opposition to the commune.

f. A *desiatina* normally measured 2.7 acres, although there were also larger plots called *desiatina* that went up to about 4 acres.

g. The collectivism discussed here was a precursor of work collectives, especially artels, developed in the 1920s and 1930s, but the earlier forms were voluntary, whereas "collectivization" became forced.

h. For more on Old Believers and their "enterprising spirit" see Valentine Bill, *The Forgotten Class: The Russian Bourgeoisie from the Earliest Beginnings to 1900* (New York: Praeger, 1959); William L. Blackwell, *The Beginnings of Russian Industrialization 1800-1860* (Princeton: Princeton University Press, 1968); Robert O. Crummey, *The Old Believers and the World of Antichrist: The Vyg Community and the Russian State 1694-1855* (Madison: University of Wisconsin Press, 1970); and Henry Rosovsky, "The Serf Entrepreneur in Russia," in *Explorations in Entrepreneurial History*, vol. 6 (May 1954), pp. 207–33.

Notes

1. The Book of Iakhontov, 1579, published in: A. A. Dmitriev, *Permskaia starina (Sb. ist. statei i materialov preimushchestvenno o Permskom krae)* (Perm', 1891), issue 3, pp. 31–50, 140–42; 1892, issue 4, pp. 74–92; *Kniga Kaisarova 1623 g.*; ibid., issue 3, pp. 54–115, 143–56; issue 4, p. 97; "Kopiia s vypisi iz pistsovykh knig Usol'skogo u. 1672–1682 gg.," *RO GPB*, f.IV.620.
2. TsGADA, f. 214, d. 1468, 1511.
3. LOII, f. 36, op. 1, d. 482.
4. AGO, r. 29, op. 1, d. 79, 92; op. 2, d. 20; r. 7, d. 38, etc.
5. "Opisanie s. Seregova Cherdynskogo uezda za 1865–1880 gg.," GAPO, f. 680, op. 1, d. 180; "Primery issledovaniia byta krest'ian v khoziaistvennom otnoshenii," ibid., f. 613, op. 1, d. 300. "Sobranie geograficheskikh, statisticheskikh i etnograficheskikh svedenii o Gainskom sele. Anketa RGO," ChM. RO, d. 3011; "Vladennaia zapis' Permskoi gub. Cherdynskogo u. Anisimovskoi vol. d. Vottskovoi," ibid., d. 2869. M. V. Mazunin, "Opisanie bytovykh storon naseleniia Iurlinskogo raiona za vremia s 1870-x godov po 1917 g.," ibid., d. 3009; "Letopis' . . . tserkvi . . . s. Shaksher Cherdynskogo u. Permskoi eparkhii 1912," ibid., d. 3742; "Opisanie s. Vil'gort Cherdynskogo u.," ibid., d. 2689/3.
6. I. Blankfel'd, "Opyt sanitarno-epidemiologicheskogo obsledovaniia d. N.-Vortsvoi Bondiuzhskoi vol. Cherdynskogo u.," ChM. RO, d. 2187; "Vedomost' o kolichestve zemel' i lesov Cherdynskogo u. 1887 g.," ibid., f. 4, op. 18, d. 81; V. E. Bokov, *K voprosu o kolonizatsii Cherdynskogo kraia v sviazi s razvitiem ekspluatatsii lesov* (Perm', 1898); POKM, d. 14934.
7. TsGIA, f. 1290, op. 4, d. 323–25.
8. Ibid., f. 91, op. 2, d. 775, 786, 821.
9. Ibid., f. 880, op. 1, d. 469, 470 (1860-e gody).
10. TsGIA, f. 391, op. 2, d. 322, 375, 1197, etc.; f. 381, op. 46, d. 126.
11. V. A. Aleksandrov, *Sel'skaia obshchina v Rossii (XVII–nachalo XIX v.)* (Moscow, 1976); idem, "Vozniknovenie sel'skoi obshchiny v Sibiri (XVII v.)," *Istoriia SSSR*, 1987, no. 1, pp. 54–69.
12. P. N. Krylov, *Visherskii krai: Istoricheskii i bytovoi ocherk Severnogo Prikam'ia (Zametki iz puteshestviia po Permskoi gubernii 1870–1878 gg.)* (Sverdlovsk, 1926).
13. I. Ia. Krivoshchekov, *Ukazatel' k karte Solikamskogo uezda Permskoi gubernii* (Ekaterinburg, 1897); idem, *Slovar' geografichesko-statisticheskii Cherdynskogo uezda Permskoi gubernii* (Perm', 1914).
14. Kh. Mozel', *Materialy dlia geografii i statistiki Rossii, izdannye ofitserami General'nogo shtaba: Permskaia gub.* (St. Petersburg, 1864), vol. 2.
15. A. A. Preobrazhenskii, *Ural i Zapadnaia Sibir' v kontse XVI–nachale XVIII v.* (Moscow, 1972).
16. P. A. Kolesnikov, *Severnaia derevnia v XV–pervoi polovine XIX v.* (Vologda, 1976).
17. N. N. Pokrovskii, "Uralo-sibirskaia krest'ianskaia obshchina XVIII v. i problema staroobriadchestva," in *Krest'ianskaia obshchina v Sibiri XVIII–nachala XIX v.* (Novosibirsk, 1977).
18. V. A. Oborin, "Sotsial'no-ekonomicheskoe razvitie Urala v XVII v.," in *Istoriia Urala* (Perm', 1963), vol. 1, etc.
19. *Iz istorii rabochego klassa Urala* (Perm', 1961); *Iz istorii krest'ianstva i agrarnykh otnoshenii na Urale* (Sverdlovsk, 1963); *Voprosy agrarnoi istorii Urala i Zapadnoi Sibiri* (Sverdlovsk, 1966); *Na Zapadnom Urale* (Perm', 1974), issue 6: *Permskii obl. kraevedcheskii muzei*, etc.
20. S. B. Veselovskii, *Soshnoe pis'mo* (Moscow, 1916), vol. 2, p. 345; A. D. Gorskii, *Ocherki ekonomicheskogo polozheniia krest'ian Severo-Vostochnoi Rusi XIV–XV vv.* (Moscow, 1960), p. 149.

21. TsGADA, f. 1161, d. 3, l. 1; d. 6, l. 1.
22. Ibid., d. 32, l. 1, 3; M. M. Bogoslovskii, *Zemskoe samoupravlenie na russkom Severe v XVII v.* (Moscow, 1909), vol. 1, p. 56.
23. "Otvety na programmu VEO dlia sobiraniia svedenii o sel'skoi pozemel'noi obshchine. Permskaia guberniia," TsGIA, f. 91, op. 2, d. 775 (1879 g.), l. 77, 82-ob., 83.
24. "Sobranie geograficheskikh, statisticheskikh i etnograficheskikh svedenii o Gainskom sele," ChM. d. 3011, l. 4; "Spisok naselennykh mestnostei vo vtorom stane Solikamskogo uezda za 1869 g. i Vedomost' so statisticheskimi dannymi po Cherdynskomu uezdu 1884 g.," TsGAI, f. 1290, op. 4, d. 323, 324, 325.
25. "O komandirovanii chinovnika osobykh poruchenii A. Charushina v Vologodskuiu, Viatskuiu i Permskuiu gub.," TsGAI, f. 391, op. 2, l. 23; A. Tret'iakov, "Etnograficheskie svedeniia o s. Arkhangel'skom Solikamskogo uezda Permskoi gub.," AGO, r. 29, op. 2, d. 20, l. 13-ob., 14.
26. I. Blankfel'd, "Opyt sanitarno-epidemiologicheskogo obsledovaniia"; idem, "Spisok naselennykh mestnostei"; idem, "Vedomost' so statisticheskimi dannymi," all in TsGIA, f. 1290, op. 4, d. 323, 324, 325.
27. AIE, "Permskii otriad 1982 g.," d. 789, l. 37-ob.
28. "Vladennaia zapis' . . . d. Vottskovoi," l. 1–1-ob., 2–4; P. I. Khitrov, "K istorii krest'ianstva i zemledeliia na Urale v period imperializma," in *Voprosy agrarnoi istorii Urala*, p. 279.
29. AIE, "Permskii otriad 1979 g," d. 6964, l. 175-ob.
30. Ibid., 1982 g., d. 789, l. 41-ob.
31. TsGIA, f. 381, op. 46, d. 126, l. 33–33-ob.
32. Mazunin, "Opisanie bytovykh storon," l. 4–6.
33. "Opisanie s. Seregova," l. 14-ob.; Krylov, "Visherskii krai," pp. 34–35.
34. "Opisanie s. Vil'gort," l. 96; "Anketnye svedeniia," TsGIA, f. 91, op. 2, d. 821, l. 38.
35. AIE, "Permskii otriad 1981 g.," d. 7548, l. 2-ob., 8, 12.
36. "Opisanie s. Seregova," l. 18–18-ob.
37. "Otvety na programmu VEO," TsGIA, f. 91, op. 2, d. 775, l. 42–43.
38. Sheshukov and Krivoshchekov, "O permiakakh raionov pritokov Kamy-In'vy i Kosy," AGO, r. 29, op. 1, d. 92, l. 4.
39. "Letopis' . . . tserkvi . . . s. Shaksher," l. 16-ob.
40. AIE, "Permskii otriad 1982 g.," d. 789, l. 41; Krylov, "Visherskii krai," p. 35.
41. Ibid., "Permsko-Pechorskii otriad 1983 g.," d. 7958, l. 6-ob., 25.
42. Ibid., "Permskii otriad 1979 g.," d. 6964, l. 176-ob., 190-ob.
43. "Anketnye svedeniia po issledovaniiu krest'ianskogo khoziaistva," TsGIA, f. 91, op. 2, d. 821, l. 38.
44. AIE, "Permskii otriad 1978 i 1979 gg.," d. 7054, l. 3-ob., 61-ob., 177-ob., 192–93-ob.; d. 6964, l. 11, 175-ob., 176-ob.
45. AIE, "Permskii otriad 1978 g.," d. 7054, l. 61.
46. Ibid., l. 7, 70.
47. *Istoriia Urala* (Leningrad, 1976), vol. 1, pp. 100, 192; F. R. Diagilev, "Selo Kopal'no Permskogo uezda 1891 g.," AGO, r. 29, op. 1, d. 79, l. 32.
48. Khitrov, "K istorii krest'ianstva," p. 283.
49. L. P. Matveenko, "Stolypinskaia agrarnaia reforma kak odin iz faktorov, vliiavshikh na formirovanie rabochego klassa Permskoi obl.," in *Iz istorii rabochego klassa Urala*, p. 274.
50. TsGIA, f. 91, op. 2, d. 775, l. 25-ob.
51. "Istochniki XVII v. otmechaiut vladeniia neskol'kikh dvorov zhereb'iami 'c tovarishchi,' " in *Kopiia s vypisi*; GPB, f.IV.620, l. 15-ob., 19-ob.
52. "Opisanie s. Seregova," l. 1; AIE, "Permskii otriad 1978 g.," d. 7054, l. 8.
53. AIE, "Permskii otriad 1978–1982 gg.," d. 6964, 7054, 7548, 789.
54. "Opisanie bytovykh storon," l. 13.
55. AIE, "Permskii otriad 1981 g.," d. 7548, l. 4, 8-ob., 13, 18-ob., 21-ob., 30-ob.–31, 33-ob.; 1982 g., d. 789, l. 42–42-ob.; "Opisanie s. Seregova," l. 13.
56. AIE, "Permsko-Pechorskii otriad 1983 g.," d. 7958, l. 6-ob., 20-ob.
57. Ibid., "Permsko-Pechorskii otriad 1978–1982 gg.," d. 789, 7054, 6964, 7548.
58. Ibid., "Permsko-Pechorskii otriad 1983," d. 7958, l. 21.
59. "Otvety na programmu VEO," l. 76-ob., 77; M. M. Gromyko, "Obychai pomochei u russkikh krest'ian v XIX v. (K probleme kompleksnogo issledovaniia trudovykh traditsii)," *SE*,

1981, no. 4., pp. 29, 34, 37; no. 5, p. 41; idem, *Traditsionnye normy povedeniia i formy obshcheniia russkikh krest'ian XIX v.* (Moscow, 1986), pp. 32–92.

60. AIE, "Permsko-Pechorskii otriad 1983 g.," d. 7958, l. 20, 21-ob., 25–26.

61. Mozel', *Materialy dlia geografii*, pp. 34–35.

62. TsGIA, f. 91, op. 2, d. 775, l. 22-ob., 73, 76-ob.; Gromyko, "Obychai pomochei," pp. 29–37.

63. TsGIA, f. 91, op. 2, d. 775, l. 60, 70-ob.

64. "Raporty Permskogo (Chermozskogo) glavnogo pravleniia i predpisaniia emu po upravleniiu zavodamii promyslami," TsGIA, f. 880, op. 1, d. 469, l. 64.

65. AIE, "Permskii otriad 1981 g.," d. 7548, l. 6, 12-ob.

66. Ibid., l. 8, 11-ob., 12; "Raporty Permskogo," d. 470, l. 88; "Otvety na programmu VEO," l. 77; "O pereselenii krest'ian Permskoi gub. 1898 g.," TsGIA, f. 391, op. 2, d. 375, l. 3-ob.

67. "Ankety so svedeniiami po agrarnomu dvizheniiu," TsGIA, f. 91, op. 2, d. 786, l. 25, 27–27-ob.

68. Diagilev, "Selo Kopal'no," l. 45.

69. AIE, "Permskii otriad 1981 g.," d. 7548, l. 4, 8-ob., 13, 18-ob.

70. I. V. Pozdeeva, "Vereshchaginskoe territorial'noe knizhnoe sobranie i problemy istorii dukhovnoi kul'tury russkogo naseleniia verkhov'ev Kamy," in *Russkie pis'mennye i ustnye traditsii i dukhovnaia kul'tura* (Moscow, 1982), pp. 70–71.

71. Pokrovskii, "Uralo-Sibirskaia krest'ianskaia obshchina," p. 195.

72. Ibid., pp. 196–97.

73. B. A. Sutyrin, "Krest'iane-otkhodniki na rechnom transporte Urala v pervoi polovine XIX v.," in *Iz istorii krest'ianstva*, p. 69.

74. Krivonogov, "K voprosu o zemledelii," p. 65.

75. F. S. Gorovoi, "Vliianie reformy 1861 g. na formirovanie rabochego klassa Urala," in *Iz istorii rabochego klassa*, p. 161.

76. D. V. Gavrilov, "O zemlepol'zovanii gornozavodskikh rabochikh Urala v kontse XIX v.," in *Iz istorii krest'ianstva*, pp. 106–8.

77. Ibid., "Raporty Permskogo," d. 469, l. 60–60-ob., 64-ob.

78. Gavrilov, "O zemlepol'zovanii," p. 107.

79. Ia. B. Rabinovich, "Ob agrarnykh trebovaniiakh rabochikh Urala v 70–80-kh godakh XIX v.," in *Iz istorii rabochego klassa*, p. 209.

80. F. S. Gorovoi, "Ob izmenenii zemlevladeniia i zemlepol'zovaniia gornozavodskogo naseleniia zavodov Abamelik-Lazareva v poreformennyi period," in *Voprosy agrarnoi istorii Urala*, p. 247.

81. Gorovoi, "Vliianie reformy 1861 g.," p. 163.

82. Krivonogov, "K voprosu o zemledelii," p. 66.

83. "Raporty Permskogo," d. 470, l. 53–53-ob.

84. N. D. Alenchikova, "Izmeneniia v zemlepol'zovanii rabochikh zavodov naslednikov A. V. Vsevolozhskogo v predreformennyi period," in *Iz istorii rabochego klassa*, pp. 168, 169, 177.

85. F. P. Bystrykh, "O zemlepol'zovanii gornozavodskogo naseleniia Urala v kontse XIX–nachale XX v.," in *Iz istorii krest'ianstva*, p. 96.

86. V. A. Aleksandrov, "Russkoe naselenie Sibiri XVII–nachala XVIII v. (Eniseiskii krai) (Moscow, 1964), pp. 176–85; Z. Ia. Boiarshinova and V. V. Lozinskii, "O sovmestnom vladenii zemlei v Tomskom uezde (Po dannym perepisnykh knig 1703 i 1720 gg.)," in *Iz istorii Sibiri* (Tomsk, 1972), issue 4, pp. 328–30; M. M. Gromyko, *Trudovye traditsii russkikh krest'ian Sibiri (XVIII–pervaia polovina XIX v.)* (Novosibirsk, 1975), pp. 30–36; I. V. Vlasova, *Traditsii krest'ianskogo zemlepol'zovaniia v Pomor'e i Zapadnoi Sibiri v XVII–XVIII vv.* (Moscow, 1984), pp. 106–28.

APPENDICES

A Program for Collection of Material on the Customs and Rituals Associated with Childbirth

T. A. LISTOVA

I. The time prior to birth

1. Attitude toward infertility, causes of infertility. Attitude toward a childless woman in the family.

2. Measures against infertility (magical—amulets, spells, herbal cures, prayers—to whom). Rational remedies.

3. Ritual actions at the wedding and during the first nuptial night, for the purpose of ensuring childbirth.

4. The desired gender. Methods of determining gender (from the belly, from the length of pregnancy). Methods of influencing the child's gender.

5. Attitude toward artificial interruption of pregnancy. Which agencies were used.

6. Prohibitions on eating, working, behavior of a pregnant woman. (For example, she may not step across a fence, a rope, or an animal, or look at a flame or a corpse.) On which holidays was the work ban especially rigorous, were all kinds of work forbidden, did the ban extend to the husband's work?

7. Could a pregnant woman be a godparent? Which beliefs existed on this score (if her own child dies, the godchild will die). Why?

8. Granting of the pregnant woman's requests. Consequences of a refusal for the pregnant woman and the person refusing (e.g., mice will consume the clothing). Can things be loaned to a pregnant woman?

9. Is the pregnant woman considered impure?

Russian text © 1989 by "Nauka" Publishers. "Programma sbora materiala po obychaiam i obriadam, sviazannym s rozhdeniem rebenka," in *Russkie: semeinyi i obshchestvennyi byt* (Moscow: "Nauka" Publishers, 1989), pp. 292–307. A publication of the Order of Friendship among Peoples, N. N. Miklukho-Maklai Institute of Ethnography, USSR Academy of Sciences.

The program was drawn up using the programs compiled by the Russian Geographical Society, the V. N. Tenishev Ethnography Bureau, V. N. Kharuzina, and the Institute of Slavic Studies.

10. Attitude toward the pregnant woman in the family. Did pregnant women work alongside everyone else up to the time of birth, or were they exempted (in the family, in collective chores)?

II. Childbirth

11. Concealment of the onset of childbirth. Reasons for concealment.

12. Where did the birth occur (home, outside the home— where?). Why?

13. Notions about impurity of the birth, impurity of the place where it occurred. Are there bans on visiting a home where a birth has occurred, and if so, for whom (maidens, elderly persons . . .), for how long?

14. Did the woman take leave of household members before birth? Did she ask forgiveness of relatives or outsiders as the birth drew near? Did she take confession?

15. Were there special prayers to facilitate birth, and if so, to whom?

16. Could girls or the husband be present at birth? Was it believed that certain actions of the husband could facilitate the birth (for example, the husband steps over the wife, etc.)?

17. Was it believed that labor pains could be transferred from the wife to the husband? Who could do this, and how?

18. Actions to facilitate birth: procession around the table, opening all doors and shutters, loosening the belt, administering a substance to produce contractions, opening the "heavenly" gates in the church, etc.

19. Is notice given of the birth occurring, and how?

III. The midwife

20. Were there special kinds? Who could be one—widow, elderly, any experienced woman?

21. When was she called—onset of birth, after birth to care for the newborn and mother?

22. Actions of the midwife aimed at facilitating birth (magical, rational).

23. To which saints did the midwives appeal for help? Did they regard any of them as being the immediate patron of their profession? Did any legends exist as to a particular saint engaging in midwifery?

24. Did the midwife bring anything for the mother and child when coming to perform a delivery, did she bring bread?

25. Actions of the midwife with the newborn, what does it mean to "remidwife" [*perebabit'*] the child?

26. Did the midwife offer any help to the mother after birth—cleaning, household chores?

27. Time spent by the midwife at the mother's home or the time of the visit. Reasons. Did the midwife bring anything?

28. Remuneration of the midwife. When was it received (at once, whenever convenient, at the christening, etc.)? Was it attended by any rituals? If the midwife was replaced by other persons (e.g., a neighbor, the mother-in-law, etc.), were they to be remunerated?

29. In what form was the remuneration received—monetary, presents? Could the

midwife demand remuneration, was it considered a sin to take money for midwifing?

30. Could the midwife refuse to attend the childbirth for any reasons?

31. Was the midwife considered "impure" after delivering the infant, could she immediately deliver another infant? Did the ritual of "washing the hands" exist? When did they "wash hands" (before the christening, two days after birth, twelve days after birth, etc.). Where did they wash hands (before the "saints," on the threshold, etc.)? What kind of water (holy, "charmed") was used? Did the midwife and the mother wash each other's hands, or one of them? Did the mother give the midwife a gift (cloth, a glove) during this? Who, besides the midwife, was present (only the parents of the newborn, the godparents)? Did the midwife use holy water for washing?

32. What did the midwife call the children delivered by her?

33. Was it the custom for women whose children had been delivered to visit the midwife and help her with her chores?

34. Was a special day set aside—"midwife's day," "midwife's porridge"— the holiday of midwives and new mothers on the second or third day of Christmas? Who visited the midwife on this day (husbands and wives having children, only women)? What did they bring her? Did mothers invite midwives to their houses on this day? What gifts did they give them? Did they serve them porridge?

35. What was the attitude of the community to the profession of midwife? How were these views reflected in the notions concerning the midwife's life after death?

36. Was it believed that a connection existed after death between the midwife and the children that she delivered (e.g., would the children attend her).

IV. The infant

37. Was a distinction drawn in rituals for the birth of a boy and a girl, birth of the first child?

38. The propitious time for birth. Did the child's future depend on the time of birth?

39. Omens regarding the health of the newborn.

40. Notions concerning twins. How is their birth explained?

41. Notions about the soul. Is the child born with a soul, is it imparted after birth, by whom?

42. Handling of the afterbirth and umbilical cord. Were they washed, where were they hidden, who performed the necessary actions? Was anything placed together with the afterbirth and umbilical cord, and why? Was it considered possible to influence the fate of the mother or child through the afterbirth?

43. First bathing of the newborn. Who did it, what was put in the water, when was the first washing, how often? Where was the water poured after the bath?

44. Was the newborn wrapped in the father's shirt and why?

45. Was anything sprinkled on him (for example, salt)? Why?

46. What was placed in the cradle? On what day was the infant placed in the cradle, were there any attendant rituals? Who was the first to place the newborn in the cradle (midwife, godmother, mother)? Was the cradle fumigated, by whom (midwife, godmother), with what (incense, herbs)? Was the blanket, pillow, etc., sprinkled with holy water? What was said when first placing the child in the cradle? Necessary number of first rockings. Was a crucifix hung over the child's cradle?

47. How were the swaddling clothes cleaned, where were they dried?

48. Was it possible to rock an empty cradle?

49. What was done to make the infant walk more quickly, were there certain spells and prayers? What was done during the first steps of the infant (for example, did they "cut the cracks")?

50. Was it possible to lift the infant up to a mirror?

51. When did they begin to suckle the infant, how long usually did the women nurse the children, which breast was to be given first?

52. Were there any rituals in weaning the child?

53. When was the child first taken outside the home, was it shown to strangers before this?

54. What was the attitude toward children born with physical defects? Was it believed that they were changed by evil power?

55. How to recognize a "changeling." Is there a way to return the real child?

56. Did the ritual of "rebirth" (symbolic birth) exist for sick children? Was there a "rebaking" [perepechenie] of the children in the same instances?

57. Where were the stillborn buried: the cemetery, beyond the fence, beneath the threshold? Why?

58. What were the ways of protecting against evil eye? Methods of healing "blight," "crying," and various illnesses. Were special persons invited for the spells? Texts of the spells. What rituals accompanied them?

59. When was the child's first haircut, by whom, where was the child placed during this? Were the nails clipped? Were the hair and nail clippings preserved?

60. Was a belt placed on the child—during the christening, on the fortieth day, after a week, etc.? By whom? Was there a special ritual for this? To what other rituals did it belong? Was this ritual accompanied by gifts?

V. The mother

61. How much time did the mother spend in bed?

62. Was the mother given anything to strengthen her (vodka with salt, bread with salt, medicinal herbs)? When (immediately after birth, the first week, etc.)?

63. Washing of the mother. Where did it take place, who helped, on what day?

64. Notions as to the mother's impurity. Could she go out into the street, perform any work, eat along with everyone else, etc.? Was she forbidden to touch fire, the oven, to bake bread, milk the cow, go out in the street, visit other houses?

65. Was it the custom to visit one's mother after giving birth and then return home? For how long?

66. For how long was it forbidden the mother to attend church? Was the mother considered "cleansed" after the christening of the infant, after the washing of the hands, after the prayer on the fortieth day?

67. What was the attitude toward women during menstruation? What kinds of work were they forbidden to perform (for example, planting, pickling)? Could they go to the steam bath along with everyone else? Go to church, or worship at home? Could they perform various ritual duties (e.g., matchmaking)? Were there any explanations for the prohibitions? Were there notions about the harmful power of menstrual blood, ways of being harmed?

68. Where did the mother stay after birth (if the birth took place at home, away from home)? Was the mother left alone?

69. How were the mother and child buried when they died at the same time?

70. Was it believed that a deceased mother would arise from the grave to nurse her infant?

VI. The custom of women visiting the new mother

71. How was it called, when did they visit, who came, could pregnant women, maidens, menstruating women come? What did they bring, were there obligatory dishes to be brought to the mother? Was there a common repast?

72. The need for a return visit. The need to invite those who visited to the christening.

73. Was it a custom to celebrate the birth of a child? When? Who was invited?

VII. The christening

74. Was a newborn considered impure, for how long? Why?

75. Attitude toward an unchristened child. Why was it necessary to christen as soon as possible? What was said about a child dying unchristened (e.g., the souls turn into birds, the souls fly away, ask for a name, etc.)? Could a funeral prayer be said for an unchristened infant?

76. What was the child called before the christening? Was it a custom to call all unchristened boys Ivan, and girls Mar'ia?

77. Which names were most common in the given locality? Why?

78. The magic of namesakes. Was it a custom, if the child were near death, to shout the name of the father or mother into its ear? Was it customary to give the name of the parents or godparents if the children in the family did not live?

79. How was the name chosen (by saint's days, by a particular relative, by the parents, etc.)? What was the attitude toward children having identical names in the same family (if the names were given by saint's days)?

80. Could the midwife christen or "lay a name" on the newborn? How did this ritual take place? If the infant survived, was church christening necessary, or only certain supplementary rituals? What name did the priest give the child in this case?

81. On which day was the christening performed? Was the christening performed in church before a particular service, and why?

82. Who was present at the christening besides the godparents? Was the midwife present?

83. Was the rite of christening performed at home? Was there a difference in this respect between poor and rich peasants (christening and anointing at home for the rich, in church for the poor)? How was the house prepared for the rite? Were outsiders present?

84. Was the "fortieth prayer" performed on the "fortieth day" after birth of the child? Could it be sooner or later than this day? Did the peasant and church views differ in this? Was the presence of the mother essential?

85. Whom was it preferable to select as godparent—relatives (on the mother's or

father's side), neighbors, friends? Was it possible to select widows, widowers, the childless, those unhappy in marriage, pregnant women, menstruating women? Was it preferred to select the affluent and respected, and why?

86. What was the preferred age of the godparents? Was it important for the age of the godparents and that of the parents to match?

87. If the children did not live in the family, who was chosen as godparent?

88. Was there a special ritual in making someone a godparent? Were the parents of the future godparents asked, if the latter were young? Who invited them to become godparents?

89. Were the same godparents chosen for subsequent children? Was it deemed preferable to have different godparents for each child? What accounted for this?

90. Was it held to be lucky to be the godparents of illegitimate children?

91. Could there be a single godparent (for a boy, for a girl), and of what gender? Did the godparents have to be present?

92. Possibility of refusing to become a godparent. Were people eager to become godparents? Did the young consider this an opportunity to find a match in this family or enter into marriage with the one alongside whom they "stood beneath the cross"?

93. Omens associated with the choice of gender of the first godchild (could a girl be the godparent of a first daughter, and if not, why not, etc.)?

94. What did the godparents bring (bread, cloth, calico— "chasubles," a shirt for the infant, a towel for the priest, a cross)? Did the godmother herself sew the shirt for the child, was it essential to use homespun cloth? Who paid for the christening? Did the godmother, arriving at the house for the child, bring the mother a "chasuble" (piece of fabric)? Did she bring *makhotka*—porridge— wrapped in a clean piece of cloth?

95. Were the godparents given refreshment before the christening? Rituals of departing for the church. Was the child bathed before the christening and by whom, who gave the child to the godparents, who carried it to church?

96. What articles were given to the godparents to protect the child from the evil eye on the way to church?

97. Who brought water for the christening, and how? Could several children be christened in the same water, how were such children called? Where was the water poured out after the christening?

98. What did the godfather do with the child's hair clipped during the christening (e.g., did he roll it in wax and throw it into the font)?

VIII. Rituals upon returning home

99. How did they return from church: the same way, or a different one?

100. Was it the custom, in families where children did not live, to hand over the child after christening through the window, with the back to the door, etc. For what purpose?

101. Was it a custom to place the child on a fur coat, spread out with the fur side on top? When was this done (before or after the christening, twice—before and after the christening, after the christening party)? Where was the fur coat spread out (in the front corner, on the threshold, etc.)? Who performed the ritual, and how? How were these actions explained?

102. Was money placed alongside the child, in his hand, on the fur coat?

103. Were the godparents with the child greeted in the hall by the midwife, wearing a fur coat with the fur side outwards? Did she (or the godfather or godmother) lift the child onto the oven? What was cooked on this occasion? Did the grandfather and grandmother of the newborn greet the guests with bread and salt?

104. Were the godfather and godmother met returning with the child after the christening? Were they supposed to get pies down from the top shelf or perform any other rituals?

IX. The christening dinner

105. When was it held?

106. Who was invited—only the godparents, midwife, young people, children, neighbors, relatives (on whose side), relations of the godfather and godmother, the women who visited the mother?

107. Who invited them, the formula of invitation, were they invited "for porridge"?

108. Were the invited supposed to bring anything? Certain articles essential to bring (e.g., the father-in-law brings a live rooster, the women bring *makhotka* or cookies, etc.).

109. Did the mother appear before the guests, if not, why? Did the invited women go to her with presents?

110. Who cooked the food, was the midwife invited to do the cooking?

111. Peculiarities in the table service for the christening meal. Was there a tablecloth? Were the spoons supposed to be red? Was a certain collection of articles (salt, bread, knife, red spoons) placed on the table before the dishes were served?

112. Who served the food to the table? Who supervised the entire meal (midwife, mistress of the house, master of the house)? Did the master of the house perform any ritual with the bread at the start of the meal? The order of serving wine.

113. Assignment of places at the table for the christening meal. Were the family members seated at the table? Did everyone pray before dinner, light candles at the icon?

114. What was cooked, were there compulsory dishes?

115. Rituals with the porridge ("baba's porridge"):

a. was the christening dinner known as "porridge"?

b. was porridge served, when during the meal? Who cooked it—the mother, the midwife, the godparents? Were several porridges made at the same time? Was the "common porridge" served separately in a red cup, and the "midwife's porridge" in a clay pot?

c. what rituals accompanied the serving of the porridge, who performed them—the midwife, the godparents, everyone present? (For example, did the midwife cover her head with the tablecloth, did the godparents cover themselves together with a *ruchnik*, was the child brought in for this ritual, what did the midwife say. Did the godparents repeat her sayings after her, etc.?)

d. was the pot in which the porridge was served smashed? Who smashed it (midwife, godfather)? What rituals and sayings accompanied this?

e. was money collected for the porridge, to whom did it go? In what form was it collected (e.g., did they buy a spoon, place it beneath a pie, set it on top of a pot with porridge; put the money at the bottom of a glass after drinking vodka from it)? Traditional names for this money (for the child's teeth, for the midwife's teeth, for the midwife's porridge, for the mother's porridge)? What was said when they ate the porridge?

116. Did they feed the child's father spoiled food, how was this explained, who served the food? What actions was he supposed to perform on this occasion?

117. Was a rye pie—"midwife's tooth"—served at the end of the meal? Did the midwife distribute this to all she encountered on the road (returning from the christening party), what did she say on this occasion?

118. Did the godparents give gifts to each other during the dinner? Was this accompanied by kisses? Was there a special meaning for the ritual between godfather and godmother? Were godparents who had already been godparents before matched up?

119. Was a gift given to the midwife from the mother; what rituals accompanied it?

120. Were the godparents the last to leave the christening meal? Did they leave gifts for the newborn (money, bread rolls, calico cloth, in which the infant was placed when taken from the font)? How was this done? Did the godfather perform a ritual with a round loaf (or bread) to exchange gifts with the mother? What did she put in this?

121. a. Was a "godparent's dinner" organized at the christening for the godparents alone, before inviting the other guests into the home? What were they given as refreshment, and by whom, was porridge served, a chicken, were these dishes mandatory, what sentiments were expressed and how?

b. Was a "repayment" organized for the godparents alone after the christening dinner? What kind of refreshment was served? Did the godfather and godmother exchange presents? What kind? Did the towel given to the godfather have to possess red ends?

122. Were children present in the house during the feast of the adults? Where did they stay? Were they given refreshment? What exactly (porridge, pancakes)? Were children fed separately at the christening party after the adult guests left? Who did this? What food was prepared? How old were the children? Was there a gender distinction (boys for a male child, girls for a female)? Were the girls supposed to catch a chicken in the yard (the boys a rooster) on this occasion? Was this bird served at table? In what way? Did the godfather and godmother participate in this ritual?

X. Visiting of the mother and newborn after the christening

123. Was a visit to the mother and newborn organized after the christening, when (e.g., one week later)? Who came (e.g., women who attended the christening dinner)? What did they bring to the newborn (*na naveski*) (porridge, a chick, an egg, bagels)? Were any dishes mandatory? Was the food lifted up and a pronouncement made?

124. Were the godfather and godmother invited to this visit? What gifts did they bring? Was the midwife invited?

125. Did the hosts organize a dinner for those who visited the mother after the christening? Did the persons arriving (women only, godfather and godmother, or all of these) bring refreshments to the hosts?

126. Did the midwife on this occasion produce the pot in which porridge was served

(or cooked) at the christening? What ritual was performed with this pot, and what was said (for example, in Orel province, the godfather lifted the midwife's pot, uttered something, and smashed it, while the godmother collected the fragments in her apron, took them out to the yard, and threw them away with an utterance)?

127. Did they bid farewell to the mother after this? Did the godmother place a shirt on the godchild and tie a belt on him? What took place?

XI. Godparents in later relationships

128. Relations between the parents and the godparents. Did they go to visit them, on what days? On what family and calendar holidays were the godparents invited? What was the attitude toward disputes with the godparents? Did the godparents provide mutual support?

129. Relations between the godparents and the godchildren. Was it considered that the godparents are answerable to God for the godchild? Were the godchildren required to respect the godparents like their own ("Each person has three mothers: the birth mother, the godmother, and the damp mother earth")?

130. Did the godchildren go with their parents on the "days of forgiveness" of Shrovetide to the godparents to be "forgiven" (ask mutual forgiveness)?

131. Relations between godfather and godmother. Could the godfather say obscene things to the godmother, "joke" with her?

132. Were the godparents considered related to each other and to the parents of the newborn?

133. Bans on marriage between godparents. Were they passed on to the children? To what generation? Possibility of sexual relations between godparents.

134. Did the godmother take part in the family council when choosing a bride for the godson? Did she go (with another woman) to arrange the marriage for the godson?

135. Role of the godparents at the wedding. Need to invite them. Was any wedding function assigned to the godparents, what was the procedure if the godparents were absent? What were the duties of the godparents—supervise the wedding, hold the wreath, carry the dowry, etc.? Did the godparents (or one of them, and which one, at what point in the wedding) bless the bride and groom? How did this take place? Where did the godparents sit at the wedding? Were gifts given to them?

136. Was the godmother subjected to any shameful actions if her goddaughter was unchaste? (For example, was a yoke placed on her?)

137. Did the groom's godparents perform the ritual with the round loaf (or what part of the ritual) at the wedding? What actions did each godparent perform? Was the godmother supposed to sit on the oven?

138. Role of the godparents at the wedding of orphan godchildren. Did they replace the parents? Did the bride accompanied by godfather or godmother ride to the grave of the parents?

139. Role of the godparents when the godson was inducted into the army. Did the godparents bless the new recruit along with the parents, and how?

140. Was it believed that relations between godparents and godchildren continued in the next life? (For example, godchildren protect their godparents against attack by devils.)

Supplement to the Main Program

Current Status
of Rituals and Customs
Associated with Childbirth

I. The time before birth

1. Which of the indicated bans and precautions do pregnant women observe today? Do young people observe the ban on working on church holidays? How do people of different ages account for the preservation of the various bans?

2. Are there omens for determining the gender of a child? Which gender do the parents prefer? Why?

II. Birth

Are there omens for detecting the onset of birth? When is the child's "dowry" bought?

III. The child

1. Who performs the first bathing of the child when the mother returns home, is the bathing accompanied by any ritual actions? What is placed in the water?

2. Does the belief in the "evil eye" and "blighting" of the child survive? Is anything done to avoid this? Who is asked to heal the child in these cases?

3. Do any ritual actions survive when the child is first placed in the cradle?

4. Are the first-year bans observed (not to place the child in front of a mirror, not to make it laugh, etc.)?

5. What is done to make the infant walk more quickly?

6. When are the nails and hair clipped?

7. Does the custom of girding the infant exist? At what age is it usually performed, by whom?

IV. The mother

Attitude toward the mother. Are there any bans on preparation of food, working, eating? What do women of different age groups know about the bans during menstruation? Are these bans observed?

V. Visiting the mother

1. Is it considered mandatory to visit the mother? How is this custom regarded (mutual help, respect, done "out of custom"). When does it occur (immediately after discharge, as she recuperates, etc.)?

2. Do they usually come individually or in a body to the other?

3. Makeup of the visiting party (women, girls, men; girlfriends, relatives, fellow workers).

4. Is advance notice given of the visit? Is a special invitation required? Who invites them: the mother, her husband, grandmothers and grandfathers?

5. What do they bring (to the child, to the mother). Is it customary to bring any food?

6. Is it customary to give the visitors refreshment?

VI. Celebration of various dates in the life of the child

1. Celebration of the birthday.

a. Celebration mandatory? Is the gender of the newborn important, first child in a family?

b. When is it organized (immediately after discharge from the maternity hospital, after formal registration of the birth, when the parents decide, etc.)?

c. Whom is invited (friends, relatives, fellow workers, neighbors)? Age makeup?

d. Description of presents (collective or individual), things or money? Approximate price of a gift? Who gives the most valuable presents? Do any ritual actions accompany the gift giving?

e. Sentiments expressed, are any ritual actions formerly performed at the christening performed?

f. Refreshment. Mandatory foods?

g. Are any ritual actions performed with the porridge or a substitute food? By whom?

2. Formal registration of the birth; name-giving ritual.

a. Who chooses the name of the child? Is it the custom to give the child the name of the parents, grandmothers, grandfathers, certain famous people?

b. Attitude toward the civil registration procedure.

c. How carried out (strictly by the received instructions, inclusion of elements of traditional local rituals associated with childbirth, what do the performers feel is the most effective part of the procedure?)

d. Is there a ceremony for the registration of the house, how? What is the dinner called?

3. Christening

a. Is it considered essential to christen the child? Why? View of various age and social groups as to the necessity for christening.

b. What is the usual age of christening of the child? What influences the choice of the time of christening?

c. Where does the christening take place (at home, in the church)? Can christening be done without the child being present?

d. Is it deemed necessary to conceal the christening of the child from the community?

e. Is a dinner given at home on the occasion of the christening? Who is invited, what gifts are given? Are any ritual actions performed?

4. Celebration of the first year of the child.

a. Is it mandatory to celebrate the first year?

b. Who is invited?

c. Gifts given.

5. Which of the aforesaid events are celebrated most solemnly (celebration of child's birth, christening, formal registration, first year)? Is there a tendency to combine the celebration of these events? Do ritual actions survive, formerly performed at the christening dinner?

VII. Godparents and "honorary" parents

1. Who is chosen to be godparents and "honorary" parents? Age, importance of family, neighborhood, friendship relations.

2. Ideas on the obligations of godparents and "honorary" parents to the child. Are the honorary parents known as godparents?

3. Is it mandatory for the same individuals to perform the role of godparent and honorary parent?

4. Does a godparent relationship exist if the christening rite is not performed? Who is chosen as godparent in such case, and for what purpose?

5. Notions on marriage bans of godparents. Do these bans extend to "honorary" parents?

6. Role of godparents at the wedding and send-off to the army of their godchildren, notions of their mandatory attendance of the wedding. Does anyone play the part of the godparents in their absence (including an unchristened child)? Do the obligations of godparents (of an unchristened child) extend to the "honorary" parents?

7. Must godchildren and their parents visit the godparents, and on which days? Are the godparents invited on solemn occasions in the family of the godchildren? Are the same relations preserved with "honorary" parents?

A Program for Gathering Information on the Peasant Commune and Family

Structure and Composition of Community and Family Groupings

Land and Property Relationships
(On the Example of the Provinces of the European North)

I. V. Vlasova

Commune

I. Existence of the commune

Its type in the late nineteenth and early twentieth centuries. Commune and rural socie-ty. The *mir* meeting and its connection with the type of commune. The land fund of the commune. Contiguous land borders, farming in strips (between villages, within vil-lages), peasant allotments. Preservation of land use by seizure, its connection with commune land use. Collective associations in the community; makeup, nature of activity, basis of the joint economy (tradition; necessity of association). Type of associa-tion: joint household or work assistance.

Specifics of the commune in terms of regions, depending on economic zones (associ-ations in the farming or industrial zone, etc.) and depending on the makeup of the local population: (1) social classes (for the prereform period, the government, land-owner, monastery peasants); (2) religious affiliation (members of the official faith, Old Believers).

Russian text © 1989 by "Nauka" Publishers. "Programma dlia sobiraniia svedenii po voprosam: 'Krest'ianskaia obshchina i sem'ia. Struktura i sostav obshchinnykh i semeinykh kollektivov. Pozemel'nye i imushchestvennye otnosheniia' (na primere oblastei evropeiskogo Severa)," in *Russkie: semeinyi i obshchestvennyi byt* (Moscow: "Nauka" Publishers, 1989), pp. 326–31. A publication of the Order of Friendship among Peoples, N. N. Miklukho-Maklai Institute of Ethnography, USSR Academy of Sciences.

II. Land functions of the commune

1. Redistribution of plowlands.

Peasant allotments and their determination by the *mir*: the principle of allotment during different historical periods (in terms of the number of workers, the number of males, the number of mouths to feed, etc.). Land reapportionment: time frame, principle of reapportionment. Reapportionment and use of farmland/clearings and meadows: limits (time, place) on their use or prohibitions, incorporation of them in reapportionment. Determination of surplus or shortage of land allotment, allotment of land under these circumstances.

Wasteland: distribution by commune or seizure. Clearings: commune's permisssion for them, restriction in time, transfer to reapportionment. Forfeited plots: inheritance or transfer to reapportionment. Evacuated plots: conversion to wasteland or re-cultivated (collectively, individually). Use of privileged and leased plots and commune supervision. Approval to purchase or lease land in the commune fund, in the Exchequer, in private ownership. Transfer of land in case of resettlement and division of families. Preservation or liquidation of collective households in case of divisions.

Specifics of reapportionment and various land redistributions by zone (lack of reapportionment in industrial regions) and in areas with different land ownership (especially in places with patrimonial ownership).

2. Existence of land sale in conditions of the commune and land reapportionment. Forms of sale. Preservation under sale of certain rights of law   disposal of land (use of clearings, customary meadows, purchased lots). Continuance of sales in second half of nineteenth and especially early twentieth century.

3. Commune regulation of agriculture on plowland. Sowing, harvesting, pasturing of cattle, haw mowing. Chores on plowlands: time frame of chores, necessity of crop rotation in the three-field system, sequence of utilization of land near the village and other land.

4. Peasant land possession. Degree of land possession of peasants. Identification of strata among the peasant population in terms of land possession.

III. Breakup of the commune

"Stolypin homesteads," their extent in the regions in the early twentieth century, and their land use. The 1917 revolution and the land reform of Soviet power. Authorization of free choice of any form of land use by the peasants. The commune, the homesteads of the postrevolutionary period, the first collective farms (communes, artels, state farms, comradeships). Land use of communities, homesteads, collectives. The relationship between collective and individual usage. Authorization of community and farmstead land use under collectivization. The new system of husbandry and land distribution.

Family

I. Types of families

1. Form of family: small, undivided, variants thereof. Numerical makeup in different

forms of families. Their structure: number of generations, degree of kinship (direct, collateral), affinity. Presence of distant relatives and unrelated persons in the family. Family associations as economic units in the past.

2. Differences among types of family in the past for the different categories of the population: state, landowner peasants in the first half of the nineteenth century, different strata of peasantry in the late nineteenth and early twentieth centuries—rich [*kulaki*], middle [*seredniaki*], poor [*bednoty*]. Differences in form of family (especially presence of undivided families), in number of members, in structure.

3. Local differences in types of families. Degree of occurence of family forms in different localities as function of socioeconomic development, economic role of the regions (the peasant family in agricultural and industrial regions).

II. Historic past of the family in each region, conditions of its formation and development, connection with socioeconomic and social life

1. The family and settlement of the territory.

External and internal sources of growth of families and settlements during different times. The role of population migrations, external and internal. Reports on the first settlements and their founders. Squatters, their growth and conversion to villages and other types of settlements (at first, single-family). Moves to new places and settling down with relatives, conversion of single-family settlements into unrelated types. The family core and "foreign elements." Their relationship in the economic role, in land use and social life. Conditions of family building, types of families during capitalism: the role of migrations and growth of commercial-monetary relations. Composition of families in subsequent epochs—the Stolypin reforms, the 1917 revolution and formation of collective farms: resettlement of separate farms, leaving the community and family divisions; the revolutionary land system— communes, separate farms and communities and family divisions; collectivization, desettlement and families.

2. Families and the peasant commune.

Associations of related and unrelated families into peasant communes. Commune land use and land use of family homesteads: nature of land ownership and use, land occupancy, seizure of land and the commune, land reapportionment and allotment of land to families. Collective chores of the *mir* and the family *pomochi*. Community holidays (feasts, etc.). Collective associations, artels (industrial, craftsmen), participation of the community and family in them. Social strata of peasants and the community: the wealthy peasantry and the *mir*.

3. Family divisions and the commune.

Forms of divisions during different times. Involvement of the commune in divisions (cf. division of the property and legal standing of family members).

4. The peasant commune and the religious community (for places with Old Believer population). Their relationship, or coincidence, their role in family and social life.

III. Internal organization of the family and family relations depending on family form and structure, social milieu

The family household and property. The farmstead, the nature of structures on the farmstead and their use by the family: accommodation of family members in the house. Divisions and abodes (full and partial divisions).

Family members and their functions. The head of the family and other members. Role of women in the family. Children. Male in-laws, brides. Widows. Foster children: in-laws and husbands; adopted children. The role of each family member in the economic and the entire domestic life. Age/sex division of labor in the family. Family leisure.

IV. Family-property relations among the peasantry (inheritance, family divisions)

1. Customary law in the inheritance of the entire household and family property. How was the functioning of the household assured when property was inherited? Taking care of non-able-bodied or indigent family members. Separation of the common household and personal property during inheritance.

2. The rights of each family member in apportionment. The rights of the men: the share of the father, sons (in divisions of the father's, brother's family). The rights of the widow-mothers: (a) after the husband's death; (b) if adult sons are present; (c) primary rights [*primachestvo*] of husbands or male in-laws.

3. Commune rights of land ownership and principles of division during family allotments. Equal and proportional divisions in terms of family makeup and taxpaying ability. Allotment for widows with male children taking account of the rights of the future worker/children; the local principle of allotment for widows with female children. *Primachestvo*, the rights of *primaki* to the farm, land, including rights of aged parents, unmarried female members to inherit the property and land by common law. Non-able-bodied family members and their support during divisions of land and family property.

4. Personal property and rights to it by family members. (a) Dowry: endowerment of daughters (after the father's death, brother's endowering of sisters). Inheritance of the dowry: through the maternal line; if no female heirs are present, to the husband. (b) Clothing: personal (especially holiday clothing), its noninclusion in the division. (c) Temporary external labor [*otkhod*] and earnings. Personal earnings, noninclusion of them in the division.

5. Succession without heirs. Role of the will. Noninclusion of taxable land in testamentary succession. Testamentary succession of purchased land (personal property), possibly by women.

V. Mixed marriages

Class, religious, ethnic mixtures. Conditions under which such marriages appear. Degree of miscegenation. Rights of family members in mixed marriages, their internal relations.

VI. Kinship systems

Terminology of kinship and affinity and family relations. Connections with the history of the family, the social organization, economic and social factors. Connection with the local conditions of development of the family, customs and marriage norms.

Reflection of the family form in the terminology. Kinship terms and the wealth and legal status of the person. Role of kin and in-laws in the social, economic, and domestic life in cases of direct, collateral kinship, and relation by marriage. Common chores and *pomochi* and participation of kin and in-laws in them. Their role in the economic, industrial, and other associations. The *mir* and evidence of family-kinship relations. Family rituals and the role of kin and in-laws in them. The wedding, wedding rituals. Christening, godparents. Relationship between parents and godparents. Participation of relatives in the burial ritual. Participants in the ritual (permanent in the village, or special for each family), their connection to family members, role in the ritual, in the family's everyday life.

Family leisure. Education of children. Role of kin and in-laws.

Concept of kinship and relation by marriage and the body of acknowledged relatives in different social environments, in different generations.

Bibliography

MARJORIE M. BALZER, BEN EKLOF, AND LESLIE ENGLISH, COMPILERS

Western-language sources

Afanasyev, Aleksandr N. *Russian Fairy Tales*. New York: Pantheon, 1945.
———. *Russian Secret Tales: Bawdy Folktales of Old Russia*. New York: Brussel and Brussel, 1966 (original 1872).
Aksakov, Sergei. *A Russian Gentleman*, trans. J. D. Duff. Oxford, 1982 (first published as *Semeinaia khronika*, 1846).
Alexander, A. E. *Bylina and Fairy Tale: The Origins of Russian Heroic Poetry*. The Hague: Mouton, 1973.
———. *Russian Folklore: An Anthology in English Translation*. Belmont: Nordland, 1974.
Alexinsky, G. "Slavonic Mythology." *Larousse Encyclopedia of Mythology*. New York: Prometheus, 1960.
Allworth, Edward, ed. *Ethnic Russia in the USSR: The Dilemma of Dominance*. New York: Pergamon, 1980.
Anderson, Bonnie, and Zinsser, Judith P. *A History of Their Own: Women in Europe from Prehistory to the Present*, vol. 1. New York: Harper & Row, 1988.
Andreyev, Nikolai. "Pagan and Christian Elements in Old Russia." *Slavic Review*, 1962, no. 21.
Anfimov, A. M., and Zyrianov, P. N. "Elements of the Evolution of the Russian Peasant Commune in the Post-Reform Period (1861–1914)." *Soviet Studies in History*, vol. 21, no. 3 (Winter 1982–83).
Armstrong, Terence. *Russian Settlement in the North*. Cambridge: Cambridge University Press, 1965.
Atkinson, Dorothy. "The Statistics on the Russian Land Commune, 1905–1917." *Slavic Review*, vol. 32, no. 4 (December 1973).
Atkinson, Dorothy; Dallin, Alexander; and Lapidus, Gail Warshofsky, eds. *Women in Russia*. Stanford: Stanford University Press, 1977.
Avrich, Paul. *Russian Rebels, 1600–1800*. New York, 1972.
Avvakum. *The Life of Archpriest Avvakum by Himself*, trans. J. Harrison and H. Mirrlees. London: Hogarth Press, 1924.
Aytova, Alla. *The Lubok: Russian Folk Pictures, Seventeenth to Nineteenth Century*. Leningrad, 1984.
Babcock, Barbara A., ed. *The Reversible World: Symbolic Inversion in Art and Society*. Ithaca: Cornell University Press, 1978.

Balzer, Marjorie Mandelstam. "Sibiriaki." In *Encyclopedia of World Cultures: The USSR*, ed. Paul Freidrich. Yale: Human Relations Area Files, forthcoming.

Bartlett, John, ed. *Land, Commune and Peasant Community: Russia*. New York: MacMillan, 1990.

Bartlett, Roger, ed. *Land Commune and Peasant Community in Russia: Communal Forms in Imperial and Early Soviet Society*. London, 1990.

Bater, James, and French, R. A., eds. *Studies in Russian Historical Geography*, vols. 1 & 2. London, 1983.

Benet, Sula, ed. *The Village of Viriatino*. New York: Doubleday, 1970 (original Russian edition, ed. I. P. Kushner, Moscow, 1958).

Bill, Valentine. *The Forgotten Class: The Russian Bourgeoisie from the Earliest Beginnings to 1900*. New York: Praeger, 1959.

Billington, James. *The Icon and the Axe*. New York: Vintage, 1970.

Birnbaum, Henrik, and Flier, Michael S., eds. *Medieval Russian Culture*. Berkeley: University of California Press, 1984.

Blackwell, William L. *The Beginnings of Russian Industrialization 1800–1860*. Princeton: Princeton University Press, 1968.

Blake, Patricia, and Hayward, Max, eds. *Half-way to the Moon*. New York: Anchor, 1965.

Blum, Jerome. *The End of the Old Order in Rural Europe*. Princeton: Princeton University Press, 1978.

———. *Lord and Peasant in Russia: From the Ninth to the Nineteenth Century*. Princeton, 1961.

Bohac, Rodney D. "Family, Property and Socioeconomic Mobility: Russian Peasants on Manuilovskoe Estate (1810–1861)." Unpublished Ph.D. dissertation, University of Illinois, 1982.

———. "The Mir and the Military Draft." *Slavic Review*, vol. 47, no. 4 (Winter 1988).

Bourdeaux, Michael. *Patriarchs and Prophets: Persecution of the Russian Orthodox Church Today*. New York: Praeger, 1970.

Bradley, Joseph. *Muzhik and Muscovite: Urbanization in Late Imperial Russia*. Berkeley: University of California Press, 1985.

Bromlei, Iu. V., and Voronov, A. A. "Folk Medicine as a Subject of Ethnographic Investigation." *Soviet Anthropology and Archeology*, vol. 18, no. 1 (Summer 1979). Original Russian text in *Sovetskaia etnografiia*, 1976, no. 5.

Brooks, Jeffrey. *When Russia Learned to Read: Literacy and Popular Literature 1861–1917*. Princeton: Princeton University Press, 1985.

Brumfield, William C., and Velimirovich, Milos, eds. *Christianity and the Arts in Russia*. New York: Cambridge University Press, 1991.

Buckley, Thomas, and Gottlieb, Alma, eds. *Blood Magic: The Anthropology of Menstruation*. Berkeley: University of California Press, 1988.

Burke, Peter. *Popular Culture in Early Modern Europe*. London, 1978.

———. "Religion and Secularisation." In *The New Cambridge Modern History*. Vol. 12, *Companion Volume*, ed. P. Burke. Cambridge, 1979.

Bushnell, John. "Peasant Economy and Peasant Revolution at the Turn of the Century: Neither Immiseration nor Autonomy." *The Russian Review*, vol. 47, no. 1 (January 1988).

Chayanov, A. V. *The Theory of Peasant Economy*, eds. and trans. D. Thorner, B. Kerblay, R. E. F. Smith. Homewood, IL, 1966.

Chekhov, Anton. "Peasants" [Muzhiki]. E.g., in *Muzhiki i drugie rasskazy* [Moscow: Akademiia, 1932, original 1897], or *Peasants and Other Stories*, trans. Edmund Wilson. New York: Doubleday, 1956.

Cherniavsky, Michael. "The Old Believers and the New Religion." In *The Structure of Russian History*, ed. M. Cherniavsky. New York, 1970.

Christian, David, and Smith, R. E. F. *Bread and Salt: A Social and Economic History of Food and Drink in Russia*. Cambridge: Cambridge University Press, 1984.

Clements, Barbara Evans; Engel, Barbara Alpern; and Worobec, Christine D., eds. *Russia's Women: Accommodation, Resistance, Transformation*. Berkeley: University of California Press, 1991.

Cohn, Norman. *The Pursuit of the Millennium* (revised ed.). New York, 1961.

Conybeare, F. C. *Russian Dissenters*. New York, 1962.

Coquin, François-Xavier. *La Sibérie: Peuplement et immigration paysanne au XIXᵉ siècle*. Paris, 1975.

Crisp, Olga. *Studies on the Russian Economy before 1914*. London, 1976.

Crisp, Olga, and Edmondson, Linda, eds. *Civil Rights in Imperial Russia*. Oxford: Oxford University Press, 1989.

Crone, Patricia. *Pre–Industrial Societies*. Oxford: Blackwell, 1989.

Cross, Samuel Hazard, and Sherbowitz-Wetzor, Olgerd P. *The Russian Primary Chronicle*. Cambridge: Medieval Academy of America, 1953.

Crummey, Robert O. *The Old Believers and the World of Antichrist: The Vyg Community and the Russian State 1694–1855*. Madison: University of Wisconsin Press, 1970.

Crumrine, N. Ross. "Ritual Drama and Culture Change." *Comparative Studies in Society and History*, 1970, vol. 12, no. 4.

Czap, P. "Peasant–Class Courts and Peasant Customary Justice in Russia, 1861–1912." *Journal of Social History*, 1967, vol. 1.

Danilov, V. P. *Rural Russia under the New Regime*. Bloomington: Indiana University Press, 1988.

Davies, R. W. *Soviet History in the Gorbachev Revolution*. Bloomington: Indiana University Press, 1989.

Dioszegi, V., ed. *Popular Beliefs and Folklore Tradition in Siberia*. The Hague: Mouton, 1968.

Dmytryshyn, Basil; Crownhart-Vaughan, E. A. P.; and Vaughan, Thomas, eds. *Russia's Conquest of Siberia, 1558–1700: A Documentary Record*. Portland: Oregon Historical Society North Pacific Studies Series, 1985.

Douglas, Mary. *Purity and Danger: An Analysis of Concepts of Pollution and Taboo*. London: Routledge & Kegan Paul, 1966.

Druzhinin, M. N. "The Liquidation of the Feudal System in the Russian Manorial Village (1862–1882)." *Soviet Studies in History*, vol. 21, no. 3 (Winter 1982–83). Original Russian text, "Likvidatsiia feodal'noi sistemy v russkoi pomeshchich'ei derevni." *Voprosy istorii*, 1968, no. 12.

Dunlop, John. "A Conversation with Dmitrii Vasil'ev, the Leader of Pamyat'." *Radio Liberty Report on the USSR*, 15 December 1989.

———. *The Faces of Contemporary Russian Nationalism*. Princeton: Princeton University Press, 1983.

———. "Soviet Cultural Politics." *Problems of Communism*, November–December 1987.

———. "Two Noteworthy Russian Nationalist Initiatives." *Radio Liberty Report on the USSR*, 26 May 1989.

Dunn, Patrick P. "That Enemy Is the Baby: Childhood in Imperial Russia." In *The History of Childhood*, ed. Lloyd de Mause. New York, 1974.

Dunn, Stephen P., and Dunn, Ethel. "The Great Russian Peasant: Culture Change or Cultural Development." *Ethnology*, vol. 2 (July 1963).

———, eds. *Introduction to Soviet Ethnography*. Vol. 1. Berkeley: Highgate Road Social Science Research Station, 1974.

———. *The Peasants of Central Russia*. New York: Holt, Rinehart & Winston, 1967 (reprint: Prospect Heights, IL: Waveland Press, 1988).

Edelman, Robert. *Proletarian Peasants: The Revolutions of 1905 in Russia's Southwest*. Ithaca: Cornell University Press, 1987.

Eklof, Ben. *Russian Peasant Schools: Officialdom, Village Culture, and Popular Pedagogy, 1861–1914*. Berkeley: University of California Press, 1987.

———. "Ways of Seeing: Recent Anglo-American Studies of the Russian Peasant. 1861–1914)." *Jahrbücher für Geschichte Osteuropas*, 1988, vol. 36, no. 1.

Eklof, Ben, and Frank, Stephen, eds. *The World of the Russian Peasant: Post-Emancipation Culture and Society*. Boston: Unwin Hyman, 1990.

Eklof, Ben, and Gagle, Reid. "Serfs, Emancipation of." In *Modern Encyclopedia of Russian and Soviet History*, forthcoming. Ed. Joseph L. Wieczynski. Gulf Breeze, FL: Academic International Press.

Emmons, Terence, ed. *The Emancipation of the Russian Serfs*. New York, 1970.

Engel, Barbara. "Peasant Morality and Pre-Marital Relations in Late 19th Century Russia." *Journal of Social History*, 1990, vol. 23, no. 4.

Engelstein, Laura. "Morality and the Wooden Spoon: Russian Doctors View Syphilis, Social Class, and Sexual Behavior, 1890–1905." *Representations*, 14 (Spring 1981).

Ericson, Eric. "The Legend of Maxim Gorky's Youth." In idem, *Childhood and Society*, ch. 10. New York, 1963.

Falkus, M. E. *The Industrialization of Russia, 1700–1914*. London: Macmillan, 1972.

"Family History at the Crossroads." *Journal of Family History*, 1987, vol. 12, no. 1–3 (special issue).

Farnsworth, Beatrice. "The Litigious Daughter-in-Law: Family Relations in Rural Russia in the Second Half of the Nineteenth Century." *Slavic Review*, vol. 45, no. 1 (Spring 1986).

———. "The Soldatka: Folklore and Court Record," *Slavic Review*, vol. 49, no. 1 (Spring 1990).

Farrell, Dianne Ecklund. "Popular Prints in the Cultural History of Eighteenth-Century Russia." Unpublished PhD. dissertation, University of Wisconsin, 1980.

Fedotov, George P. *The Russian Religious Mind: Kievan Christianity*. New York: Harper & Row, 1960.

———. *The Russian Religious Mind: The Middle Ages*, ed. John Meyendorff. Cambridge: Harvard University Press, 1966.

Field, Daniel. *Rebels in the Name of the Tsar*. Boston: Unwin Hyman, 1976, 1989.

———. "The Reforms of the 1860s." In *Windows on the Russian Past: Essays on Soviet Historiography Since Stalin*, eds. Samuel H. Baron and Nancy W. Heer. Columbus, OH, 1977.

Figes, Orlando. "The Russian Land Commune and the Agrarian Question 1905–1930" (review of Dorothy Atkinson, *The End of the Russian Land Commune, 1905–1930* [Stanford, 1983]). *Peasant Studies*, vol. 11, no. 2 (Winter 1984).

Florovsky, George. *Collected Works*. Belmont: Norland, 1976.

Frank, Stephen P. *Cultural Conflict, Law, and Criminality in Rural Russia 1861–1907*. Forthcoming.

Freeze, Gregory L. *From Supplication to Revolution: A Documentary Social History of Imperial Russia*. New York, 1987.

———. *The Parish Clergy in the Nineteenth Century: Crisis, Reform, and Counter-Reform*. Princeton: Princeton University Press, 1983.

———. *The Russian Levites: Parish Clergy in the Eighteenth Century*. Cambridge: Harvard University Press, 1977

Frieden, Nancy M. "The Russian Cholera Epidemic, 1892–93, and Medical Professionalization." *Journal of Social History*, vol. 10 (June 1977).

Frierson, Cathy. "Crime and Punishment in the Russian Village: Rural Concepts of Criminality at the End of the Nineteenth Century." *Slavic Review*, vol. 46, no. 1 (Spring 1987).

———. "Rural Justice in Russia: the Volost' Court Debate, 1861–1912." *Slavonic and East European Review*, vol. 64 (October 1986).

Galeotti, Mark. "The Soviet Army's New Interest in Imperial Traditions." *Radio Liberty Report on the USSR*, 28 December 1990.

Gatrell, Peter. *The Tsarist Economy 1850–1917*. London, 1986.

Gibson, James R. *Feeding the Russian Fur Trade: Provisionment of the Okhotsk Seaboard and the Kamchatka Peninsula 1639–1856*. Madison: University of Wisconsin Press, 1969.

Gillis, John R. *Youth and History: Tradition and Change in European Age Relations, 1770–Present*. New York: Academic Press, 1981.

Gimbutas, Marija. "Ancient Slavic Religion: A Synopsis." In *To Honor Roman Jakobson: A Collection of Essays*. Vol. 1. The Hague and Paris: Mouton, 1967.

Glickman, Rose. "An Alternative View of the Peasantry: The *Raznochintsy* Writers of the 1860s." *Slavic Review*, 1973, vol. 32, no. 4.

Goble, Paul. "Siberian Regionalism as a Political Force." *Soviet Economy*, 1991, vol. 7.

Gorer, Geoffrey, and Rickman, John. *The Peoples of Great Russia: A Psychological Study*. New York: Norton, 1962 (original Cresset, 1949).

Gorky, Maxim. "On the Russian Peasantry." *Journal of Peasant Studies*, vol. 4 (October 1976).

Grant, Steven. "*Obshchina* and *Mir*." *Slavic Review*, vol. 35 (December 1976).

Gregory, Paul R. "The Russian Agrarian Crisis Revisited." In *The Soviet Rural Economy*, ed. Robert C. Stuart. Totowa, NJ: Rowman and Littlefield, 1984.

Gutman, Peter. "The Serf Entrepreneur in Russia: A Comment." In *Explorations in Entrepreneurial History*, ed. Henry Rosovsky, 1954, vol. 7.

Habbakuk, H. J. "Family Structure and Economic Change in Nineteenth Century

Europe." *The Journal of Economic History*, 1955, vol. 15, no. 1.

Haimson, Leopold H., ed. *The Politics of Rural Russia 1905–1914*. Bloomington, IN, 1979.

Hajnal, J. "European Marriage Patterns in Perspective." In *Population in History*, eds. D. E. C. Eversley and D. V. Glass. Chicago, 1965.

Harrison, Mark. "Resource Allocation and Agrarian Class Formation: The Problem of Social Mobility among Russian Peasant Households, 1880–1930." *Journal of Peasant Studies*, 1977, vol. 4, no. 2.

Heer, D. M. "The Demographic Transition in the Russian Empire and the Soviet Union." *Journal of Social History*, 1968, no. 1.

Hellie, Richard. *Enserfment and Military Change in Muscovy*. Chicago: University of Chicago Press, 1971.

Hoch, Stephen L. *Serfdom and Social Control in Russia. Petrovskoe, a Village in Tambov*. Chicago: University of Chicago Press, 1986.

Hodges, Richard. *Primitive and Peasant Markets*. Oxford: Blackwell, 1988.

Holquist, Peter I. "The Transformation of Peasant Identities: Changing Attitudes among Orthodox and Old Believers in Western Siberia, 1875–1900." Unpublished master's thesis, Columbia University, 1989.

Hourwich, Isaac A. *The Economics of the Russian Village*. New York, 1970 (reprint of 1892 edition).

Howe, Jovan E. *The Peasant Mode of Production As Exemplified by the Russian Obshchina-Mir*. Tampere, Finland: University of Tampere, 1991.

Hubbs, Joanna. *Mother Russia: The Feminine Myth in Russian Culture*. Bloomington: Indiana University Press, 1988.

Il'in, Viktor. "My Village of Rechnoe." *Soviet Anthropology & Archeology*, vol. 24, no. 3 (Winter 1985–86).

Ivanits, Linda J. *Russian Folk Belief*. Armonk, NY: M. E. Sharpe, 1989.

———. "Russian Folk Narratives about the Supernatural." *Soviet Anthropology & Archeology*, vol. 26, no. 2 (Fall 1987).

Jacobsen, Roman. "Slavic Folklore and Slavic Mythology." In *Standard Dictionary of Folklore and Mythology*, ed. Maria Leach. Vol. 2. New York: Funk and Wagnell, 1950.

Kahan, Arcadius. *Russian Economic History: The Nineteenth Century*. Chicago, 1989.

Kaiser, Dan. *The Growth of Law in Medieval Russia*. Princeton: Princeton University Press, 1980.

Kearney, Michael, and Nagengast, Carole. *Reconceptualizing the Peasantry*. Boulder: Westview (forthcoming).

Keenan, Edward L. "Moscovite Political Folkways." *The Russian Review*, 1986, vol. 45.

Keep, J. L. H. "Emancipation by the Axe? Peasant Revolts in Russian Thought and Literature." *Cahiers du monde russe et soviétique*, 1982, vol. 23, no. 1.

Kemp, Tom. *Industrialization in Nineteenth Century Europe*. London, 1969.

Kennan, George. *Siberia and the Exile System*. New York: Praeger, 1970 (original 1891).

Kennard, Howard P. *The Russian Peasant*. New York, 1980 (reprint of 1908 edition).

Kingston-Mann, Esther. *Lenin and the Problem of Marxist Peasant Revolution*. New York: Oxford University Press, 1983.

Kingston-Mann, Esther, and Mixter, Timothy, eds. *Peasant Economy, Culture, and Politics of European Russia, 1800–1921.* Princeton: Princeton University Press, 1991.

Kleinman, Arthur. *Patients and Healers in the Context of Culture: An Exploration of the Borderland between Anthropology, Medicine, and Psychiatry.* Berkeley: University of California Press, 1980.

Klibanov, A. I. "Fifty Years of Scientific Study of Religious Sectarianism." *Soviet Sociology*, 1970, vol. 8, no. 3–4.

———. *History of Religious Sectarianism in Russia (1860s–1917)*, trans. Ethel Dunn and ed. Stephen P. Dunn. New York: Pergamon, 1982.

Kolchin, Peter. *Unfree Labor: American Slavery and Russian Serfdom.* Cambridge: Harvard University Press, 1987.

Kollmann, Jack Edward. "The *Stoglav* Council and Parish Priests." *Russian History*, 1980, vol. 7, nos. 1–2.

Kollmann, Nancy Shields. *Kinship and Politics: The Making of the Muscovite Political System, 1345–1547.* Stanford: Stanford University Press, 1987.

———. "The Seclusion of Elite Muscovite Women." *Russian History*, 1983, vol. 10, pt. 2.

Kourenoff, Paul M., and St. George, George. *Russian Folk Medicine.* New York: Pyramid, 1971.

Krader, Lawrence. "Recent Studies of the Russian Peasant." *American Anthropologist*, 1956, vol. 58.

Krukones, James H. *To the People: The Russian Government and the Newspapers "Sel'skii Vestnik" ("Village Herald"), 1881–1917.* New York: Garland Publishing, 1987.

Kushner, P. I. *The Village of Viriatino*, ed. and trans. Sula Benet. New York, 1970 (original Russian edition, Moscow, 1958).

Kuzmina, L. P. "Ethnocultural Aspects of Research in the Oral Tradition of the Russian Population of Siberia." *Review of Ethnology*, 1982, vol. 8.

Lantzeff, George V., and Pierce, Richard A. eds. *Eastward to Empire: Exploration and Conquest on the Russian Open Frontier.* Montreal: McGill-Queens University Press, 1973.

Lapidus, Gail Warshofsky, ed. *Women, Work and Family in the Soviet Union.* Armonk, NY: M. E. Sharpe, 1982.

"Law on Freedom of Conscience." *Current Digest of the Soviet Press*, vol. 42, no. 40.

Leroy-Beaulieu, A. *The Empire of the Tsars and the Russians*, trans. Z. A. Rogosin. Vol. 3. London, 1905.

Le Roy-Ladurie, Emmanuel. "The Historian in the Countryside" and "History without People." In idem, *The Territory of the Historian.* Chicago: University of Chicago Press, 1982.

———. "Peasants." In *The New Cambridge Modern History.* Vol. 12, *Companion Volume*, ed. P. Burke. Cambridge: Cambridge University Press, 1979.

Levin, Eve. *Sex and Society in the World of the Orthodox Slavs 900–1700.* Ithaca: Cornell University Press, 1989.

Lewin, Moshe. "Customary Law and Russian Rural Society in the Post-Reform Era." *The Russian Review*, 1985, vol. 44.

————. *Russian Peasants and Soviet Power*. Evanston: Northwestern University Press, 1968.

Likhachev, D. S. "Russian Culture in the Modern World." Harriman Institute seminar report, Columbia University, 13 November 1990.

————. "Preliminary Results of a Thousand-year Experiment." *The Soviet Multinational State*. Armonk, NY: M. E. Sharpe, 1990.

Lomnitz-Adler, Claudio. "Concepts for the Study of Regional Culture." *American Ethnologist*, vol. 18, no. 2.

Longworth, Philip. "Peasant Leadership and the Pugachev Revolt." *The Journal of Peasant Studies*, 1975, vol. 2, no. 2.

Macey, David A. J. *Government and Peasant in Russia, 1861–1906: The Prehistory of the Stolypin Reforms*. Dekalb, IL: Northern Illinois University Press, 1987.

Matossian, Mary. "Climate, Crops and Natural Increase in Rural Russia, 1861–1913." *Slavic Review* vol. 45 (Fall 1986).

Maynard, Sir John. *The Russian Peasant and Other Studies*. New York: Collier, 1942.

Mead, Margaret. *Soviet Attitudes toward Authority: An Interdisciplinary Approach to Problems of Soviet Character*. New York: Schocken, 1951.

Mead, Margaret, and Metraux, Rhoda, eds. *The Study of Culture at a Distance*. Chicago: University of Chicago Press, 1953.

Melton, Herman E., Jr. "Serfdom and the Peasant Economy in Russia, 1780–1861." Ph.D. dissertation, Columbia University, 1984.

Meyendorff, John. "The Church." In *An Introduction to Russian History*. Vol. 1 of *Companion to Russian Studies*, eds. R. Auty and D. Obolensky. Cambridge, England, 1976.

Miliukov, P. N. *Outlines of Russian Culture: Religion and the Church*. New York: Barnes, 1960. Originally published in Russian as *Ocherki po istorii russkoi kul'tury*.

Minenko, N. A. "Traditional Forms of Investigation and Trial among the Russian Peasants of Western Siberia in the Eighteenth and First Half of the Nineteenth Centuries." *Soviet Anthropology & Archeology*, vol. 21, no. 3 (Summer 1982) (originally published in Russian in *Sovetskaia etnografiia*, 1980, no. 5).

Mitterauer, Michael, and Sieder, Reinhard, eds. *The European Family: Patriarchy to Partnership from the Middle Ages to the Present*, trans. K. Oosterveen and M. Horzinger. Chicago: University of Chicago Press, 1982.

Mixter, Timothy. "Peasant Collective Action in Saratov Province, 1902–1906." In *Politics and Society in Provincial Russia, 1590–1917*, eds. Rex A. Wade and Scott J. Seregny. Columbus, OH, 1990.

Mongait, A. L. *Archeology in the USSR*, trans. M. W. Thomson. Baltimore: Penguin, 1961 (original 1955).

Moon, David Gerrard. "The Russian Seigneurial Peasantry and Tsarist Legislation: Aspects of 'The Peasant Movement' 1825–1855." Unpublished Ph.D. dissertation, University of Birmingham, 1987.

Moore, Barrington, Jr. *Social Origins of Dictatorship and Democracy: Lord and Peasant in the Making of the Modern World*. Boston: Beacon Press, 1966.

Moore, Sally Falk. *Law as Process: An Anthropological Approach*. London: Routledge & Kegan Paul, 1978.

Moore, Sally Falk, and Myerhoff, Barbara G. *Secular Ritual*. Amsterdam: Van Gorkum, 1977.

Moskoff, William. "Divorce in the USSR." *Journal of Marriage and the Family*, 1983, vol. 45.

Norton, Henry K. *The Far Eastern Republic of Siberia*. New York: Hyperion Press, 1982.

Nosova, G. A. "Mapping of Russian Shrovetide Rituals (from Materials of the Nineteenth and Early Twentieth Centuries)." *Soviet Anthropology & Archeology*, vol. 14, no. 1–2 (Summer–Fall 1975).

Obolensky, Dimitri. "Popular Religion in Medieval Russia." In *The Religious World of Russian Culture: Russia and Orthodoxy* ed. A. Blane. Vol. 2 of *Essays in Honor of Georges Florovsky*. The Hague and Paris, 1975.

O'Flaherty, Wendy D. *Women, Androgynes, and Other Mythical Beasts*. Chicago: Chicago University Press, 1980.

Oinas, Felix J. *Essays on Russian Folklore and Mythology*. Columbus, OH: Slavica Publishers, 1985.

Oinas, Felix J., and Soudakoff, Stephen, eds. *The Study of Russian Folklore*. The Hague: Mouton, 1975.

Ouspensky, L. *Essai sur la théologie de l'icone dans l'Eglise orthodoxe*. Paris, 1960.

Owen, Launcelot A. *The Russian Peasant Movement 1906–1917*. New York, 1963.

Paige, Jeffery M. *Agrarian Revolution: Social Movements and Export Agriculture in the Underdeveloped World*. New York, 1975.

Pascal, Pierre. *The Religion of the Russian People*, trans. Rowan Williams. Oxford: Mobray, 1976.

Pearson, Thomas S. "Russian Law and Rural Justice: Activity and Problems of the Russian Justices of the Peace, 1865–1889." *Jahrbücher für Geschichte Osteuropas*, 1984, vol. 32, no. 1.

———. *Russian Officialdom in Crisis: Autocracy and Local Self-Government, 1861–1900*. Cambridge: Cambridge University Press, 1989.

Perrie, Maureen. *The Agrarian Policy of the Russian Socialist-Revolutionary Party from Its Origins through the Revolution of 1905–1907*. Cambridge, England, 1976.

———. "Folklore as Evidence of Peasant *Mentalité*." *The Russian Review*, vol. 48, no. 2 (April 1989).

Plakans, Andrejs. *Kinship in the Past: An Anthropology of European Family Life, 1500–1900*. Oxford, 1984.

Pounds, Norman J. G. *Hearth and Home: A History of Material Culture*. Bloomington, IN: Indiana University Press, 1989.

Pushkarev, Sergei. "The Russian Peasants' Reaction to the Emancipation of 1861." *The Russian Review*, 1968, vol. 27.

———. *Dictionary of Russian Historical Terms from the Eleventh Century to 1917*. New Haven: Yale University Press, 1970.

Radishchev, Aleksandr. "Journey from St. Petersburg to Moscow." In *Imperial Russia: A Source Book, 1700–1917*, ed. Basil Dmytryshyn. 2nd ed. Hinsdale, IL, 1974.

Raeff, Marc. "Pugachev's Rebellion." In *Preconditions of Revolution in Early Modern Europe*, eds. R. Forster and J. P. Greene. Baltimore, 1970.

Ramet, S. P., ed. *Religious Policy in the Soviet Union*. Cambridge: Cambridge University Press, 1992.

Ransel, David L., ed. *The Family in Imperial Russia: New Lines of Historical Research*. Urbana-Champaign: University of Illinois Press, 1978.

————. "Mothering, Medicine and Infant Mortality in Russia." Kennan Institute Occasional Paper no. 236, 1990.

————. *Mothers of Misery: Child Abandonment in Russia.* Princeton: Princeton University Press, 1988.

Rice, T. Talbot. *The Russian Icon.* London, 1947.

Robinson, Geroid Tanquary. *Rural Russia under the Old Regime.* Berkeley: University of California Press, 1969 (original, 1932).

Roeder, Philip G. "Legitimacy and Peasant Revolution: An Alternative to Moral Economy." *Peasant Studies,* vol. 11, no. 3 (Spring 1984).

Romanucci-Ross, Lola; Moerman, Daniel R.; and Tancredi, Laurence, eds. *The Anthropology of Medicine: From Culture to Method.* Westport: Bergin and Garvey, 1991, revised.

Rosovsky, Henry. "The Serf Entrepreneur in Russia." *Explorations in Entrepreneurial History,* vol. 6 (May 1954).

Rothemund, N. J. *Ikonenkunst. Ein Handbuch.* Munich, 1954.

Rueshchemeyer, Marilyn. *Professional Work and Marriage: An East-West Comparison.* New York: St. Martin's Press, 1986.

Sadovnikov, D. *Riddles of the Russian People: A Collection of Riddles, Parables and Puzzles,* trans. A. C. Bigalow. Ann Arbor, 1986.

Scott, James C. *Weapons of the Weak: Everyday Forms of Peasant Resistance.* New Haven: Yale University Press, 1986.

Seregny, Scott J. *Russian Teachers and Peasant Revolution: The Politics of Education in 1905.* Bloomington, IN, 1989.

Shanin, Teodor. *The Awkward Class: The Political Sociology of the Peasantry in a Developing Society: Russia, 1910–1925.* New York: Clarendon, 1972.

————, ed. *Peasants and Peasant Societies.* Baltimore: Penguin, 1971.

————. *The Roots of Otherness: Russia's Turn of the Century.* Vol. 1: *Russia as a "Developing" Society.* London, 1985; vol. 2: *Russia, 1905–1907: Revolution as a Moment of Truth.* London, 1986.

Shimkin, Dmitri B. "National Forces and Ecological Adaptations in the Development of Russian Peasant Societies." In *Process and Pattern in Culture,* ed. R. A. Manners. Chicago, 1964.

Shimkin, Dmitri B., and Sanjuan, Pedro. "Culture and World View: A Method of Analysis Applied to Rural Russia." *American Anthropologist,* vol. 55.

Shinn, William T. "The Law of the Russian Peasant Household." *Slavic Review,* 1961, vol. 20, no. 4.

Silverman, Sydel. "The Peasant Concept in Anthropology." *Journal of Peasant Studies,* 1979, vol. 7.

Smith, Hedrick. *The New Russians.* New York: Random House, 1990.

Smith, R. E. F., ed. "The Russian Peasant 1920 and 1984." *The Journal of Peasant Studies,* vol. 4, no. 1.

Stewart, John Massey, and Wood, Alan, eds. *Siberia: Two Historical Perspectives.* London: School of Slavonic and East European Studies, 1984.

Szczesniak, Boleslaw, ed. *The Russian Revolution and Religion: A Collection of Documents Concerning the Suppression of Religion by the Communists 1917–1925.* Notre Dame: University of Notre Dame Press, 1959.

Szporluk, Roman. "Dilemmas of Russian Nationalism." *Problems of Communism*, July–August 1989.

Thomas, Keith V. *Religion and the Decline of Magic*. London, 1971.

Tilly, Charles. "Did the Cake of Custom Break?" In *Consciousness and Class Experience in Nineteenth Century Europe*, ed. John Merriman. New York, 1979.

Todd, William Mills III, ed. *Literature & Society in Imperial Russia, 1800–1914*. Stanford, 1978.

Treadgold, Donald W. *The Great Siberian Migration: Government and Peasant in Resettlement from Emancipation to the First World War*. Princeton, 1957.

Tsipko, Aleksandr S. "The Sources of Stalinism." *Soviet Law and Government*, vol. 29, nos. 1 and 2 (Summer and Fall 1990).

Tultseva, L. A. "Calendrical Religious Festivals in the Life of the Contemporary Peasantry (Based on Materials from Riazan' Oblast')." *Soviet Anthropology & Archeology*, vol. 13, no. 1 (Summer 1974).

Turgenev, Ivan. *A Sportsman's Sketchbook* [Zapiski otkhotnika]. Any edition.

Turner, Victor, ed. *Celebration: Studies in Festivity and Ritual*. Washington: Smithsonian Institution Press, 1982.

von Haxthausen, August. *Studies on the Interior of Russia*, ed. and intro. S. Frederick Starr. Chicago, 1972.

Von Laue, Theodore. "Russian Peasants in the Factory." *Journal of Economic History*, 1961, vol. 26.

Vucinich, Wayne S., ed. *The Peasant in Nineteenth-century Russia*. Stanford: Stanford University Press, 1968.

Vucinich, W., and Emmons, T. eds. *The Zemstvo in Russia: An Experiment in Local Self-Government*. Cambridge: Cambridge University Press, 1982.

Wada, Haruki. "The Inner World of Russian Peasants." *Annals of the Institute of Social Science*, vol. 20 (Tokyo, 1979).

Wall, Richard, ed. *Family Forms in Historica Europe*. Cambridge, England, 1983.

Wallace, Sir Donald Mackenzie. *Russia on the Eve of War and Revolution*, ed. Cyril E. Black. Princeton: Princeton University Press, 1984 (reprint of 1877 edition).

Wcislo, Francis William. *Reforming Rural Russia: State, Local Society, and National Politics, 1855–1914*. Princeton: Princeton University Press, 1990.

Weber, Frederick C., ed. *The Present State of Russia*. Vol. 2. London: Taylor, Innys and Osborn, 1722.

Weissman, Neil. "Rural Crime in Tsarist Russia: The Question of Hooliganism, 1905–1914." *Slavic Review*, vol. 37 (June 1978).

Willets, H. T. "The Agrarian Problem." In *Russia Enters the Twentieth Century*, ed. Erwin Oberlander. New York, 1971.

Wilson, Edmund, ed. *Peasants and Other Stories*. New York: Doubleday, 1956.

Wirtschafter, Elise Kimerling. *From Serf to Russian Soldier*. Princeton: Princeton University Press, 1990.

———. *Peasants*. Englewood Cliffs, NJ, 1966.

———. *Peasant Wars of the Twentieth Century*. New York, 1968.

Wolf, Eric R. *Europe and the People without History*. Berkeley: University of California Press, 1982.

Wolf, Eric R. *Peasants*. Englewood Cliffs, NJ: Prentice-Hall, 1966.

Worobec, Christine D. "Horse Thieves and Peasant Justice in Post-Emancipation Imperial Russia." *Journal of Social History*, vol. 21 (Winter 1987).

―――. *Peasant Russia: Family and Community in the Post-Emancipation Period.* Princeton, 1991.

―――. "Temptress or Virgin? The Precarious Sexual Position of Women in Post-Emancipation Ukrainian Peasant Society." *Slavic Review*, 1990, vol. 49, no. 2.

Yaney, George L. *The Urge to Mobilize: Agrarian Reform in Russia, 1861–1930.* Urbana, IL: University of Illinois Press, 1982.

Zaionchkovskii, P. A. *The Abolition of Serfdom in Russia.* Trans. and ed. Susan Wobst. Gulf Breeze, FL: Academic International Press, 1978

Zenzinov, Vladimir. *The Road to Oblivion.* New York: National Travel Club, 1931.

Zenkovsky, Serge A. *Medieval Russia's Epics, Chronicles and Tales.* 2nd ed. New York: Dutton, 1974.

Zguta, Russell. "The Pagan Priests of Old Russia: Some New Insights." *Slavic Review*, 1974, vol. 33, no. 2.

―――. *Russian Minstrels: A History of the Skomorokhi.* Philadelphia: University of Pennsylvania Press, 1978.

―――. "Witchcraft and Medicine in Pre-Petrine Russia." *Russian Review*, 1978, vol. 37, no. 4.

Zhirnova, G. V. "The Russian Wedding Ritual in the Late Nineteenth and Early Twentieth Centuries." *Soviet Anthropology & Archeology*, vol. 14, no. 3 (Winter 1975).

Russian-language sources

Abramov, N. "Gorod Ialutorovsk s ego okrugom." *Tobol'skie gub. vedomosti*, 1864, no. 27.

―――. "Reka Tobol' s ee pritokami." *Tobol'skie gub. vedomosti*, 1863, no. 3.

Adrianova-Peretts, V. P. *Povest' vremennykh let.* Moscow-Leningrad, 1950.

Afanas'ev, A. *Drevo zhizni. Izbrannye stat'i.* Moscow, 1983.

―――. *Poeticheskie vozzreniia slavian na prirodu.* Vol. 2. Moscow, 1868.

―――. *Narodnye russkie skazki A. N. Afanas'eva, v 3-kh tomakh.* Moscow, 1957.

Akimova, T. M., et al. *Russkoe narodnoe poeticheskoe tvorchestvo: posobie k seminarskim zaniatiam.* Moscow, 1983.

Aleksandrov, V. A., ed. *Na putiakh iz zemli Permskoi v Sibir: ocherki etnografii severnoural'skogo krest'ianstva XVII–XX vv.* Moscow: Nauka, 1989.

Aleksandrov, V. A. *Obychnoe pravo krepostnoi derevni Rossii XVIII–nachalo XIX v.* Moscow, 1984.

―――. *Russkoe naselenie Sibiri XVII–nachala XVIII v. (Eniseiskii krai).* Moscow, 1964.

―――. *Sel'skaia obshchina v Rossii (XVII–nachalo XIX v.).* Moscow, 1976.

―――. "Vozniknovenie sel'skoi obshchiny v Sibiri (XVII v.)." *Istoriia SSSR*, 1987, no. 1.

Alekseichenko, G. A. "Prigovory sel'skikh skhodov kak istochnik po istorii krest'ianskoi obshchiny v Rossii vtoroi poloviny XIX v." *Istoriia SSSR*, 1981, no. 6.

Andreev, I. "Domovaia letopis'." In *Chteniia v obshchestve istorii i drevnostei Rossiiskikh pri Moskovskom universitete (ChOIDR).* Bk. 4. Moscow, 1870.

Anfimov, A. M. *Krest'ianskoe khoziaistvo evropeiskoi Rossii 1881–1904*. Moscow, 1980.

Anichkov, A. *Iazychestvo i drevniaia Rus'*. St. Petersburg, 1914.

Anichkov, E. V. *Vesenniaia obriadovaia pesnia na Zapade i u slavian*. St. Petersburg, 1903.

Anisimov, E. V. "Petr I: Rozhdenie imperii." *Voprosy istorii*, 1989, no. 7.

Anokhina, L. A., and Shmeleva, M. N. *Byt gorodskogo naseleniia srednei polosy RSFSR v proshlom i nastoiashchem*. Moscow, 1977.

———. *Kul'tura i byt kolkhoznikov Kalininskoi oblasti*. Moscow, 1964.

Aref'ev, V. S. "Obraztsy narodnoi slovesnosti: primety, gadan'ia, koldovstvo, nagovory i sueveriia." *Izv. VSORGO*, 1901, vol. 32, no. 1–2.

Astakhova, A. M. *Khudozhestvennyi obraz i mirovozzrencheskii element v zagovorakh*. Moscow, 1964.

Astyrev, N. M. *V volostnykh pisariakh: Ocherki krest'ianskogo samoupravleniia*. Moscow, 1896.

Avdeeva, E. "Ocherki maslenitsy v Evropeiskoi Rossii i Sibiri, v gorodakh i derevniakh." *Otechestvennye zapiski*, 1849, vol. 62, no. 2.

Azadovskii, M. K. "Zagovory amurskikh kazakov." *Zhivaia starina*, 1914, issue 3–4.

Bakhrushin, S. V. *Nauchnye trudy*. 3 vols. Moscow, 1952–54.

Barsukov, I. V. *O zhizni i podvigakh Innokentiia*. St. Petersburg: Tip. Katankogo, 1893.

Basilov, V. N. "Sledy kul'ta umiraiushchego i voskresaiushchego bozhestva v khristianskoi i musul'manskoi agiologii." In *Fol'klor i istoricheskaia etnografiia*. Moscow, 1983.

Belov, I. *Putevye zametki i vpechatleniia po Zapadnoi Sibiri*. Moscow, 1852.

Bernshtam, T. A. *Molodezh' v obriadovoi zhizni russkoi obshchiny XIX– nachala XX v. Polyvozrastnoi aspekt traditsionnoi kul'tury*. Leningrad, 1988.

———. "Russkaia narodnaia kul'tura i narodnaia religiia." *Sovetskaia etnografiia*, 1989, no. 1.

Bezsonov, P. *Kaliki perekhozhie*. Vol. 1, nos. 1–3. Moscow, 1861.

Biriukov, Ia. O., ed. *Altaiskii sbornik*, 1911, vol. 11.

Bleklov, S. M. "Krest'ianskoe obshchestvennoe upravlenie." In *Istoriia Rossii v XIX veke* (9 vols.), ed. M. N. Pokrovskii. Vol. 5.

Bogoslovskii, M. M. *Zemskoe samoupravlenie na russkom Severe v XVII v.* Vol. 1. Moscow, 1909.

Bogatyrev, P. G., ed. *Russkoe narodnoe poeticheskoe tvorchestvo*. Moscow, 1954.

Bogdanov, V. " 'Dushila' u russkikh raskol'nikov." *Etnograficheskoe obozrenie*, 1904, no. 2.

Boguslavskaia, I. Ia. *Russkoe narodnoe iskusstvo v sobranii Gosudarstvennogo Russkogo Muzeia*. Leningrad: Khudozhnik, 1984.

Boiarshinova, Z. Ia., and Lozinskii, V. V. "O sovmestnom vladenii zemlei v Tomskom uezde (Po dannym perepisnykh knig 1703 i 1720 gg.)." *Iz istorii Sibiri*, issue 4. Tomsk, 1972.

Bolonev, F. F. *Narodnyi kalendar' semeiskikh Zabaikal'ia (vtoraia polovina XIX–nachalo XX v.)*. Novosibirsk, 1978.

———. "O nekotorykh sposobakh narodnogo vrachevaniia u semeiskikh Zabaikal'ia."

In *Etnograficheskie aspekty izucheniia narodnoi meditsiny: Tezisy vsesoiuznoi konferentsii.* Leningrad, 1975.

Bokov, V. E. *K voprosu o kolonizatsii Cherdynskogo kraia v sviazi s razvitiem ekspluatatsii lesov.* Perm', 1898.

Boltrik, Iu. V. "Sukhoputnye kommunikatsii skifii (po materialam novostroechenykh issledovanii ot Priazov'ia do Dnepra)." *Sovetskaia arkheologiia,* 1990, no. 4.

Brokgauz, F. A., and Efron, I. A., eds. *Entsiklopedicheskii slovar'.*

Bromlei, Iu. V., and Voronov, A. A. "Narodnaia meditsina kak predmet etnograficheskikh issledovanii." *Sovetskaia etnografiia,* 1976, no. 5.

Budovnits, I. U. *Monastyri na Rusi i bor'ba s nimi krest'ian v XIV–XVI vv.* Moscow, 1966.

Bulgakov, S. V. *Nastol'naia kniga dlia sviashchennotserkovnosluzhitelei.* Kiev, 1913.

Bulygin, Iu. S. "Nekotorye voprosy kul'tury pripisnoi derevni Kolyvano-Voskresenskikh gornykh zavodov XVIII v." In *Krest'ianstvo Sibiri XVIII–nachala XX v.* Novosibirsk, 1975.

Bunak, V. V., and Zolotareva, I. M., eds. *Russkie starozhily Sibiri.* Moscow: Nauka, 1973.

Buslaev, F. I. *Istoricheskie ocherki russkoi narodnoi slovesnosti i iskusstva.* Vol. 1, *Epicheskaia poeziia.* St. Petersburg, 1861.

Busygin, E. P. *Obshchestvennyi i semeinyi byt russkogo sel'skogo naseleniia Srednego Povolzh'ia.* Kazan', 1973.

Butkevich, (Archpriest) T. I. *Obzor russkikh sekt i ikh tolkov.* Khar'kov, 1910.

"Byt belorusskikh krest'ian (Vitebskaia gub.)." *Etnograficheskii sbornik.* Issue 2. St. Petersburg, 1854.

"Byt krest'ian Kurskoi gub. Oboianskogo u." *Etnograficheskii sbornik.* Issue 5. St. Petersburg, 1862.

"Byt krest'ian Tverskoi gubernii Tverskogo uezda." *Etnograficheskii sbornik.* Issue 1. St. Petersburg, 1853.

Cherepnin, L. V. "Iz istorii drevnerusskogo koldovstva XII v." *Etnografiia,* 1929, no. 2.

———. *Obrazovanie russkogo tsentralizovannogo gosudarstva v XIV–XV vv.* Moscow, 1960.

Cherniakovskii, N. "Statisticheskoe opisanie Ishimskogo okruga Tobol'skoi gubernii." *ZhMVD,* 1843, pt. 2.

Chernov, I. A. "O strukture russkikh liubovnykh zagovorov." In *Trudy po znakovym sistemam.* Tartu, 1965.

Chernykh, E. N. *Metall, chelovek, vremia.* Moscow, 1972.

Chicherin, B. *Opyty po istorii russkogo prava.* Moscow, 1858.

Chicherov, V. I. *Shkoly skazitelei Zaonezh'ia.* Moscow, 1982.

———. *Zimnii period russkogo narodnogo zemledel'cheskogo kalendaria XVI–XIX vv.* Moscow, 1957.

Chistov, K. V. *Narodnyi traditsii i fol'klor: ocherk teorii.* Leningrad, 1986.

———. *Russkie narodnye sotsial'no-utopicheskie legendy.* Moscow, 1967.

———. *Russkie skaziteli Karelii. Ocherki i vospominaniia.* Petrozavodsk, 1980.

Chukmaldin, N. *Moi vospominaniia.* St. Petersburg, 1899.

Dal', V. I. *Poslovitsy russkogo naroda.* Moscow: Nauka, 1957 (original 1878).

———. *Tol'kovyi slovar' zhivogo velikorusskogo iazyka.* Moscow: Russkii iazyk, 1978 (original 1863–66).

Demidova, N. F. *Sluzhilaia biurokratiia v Rossii XVII v. i ee rol' v formirovanii absoliutisma.* Moscow, 1988.

Dergacheva-Skop, E. I., and Romodanovskaia, E. K. "Sobranie rukopisnykh knig Gosudarstvennogo arkhiva Tiumenskoi oblasti v Tobol'ske." In *Arkheografiia i istochnikovedenie Sibiri.* Novosibirsk, 1975.

Dintses, L. A. "Dokhristianskie khramy Rusi v svete pamiatnikov narodnogo iskusstva." *Sovetskaia etnografiia*, 1947, no. 2.

Dmitriev, A. *Pisatel'-samouchka Aleksandr Nikiforovich Zyrianov.* Kazan', 1885.

Dmitriev, A. A. *Permskaia starina. (Sb. ist. statei i materialov preimushchestvenno o Permskom krae)*, issue 3, Perm', 1891; issue 4, 1892.

Dmitriev, L. A. *Zhitiinye povesti russkogo Severa kak pamiatniki literatury XIII–XVII vv.* Leningrad, 1973.

Dmitrieva, S. I. "Slovo i obriad v mezenskikh zagovorakh." *Obriady i obriadovyi fol'klor.* Moscow, 1982.

Dneprov, E. D. ed. *Ocherki istorii shkoly i pedagogicheskoi mysli narodov SSSR: s drevneishikh vremen do kontsa xvii v.* Moscow, 1989.

Dobrovol'skii, V. N. *Smolenskii etnograficheskii sbornik.* Pt. 2. St. Petersburg, 1893.

Domostroi po spisku Obshchestva istorii i drevnostei rossiiskikh. Moscow, 1882.

Drevnerusskie kniazheskie ustavy XI–XV vv. Moscow, 1976.

"Drevnerusskie letopisi i khroniki." In *Trudy Otdela drevnerusskoi literatury.* Vol. 39. Leningrad, 1985.

Druzhinin, M. N. "Likvidatsiia feodal'noi sistemy v russkoi pomeshch'ei derevne (1862–1882)." In idem, *Izbrannye trudy.* Moscow, 1987.

———. *Russkaia derevnia na perelome 1861–1880.* Moscow, 1978.

Dubov, I. V. "Spornye voprosy etnicheskoi istorii severovostochnoi Rusi IX–XIII vekov." *Voprosy istorii*, 1990, no. 5.

Dubrovskii, S. M. "Rossiiskaia obshchina v literature XIX i nachala XX vekov: Bibliograficheskii obzor." In *Voprosy istorii sel'skogo khoziaistva, krest'ianstva, i revoliutsionnogo dvizheniia v Rossii.* Moscow: Nauka, 1961.

Dzhivelegov, A., et al., eds. *Velikaia reforma: Russkoe obshchestvo i krest'ianskii vopros v proshlom i nastoiashchem.* 6 vols. Moscow, 1911.

Efimenko, A. *Issledovanie narodnoi zhizni.* 3 vols. Moscow, 1884.

Efimenko, P. S. "Materialy po etnografii russkogo naseleniia Arkhangel'skoi gubernii." Pt. 1. *Izv. OLEAE*, 1877.

Eleonskaia, E. *K izucheniiu zagovora i koldovstva v Rossii.* Issue 1. Moscow, 1917.

El'nitskii, L. A. "Vizantiiskii prazdnik brumalii i rimskie saturnalii." In *Antichnost' i Vizantiia.* Moscow, 1975.

Engel'gardt, A. N. *Iz derevni: 12 pisem 1872–1887.* St. Petersburg, 1882 (most recent edition Moscow, 1987, reprint of 3rd ed.: Moscow, 1897) [English translation forthcoming by C. Frierson].

Engels, F. *Dialektika prirody.* Moscow, 1957.

Etimologicheskii slovar' russkogo iazyka. Vol. 2, issue 8. Moscow, 1982.

"Etnograficheskie nabliudeniia po puti po Volge i ee pritokam." *Izv. OLEAE*, vol. 28, bk. 4. Moscow, 1877.

Evreinov, N. N. *Azazel i Dionis.* Leningrad, 1924.

———. *Istoriia telesnykh nakazanii v Rossii.* New York, 1979 (reprint of prerevolutionary ed., n.d., n.p.).

F. (F. N. Usov), "Izvestiia, soobshchennye iz Omska." *Tobol'skie gubernskie vedomosti*, 1858, no. 8.

Famintsyn, A. S. *Bozhestva drevnikh slavian*. St. Petersburg, 1884.

Fedorova, M. E., and Sumnikova, T. A. *Khrestomatiia po drevnerusskoi literature*. Moscow, 1969.

Froianov, I. Ia. *Genezis i razvitie feodalizma v Rossii*. Leningrad, 1987.

———. *Kievskaia Rus'. Ocherki sotsial'no-politicheskoi istorii*. Leningrad, 1980.

———. "Nachalo khristianstva na Rusi." *Khristianstvo: Antichnost'. Vizantiia. Drevniaia Rus'*. Leningrad, 1988.

Froianov, I. Ia., and Dvornichenko, A. Iu. *Goroda-gosudarstva drevnei Rusi*. Leningrad: LGU Press, 1988.

Gal'kovskii, N. M. *Bor'ba khristianstva s ostatkami iazychestva v drevnei Rusi*. Vol. 1. Khar'kov, 1916.

Garkavi, A. Ia. *Skazaniia musul'manskikh pisatelei o slavianakh i russkikh*. St. Petersburg, 1870.

Gavriliuk, N. K. *Kartografirovanie iavlenii dukhovnoi kul'tury*. Kiev, 1981.

Golodnikov, K. "Ialutorovskii okrug gubernii Tobol'skoi." *ZhMVD*, 1846, pt. 15.

Golovin, K. *Sel'skaia obshchina v literature i deistvitel'nosti*. St. Petersburg, 1887.

Golovko, A. B. "Khristianizatsiia vostochnoslavianskogo obshchestva i vneshniaia politika drevnei rusi v IX–pervoi treti XIII veka." *Voprosy istorii*, 1988, no. 9.

Golubinskii, E. *Istoriia kanonizatsii sviatykh v russkoi tserkvi*. Moscow, 1903.

———. *Istoriia russkoi tserkvi*. Vol. 1. Moscow, 1901.

Gorbunov, B. V. "Narodnye vidy sportivnoi bor'by kak element traditsionnoi kul'tury russkikh (XIX–nachalo XX v.)." *Sovetskaia etnografiia*, 1989, no. 4.

Gorchakov, M. *O taine supruzhestva. Proiskhozhdenie, istoriko-iuridicheskoe znachenie i kanonicheskoe dostoinstvo 50 glavy pechatnoi Kormchei knigi*. St. Petersburg, 1880.

Gorodtsov, N. A. "Prazdniki i obriady krest'ian Tiumenskogo uezda." *EGTM*, 1915, issue 26.

Gorovoi, F. S. "Ob izmenenii zemlevladeniia i zemlepol'zovaniia gornozavodskogo naseleniia zavodov Abamelik-Lazareva v poreformennyi period." In *Voprosy agrarnoi istorii Urala*.

———. "Vliianie reformy 1861 g. na formirovanie rabochego klassa Urala." In *Iz istorii rabochego klassa*.

Gorskii, A. D. *Ocherki ekonomicheskogo polozheniia krest'ian Severo-Vostochnoi Rusi XIV–XV vv.* Moscow, 1960.

Grekov, B. D. *Kievskaia Rus'*. Moscow, 1953.

Grigorovskii, N. P. "Krest'iane-starozhily Narymskogo kraia." In *Zapiski Zap.-Sib. otd. RGO*. Bk. 1. Omsk, 1879.

Grinkova, N. "Odezhda bukhtarminskikh staroobriadtsev." In *Bukhtarminskie staroobriadtsy*. Leningrad, 1930.

———. "Materialy dlia slovaria." In *Bukhtarminskie staroobriadtsy*. Leningrad, 1930.

Gromyko, M. M. "Dokhristianskie verovaniia v bytu sibirskikh krest'ian XVIII–XIX vv." In *Iz istorii sem'i i byta sibirskogo krest'ianstva XVII–nachala XX v.* Novosibirsk, 1975.

———. "Dukhovnaia zhizn' russkogo krest'ianstva vo vtoroi polovine XVII–pervoi polovine XIX v." In *Istoriia krest'ianstva v Evropi*. Moscow, 1986.

―――. "Kul'tura russkogo krest'ianstva XVIII–XIX vekov kak predmet istoricheskogo issledovaniia." *Istoriia SSSR*, 1987, no. 3.

―――. "Obychai pomochei u russkikh krest'ian v XIX v. (K probleme kompleksnogo issledovaniia trudovykh traditsii)." *Sovetskaia etnografiia*, 1981, no. 4.

―――. "Problemy, metody i istochniki issledovaniia eticheskikh traditsii vostochnykh slavian (XVIII–XIX vv.)." In *Istoriia, kul'tura, etnografiia i fol'klor slavianskikh narodov*. Moscow, 1983.

―――. "Territorial'naia krest'ianskaia obshchina Sibiri (30-e gody, XVIII–60-e gody XIX v.)." In *Krest'ianskaia obshchina v Sibiri XVIII–nachala XX v.* Novosibirsk, 1977.

―――. *Traditsionnye normy povedeniia i formy obshcheniia russkikh krest'ian XIX v.* Moscow, 1986.

―――. *Trudovye traditsii russkikh krest'ian Sibiri. XVIII–pervaia polovina XIX v.* Novosibirsk, 1975.

Gromyko, M. M., and Listova, T. A., eds. *Russkie: semeinyi i obshchestvennyi byt.* Moscow: Nauka, 1989.

Gubarev, K. "Ot Tobol'ska do Berezova." *Sovremennik*, 1863, no. 2.

Guliaev, S. I. "Etnograficheskie ocherki Iuzhnoi Sibiri." In *Biblioteka dlia chteniia*, 1848, vol. 90.

―――. "O sibirskikh krugovykh pesniakh." *Otechestv. zap.*, 1839, vol. 111, no. 5.

Gumilev, Lev N. *Drevniaia Rus' i velikaia step'.* Moscow: Mysl', 1989.

Gurevich, A. Ia. "Ved'ma v derevne i pred sudom (narodnaia i uchenaia traditsii v ponimanii magii)." In *Iazyki kul'tury i problemy perevodimosti*. Moscow, 1987.

Gur'ianov, N. S. *Krest'ianskii antimonarkhiskii protest v staroobriadcheskoi eskhatologicheskoi literatury perioda pozdnego feodalizma.* Novosibirsk, 1988.

Iadrintsev, N. M. *Sibir' kak koloniia.* St. Petersburg, 1882.

―――. "Poezdka po Zapadnoi Sibiri i v Gornyi Altaiskii okrug." In *Zapiski Zap.-Sib. otd. RGO.* Bk. 2. Omsk, 1880.

Ianin, V. L. "Kompleks gramot no. 519–521 iz Novgoroda." *Obshchestvo i gosudarstvo feodal'noi Rossii.* Moscow, 1975.

Ilovaiskii, D. I. *Istoriia Rossii.* Vol. 1. Moscow, 1876.

Iordanskii, V. B. *Khaos i garmoniia.* Moscow, 1982.

Istoricheskie sochineniia o Rossii XVI v. Moscow, 1983.

Istoriia russkoi arkhitektury. Moscow, 1951.

Iudin, Iu. I. "Russkaia narodnaia bytovaia skazka." Author's abstract of doctor of philology dissertation. Leningrad, 1979.

Ivancha, I. A., and Koshevarov, M. S. "Aleksandr Nikiforovich Zyrianov." In *Isetsko-Pyshminskii krai.* Shadrinsk, 1930.

Ivanov V. V., and Toporov, V. N. *Issledovaniia v oblasti slavianskikh drevnostei.* Moscow, 1974.

Ivanitskii, N. A. "Materialy po etnografii Vologodskoi gub." *Izv. OLEAE*, 1890, vol. 1, issue 1/2.

Ivina, L. I. *Vnutrennee osvoenie zemel' Rossii v XVI v.* Leningrad, 1985.

Iz istorii krest'ianstva i agrarnykh otnoshenii na Urale. Sverdlovsk, 1963.

Iz istorii rabochego klassa Urala. Perm', 1961.

Kabytov, P. S.; Kozlov, V. A.; and Litvak, G. G. *Russkoe krest'ianstvo: etapy dukhovnogo osvobozhdeniia.* Moscow, 1988.

Kaidash, S. N. *Sila slabykh. Zhenshchiny v Rossii (XI–XIX vv.)*. Moscow: Sovetskaia Rossiia, 1989.

Kalendarno-obriadovaia poeziia sibiriakov. Novosibirsk, 1981.

Kalendarnye obychai i obriady v stranakh zarubezhnoi Evropy. Zimnie prazdniki, Moscow, 1973; *Vesennie prazdniki*, Moscow, 1977.

Karamzin, N. M. *Istoriia gosudarstva rossiiskogo*. Vol. 1. St. Petersburg, 1892.

Kashin, I. "Svadebnye obychai priarguntsev." *VRGO*, 1860, vol. 30.

Kazakova, N. A., and Lur'e, Ia. S. *Antifeodal'nye ereticheskie dvizheniia na Rusi XIV–nachala XVI veka*. Moscow: Nauka, 1955.

Kazimir, E. P. "Iz svadebnykh i rodil'nykh obychaev Khotinskogo u. Bessarabskoi gub." *Etnograficheskoe obozrenie*, 1907, no. 1/2.

Khanykov, D. D. *Russkie byliny*. Moscow, 1860.

Kharlampovich, K. V. *Arkhimandrit Makarii*. St. Petersburg, 1905.

Kharuzin, N. N. *Etnografiia*. St. Petersburg, 1905.

Kharuzina, V. N. "Neskol'ko slov o rodil'nykh i krestil'nykh obriadakh i ob ukhode za det'mi v Pudozhskom u. Olonetskoi gub." *Etnograficheskoe obozrenie*, 1906, no. 1/4.

Khlebnikov, N. *Obshchestvo i gosudarstvo v domongol'skii period russkoi istorii*. St. Petersburg, 1872.

Kireevskii, P. V., ed., coll. *Pesni*. Vol. 1. St. Petersburg, 1860.

Klein, L. S. "Pokhorony boga i sviatochnye igry s umrunom." In *Konferentsiia "Baltoslavianskie etnokul'turnye i arkheologicheskie drevnosti. Pogrebal'nyi obriad." Tez. dokl.* Moscow, 1985.

Klements, D. A. "Nagovory i primety u krest'ian Minusinskogo okruga." In *Izv. VSORGO*, 1902, vol. 19.

Kletnova, E. N. "Zapiska o metakh i znakakh sobstvennosti Viazemskogo uezda." *Etnograficheskoe obozrenie*. Moscow, 1916.

Klibanov, A. I. *Reformatsionnye dvizheniia v Rossii v XIV–pervoi polovine XVI vv.* Moscow: Nauka, 1960.

Kolesnikov, P. A. *Severnaia derevnia v XV–pervoi polovine XIX v.* Vologda, 1976.

Kolmogorov, G. "Ocherk prostonarodnogo byta v uezdnykh gorodakh i selakh Sibiri." *Severnaia pchela*, 1859, no. 67.

Komarev, M., ed. *Opisanie trinadtsati starinnykh svadev*. Moscow, 1785.

Kopylov, A. N. *Ocherki kul'turnoi zhizni Sibiri XVII–nachala XIX vv.* Novosibirsk: Nauka, 1974.

Korablev, S. *Moskovskie gulianiia*. Moscow, 1855.

Korobka, N. I. " 'Kamen' na more' i kamen' alatyr'." *Zhivaia starina*. Issue 4. St. Petersburg, 1909.

Kostomarov, N. I. *Istoricheskie monografy i issledovaniia*. Vol. 1. St. Petersburg, 1872.

Kostrov, N. A. *Iuridicheskie obychai krest'ian-starozhilov Tomskoi gubernii*. Tomsk, 1876.

———. "Koldovstvo i porcha mezhdu krest'ianami Tomskoi gubernii." In *Zapiski Zap.-Sib. otd. RGO*. Bk. 1. Omsk, 1879.

———. "Sviatki v Minusinskom okruge Eniseiskoi gubernii." In *Zap. Sib. otd. RGO*. Bk. 5. St. Petersburg, 1858.

Kosven, M. O. *Ocherki istorii pervobytnoi kul'tury*. Moscow, 1957.

Kotsebu, A. *Dostopamiatnyi god moei zhizni*. Pt. 1. St. Petersburg, 1879.

Koval'chenko, I. D. "O burzhuaznom kharaktere krest'ianskogo khoziaistva evropei-skoi Rossii v kontse XIX–nachale XX veka: po biudzhetnym dannym sredne-chernozemnykh gubernii." *Istoriia SSSR*, 1983, no. 5.

Kovalev, S. I. *Proiskhozhdenie khristianstva: osnovnye voprosy*. Moscow-Leningrad, 1964.

Kozachenko, A. I. "K istorii velikorusskogo svadebnogo obriada." *Sovetskaia et-nografiia*, 1957, no. 1.

Krachkovskii, Iu. F. *Byt zapadnorusskogo selianina*. Moscow, 1874.

Kramer, S. N. *Istoriia nachinaetsia v Shumere*. Moscow, 1965.

Krasnobaev, B. I. *Russkaia kul'tura vtoroi poloviny XVII–nachala XIX v*. Moscow: MGU Press, 1983.

Krasnovskaia, N. A. *Proiskhozhdenie i etnicheskaia istoriia sardintsev*. Moscow, 1986.

Krasnozhenova, M. V. "Materialy po narodnoi meditsine Eniseiskoi gubernii." *Izv. VSORGO*. Irkutsk, 1908, vol. 39; 1911, vol. 42.

Kravtsov, N. I., and Lazutin, S. G. *Russkoe ustnoe narodnoe tvorchestvo*. Moscow, 1983.

Krest'ianskaia reforma v Rossii 1861 goda: sbornik zakonodatel'nykh aktov. Moscow, 1954.

Krest'ianstvo Sibiri v epokhu feodalizma. Novosibirsk, 1982.

Krivoshapkin, M. F. *Eniseiskii okrug i ego zhizn'*. Vol. 1. St. Petersburg, 1865.

Krivoshchekov, I. Ia. *Slovar' geografichesko-statisticheskii Cherdynskogo uezda Permskoi gubernii*. Perm', 1914.

———. *Ukazatel' k karte Solikamskogo uezda Permskoi gubernii*. Ekaterinburg, 1897.

Krivosheev, Iu. V. "Sotsial'naia bor'ba i problema genezisa feodal'nykh otnoshenii v severo-vostochnoi Rusi XI–nachala XII veka." *Voprosy istorii*, 1988, no. 9.

"Kruglyi stol. Rol' pravoslavnoi tserkvi v istorii Rossii." *Voprosy istorii*, 1990, no. 3.

Krupianskaia, V. Iu., and Polishchuk, N. S. *Kul'tura i byt rabochikh gornozavodskogo Urala (konets XIX–nachalo XX v.)*. Moscow, 1971.

Krylov, P. N. *Visherskii krai: Istoricheskii i bytovoi ocherk Severnogo Prikam'ia (Zametki iz puteshestviia po Permskoi gubernii 1870–1878 gg.)*. Sverdlovsk, 1926.

Kryvelev, I. A. *Istoriia religii*. Vol. 1. Moscow, 1975.

Kurmacheva, M. D. *Krepostnaia intelligentsiia Rossii: vtoraia polovina XVIII–nachalo XIX veka*. Moscow, 1983.

Kushner, P. I. *Selo Viriatino v proshlom i nastoiashchem*. Moscow, 1958.

Kushner, P. I., et al., eds. *Russkie: istoriko-etnograficheskii atlas. Seredina XIX–nachalo XX veka*. 2 vols. and supplementary map volume. Moscow, 1967–70.

Latyshev, V. V. *Izvestiia drevnikh pisatelei grecheskikh i latinskikh o Skifii i Kavkaze*. Vol. 1. St. Petersburg, 1890.

Lebedeva, A. A. "K istorii formirovaniia russkogo naseleniia Zabaikal'ia, ego

Koval'chenko, I. D. "O burzhuaznom kharaktere krest'ianskogo khoziaistva evropei-skoi Rossii v kontse XIX–nachale XX veka: po biudzhetnym dannym sred-nechernozemnykh gubernii." *Istoriia SSSR*, 1983, no. 5.

Kovalev, S. I. *Proiskhozhdenie khristianstva: osnovnye voprosy*. Moscow-Leningrad, 1964.

Kozachenko, A. I. "K istorii velikorusskogo svadebnogo obriada." *Sovetskaia etnografiia*, 1957, no. 1.

Krachkovskii, Iu. F. *Byt zapadnorusskogo selianina*. Moscow, 1874.

Kramer, S. N. *Istoriia nachinaetsia v Shumere*. Moscow, 1965.

Krasnobaev, B. I. *Russkaia kul'tura vtoroi poloviny XVII–nachala XIX v.* Moscow: MGU Press, 1983.

Krasnovskaia, N. A. *Proiskhozhdenie i etnicheskaia istoriia sardintsev*. Moscow, 1986.

Krasnozhenova, M. V. "Materialy po narodnoi meditsine Eniseiskoi gubernii." *Izv. VSORGO*. Irkutsk, 1908, vol. 39; 1911, vol. 42.

Kravtsov, N. I., and Lazutin, S. G. *Russkoe ustnoe narodnoe tvorchestvo*. Moscow, 1983.

Krest'ianskaia reforma v Rossii 1861 goda: sbornik zakonodatel'nykh aktov. Moscow, 1954.

Krest'ianstvo Sibiri v epokhu feodalizma. Novosibirsk, 1982.

Krivoshapkin, M. F. *Eniseiskii okrug i ego zhizn'*. Vol. 1. St. Petersburg, 1865.

Krivoshchekov, I. Ia. *Slovar' geografichesko-statisticheskii Cherdynskogo uezda Permskoi gubernii*. Perm', 1914.

———. *Ukazatel' k karte Solikamskogo uezda Permskoi gubernii*. Ekaterinburg, 1897.

Krivosheev, Iu. V. "Sotsial'naia bor'ba i problema genezisa feodal'nykh otnoshenii v severo-vostochnoi Rusi XI–nachala XII veka." *Voprosy istorii*, 1988, no. 9.

"Kruglyi stol. Rol' pravoslavnoi tserkvi v istorii Rossii." *Voprosy istorii*, 1990, no. 3.

Krupianskaia, V. Iu., and Polishchuk, N. S. *Kul'tura i byt rabochikh gornozavodskogo Urala (konets XIX–nachalo XX v.)*. Moscow, 1971.

Krylov, P. N. *Visherskii krai: Istoricheskii i bytovoi ocherk Severnogo Prikam'ia (Zametki iz puteshestviia po Permskoi gubernii 1870–1878 gg.)*. Sverdlovsk, 1926.

Kryvelev, I. A. *Istoriia religii*. Vol. 1. Moscow, 1975.

Kurmacheva, M. D. *Krepostnaia intelligentsiia Rossii: vtoraia polovina XVIII–nachalo XIX veka*. Moscow, 1983.

Kushner, P. I. *Selo Viriatino v proshlom i nastoiashchem*. Moscow, 1958.

Kushner, P. I., et al., eds. *Russkie: istoriko-etnograficheskii atlas. Seredina XIX–nachalo XX veka*. 2 vols. and supplementary map volume. Moscow, 1967–70.

Latyshev, V. V. *Izvestiia drevnikh pisatelei grecheskikh i latinskikh o Skifii i Kavkaze*. Vol. 1. St. Petersburg, 1890.

Lebedeva, A. A. "K istorii formirovaniia russkogo naseleniia Zabaikal'ia, ego khoziaistvennogo i semeinogo byta." In *Etnografiia russkogo naseleniia Sibiri i Srednei Azii*. 1964.

Leont'ev, A. A. *Krest'ianskoe pravo*. 2nd ed. St. Petersburg, 1914.

Leont'ev, A. K. "Nravy i obychai." *Ocherki russkoi kul'tury XVI v.* Pt. 2. Moscow, 1977.

Lezhe, L. *Slavianskaia mifologiia*. Voronezh, 1908.

Liashchenko, P. L. *Ocherki agrarnoi evoliutsii Rossii*. 2 vols. St. Petersburg–Leningrad, 1913–26.

Likhachev, D. S. *Chelovek v literature drevnei Rusi*. Moscow, 1970 (original, 1958).

———. *Poetika drevnerusskoi literatury*. Moscow, 1979.

———. "Rossiia." *Literaturnaia gazeta*, 12 October 1988, no. 41.

Likhachev, N. P. *Inoka Fomy slovo pokhval'noe o blagorodnom i velikom kniaze*

Borise Aleksandroviche. St. Petersburg, 1908.

Likhacheva, V. D., and Likhachev, D. S. *Khudozhestvennoe nasledie drevnei Rusi i sovremennost'*. Leningrad, 1971.

Linder, N. "Raskol'nich'ia sekta 'kalagury.'" *Novoe vremia*, 1891, no. 5243.

Lipinskaia, V. A. *Russkoe naselenie Altaiskogo kraia*. Moscow: Nauka, 1987.

Listova, T. A. "Chiny v rodil'no–krestil'noi obriadnosti russkikh severnykh i zapadnykh oblastei RSFSR." In *Vsesoiuznaia sessiia po polevym etnograficheskim issledovaniiam 1981–1982 gg.* Nal'chik, 1983.

Litvak, V. G. *Russkaia derevnia v reforme 1861 goda*. Moscow, 1972.

Litvinova, P. "Kak sazhali v starinu liudei starykh na lubok." *Kievskaia starina*, June 1885.

Loparev, Kh. *Samarovo selo Tobol'skoi gubernii i okruga*. St. Petersburg, 1896.

Magnitskii, V. *Pover'ia i obriady (zapuki) v Urzhumskom u. Viatskoi gub*. Viatka, 1883.

Maikov, L. N. "Velikorusskie zaklinaniia." In *Zapiski imperatorskogo russkogo geograficheskogo obshchestva po otdeleniiu etnografii*. Vol. 2. 1869.

Makarenko, A. A. "Materialy po narodnoi meditsine Uzhurskoi volosti Achinskogo okruga Eniseiskoi gub. S prilozheniem sbornika narodno-meditsinskikh sredstv toi zhe volosti." *Zhivaia starina*. Issue 1–4. St. Petersburg, 1898.

Maksimov, S. *Lesnaia glush': Kartiny narodnogo byta*. Vol. 2. St. Peterburg, 1871.

Maksimov, S. V. *Nechistaia, nevedomaia i krestnaia sila*. St. Petersburg, 1903.

———. *Sobranie sochinenie*. St. Petersburg, 1908–13.

Mamsik, T. S. "Iz istorii razvitiia gramotnosti v zapadno-sibirskoi derevne (po materialam sudebnykh del pervoi poloviny XIX v.)." In *Kul'turno-bytovye protsessy u russkikh Sibiri XVIII–nachala XX v*. Novosibirsk, 1985.

Markov, (Reverend) S. *O prave tserkvi izmeniat' tserkovnye postanovleniia, obriady i obychai, sushchestva very ne kasaiushchiesia*. Moscow, 1901.

Markova, I. B. "Dosug sibirskikh chinovnikov v pervoi polovine XIX v." In *Kul'turno-bytovye protsessy u russkikh Sibiri XVIII–nachala XX v*. Novosibirsk, 1985.

Martynov, S. V. *Pechorskii krai*. St. Petersburg, 1905.

Maslova, G. S. *Ornament russkoi narodnoi vyshivki kak istoriko-etnograficheskii istochnik*. Moscow, 1978.

Maslova, G. S., and Saburova, L. M. eds. *Etnografiia Russkogo naseleniia Sibiri i srednei Azii*. Moscow: Nauka, 1969.

Materialy dlia istorii drevneruskoi pokaiannoi distsipliny XII–XV vv. Moscow, 1913.

Matveeva, R. P. *Tvorchestvo sibirskogo skazitelia E. I. Sorokovinkova-Magaia*. Novosibirsk, 1976.

Mazaev, A. I. *Prazdnik kak sotsial'no-khudozhestvennoe iavlenie. Opyt istoriko-teoreticheskogo issledovaniia*. Moscow, 1978.

Mel'nikova, E. A., and Petrukhin, V. Ia. "Nazvanie 'Rus'' v etnokul'turnoi istorii drevnerusskogo gosudarstva (IX–X vv.)." *Voprosy istorii*, 1989, no. 8.

Meves, I. "Tri goda v Sibiri i Amurskoi strane." *Otechestvennye zapiski*, 1863, vol. 148, bk. 5.

Miliukov, P. *Ocherki po istorii russkoi kul'tury*. Vol. 2. St. Petersburg, 1902.

Miller (Muller), G. F. *Istorii Sibiri*. 2 vols. Moscow: Nauka, 1941 (original 1763).

Minenko, N. A. "Dosug i razvlecheniia u russkikh krest'ian Zapadnoi Sibiri v XVIII–pervoi polovine XIX v." *Sovetskaia etnografiia*, 1979, no. 6.

————. *Istoriia kul'tury russkogo krest'ianstva Sibiri v period feodalizma.* Novosibirsk, 1986.

————. "K istorii russkoi narodnoi meditsiny v Sibiri XVIII–pervoi poloviny XIX v." In *Traditsii i innovatsii v bytu i kul'ture narodov Sibiri.* Novosibirsk, 1983.

————. "Obshchina i russkaia krest'ianskaia sem'ia v iugo–zapadnoi Sibiri, XVIII– pervaia polovina XIX v." In *Kresti'anskaia obshchina v Sibiri XVII–nachala XX v.* Novosibirsk, 1977.

————. *Russkaia krest'ianskaia sem'ia v Zapadnoi Sibiri. XVIII–pervoi poloviny XIX v.* Novosibirsk, 1979.

————. "Svadebnye obriady russkikh krest'ian Zapadnoi Sibiri v XVIII–pervoi polovine XIX v." *Sovetskaia etnografiia,* 1977, no. 3.

————. *Zhivaia starina: budni i prazdniki sibirskoi derevni.* Novosibirsk, 1989.

Mironov, Boris N. "Traditsionnoe demograficheskoe povedenie krest'ian v XIX–nachale XX v." In *Brachnost', rozhdaemost', smertnost' v Rossii i v SSSR,* ed. A. G. Vishnevskii. Moscow, 1977.

Mogil'nitskii, B. G. "Alternativnost' v istorii sovetskogo obshchestva." *Voprosy istorii,* 1989, no. 11.

Mozel', Kh. *Materialy dlia geografii i statistiki Rossii, izdannye ofitserami General'nogo shtaba: Permskaia gub.* Vol. 2. St. Petersburg, 1864.

Myl'nikov, A. S. *Etnograficheskoe izuchenie znakovykh sredstv kul'tury.* Leningrad: Nauka, 1989.

Narodnye russkie legendy. Kazan', 1914.

Na Zapadnom Urale. Issue 6. Perm', 1974.

Nebol'sin, P. I. "Zametki na puti iz Peterburga v Barnaul." *Otechestvennye zapiski,* 1849, vol. 64.

Nekrylova, A. F. *Russkie narodnye gorodskie prazdniki, uveseleniia i zrelishcha: Konets XVIII–nachalo XX veka.* Leningrad, 1984.

Niderle, L. *Slavianskie drevnosti.* Moscow, 1956.

Nikitin, N. A. "K voprosu o russikh koldunakh." *Sbornik Muzei antropologii i et-nografii,* 1928, vol. 7.

Nikitina, S. E. "Zhanr zagovora v narodnom predstavlenii." In *Etnolingvistika teksta: semiotika malykh form fol'klora.* Vol. 1. *Tez. v predvaritel'nye materialy k simpoziumu.* Moscow, 1988.

Nikol'skii, N. K. "O drevnerusskom khristianstve." *Russkaia mysl',* 1913, bk. 6.

Nikol'skii, N. M. *Istoriia russkoi tserkvi.* Moscow, 1985.

Nosova, G. A. *Iazychestvo i pravoslavii.* Moscow, 1975.

Novgorodskaia pervaia letopis' starshego i mladshego izvodov. Moscow-Leningrad, 1950.

Novombergskii, N. I. *Koldovstvo v moskovskoi Rusi XVII veka.* St. Petersburg: Suvorin, 1906.

Oborin, V. A. "Sotsial'no-ekonomicheskoe razvitie Urala v XVII v." In *Istoriia Urala.* Perm', 1963.

Okladnikov, A. P. ed. *Istoriia Sibiri.* 5 vols. Leningrad: Nauka, 1968.

Opisanie Tobol'skogo namestnichestva. Novosibirsk, 1982.

Ostroumov, N. I. *Svadebnye obychai v Drevnei Rusi.* Tula, 1905.

Ostrovskaia, L. V. "Nekotorye zamechaniia o kharaktere krest'ianskoi religioznosti."

In *Krest'ianstvo Sibiri XVIII–nachala XX v.: Klassovaia bor'ba, obshchestvennoe soznanie i kul'tura.* Novosibirsk, 1975.

Ovchinnikov, V. G. "Pravoslavnaia tserkov v istorii nashei stranei." *Voprosy istorii,* 1988, no. 5.

Pakhman, S. V. *Obychnoe grazhdanskoe pravo v Rossii.* 2 vols. St. Petersburg, 1877.

Pallas, D. S. *Puteshestvie po raznym provintsiiam Rossiskoi imperii.* St. Petersburg, 1773–88.

Pamiatnaia knizhka Vitebskoi gub. na 1865 g. St. Petersburg, 1865.

Pamiatniki russkogo prava. No. 4. Moscow, 1956.

Pavlenko, N. I. "U istokov rossiiskoi biurokratii." *Voprosy istorii,* 1989, no. 12.

Petrov, V. P. "Zagovory." In *Iz istorii russkoi sovetskoi fol'kloristiki.* Leningrad, 1981.

Platonov, Andrei. "Iamskaia sloboda." *Povesti i rasskazy.* Leningrad: Lenizdat, 1985.

Pokrovskii, N. N. *Puteshestvie za redkimi knigami.* Moscow, 1984.

———. "Uralo-sibirskaia krest'ianskaia obshchina XVIII v. i problema staroobriadchestva." In *Krest'ianskaia obshchina v Sibiri XVIII–nachala XIX v.* Novosibirsk, 1977.

Polnoe sobranie russkikh letopisei. St. Petersburg. Vol. 1, 1846; vol. 2 (*Gustynskaia letopis'*), 1846; vol. 3 (*Novgorodskie i pskovskie letopisi*), 1841; vol. 5, 1851; vol. 6, 1853; vol. 7, 1856; vol. 8, 1859; vol. 21, 1908.

Pomerantseva, E. V. *Mifologicheskie personazhi v russkom fol'klore.* Moscow, 1975.

Ponomarev, A. I., ed. *Pamiatniki drevnerusskoi tserkovno-uchitel'noi literatury.* Vol. 4, no. 60. St. Petersburg, 1898.

Popov, G. I. *Russkaia bytovaia meditsina.* St. Petersburg: Suvorin, 1903.

Popov, N. *Khoziaistvennoe opisanie Permskoi gubernii.* Pt. 2. Perm', 1804.

Popov, T. "Sloboda Takmytskaia." *Tobol'skie gub. vedomosti,* 1864, no. 7.

Potanin, G. N. "Iugo-zapadnaia chast' Tomskoi gubernii v etnograficheskom otnoshenii." In *Etnograficheskii sbornik.* Issue 6. St. Petersburg, 1864.

———. "Polgoda v Altae." *Russkoe slovo,* 1859, no. 12.

Pozdeeva, I. V. "Vereshchaginskoe territorial'noe knizhnoe sobranie i problemy istorii dukhovnoi kul'tury russkogo naseleniia verkhov'ev Kamy." In *Russkie pis'mennye i ustnye traditsii i dukhovnaia kul'tura.* Moscow, 1982.

Poznanskii, N. F. "Zagovory: Opyt issledovaniia proiskhozhdeniia i razvitiia zagovornykh formul." In *Zapiski istoricheskogo-filosoficheskogo fakul'teta Petrogradskogo universiteta.* Petrograd, 1917.

Pravda russkaia. Vol. 1. Moscow-Leningrad, 1940.

Predtechenskii, A. V. "O. V. Gorskii i ego 'Zapiska.'" In *Vospominaniia i rasskazy deiatelei tainykh obshchestv 1820-kh godov.* Moscow, 1933.

Preobrazhenskii, A. A. *Ural i Zapadnaia Sibir' v kontse XVI–nachale XVIII v.* Moscow, 1972.

Preobrazhenskii, A. G. *Etimologicheskii slovar' russkogo iazyka.* Vol. 1. Moscow, 1959.

Prokhorov, Gelian M. "Proshloe i vechnost' v kul'ture kievskoi Rusi." In *Chelovek i istoriia v srednevekovoi filosofskoi mysli russkogo, ukrainskogo i belorusskogo narodov.* Kiev: Naukova dumka, 1987.

Prokof'eva, L. S. *Krest'ianskaia obshchina v Rossii: vo vtoroi polovine XVIII–pervoi polovine XIX veka.* Leningrad, 1981.

Pronshtein, A. P., and Kiiashko, V. Ia. *Khronologiia.* Moscow, 1981.

Propp, V. Ia. *Istoricheskie korni volshebnoi skazki.* Leningrad, 1946.

———. *Problemy komizma i smekha.* Moscow, 1976.

———. *Russkie agrarnye prazdniki.* Leningrad, 1963.

———. *Russkoi geroicheskoi epos.* Leningrad, 1955.

Prugavin, A. S. *Raskol i sektantstvo v russkoi narodnoi zhizni.* Moscow, 1905.

Pskovskie letopisi. Issue 1. Moscow-Leningrad, 1941.

Pushkarenko, A. A. *Obychnoe pravo pozdne-feodal'noi epokhi: Sotsial'no-politi-cheskoe i pravovoe polozhenie krest'ianstva v dorevoliutsionnoi Rossii.* Voronezh, 1983.

Pushkarev, S. G. *Krest'ianskaia pozemel'no peredel'naia obshchina v Rossii.* Prague, 1939–41; reprinted Newtonville, Massachusetts, 1976.

Pushkareva, N. L. "Imushchestvennye prava zhenshchin v russkom gosudarstve X–XV vv." In *Istoricheskie zapiski.* Vol. 114. Moscow, 1986.

———. "Pravovoe polozhenie zhenshchiny v Drevnei Rusi X–XV vv." *Sovetskoe gosudarstvo i pravo,* 1985, no. 4.

Pypin, A. N. *Istoriia russkoi etnografii.* 4 vols. St. Petersburg, 1890–92.

Rabinovich, Ia. B. "Ob agrarnykh trebovaniiakh rabochikh Urala v 70–80-kh godakh XIX v." In *Iz istorii rabochego klassa.*

———. *Ocherki etnografii russkogo feodal'nogo goroda.* Moscow, 1978.

Rabinovich, M. G. *Ocherki etnografii russkogo feodal'nogo goroda. Gorozhane, ikh ob-shchestvennyi i domashnii byt.* Moscow, 1978.

———. "Svadba v russkom gorode XVI v." In *Russkii narodnyi svadebnyi obriad.* Leningrad, 1978.

Rakhmatullin, M. A. "Sotsial'noe nastroenie krepostnogo krest'ianstva i klassovaia bor'ba. 1826–1857." *Istoriia SSSR,* 1988, no. 3.

Romanov, B. A. *Liudi i nravy Drevnei Rusi (istoriko-bytovye ocherki. XI–XIII vv.).* Moscow, 1948 (2nd ed., Leningrad, 1966).

Romanov, E. R. *Belorusskii sbornik.* Issue 8. Vil'no, 1912.

Rovinskii, D. A. *Russkie narodnye kartinki.* Vol. 5. St. Petersburg, 1881.

Rozen, A. E. "Zapiski." Otechestvennye zapiski, 1876, no. 8.

Rusakova, L. M., and Minenko, N. A. eds. *Kul'turno-bytovye protsessy u Russkikh Sibiri (XVIII–nachalo XX vv.).* Novosibirsk: Nauka, 1985.

Russkaia istoricheskaia biblioteka. Vol. 6. St. Petersburg, Russkaia starina, 1908.

Rybakov, B. A. "Drevnie elementy v russkom narodnom tvorchestve." *Sovetskaia etnografiia,* 1948, no. 1.

———. "Iazycheskoe mirovozzrenie russkogo srednevekov'ia." *Voprosy istorii,* 1974, no. 1.

———. *Iazychestvo drevnikh slavian.* Moscow, 1981.

———. *Iazychestvo drevnei Rusi.* Moscow: Nauka, 1987.

———, ed. *Ocherki russkoi kul'tury XVIII veka.* Moscow, 1985.

———. "Prosveshchenie." In *Ocherki russkoi kul'tury XIII–XV vv.* Pt.2 Moscow, 1970.

Rybnikov, P. N., ed., coll. *Pesni.* St. Petersburg, 1861.

Ryndiunskii, P. G. "Ideinaia storona krest'ianskikh dvizhenii 1770–1850-kh godov i metody ee izucheniia." *Voprosy istorii,* 1983, no. 5.

———. *Krest'iane i gorod v kapitalisticheskoi Rossii vtoroi poloviny XIX veka.* Moscow, 1983.

Saburova, L. M. *Kul'tura i byt russkogo naseleniia Priangar'ia.* Leningrad, 1967.

Sakharov, A. M. "Religiia i tserkov'." In *Ocherki russkoi kul'tury XVI v.* Pt. 2. Moscow, 1977.

Sakharov, I. *Skazaniia russkogo naroda o semeinoi zhizni svoikh predkov.* Pt. 3, bk. 2. St. Petersburg, 1837.

Sapozhnikov, D. I. *Samosozhzhenie v russkom raskole.* Moscow, 1891.

Savushkina, N. I. *Russkii narodnyi teatr.* Moscow, 1976.

Sbornik otdeleniia russkogo iazyka i slovesnosti Akademii nauk. Vol. 38. St. Petersburg, 1858.

Sbornik Russkogo istoricheskogo obshchestva. St. Petersburg, 1882.

Seleshnikov, S. I. *Istoriia kalendaria i khronologiia.* Moscow, 1970.

"Selo Golun' i Novomikhailovka Tul'skoi gub. Novosil'skogo u." *Etnograficheskii sbornik.* Issue 2. St. Petersburg, 1854.

Selo Viriatino v proshlom i nastoiashchem. Moscow, 1958.

Semenev, S. T. *Dvadtsat' piat let v derevne.* Petrograd, 1915.

Semenov, S. "Dekabristy v Ialutorovske." *Sibirskii arkhiv,* 1913, no. 6–8.

Semenov, S. A. "Dobyvanie ognia treniem." In *Materialy po etnografii: Doklady za 1962 g.* Issue 3. Leningrad, 1963.

Semenova Tian-Shanskaia, O. P. "Zhizn' 'Ivana.' " *Zapiski imperskogo Russkogo geograficheskogo obshchestva po otdeleniiu etnografiia.* Vol. 39. St. Petersburg, 1914 (forthcoming in English, trans. David L. Ransel).

Semevskii, V. I. "Domashnyii byt i nravy krest'ian vo vtoroi polovine XVIII veka." *Ustoi,* 1882, no. 2.

———. *Krest'ianskii vopros v Rossii v XVIII i pervoi polovine XIX veka.* 2 vols. St. Petersburg, 1888.

Seniunina, M. G. *Potanin i Iadrintsev: ideologi sibirskogo oblastnichestva.* Tomsk: Tomsk University Press, 1974.

Shashkov, S. S. *Istoriia russkoi zhenshchiny.* St. Petersburg, 1879.

———. "Iz putevykh vospominanii." *Sibirskaia zhivaia starina,* 1926, no. 7.

Shchapov, A. P. "Istoriko-etnograficheskaia organizatsiia russkogo narodonaseleniia." *Russkoe slovo,* 1985, February.

———. *Russkii raskol staroobriadchestva.* Kazan', 1859.

Shchapov, Ia. N. "Brak i sem'ia v drevnei Rusi." *Voprosy istorii,* 1970, no. 10.

———. "Novyi pamiatnik russkogo prava XV v." In *Slaviane i Rus'.* Moscow, 1968.

Shcheglova, S. A. *"Pchela" po rukopisiam kievskikh bibliotek.* St. Petersburg, 1910.

Shein, P. V. *Belorusskie narodnye pesni.* St. Petersburg, 1874.

Sherotskii, K. V. *Kiev,* 1917.

Shingarev, A. I. *Vymiraiushchaia derevnia: opyt sanitarno-ekonomicheskogo issledovaniia dvukh selenii Voronezhskogo uezda.* 2nd ed. St. Petersburg, 1907 (reprinted in K. M. Shuvaev, *Staraia i novaia derevniia.* Moscow, 1937).

Shirokov, A. "Sibirskii karnaval." *Maiak,* 1844, vol. 17.

Shiuts, P. "Pis'ma o Sibiri." *Severnaia pchela,* 1839, no. 83.

Shkoldin, P. "Khoziaistvenno-statisticheskoe opisanie Burlinskoi volosti." *ZhZMOSKh,* 1863, bk. 1.

Skrebitskii, A. *Krest'ianskoe delo v tsarstvovanie imperatora Aleksandra II.* Vol. 4. St. Petersburg, 1862–68.

Skripil', M. O. "Povest' o Petre i Fevronii Muromskikh i ee otnoshenie k russkoi skazke." In *Tr. Otdela drevnerusskoi literatury*. Vol. 7. Moscow-Leningrad, 1949.

Slovar' knizhnikov i knizhnosti Drevnei Rusi. Vol. 1 (eleventh century to first half of thirteenth century). Leningrad, 1987.

Slovar' tserkovno-slavianskogo i russkogo iazyka. Vol. 2. St. Petersburg, 1867.

Slovtsov, P. A. *Progulki vokrug Tobol'ska v 1830 g*. Moscow, 1834.

Smirnov, V. *Narodnye pokhorony i prichitaniia v Kostromskom krae*. Kostroma, 1920.

Smirnova, M. "Rodil'nye i krestil'nye obriady krest'ian sela Golitsyna Kurganskoi volosti Serdobskogo u. Saratovskoi gub." *Etnograficheskoe obozrenie*, 1911, no. 1/2.

Smyshliaev, D. *Sbornik statei o Permskoi gubernii*. Perm', 1891.

Snegirev, I. M. *Russkie prostonarodnye prazdniki i suevernye obriady*. Vol. 3. Moscow, 1838.

Sobolev, A. *Svadebnyi obriad v Sudogodskom u. Vladimirskoi gub*. Vladimir, 1912.

Sobolevskii, A. *Velikorusskie narodnye pesni*. Vol 7. St. Petersburg, 1902.

Sokolov, Iu. M. *Russkii fol'klor*. Leningrad, 1941.

Soldatov, G. M. *Mitropolit Filofei, v skhime Feodor, Prosvetitel' Sibiri*. Minneapolis, 1972.

Sosenko, K. *Kulturno-istorychna postat' staroukrains'kykh sviat Rizdva i Shchedrogo Vechera*. L'viv, 1928.

Sreznevskii, I. I. *Materialy dlia slovaria drevnerusskogo iazyka*. Vol. 1. St. Petersburg, 1893; Moscow, 1958.

Steblin-Kamenskii, M. I. "Mir sagi. Stanovlenie literatury." Leningrad, 1984.

"Stoglav." In *Rossiiskoe zakonodatel'stvo X–XX vv*. Vol. 2. Moscow, 1985.

Stepanov, A. P. *Eniseiskaia guberniia*. Pt. 2. St. Petersburg, 1835.

Stepanov, V. I. "Svedeniia o rodil'nykh i krestil'nykh obriadakh v Klinskom u. Moskovskoi gub." *Etnograficheskoe obozrenie*, 1906, no. 3/4.

Sulotskii, A. I. *Istoricheskie svedeniia ob ikonopisanii v Sibiri*. Omsk, 1863.

Sumtsov, N. I. *O svadebnykh obriadakh, preimushchestvenno russkikh*. Khar'kov, 1881.

Sutyrin, B. A. "Krest'iane-otkhodniki na rechnom transporte Urala v pervoi polovine XIX v." In *Iz istorii krest'ianstva*.

Suvorov, N. *Kurs tserkovnogo prava*. Vol. 1. Iaroslavl', 1889.

Sventsitskaia, I. S. *Ot obshchiny k tserkvi*. Moscow, 1985.

Sviatskii, D. O. "Ocherki istorii astronomii v Drevnei Rusi." In *Istoriko-astronomicheskie issledovaniia*. Pt. 1, issue 7. Moscow, 1961.

Tatishchev, V. N. *Istoriia Rossiiskaia v 7-mi tomakh*. Moscow-Leningrad, 1963, 1967 (original 1769).

Tenishev, V. V. *Pravosudie v russkom krest'ianskom bytu, svod dannykh, dobytykh etnograficheskimi materialami pokoinogo kniazia V. N. Tenisheva*. Briansk, 1907.

Tikhomirov, M. N. "Moskva i kul'turnoe razvitie russkogo naroda XIV–XVII vv." *Voprosy istorii*, 1947, no. 9.

———. *Srednevekovaia Moskva v XIV–XV vv*. Moscow, 1957.

Tikhonitskaia, N. N. "Sel'skokhoziaistvennaia toloka u russkikh." *Sovetskaia etnografiia*, 1934, no. 4.

Timofeev, A. G. *Istoriia telesnykh nakazanii v russkom prave*. 2nd ed., pt. 2. St. Petersburg, 1904.

Tishkov. Valerii A. "Vystupleniia." *Vestnik akademii nauk SSSR*, 1990, no. 7.

Tokarev, S. A. *Istoriia russkoi etnografii*. Moscow, 1966.

———. "O religii kak sotsial'nom iavlenii: mysly etnografa." *Sovetskaia etnografiia*, 1979, no. 3; "Eshche raz," ibid., 1981, no. 1. English translation: *Soviet Anthropology & Archeology*, vol. 18, no. 3 (Winter 1979–80); vol. 20, no. 4 (Spring 1982).

———. *Religioznye verovaniia vostochnoslavianskikh narodov XIX–nachala XX vekov*. Moscow–Leningrad, 1957.

———. "Vvedenie." In *Kalendarnye obychai i obriady v stranakh zarubezhnoi Evropy: Istoricheskie korni i razvitie obychaev*. Moscow, 1983.

Tokarev, S. A., and Filimonova, T. D. "Obriady i obychai, sviazannye s rastitel'nost'iu." In *Kalendarnye obychai i obriady v stranakh zarubezhnoi Evropy: Istoricheskie korni i razvitie obychaev*. Moscow, 1983.

Tolmachev, P. M. "Zagovory i pover'ia v Zabaikal'e." *Sib. arkhiv*. Irkutsk, 1911, nos. 2 & 3.

Tolochko, P. P. *Drevnii Kiev*. Kiev, 1983.

Tolstoi, N. I. "Iz nabliudenii nad polesskimi zagovorami." In *Slavianskii i balkanskii fol'klor: dukhovnaia kul'tura Poles'ia na obshcheslavianskom fone*. Moscow, 1986.

Toporov, V. N. "K proizkhozhdeniiu nekotorykh poeticheskikh simvolov. Paleoliticheskaia epokha." In *Rannie formy iskusstva*. Moscow, 1972.

———. "K rekonstruktsii indoevropeiskogo rituala i ritual'no-poeticheskikh formul (na materiale zagovorov)." In *Trudy po znakovym sistemam*. Issue 4. Tartu, 1969.

Tret'iakov, A. "Shadrinskii uezd Permskoi gubernii v sel'skokhoziaistvennom otnoshenii." *ZhMGI*, 1852, pt. 45, no. 12.

Trubetskoi, E. *Inoe tsarstvo i ego iskateli v russkoi narodnoi skazke*. Moscow, 1922.

Tul'tseva, L. A. "Religioznye verovaniia i obriady russkikh krest'ian na rubezhe XIX i XX vekov." *Sovetskaia etnografiia*, 1978, no. 3.

Turbin, S. *Strana izgnaniia i ischeznuvshie liudi*. St. Petersburg, 1872.

Uspenskii, B. A. *Filologicheskie razyskaniia v oblasti slavianskikh drevnostei (Relikty iazychestva v vostochnoslavianskom kul'te Nikolaia Mirlikiiskogo)*. Moscow, 1982.

Uspenskii, D. I. "Rodiny i krestiny, ukhod za rodil'nitsei i novorozhdennym." *Etnograficheskoe obozrenie*, 1895, no. 4.

Uspenskii, T. "Ocherk iugo-zapadnoi poloviny Shadrinskogo uezda." *Permskii sbornik*, bk. 1.

"Ustav kniazia Iaroslava Vladimirovicha (XII v.)." In *Pamiatniki russkogo prava*. Vol. 1. Moscow, 1952.

Vagner, G. K. *Kanon i stil' v drevnerusskom iskusstve*. Moscow, 1987.

Valek, S. N., ed. *Gramoty Velikogo Novgoroda i Pskova*. Moscow-Leningrad, 1949.

Vedernikova, N. M. *Russkaia narodnaia skazka*. Moscow, 1975.

Veletskaia, N. N. "Iazycheskaia simvolika antropomorfnoi ritual'noi skul'ptury." In *Kul'tura i iskusstvo srednevekovogo goroda*. Moscow, 1984.

———. *Iazycheskaia simvolika slavianskikh arkhaicheskikh ritualov*. Moscow, 1978.

———. "Iz istorii kupal'skikh ritualov u slavian." In *Materialy od V Megunaroden simpozium za balkanskiot folklor. Makedonski folklor*, 1977.

———. "O rudimentakh iazycheskikh ritual'nykh deistv v slaviano-balkanskoi pogrebal'noi obriadnosti." In *Materialy od VII Megunaroden simpozium za balkanskiot folklor. Makedonski folklor*, 1982.

————. "Rudimenty indoevropeiskikh i drevnebalkanskikh ritualov v slaviano-balkanskoi obriadnosti mediatsii sil prirody." In *Materialy od VI Megunaroden simpozium za balkanskiot folklor. Makedonski folklor.* Skopje, 1979.

Verbitskii, V. "Piataia sotnia oblastnykh slov, upotrebliaemykh prialtaiskimi zhiteliami." *Tomskie gub. vedomosti*, 1863, no. 26.

————. "Predrassudki i sueveriia prialtaiskikh krest'ian." *Tomskie gub. vedomosti*, 1863, no. 12.

Veselovskii, A. N. "Zametki i somneniia o sravnitel'nom izuchenii srednevekovogo eposa." In idem, *Sobranie sochineniia.* Vol. 16. Moscow-Leningrad, 1938.

Veselovskii, S. B. *Soshnoe pis'mo.* Vol. 2. Moscow, 1916.

Vetlovskaia, V. E. "Letopisnoe osmyslenie pirov i darenii v svete fol'klornykh i etnograficheskikh dannykh." *Genezis i razvitie feodalizma v Rossii.* Leningrad, 1987.

Vetukhov, A. "Zagovory, zaklinaniia, oberegi i drugie vidy narodnogo vrachevaniia, osnovannye na vere v silu slova." *Russkii filologicheskii vestnik*, 1907, issue 1–2.

Vilchinskii, V. P., ed. *Russkoe narodno-poeticheskoe tvorchestvo protiv tserkvi i religii.* Moscow-Leningrad: Nauka, 1961.

Vinkler, G. *Vavilonskaia kul'tura v ee otnoshenii k kul'turnomu razvitiiu chelovechestva.* Moscow, 1913.

Vinogradov, G. S. "Otchet o rabote v Tunkinskom krae letom 1925 g." *Sibirskaia zhivaia starina*, 1926, issue 5.

————. "Pover'ia i obriady krest'ian-sibiriakov: materialy po etnografii Nizhneudinskogo uezda." *Sib. arkhiv.* Irkutsk, 1915, no. 3–5.

————. "Samovrachevanie i skotolechenie u russkogo starozhil'cheskogo naseleniia Sibiri." *Zhivaia starina.* Issue 4. St. Petersburg, 1915.

Vinogradov, N. N. "Zagovory, oberegi, spasitel'nye molitvy i pr." *Zhivaia starina.* St. Petersburg, 1907 (issues 1–2, 1908; issues 1–4, 1909).

Vlasov, V. G. "Khristianizatsiia russkikh krest'ian." *Sovetskaia etnografiia*, 1988, no. 3.

————. "Russkii narodnyi kalendar'." *Sovetskaia etnografiia*, 1985, no. 4.

Vlasova, I. V. *Traditsii krest'ianskogo zemlepol'zovaniia v Pomor'e i Zapadnoi Sibiri v XVII–XVIII vv.* Moscow, 1984.

Vlasova, Z. I. "K izucheniiu poetiki ustnykh zagovorov." In *Russkii fol'klor.* Vol. 13. Moscow, 1972.

Vorms, A., and Parenago, A. "Krest'ianskii sud i sudebno-administrativnye uchrezhdeniia." In *Sudebnaia reforma 1864–1914*, eds. N. V. Davydov and N. N. Polianskii. 2 vols. Vol. 2. Moscow, 1915.

Voshchanov, Pavel. "Kulaki." *Komsomol'skaia pravda*, 8 September 1989, and the ensuing debate in *Komsomol'skaia pravda*, 2 December 1989 (translated in "History and Ideology," *Joint Publications Research Service*, 11 January 1990).

Vysotskii, N. F. *Narodnaia meditsina.* Moscow, 1911.

Zabylin, M. *Russkii narod: ego obychai, obriady, predaniia, sueveriia i poeziia.* Moscow, 1990 (reprint, 1880 edition).

Zaionchkovskii, P. A. *Otmena krepostnogo prava v Rossii.* Moscow, 1968.

————. *Provedenie v zhizn' krest'ianskoi reformy 1861.* Moscow, 1958.

Zaitsev, A. I. "K voprosu o proiskhozhdenii volshebnoi skazki." In *Fol'klor i etnografiia. U etnograficheskikh istokov fol'klornykh siuzhetnykh obrazov.* Leningrad: Nauka, 1984.

Zamakhaev, S. N., and Tsvetaev, G. A. *Istoricheskaia zapiska o Tobol'skoi gimnazii.* Tobol'sk, 1889.

Zavoiko, K. "V Kostromskikh lesakh po Vetluge-reke: Etnograficheskie materialy, zapisannye v Kostromskoi gubernii v 1914–1916 gg." *Etnograficheskii sbornik.* Issue 8. Kostroma, 1917.

Zelenin, D. K. *Bibliograficheskii ukazatel' Russkoi etnograficheskoi literatury, 1700–1910.* St. Petersburg, 1913.

———. " 'Krasnaia smert" u russkikh staroobriadtsev." *Etnograficheskoe obozrenie,* 1904, no. 3.

———. *Opisanie rukopisei uchenogo arkhiva Imperatorskogo Russkogo geograficheskogo obshchestva.* Issue 2, St. Petersburg, 1915; issue 3, Petrograd, 1916.

———. "Tabu slov u narodov Vostochnoi Evropy i Severnoi Azii." In *Sbornik muzeia antropologii i etnografii.* Vol. 8. Leningrad, 1929.

———. *Totemy-derev'ia v skazaniiakh i obriadakh evropeiskikh narodov.* Moscow-Leningrad, 1937.

Zenkovskii, Serge A. *Russkoe staroobriadchestvo: Dukhovnye dvizheniia semnadtsatogo veka.* Munich: Wilhelm Fink, 1970.

Zhbankov, P. N. *Babia storona (Statistiko-etnograficheskii ocherk).* Kostroma, 1891.

Zhitiia Borisa i Gleba. Petersburg, 1916.

Zhuravlev, A. F. "Iz russkoi obriadovoi leksiki: 'zhivoi ogon'.' " *Obshcheslavianskii lingvisticheskii atlas. Materialy i issledovaniia.* Moscow, 1978.

Zobnin, F. "Iz goda v god (Opisanie krugovorota krest'ianskoi zhizni v s. Ust'-Nitsynskom Tiumenskogo okruga)." *Zhivaia starina,* 1894, issue 1.

———. "Ust'-Nitsynskaia sloboda Tiumenskogo uezda Tobol'skoi gubernii." *Zhivaia starina,* 1889, issue 2.

Zol'nikova, N. D. "Opisanie knig kirillovskoi pechati XVI–XVII vv. (sobranie IIFF SO AN SSSR)." In *Pamiatniki literatury i obshchestvennoi mysli epokhi feodalizma.* Novosibirsk, 1985.

Zolotov, P. "Neskol'ko slov ob Omske." *Akmolinskie oblastnye vedomosti,* 1872, no. 22.

Zorkin, V. I. *Vklad politicheskikh ssil'nykh v izuchenie fol'klora Sibiri.* Novosibirsk: Nauka, 1985.

Zyrianov, P. N. "Nekotorye cherty evoliutsii krestianskogo 'mira' v poreformennuiu epokhu." In *Ezhegodnik po agrarnoi istorii Vostochnoi Evropy 1971 g.* Vilnius, 1974.

Acronyms

Archives and Journals

AGO—Arkhiv Vsesoiuznogo Geograficheskogo obshchestva
AIE—Arkhiv Instituta etnografii AN SSSR
ChOIDR—Chteniia Obshchestva istorii i drevnostei Rossiiskikh pri Moskovskom Universitete
EGTM—Ezhegodnik Gosudarstvennogo Tobol'skogo muzeia
EO—Etnograficheskoe obozrenie
GAAK—Gosudarstvennyi arkhiv Altaiskogo kraia
GANO—Gosudarstvennyi arkhiv Novosibirskoi oblasti
GAOO—Gosudarstvennyi arkhiv Omskoi oblasti
GATiumO—Gosudarstvennyi arkhiv Tiumenskoi oblasti
GATO—Gosudarstvennyi arkhiv Tomskoi oblasti
GME—Gosudarstvennyi muzei etnografii narodov SSSR. Otdel pis'mennykh istochnikov
GTG—Gosudarstvennaia Tret'iakovskaia galleria
LO AAN—Leningradskoe otdelenie, arkhiv Akademii nauk SSSR
LO II—Leningradskoe otdelenie Instituta istorii SSSR, Akademii nauk SSSR
MdRPD—Materialy dlia istorii drevnerusskoi pokaiannoi distsipliny
MGSR—Materialy dlia geografii i statistiki Rossii, izdavaemye General'nym shtabom
NPL—Novgorodskaia pervaia letopis'
OLEAE—Obshchestvo liubitelei estestvoznaniia, antropologii i etnografii
POKM—Perm'skaia oblastnoi kraevecheskii muzei
PRP—Pamiatniki russkogo prava
PSRL—Polnoe sobranie russkikh letopisei
PVL—Povest' vremennykh let
RGO—Russkoe geograficheskoe obshchestvo
RIB—Russkaia istoricheskaia biblioteka
RO BAN—Rukopisnyi otdel Biblioteki Akademii nauk SSSR v Leningrade
RO GPB—Rukopisnyi otdel gosudarstvennoi publichnoi biblioteki im. M. E. Salty-kova-Shchedrina
RSZ—Russkie svadebnye zapisi
Sb. RIO—Sbornik Russkogo istoricheskogo obshchestva
SE—Sovetskaia etnografiia
SZhS—Sibirskaia zhivaia starina
TF GATiumO—Tobol'skii filial, Gosudarstvennyi arkhiv Tiumenskoi oblasti
TsGADA—Tsentral'nyi gosudarstvennyi arkhiv drevnikh aktov SSSR
TsGAOR—Tsentral'nyi gosudarstvennyi arkhiv Oktiabr'skoi revoliutsii, vysshikh organov gosudarstvennoi vlasti i organov gos. upravleniia SSSR
TsGATO—Tobol'skii filial, Gosudarstvennyi arkhiv Tomskoi oblasti
TsGIA—Tsentral'nyi Gosudarstvennyi istoricheskii arkhiv SSSR
VRGO—Vestnik Russkogo geograficheskogo obshchestva
VSORGO—Vostochno-Sibirskoe otdelenie Russkogo geograficheskogo obshchestva
ZhZMOSKh—Zhurnal zasedanii Moskovskogo obshchestva sel'skogo khoziaistva
ZhMVD—Zhurnal Ministerstva vnutrennikh del
ZhMGI—Zhurnal Ministerstva gosudarstvennykh imushchestv

Index